WHEN TRUST BREAKS DOWN

Studies in International Relations
Charles W. Kegley, Jr., and Donald J. Puchala,
Series Editors

WHEN TRUST BREAKS DOWN

Alliance Norms and World Politics

CHARLES W. KEGLEY, JR.
University of South Carolina
and
GREGORY A. RAYMOND
Boise State University

University of South Carolina Press

Published in Columbia, South Carolina, by the
University of South Carolina Press

Manufactured in the United States of America

Library of Congress Cataloging-in-Publication Data

Kegley, Charles W., Jr.
  When trust breaks down : alliance norms and world politics /
Charles W. Kegley, Jr. and Gregory A. Raymond.
    p. cm. — (Studies in international relations)
  Includes bibliographical references.
  ISBN 0–87249–644–9   ISBN 0–87249–688–0 (pbk.)
  1. Alliances. 2. International relations.   I. Raymond, Gregory
A. II. Title. III. Series: Studies in international relations
(Columbia, S.C.)
JX4005.K44 1989
327.1′16—dc20   89–16720
                                              CIP

To the loving memory of our fathers:

Charles W. Kegley *(1912–1986)*
and Andrew Raymond, Jr. *(1914–1985)*

Contents

Tables

Figures

Displays

Editor's Preface

The pace of global change has accelerated greatly in the last decades of the twentieth century, and new problems occurring under novel conditions are challenging the academic study of International Relations. There is today a renaissance in scholarship directed toward enhancing our understanding of world politics, global economics, and foreign policy. To examine the transformed structure of the international system and the expanded agenda of global affairs, researchers are introducing new concepts, theories, and analytic modes. Knowledge is expanding rapidly.

Our goal in this series of books is to record the findings of recent innovative research in International Relations, and make these readily available to a broader readership of professionals and students. Contributors to the series are leading scholars who are expert in particular subfields of the discipline. Their contributions represent the most recent work located at the discipline's research frontiers. Topics, subjects, approaches, methods and analytical techniques vary from volume to volume in the series, as each book is intended as an original contribution in the broadest sense. Common to all volumes, however, are careful research and the excitement of new discovery.

When Trust Breaks Down by Charles W. Kegley, Jr., and Gregory A. Raymond is a work of mature scholarship. Save in its expression, which is lucid, the book is in every other way very complex because the realities it addresses are themselves highly complex. The study is analytically multi-modal, eclectically philosophical, strictly scientific yet unabashedly normative, historical and contemporary, conclusive yet still provocative. This book is about alliances, which are among the most common but least understood forms of international relationships, and the authors have an almost definitive amount to say about the causes and conditions that lead governments to make, and break, their alliance commitments to one another. On a broader analytical plane, however, Kegley and Raymond are astutely concerned not merely with alliances but with the phenomenon of *commitment* in relations between states. They call it ''promissory obligation,'' and they see it emerging from an interesting process that they call ''norm formation.'' In looking into this process they carefully examine relation-

ships between kinds and characteristics of commitment and an array
of factors having to do with structure, process and people in international politics. At the deepest philosophical level, Kegley and Raymond's book is a study of peace and a penetrating look at how
complex interrelationships among commitments, global conditions
and alliances either contribute to or detract from peace. *When Trust
Breaks Down* addresses and answers questions about morality and international behavior that have long been central to the discipline of
International Relations.

Donald J. Puchala

Preface

This book originates from our conviction that alliance norms play a decisive role in world politics. Our focus on these norms evolved from a much larger and continuing research project, the Transnational Rules Indicators Project (TRIP), which was designed to investigate the sources and consequences of transnational legal norms. TRIP began in the early 1970s and has produced numerous publications dealing with various legal principles. The reception that the scholarly community has given these works strengthened our confidence in the utility of the TRIP data for evaluating the impact of alliance norms in the international community. Clearly, alliance norms deserve special attention. They speak profoundly to some of the most fundamental issues in world politics, namely, to the degree of order and level of collaboration in international life. Thus they warrant the extensive treatment that is only possible in a book-length study.

Although *When Trust Breaks Down* is an original statement on the growth and decay of alliance norms, the assumptions underpinning our alliance commitment index and data-making procedures have benefited from previous scholarly review. Our methodology has been sharpened by the many helpful suggestions offered by those editors and anonymous referees who reviewed our earlier publications in such journals as the *Harvard International Review, International Studies Quarterly, Journal of Peace Research, Conflict Management and Peace Science,* and *International Interactions.* Although we have built upon these earlier publications, the analysis offered here is a substantial revision of these works based on an enriched data base and extended time frame.

Many people have contributed to the development of this book, and their assistance is appreciated. In addition to thanking our colleagues whose research influenced our thinking on this subject, we are especially indebted to the following people. First, we acknowledge the pathbreaking work of J. David Singer and his associates with the Correlates of War project, whose data made it possible to link fluctuations in the content of alliance norms with behavioral processes and other systemic phenomena. Second, we would like to thank Dina

Zinnes, Richard Merritt, Claudio Cioffi-Revilla, Robert Keohane, and the other participants in the December 1986 Merriam Seminar on Cooperative Processes at the University of Illinois for their encouragement and constructive suggestions. Third, we appreciate the friendship and support of Earl Fry, Ladd Hollist, Ray Hillam, and the participants in the 1988 Colloquium on Paths to Peace held during November 1988 at the David M. Kennedy International Center, at Brigham Young University. Fourth, we have profited from the critical comments provided by our reviewers (James N. Rosenau, Nicholas G. Onuf, and William R. Thompson) and our colleagues Donald J. Puchala, co-editor of the *Studies in International Relations* series of which this book is a component, and William Kreml. Fifth, we are grateful for the support provided by our university administrators, in particular, James B. Holderman, Frank Borkowski, Mac Bennett, John Keiser, Larry Selland, Larry Irvin, Robert Sims, Willard Overgaard, and Gary Moncrief, for helping us present our preliminary findings on norm transformation at international conferences in Amsterdam, Brussels, Paris, Mexico City, Moscow, Rio de Janeiro, Oxford, and Toronto. The participants and audiences at these and various professional meetings in the United States provided helpful feedback on our project. Support for data acquisition by the Research and Productive Scholarship program at the University of South Carolina is also gratefully acknowledged.

Of course, no book would be possible without good staff support and technical assistance. The data collection on which the first phase of the project was based owes much to Kyungsook Choi Lee, Barron Boyd, Jane Lawther, and Jeanne Klinger, whose coding of legal treatises enabled the original data base to be tested for reliability and validity. David W. Caffry, Ken Scott, Warren Slesinger, and the staff of the University of South Carolina Press provided valuable professional advice. William A. Clark, Stephen W. Hook, Robert Waite, Karen Kelsch, Art Vanden Houten, and Kurt D. Will devoted considerable time and effort assisting us in our research. Mary Burns expertly managed the word processing for the many iterations of our manuscript carefully and cheerfully. In addition, librarians at the Peace Palace at the Hague, the Graduate Institute of International Studies in Geneva, and the headquarters of the American Society of International Law were most helpful.

Finally, on a more personal note, we would like to express our appreciation to Christine Raymond, whose faith and trust in our scholarly work never broke down.

Writing this book was truly a collaborative exercise. We shared equally in the development of all aspects of the entire book, just as we share equal responsibility for all errors of omission or commission.

C. W. K.
G. A. R.

het Vredespaleis,
Den Haag

WHEN TRUST BREAKS DOWN

Introduction

Commitment is the adhesive of human interaction. Vows between husband and wife; contracts between buyer and seller; covenants between a deity and its people; pledges of allegiance between citizens and the state; and alliance treaties between nations exemplify this bond. The degree of obligation one feels toward the commitments made to others influences all social relationships.

Of great importance for the stability of the international system are the processes by which alliance commitments are terminated. Alliances are given force by the authority and respect allies ascribe to their promissory obligations. Sometimes alliances expire according to a set, pre-established schedule. At other times they end abruptly when one party fails to keep its word. Fear of being betrayed looms large in the minds of makers of foreign policy, casting a shadow over every alliance. Whether allies can be counted on to comply with the treaty commitments they swear to execute is thus critical in estimating the potential impact of alliances. It is important to know, for example, if a commitment is viewed as an irrevocable pledge, similar to the *Nibelungentreue* given by Kaiser Wilhelm II to Austria-Hungary on July 5, 1914. Unless treaty commitments are regarded as binding by the signatories to them, the behavioral consequences of formal alliances will be marginal. Such treaties will be, in Lenin's famous words, "like piecrust, made to be broken." The amount of alliances in the international system, the number of parties to them, the distribution of capabilities they produce—none of these structural properties will matter in a cultural context where decision makers feel free to disregard their commitments ad libitum. Alliances in such an environment will be bonds that fail to bind. On the other hand, if treaty commitments are recognized as binding by members of the international system, the capacity of alliances to constrain state behavior will be substantially enlarged. Thus norms governing the nature of alliance commitments are of critical importance in explaining the impact of alliance formation in world politics. The central purpose of this book is to examine what happens if and when trust in this kind of commitment between sovereign states breaks.

1

A perusal of the writings by statesmen and theorists on this topic reveals considerable disagreement over the alleged influence of different types of alliance norms on interstate behavior. Since antiquity, alliances have been a focus of writers' hopes and fears. Some argue that alliance norms that support absolute compliance with treaty commitments limit conflict by adding predictability and mutual confidence to the relations among nations. Conversely, other writers suggest that binding commitments may actually increase the number of parties to disputes and thereby make conflict more, not less, frequent. Those writers then go on to claim that norms that support an elastic interpretation of commitment would allow national leaders the flexibility to extricate themselves from onerous burdens. The uncertainty created by the possibility of shifts in their allegiance would ostensibly breed caution, inhibit risk taking, and, in turn, reduce the possibility that disputes would escalate into wars. The literature on international statecraft, then, does not speak to us with a single voice on the issue of what tends to happen when different types of alliance norms receive wide support. The relative merits of alliance norms that support restrictive versus permissive interpretations of alliance obligations are a matter of considerable debate.

In order to examine the impact of alliance norms on world politics, we invite our readers to explore with us the available evidence that bears on contending propositions about the causes and consequences of alliance norms. The nature of the debate is introduced in Part I. In the first chapter, the environment for the making and maintenance of alliances is described as "bounded anarchy," a setting in which a variety of rules propose limits to what is permissible in statecraft. In Chapter 2 we argue that the most basic of these rules pertains to promissory obligations. How these obligations ought to be defined, however, varies widely among members of the nihilist, idealist, and realist schools of thought. Each school advances a different interpretation of the latitude for choice, as well as the place of contract in statecraft, therefore providing a different answer to the question of whether foreign policy can or should be guided by moral principles of conduct. This discussion provides the groundwork for a literature review in the third chapter, which takes a closer look at alliances and the question of whether alliances can serve as ties that bind nations together. Focus is placed upon the problematic role of promissory obligations in world politics and the reluctance of states to reduce their sovereignty by honoring commitments when changed circumstances make treaty compliance disadvantageous.

In emphasizing binding versus flexible interpretations of alliance commitment, international norms either breed a culture of shared expectations of trust or a culture in which mistrust is pervasive. Insofar as considerable disagreement exists over the consequences of each cultural climate for the stability of the international system, it is necessary to gather evidence on what happens when trust breaks down. That is, we need to know when restrictive conceptions of alliance obligations are replaced by norms advocating a relatively more permissive conception of commitment. In Part II, our interpretation of that evidence is informed by theories emanating from historical, sociological, political, philosophical, and legal scholarship, though we do not depend exclusively on a single analytic tradition or disciplinary orientation. Chapter 4 proposes a strategy for measuring changes in the content of alliance norms. It draws upon the fact that within international law the traditional quest for political consensus concerning alliance commitments has consistently been framed within a dichotomy. The debate has been defined by two rival legal and prescriptive principles—*pacta sunt servanda* and *rebus sic stantibus*—and the relative emphasis placed on each in international law since 1815 serves as an indicator of the degree to which evolutionary changes in alliance norms have occurred. Chapter 5 discusses the obstacles to making generalizations about alliance norms and world politics from an historical data base grounded in international law, a medium that communicates expectations to statesmen about treaty compliance.

Following the presentation of our methodological procedures, we explore the sources of alliance norm transformation in Part III. Discussed in Chapter 6 are the conditions that numerous theorists have suggested may foster norms that support promissory obligations. Here, we empirically analyze the impact of war termination on the emergence of alliance norms that either back the sanctity of treaty commitments or endorse a permissive interpretation of obligations between allies. Chapter 7 explores the prospects for alliance reliability and whether those prospects increase when power is concentrated in the hands of a few actors or when power is widely diffused throughout the international system.

In Part IV, we look at the consequences that emerge when those norms that promote binding versus flexible commitments gain acceptance. In Chapter 8 we analyze the impact of alliance norms on the frequency, scope, and intensity of interstate crises. This is followed in the ninth chapter with an examination of the extent to which alliance norms can inhibit the escalation of international crises to wars.

Having therein generated evidence on the causes and consequences of alliance norm transformation, in Part V we return to a review of the nature of obligation and the place of morality in world politics. Based on the historical patterns revealed through our case studies and time-series analyses, in Chapter 10 we offer some conclusions about the conditions under which particular types of alliance norms are able to promote peace, and ask the reader to evaluate, on the basis of the evidence generated, whether this interpretation is convincing or whether an alternative interpretation might be developed to better account for the roots and consequences of different conceptions of obligations among allies. In our Epilogue we advance some propositions about the policy implications of these findings for the future of world politics.

This book has been inspired by curiosity, and has been guided by two basic convictions. Epistemologically, we feel that our understanding of world politics can best be advanced by an approach that combines the positivist's reliance on empirical evidence with the postmodernist's emphasis on the meanings that statesmen attach to the concepts that organize their visions of global reality and the legal narratives that shape their thinking. We believe it necessary to probe both historical regularities (as revealed in nomothetic patterns of belief and behavior) and the discursive conventions and performances that have guided the world view of statesmen throughout various periods and circumstances. To expand knowledge, both science and postmodernism are necessary, and both macro-quantitative and hermeneutic evidence must be examined.

Our purpose is to uncover the conditions under which the prospects for a more stable international system might be enhanced. We hope to extract valid inferences about the most promising path to peace through alliances from history, so that greater order instead of continuing disorder might prevail in world politics. We thus hope to make both a theoretical and a pragmatic, policy-relevant contribution by providing evidence about the kinds of alliance norms that, if embraced, will prove most conducive to global stability. Because the diplomatic tradition advances diametrically opposed conclusions, we believe it important to disentangle the dialogue and discover the extent to which support for one or the other of these contending norms might lead to a safer and more sane world.

In its approach to these concerns, *When Trust Breaks Down* is ultimately an exercise in public philosophy, entailing a critical evaluation of the larger issues of freedom versus order. We are convinced that any philosophy of international politics must confront the fundamental dilemma around which statecraft revolves by asking how alliance obligations can be defined in such a way as to enhance the prospects for peace. In several contexts and variations, this is the issue that underlies the historical interpretations provided in this book. We hope to enlarge the discussion of this question, not to confine it, by expanding our awareness of the dangers posed by the often fallacious reasoning of incompatible conventional wisdoms. To make for a better world, sense and nonsense must be separated. It is our purpose to test competing orientations against diplomatic experience in order that the policy implications of alternate conceptions of commitment might be illuminated in an abrasive, competitive, state-centric system that continues to be predicated on self-help.

Part I

Theoretical
Foundations

Anarchy and Order in World Politics

1

The prince is not bound by the law of nations to a greater extent than by his own laws. If the law of nations is iniquitous, the prince can disregard it when making laws for his own kingdom and can forbid his subjects to observe it, even when it is truly common to all peoples.

Jean Bodin

The root of the trouble in today's world is that we believe in anarchy. We believe in the complete, or almost complete, right of every nation to do what it chooses.

Clement Attlee

During the fourth year of the Peloponnesian War, Mytilene broke its alliance with Athens and attempted to seize control of the strategically important island of Lesbos. As a result, the Athenians dispatched a fleet of forty ships to punish their former ally. While the fleet lay anchored near the coast, the Mytileneans sent envoys to Olympia in an effort to persuade Sparta and other members of the Lacaedaemonian Confederation to help them repel the imminent Athenian attack. The envoys argued that Mytilene could be trusted even though it had just broken a treaty with Athens. The crux of their argument was that although the sanctity of alliance agreements was a widely accepted norm among the Greeks, a mitigating circumstance allowed Mytilene to terminate the alliance unilaterally. According to Thucydides, that circumstance was an Athenian attempt to create an empire out of what formerly had been a league of equals.

The Mytilenean episode reveals several noteworthy things about the role of alliance norms within the ancient Greek multi-state system. First, system members acknowledged the existence of norms, or rules of conduct, that described prevailing attitudes regarding the permissibility of specific kinds of alliance behavior. Second, these norms were not neutral, immutable laws; they were challenged by those who sought to replace them with rules for behavior that were more congruent with their own interests. Finally, the sanctity of alliance agreements was a central principle underlying this normative order. Similar observations have been made about alliance norms in other multi-state systems, including the Near East in the second millennium B.C.,

8

China during the Chou dynasty, the pre-Mauryan period of ancient India, and Renaissance Italy after the Peace of Lodi (see Phillipson, 1911; Russell, 1936; and Walker, 1953). Thus, although behavior within multi-state systems frequently has been likened to a Hobbesian state of nature, the web of expectations created by prevailing norms often has made international political life something less than "nasty, brutish and short."

This book outlines the origins of alliance norms in world politics, the sources of their transformation, and the consequences that result when binding as opposed to flexible concepts of alliance commitment gain force. To treat these topics, it is necessary to describe the key characteristics of the environment in which alliance formation and dissolution occur, as well as the properties and functions of international norms. Furthermore, the various components of the international normative order need to be differentiated in order to identify those types of norms that pertain to the behavior of allies toward one another. The definitions, distinctions, and typologies developed in this chapter prepare the way for an account in subsequent chapters of the impact of alliance norms in world politics, and they frame the larger philosophical and policy questions to which that account speaks.

THE INTERNATIONAL SYSTEM AS A BOUNDED ANARCHY

As in multi-state systems of the past, diplomatic behavior in the contemporary international system occurs without a central governing body. States are sovereign: they have supreme power over their territory and populace, and no higher authority stands above them holding the legitimacy and coercive capability required to undertake the extractive, regulative, and distributive functions that governments normally perform in domestic political systems. It is for this reason that states can be said to coexist in a condition of anarchy.[1]

The twin notions of state sovereignty and international anarchy underlie most theorizing about world politics (Lijphart, 1974). Whether one examines theories of the balance of power, collective security, or world government, a common premise can be found: owing to differences in the structural and cultural characteristics of anarchic versus

---

1. Our literary use of the term "state" is neither meant to imbue it with human characteristics nor to treat it as a unitary actor in world politics. We recognize that the danger of reification exists whenever such literary conveniences are used as a shorthand way of referring to the individuals who make authoritative decisions for governments.

hierarchically centralized systems, actors of unequal power in the former behave differently from actors in the latter. This premise is backed by evidence that political structure and culture are interdependent and that they jointly affect political behavior (Barry, 1970: 48). Within a system whose structural and cultural characteristics derive from the absence of a central governing body, cooperation will be the exception to a dominant pattern of conflict. Like the participants in Rousseau's allegory of the Stag Hunt, members of the international system are highly uncertain about others' intentions and therefore engage in defensive noncooperation. In addition, states often become mired in outright conflict because of the "security dilemma" each faces (Herz, 1951: 157; Jervis, 1978). Unsure of one another's aims, each state tends to take measures to enhance its own security. But absolute security for one state may be perceived as creating absolute insecurity for the remaining members of the system, with the result that everyone becomes locked into an upward spiral of countermeasures that jeopardizes the security of all. Sir Edward Grey (1925: 92) summarized this syndrome in the following terms:

> The increase of armaments, that is intended in each nation to produce consciousness of strength, and a sense of security, does not produce these effects. On the contrary, it produces a consciousness of the strength of other nations and a sense of fear. Fear begets suspicion and distrust and evil imaginings of all sorts, til each government feels it would be criminal and a betrayal of its own country not to take every precaution, while every government regards every precaution of every other government as evidence of hostile intent.

Table 1.1 contrasts the salient characteristics of an idealized representation of anarchically and hierarchically centralized systems. Whereas hierarchical systems contain units that are linked together in superior-subordinate relationships, anarchical systems contain autonomous, legally equal units of differential power and prestige. Both systems may be stratified, but because anarchical systems lack a central governing body and their component units vary in putative strength, the leaders of these units are the final judges of whether a wrong has been committed, and they bear the ultimate responsibility for punishing the perpetrator of such perceived transgressions. Retaliatory force, in other words, is the *ultima ratio* in anarchic political systems.

Reliance upon self-help as the court of last appeal often leads to the conclusion that life in anarchic systems is like the chaos depicted in the paintings of Hieronymus Bosch. But anarchy is not anomie: "the

**Table 1.1. Characteristics of Ideal-type Anarchical
and Hierarchical Political Systems**

Anarchical	Hierarchical
Structural Characteristics	
Decentralized authority	Centralized authority
Power dispersed	Power concentrated
Sovereignty in constituent units	Sovereignty in central governmental institutions
Functional diffuseness	Functional specificity
Minimal role differentiation	Division of labor
Cultural Characteristics	
Horizontal normative order	Vertical normative order
Laws of coordination	Laws of subordination
Auto-limitation	External control
Rule making through custom and bargaining arrangements	Rule making through formal legislation
Rule interpretation by constituent political units	Rule interpretation by judicial bodies
Rule adjudication through voluntary consent	Rule adjudication through compulsory jurisdiction
Rule enforcement through self-help	Rule enforcement through institutionalized agencies
Behavioral Characteristics	
Units strive for autarchy	Units strive for specialization and interdependence
Units act in self-interest	Units act in collective interest
Substantive issues entwined with unit efforts to ensure self-preservation	Substantive issues entwined with unit efforts to influence central government
Units entrust security to deterrence through acquisition of arms and allies	Units entrust security to strength of the central government

edge of anarchy is fenced with rules'' (Bailey, 1969: xiii). As Hedley Bull persuasively argued, ''no international system . . . has operated without some regulatory rules and institutions'' (quoted in Watson, 1987: 151). Rules and order can and do exist in the absence of government. "Statesmen nearly always perceive themselves as constrained by principles, norms, and rules that prescribe and proscribe varieties of behavior" (Puchala and Hopkins, 1983: 86).

One way to conceptualize the rule-bound nature of the contemporary international system is to think of it as being analogous to a segmented society. This form of political organization was common in precolonial Africa. The Ibo of Nigeria, the Kru of Liberia and Sierra Leone, the Tallensi of Ghana, the Tonga of Zambia, and the Somali of Somalia, Ethiopia, and Kenya are a few examples of segmented societies (Eisenstadt, 1959; Fortes and Evans-Pritchard, 1940; Mair, 1964; Middleton and Tait, 1958; Radcliffe-Brown and Forde, 1952). Each was based on the principle that political power should be fragmented and localized, not concentrated in central governmental authority. Individuals in such societies recognized membership in a larger nation. Their primary affiliation and loyalty, however, were with smaller segments of the collectivity and were based on extended family groupings. Occasionally the various segments might coordinate their activities. For instance, the Masai of Kenya and Tanzania participated in a common socialization process and the Teke of Zaire cooperated during certain common religious rituals. But despite these joint activities, local autonomy was maintained, and the political culture enshrined independence as a core value.

The absence of a central governing body made it difficult to resolve disputes between competitive segments. As illustrated by the conflict between the villages of Alaikoro and Chiolu in Elechi Amadi's novel *The Great Ponds,* disputes between segments could potentially escalate into catastrophic wars. Yet fratricidal violence did not arise out of every dispute. The segments were part of a larger jural community that relied on customary rules to control the use of force. Some of these rules outlined procedures through which a third party (such as the Neur "leopard-skin chief") could take preventive action to mediate a conflict prior to the eruption of violence; others sought to reduce the severity of fighting once it broke out by restricting the amount of retaliatory force that could legitimately be used against an offender; and still others set forth symbolic acts of atonement that would deescalate and help settle conflicts that arose (Masters, 1969; Service, 1975). Thus, as the experience of segmented societies demonstrates, competitive, self-interested behavior in an anarchic system need not be arbitrary and disorderly. Even among a people as aggressive as the Philippine headhunters and the Yanomamo of northern Brazil, rules covering the use of force and military alliances were acknowledged (Barton, 1930; Chagnon, 1968). Within atomized societies that stress fierce independence, rules controlling the application of the *lex talionis* materialize and receive support. Moreover, such rules tend to be backed by sanctions, even in the absence of formal institutions to enforce compliance.

Although various observers have drawn parallels between the role of norms in segmented societies and the international system (e.g., see Hoebel, 1954; Maine, 1861; Barkun, 1968), the two are not identical. There is far more cultural pluralism within the international system (McDougal and Lasswell, 1959; Levi, 1974). But this heterogeneity does not mean, as David Fromkin (1981: 81, 84) claims, that there are no rules in international politics. As Evan Luard's (1976: 61) research on historical multi-state systems shows, "All groups of nations in regular contact have in practice adopted certain rules defining the conduct which could usually be expected among their members."

Regularized contact among independent states that acknowledge no higher authority cannot necessarily be regarded as lacking normative structure. In the absence of a superior power, international diplomacy is sustained by a diplomatic culture—"a common stock of ideas and values possessed by official representatives" (Bull, 1977: 173–183). Like the clans in a segmented society, the members of the international system have consistently developed shared beliefs about the obligations of sovereign states to one another. It is meaningful, therefore, to speak of a society of states and common normative underpinnings at the international level. To be sure, this global society is primitive in organization and support, and at times it has collapsed. But a society of states encapsulated by a diplomatic culture has not been rare in international history. Even when no hierarchically organized central institutions command authority, states still "form a society in the sense that they conceive themselves to be bound by a common set of rules in their relations with one another" (Bull, 1977: 13).

In summary, international politics unfolds in a milieu that contains "partially structured conflict relationships" (Brickman, 1974). A hierarchical environment contains fully structured conflict relationships where, as in a court of law with its quasi-religious language, dress, and protocol, the roles and behavior of the parties are clearly stipulated by codes and regulations. At the other extreme, an anomic environment contains unstructured conflict relationships where, as in terrorist confrontations such as the murder of Israeli athletes at the

1972 Olympic Games, such formal restraints are absent. But in the partially structured conflict relationships of an anarchic environment, normative rules develop despite the absence of a higher authority and these rules prescribe limits to behavior, even though the parties retain considerable latitude in the use of threats, deception, and other contentious tactics.

THE PROPERTIES OF INTERNATIONAL NORMS

Norms are "generalized formulations—more or less explicit—of expectations of proper action by differentiated units in relatively specific situations" (Parsons, 1961: 120). The expectations expressed by international norms pertain to proper action by nation-states. That is to say, norms communicate injunctions that prescribe certain actions but proscribe others. Rather than representing "average" or "normal" behavior in a statistical sense, they entail a collective evaluation of behavior by members of the state system in terms of what ought to be, as well as a collective expectation as to what behavior will be (Krummenacher, 1985: 45–83; Gibbs, 1966: 589).

These standards of conduct have three basic properties. First, they are ubiquitous. When the Romans asserted the principle *ubi societas ibi ius* (where there is society there will be law), they touched upon the pervasiveness of normative rules. Studies of hunting and gathering bands, the most primitive political systems for which we have data, indicate that groups with minimal role differentiation routinely develop rules to govern the behavior of their members. Rules controlling the use of force within and between bands have been reported among such diverse peoples as the Cheyenne (Hoebel, 1960), the Eskimo (Weyer, 1967; Hughes, 1966) and the !Kung of the Kalahari Desert (Marshall, 1967).[2] Similarly, as Ragnar Numelin (1950) has shown, norms also shaped the interactions among the earliest political communities.

A second property of international norms is that they are situational. Depending upon the context of a particular act, it may or may not be deemed permissible by prevailing norms. Consider the example of legal norms governing nonamicable modes of redress short of war. Under international law during the first half of the twentieth century, one state was permitted to take reprisals against another in retaliation

---

2. It should be remembered that organized warfare of the type found in the contemporary state system was virtually unknown among these societies. Instead, violence took the form of a feud, where attacks were sporadic and confined to relatively small groups.

for illegal acts committed by the latter. These coercive measures would have been impermissible if not performed in response to a prior illegal act. Moreover, as illustrated in the Naulilaa case (*Portugal v. Germany* 8 Trib. Arb. Mixtes 409 [1928]) in the 1920s, coercive reprisals were considered to be impermissible unless two additional conditions were met: (1) they were preceded by a request for redress that was unavailing; and (2) they were proportional to the provocation received. Hence the legitimacy of nonamicable modes of redress was dependent on context. It was contingent on the specific situation at hand (*in hoc statu*) rather than being universally applicable.[3]

The third noteworthy property of international norms is that they are mutable. Unless steps are taken to reinforce them, norms will decay and be transformed by changing practices and circumstances. To illustrate this point, let us return to our example of normative constraints on the use of force. During the early part of the eighteenth century, the prevailing intellectual mood in Europe was one of optimism. A belief in human progress had replaced the Augustinian view that divine, teleological purposes would lead to the apocalyptic end and eternal punishment of the earthly city, not to its continual improvement. Inspired by Newton's principles and Locke's critique of innate ideas, the *philosophes* demolished the Heavenly City of St. Augustine and rebuilt it on an earthly foundation (Becker, 1932: 31). Reason, enlightenment, and perfectibility now replaced grace, revelation, and salvation as the pillars of a new faith. Paralleling the growth of this new faith was the rise of international norms designed to control the use of force. Numerous treaties were concluded in which states "agreed to observe certain rules between themselves" (Clark, 1966: 23).[4] In particular, rules were established to reduce the destructiveness of war, as well as to govern the treatment of neutrals, prisoners, and civilian populations. Yet by the end of the century these

---

3. The current legal status of nonamicable modes of redress short of war is a matter of some controversy. On the one hand, most scholars assert that the Naulilaa restrictions have been superseded by Article 2, paragraph 4 of the United Nations Charter, which prohibits such acts of coercive self-help. On the other hand, some government officials have disagreed with this interpretation, as can be seen in the British and French justification of their attack on Egypt in 1956.
4. At times, these rules had chivalrous overtones, as at Fontenoy in 1745 when rival British and French commanders exhorted each other with courteous protestations, "Sir, you fire first!" (Manuel, 1951: 118). Nevertheless, historians generally agree that these normative limitations made combat a "relatively humane and well-regulated enterprise" (Guerlac, 1943: 33).

normative constraints had eroded. Unlike most of the conflicts that immediately preceded them, the French Revolutionary and Napoleonic wars were not fought with limited means for limited dynastic claims. They were secular crusades aimed at annihilating opposing governments and converting their people. Revolutionary upheaval, the spread of new ideological doctrines, and changes in the distribution of power led to the transformation of existing international norms. The norms of international society thus emerge and evolve in response to many kinds of changes in society; but regardless of their sources, they perform a common set of functions.

THE FUNCTIONS OF INTERNATIONAL NORMS

The primary function of international norms is to promote order, though some would allege that *certain* norms actually perpetuate the competitive, laissez-faire environment of the Westphalian state system (Toynbee, 1967; Lawrence, 1915). As Hedley Bull (1977: 54) has written, "Order in any society is maintained not merely by a sense of common interests in creating order or avoiding disorder, but by rules which spell out the kind of behavior that is orderly." Like members of segmented societies who attempt to reduce turmoil by developing rules that define relationships among their segments, statesmen seek predictability by forging rules that guide expectations. The judgments they make of their counterparts are "irrevocably bound up with attributions of intentions." These attributions are, in turn, bound up with "inferences concerning their knowledge of the rules and with inferences concerning their perceptions of the conditions that call forth the actions required by the rules" (Collett, 1977: 18). Because norms foster predictability, they are often believed to be more conducive to order than disorder.

To promote order in the political cosmos, international norms perform several communication functions, each of which contributes in some way to the overall goal of mitigating the effects of anarchy. Specifically, they communicate the scope of a state's entitlements, the extent of its obligations, and the range of its jurisdiction. International norms allocate legal competence in territorial, personal, material, and temporal terms (Coplin, 1970: 175). In other words, they inform governmental leaders of where their legal control begins and ends, over whom it exists, over what objects it has control, and during what period of time it operates. International norms serve as quasi-authoritative guides that present to individuals "an image of the social system—an image which has both factual and normative aspects and which contributes to social order by building a consensus on procedural as well as on substantive matters'' (Coplin, 1965: 617).

This image is communicated in at least four ways (Cohen, 1981: 16–21). First, norms delineate boundaries. Beyond defining a nation's homeland, norms establish buffer zones, neutralized areas, and spheres of influence. Examples of these extraterritorial rules include those found in the 1907 agreement between Great Britain and Russia over the status of Tibet as a buffer zone; those built into the agreement among Austria, France, Great Britain, Prussia, and Russia in 1831 to guarantee the neutrality of Belgium; and those underlying the agreements reached at the 1884–1885 Congress of Berlin over spheres of colonial influence in Africa.

Second, norms serve as signposts or heuristic mental aids that warn policymakers of prearranged actions that various states take under certain circumstances. For example, signatories to the 1908 agreement to maintain peace in the North Sea pledged that if events threatened the stability of the region, they would ''communicate with each other for concerting among themselves'' (Lauren, 1983: 51).

Third, like standard operating procedures, norms routinize many facets of transnational relations. As commercial, financial, and other contacts among nations have become more frequent in an increasingly interdependent world, the need for rules to manage these transactions has grown. Accordingly, the increase in transnational contact has expanded the willingness of states to incur obligations (Brewin, 1988). Many regimes have been devised to regulate behavior in such issue areas as trade and monetary affairs (Leive, 1976), as well as to manage access to global commons such as fisheries and resources in Antarctica (Young, 1977; Soroos, 1986). International regimes refer to the collection of principles, norms, rules, and decision-making procedures that members of the international system support in order to regularize behavior and resolve issues on their common agendas.[5] Due to the inherently competitive nature of the search for security, examples of international regimes in ''high politics'' are less common, even though historically they have ranged from institutionalized

---

5. As defined by Stephen D. Krasner (1982: 186), ''Principles are beliefs of fact, causation, and rectitude. Norms are standards of behavior defined in terms of rights and obligations. Rules are specific prescriptions or proscriptions for action. Decision-making procedures are prevailing practices for making and implementing collective action.'' Although there are other definitions of regimes, most converge on the notion of a regime as an institutionalized system of cooperation with respect to a given issue or issue area (Haas, 1980; Young, 1980).

conventions to tacit understandings about the rules of the game (see Jervis, 1982). By putting boundaries around specific functional domains in both welfare and warfare, international regimes reduce for national leaders many of the burdens of monitoring international developments. Simultaneously, they may help bureaucracies dealing with foreign affairs avoid crises and successfully manage those that erupt.

Finally, international norms can perform a tripwire function. Should a widely accepted rule be violated, attention can be focused on the transgression so that a collective response can be more easily mobilized. For instance, when France under Louis XIV occupied Strasbourg, a free city of the Holy Roman Empire, Emperor Leopold I was able to rally Catholic opponents of the Sun King. Subsequently, when Louis aroused his Protestant enemies by revoking the Edict of Nantes, the Catholic and Protestant groups formed the League of Augsburg (1686), a diverse, anti-French alliance composed of the Holy Roman Emperor, the kings of Spain and Sweden, the electors of Bavaria, Saxony, and the Palatinate, Savoy, Holland, and, following the Glorious Revolution, England. In the minds of many Europeans, by transgressing normative boundaries Louis XIV had crossed two tripwires. He violated their interpretation of the Peace of Westphalia by "reuniting" Strasbourg with the kingdom of France, and he violated the Edict of Nantes, which had dampened the protracted religious wars of the previous century. The existence of these norms alerted the victims that accepted understandings for behavior had been violated.

In summary, international norms introduce a modicum of predictability to world politics. They communicate a rudimentary consensus on the nature of the state system and they contain a set of interrelated symbols that are used to persuade members of the state system "that it makes sense to think of the problem in terms of rights and obligations" (Scheingold, 1974: 50). To conceptualize norms in this way is to see them as a medium through which prevailing opinions about acceptable patterns of state behavior are transmitted to members of the system. It is in this sense that we shall use the term "norm" in subsequent chapters.

By viewing norms as a form of communication we have departed from a more conventional, Austinian interpretation of their ontological status, that is, as commands from a sovereign that restrain states from acting in a certain manner. Nevertheless, our approach has some clear advantages over such an interpretation: not only does it allow us to examine the role of norms in international bargaining; it also sheds light on how tacit agreements coordinate state behavior through the creation of common expectations and a shared frame of reference.

Once it is granted that international norms may shape world politics in ways other than through commands backed by threats, then references to the images that norms communicate are required for the explanation of state behavior. Of course, not every member of the state system will internalize these norms even though their existence may be acknowledged. The consensus that international norms express is imperfect; it reflects what William D. Coplin (1966: 187) calls an "immature political culture" because the system's members often agree on certain values at the same time they fail to recognize the implications of these values for their own behavior. Furthermore, the consensual foundations for many norms may be weak or fragile, in which case their impact will be modest.

Any assertion that international norms exert a potential influence over the conduct of statesmen in the absence of institutionalized enforcement procedures hinges on the proposition that the ethos or mores of a particular historical period are widely shared and therefore make an impact upon decision making in foreign policy. However inviting the contentions that norm and conduct are linked (von Wright, 1963) and that foreign policy decisions are determined by cultural influences (Sampson, 1987), these propositions are difficult to verify.[6] Voluntary obedience to norms may occur, but the analyst is burdened with the need to demonstrate that state practice was indeed circumscribed by the moral climate of the day. It is one thing to show that statesmen recognized certain rules of behavior; it is quite another to determine whether they acted in accordance with them through voluntary consent.

This being the case, in what sense can we safely assume that international norms influence interstate interactions? Poststructuralists suggest an answer, namely, that norms exert influence because they enter into the discourse of diplomacy on a subconscious level (e.g., Foucault, 1979; Derrida, 1977, 1982; for a critical survey see Fisher,

---

6. Richard Ned Lebow (1981: 229) observes in this context that "It is difficult to analyze the impact of background considerations . . . because of the problems involved in reconstructing policy-makers' understandings of them. Policy-makers rarely articulate their assessment of the relative importance of the host of environmental conditions which influence any particular decision. They are more likely to acknowledge the importance of these conditions obliquely, in ways that are difficult to translate into useful analytical categories."

1987). Norms become part of the thought process and vocabulary of decision makers and are embedded in their understandings of the shared principles of appropriate conduct within international society. Makers of foreign policy inevitably become bound up with a general and unexamined theory of interstate relations, a theory whose values are rooted in their diplomatic culture and are reinforced by the vocabulary they use in their discussions. The shared diplomatic and legal narratives of statesmen are registers of opinion and sources of its dissemination. History, in other words, is "discourse-specific" (Felperin, 1985: 18). Norms reflect a set of psychological dispositions fixed within the minds of statesmen. They are produced by a ceaseless, open-ended dialogue in which statesmen appeal to socially recognized interpretative themes, articulate understandings in performing their socially established roles as policymakers, and contribute to the ongoing discourse by which these themes and understandings are affirmed.

According to this view, images of reality are shaped by diplomatic terminology: language influences thinking, perceptions, and decisions. The vocabulary of diplomatic discourse and its "key words" (R. Williams, 1976) create a normative order and endow it with strength by confining the range of choice that actors within that culture regard as available to them. The language used in negotiation and treaty making is a "prison-house" (Jameson, 1972) that exerts elocutionary force (Austin, 1962). Seen in this way, international norms have an impact that is noncoerced but powerful. In fact, when such a normative order is supported by a community consensus, statesmen may not be able to escape the pressures exerted upon their thinking and their choices.

Of course, reliance on this perspective is not necessary in order to grasp the reasons why international norms shape behavior. Indeed, the ways in which norms are internalized are diverse (Scott, 1971), and principle among them is the tendency for policymakers to actively accept, through conscious choice, particular norms as guideposts for their behavior. Diplomatic history is replete with many examples of leaders who publicly acknowledged that their decisions were affected by prevailing norms, and who demonstrated their reliance on these standards by acting in conformity with them.

Regardless of the means by which norms shape behavior, the various contending rules within the international normative order do not always rigidly define the choices facing statesmen; they often provide them with alternative policy prescriptions. This is especially true when a choice must be made to observe or ignore an alliance treaty once the conditions that led to the original decision to ally have changed. The material constraints of a given international situation have as much to do with the ways statesmen define their policy options as does the discourse, which according to poststructuralists confines their decision latitude. Thus we need not embrace an interpretative perspective in order to accept the compelling proposition that individual choice is influenced by the predominant values of a given historical epoch.

COMPONENTS OF AN INTERNATIONAL NORMATIVE ORDER

Having discussed the basic properties and functions of international norms, let us classify the various types of norms that affect state behavior, and describe how they are linked together in a normative order. In so doing, we can identify more explicitly the boundaries that delineate the focus of our study of alliance norms and the category of behavior examined here.

Norms have properly been the subject of study not only by students of international politics, but by sociologists, cultural anthropologists, linguists, legal scholars, and moral philosophers as well. Each group has approached the subject from the vantage point of its particular discipline and each discipline emphasizes different attributes of norms in its conceptualization and definition of them. Although scholars differ somewhat in their views regarding what is important about norms, they share a number of core assumptions, and their insights all have the capacity to inform our discussion of the role of normative and cultural factors in international affairs. When investigating the influence of alternative conceptions of alliance norms in world politics, we draw on all of these analytic traditions. But, as elaborated on in Chapters 4 and 5, we stress the images of moral obligation contained in alliance norms as they are symbolized and presented in international law, while recognizing the distinctions between morality, legality, and linguistic symbols that are embodied in the literature on norms.[7]

Although the field of jurisprudence contains several contending typologies of norms (see Rommetveit, 1955; Morris, 1956; Gibbs,

---

7. When alliance norms are conceptualized in terms of commitment, obligation becomes a paramount concern as efforts are made to define moral rights and duties in legal terms. But not all norms are rules of commitment. When norms are rules of direction, coercively insisted on by dominant powers, they are seen by some members of the state system as morally doubtful and subject to principled repudiation.

1966; DeLupis 1987), most of these classificatory schemes agree on some generic distinctions. One of these is the difference between substantive and procedural norms (Hart, 1961). The former are rules about permissible and impermissible conduct that imply obligation; the latter specify how these rules are ascertained and applied.

Another common distinction separates those rules that are derived from formal, written conventions from those that come from informal agreements and tacit understandings. Students of international law generally agree that if written conventions are not the "most important" source of international norms (Tung, 1968: 13), they are at least of "dominant importance" (Fenwick, 1965: 94). Between 1945 and 1965 alone, a total of 12,732 treaties were concluded to regulate international interactions (Rohn, 1976: 10). Multilateral conventions, such as the Geneva Red Cross Convention of 1864, which contain a substantial number of signatory parties and are accepted by the overwhelming majority of states, acquire the status of "law-making" treaties and are often envisioned as a form of international legislation (von Glahn, 1981: 17). Formal conventions are not, however, the only source of international norms. As Raymond Cohen (1980) points out, there are a variety of informal sources, including verbal gentlemen's agreements, the "spirit" or unwritten intent of a written agreement, and nonverbal tacit understandings. Comparisons of superpower actions in the Guatemalan (1954), Hungarian (1956), Dominican (1965), and Czechoslovakian (1968) crises reveal that informal agreements, such as those governing mutual acceptance of each other's sphere of influence, provide an important extralegal means for regulating foreign policy behavior in an anarchic environment (see Franck and Weisband, 1972; Kaufman, 1976; Keal, 1984).

Agreement also exists on the distinction between general and particular legal norms. Some norms pertain to all states. Others only bear upon a subset of that population. Among the many possible subsets are the members of an international bloc such as the Group of 77; participants in regional political (e.g., the South Pacific Forum), economic (e.g., the European Community), or sociocultural (e.g., the Islamic Conference) organizations; and countries such as the United States and Canada which claim to have a special relationship. Each of these subsets may develop its own partner-specific norms. Consider the case of the special relationship between Washington and Ottawa. Since World War II, U.S.-Canadian relations have been guided by the following rules: (1) prior notification by which one country alerts the other to impending policy shifts that may affect its interests;

Table 1.2. A Typology of International Norms

Content	Applicability	Explicitness	
		Formal	*Informal*
Substantive	Partner-Specific	I	II
	Actor-Universal	III	IV
Procedural	Partner-Specific	V	VI
	Actor-Universal	VII	VIII

(2) timely consultation concerning the implications of such shifts; and (3) willingness to seek accommodative solutions that would minimize any adverse impact of contemplated policy departures (Barry, 1980: 115; Raymond, 1987a: 222). Thus, although there are a variety of norms that may be held universally by the international community, many of the rules that affect states in their daily relations are partner-specific (Goldmann, 1971).

Taking these three generic distinctions together, we can say that international norms differ in content, degree of explicitness, and domain of applicability. Table 1.2 combines these traits to define eight types of norms. Most of these norms apply to states with cordial relations, but they can also apply to rivals and adversaries. The rise of normative rules of behavior among nations in conflict attests to the fact that norm formation is ubiquitous in all relations where recurrent problems arise and contact is frequent. This even applies to conditions of anarchy.

The first four cells in the typology are filled with substantive norms. Types I and II are both partner-specific, but differ from each other according to their explicitness. The 1494 Treaty of Tordesillas, which divided the globe between Spain and Portugal, and the 1944 Churchill-Stalin "percentages agreement," which delineated British and Soviet interests in Eastern Europe, illustrate this difference: though both entailed rules that established spheres of influence between specific states, one was a legally binding treaty while the other was merely an oral understanding.

Types III and IV also differ according to their explicitness; however, they are both instances of general rather than particular norms. Once again, we can use rules with similar content and applicability but different degrees of explicitness to contrast these two types of norms. Whereas the treaties of Münster and Osnabruck (1648) promoted the principle of religious toleration by formally affirming the rule *cujus regio eius religio* (whose the region, his the religion), religious toleration was backed by informal norms during the period of Persian supremacy over the Middle Eastern multi-state system of the sixth century B.C. (Bozeman, 1960: 47–52).

Turning to the last four cells in the typology, we encounter procedural rather than substantive norms. Types V and VI are both partner-specific but differ in their degree of explicitness. The 1794 Jay Treaty between Great Britain and the United States exemplifies the former, while what Edward McWhinney (1964) calls the tacit ground rule of "nuclear due process" exemplifies the latter. By providing for the arbitration of disputes over the boundary of the St. Croix River, American debts owed to British merchants, and losses suffered by U.S. citizens as a result of British maritime seizures, the Jay Treaty formally designated the procedure the two countries ought to follow in resolving their disagreements. Similarly, embodied within the implicit understanding that the United States and the Soviet Union should avoid surprising one another was a set of accepted procedures each should use to signal the other of its intentions. Hence bilateral rules of procedure, regardless of their degree of explicitness, help states avoid potentially explosive confrontations.

Types VII and VIII perform the same function at a more general level. For example, the Convention Respecting the Limitation of the Employment of Force for the Recovery of Contract Debts, which was adopted at the Hague Conference of 1907, formalized the rule that states ought to use arbitration rather than armed force as the procedure for recovering contract debts. Likewise, among the unwritten diplomatic rules of the last century was a belief that states should notify, solicit opinion, and discuss intended actions prior to their initiation (Lauren, 1983: 50).

With a classification of the various types of international norms behind us, we may now take up the question of how these standards or rules fit together to produce a normative order. Before proceeding with that task, however, let us emphasize that the referent of our term "normative order" is a set of linked rules. An international normative order is not simply a collection of discrete elements. Its rules are patterned and interrelated, although their linkages may vary in strength and they do not evolve monotonically in the same direction (Onuf, 1982a). Within any given order we might find a few tightly linked rules from which a statesman could derive guidance on the stance his government is expected to take in a particular situation.

Elsewhere within the same normative order, we might discover linkages so weak that such derivations would provide our statesman with far less direction when confronted with a different situation. Take, for instance, the laws of warfare during the nineteenth century. At the same time that prevailing legal norms divided enemy belligerents into combatants and noncombatants for the purpose of granting the latter certain immunities, they provided little guidance on how to conduct sieges and bombardments so that fortified cities could be captured without causing unnecessary harm to noncombatants. Simply put, those norms that pertained to the treatment of enemy belligerents were not clearly linked to norms governing military necessity, with the result that limits on the use of force against strongholds remained ambiguous and subject to different interpretations.

One of the reasons for the weakness in many of the linkages scholars draw between international norms lies in their failure to specify how normative orders evolve in world politics. It is not unusual for rules of conduct to emerge out of what Thomas C. Schelling (1960) refers to as "focal point" solutions to mixed-motive games. In other words, informal, partner-specific rules of substantive content (Type II norms) may gradually become established as collective mores (Type IV norms) and may later become embodied in bilateral or multilateral conventions (Types I and III norms). Often accompanying these conventions are formal agreements (Types V and VII norms) and unwritten understandings (Types VI and VIII norms) on procedural matters. In short, an international normative order undergoes sporadic, uneven growth, evolving clear linkages among its component rules in some issue areas but not in others.

Because of its uneven growth, an international normative order lacks symmetry and elegance. As stressed earlier, it contains a welter of norms that differ in content, degree of explicitness, and domain of applicability. At the center of this mosaic is a group of Type III and IV norms that comprise the axiology, or value orientation, of the order. These norms define the obligations of the actors in world politics, and thus underlie and ground the numerous auxiliary rules that surround them.

Several processes encourage conformity with the core and auxiliary rules in an international normative order. Some of these processes entail purposeful action by those whose interest the current order serves. One such process is deterrence by the dominant actor(s) in the political system (Axelrod, 1986). If a few powerful states promote a particular standard of behavior, the threat that they will punish viola-

tors may deter deviation from that standard. Other processes do not
require rule enforcement. As illustrated in crossover induced by critical mass, once some proportion of states observe a particular standard of behavior, a threshold will be crossed for additional states
whose acceptance of that standard may be contingent on how many
other states are already complying. Their subsequent compliance, in
turn, will cause another threshold to be crossed, and so on (Granovetter, 1978). In addition, there are other processes that do not involve
conscious choice. Like rules of etiquette, many standards of international conduct have become ritualized and are maintained by the inertia of habit (Rosenau, 1986; Mansbach and Vasquez, 1981). Finally,
norms may originate from domestic sources, where powerful constit-
uencies exert pressure for a particular rule of behavior (e.g., protec-
tionism versus free trade). Thus adherence to a certain standard of
conduct may arise from internal as well as external sources. Different
states may conform with the prescription of a given rule for different
reasons. Yet all of these pattern maintenance processes notwithstanding, international normative orders still face challenges that range in
magnitude from incremental infringement to overt defiance.

The above discussion demonstrates that the international normative
order is not homogeneous. It is composed of many different types of
norms, which together form a major part of the cultural environment
within which diplomacy unfolds. This environment is constantly in
flux, however, because many of its component norms are in tension
with one another, and acceptance of any set of norms is contingent
upon circumstance. When a group of norms are clearly articulated
and tightly linked with one another in a particular issue area, we have
the making of an international regime. Within a given normative order, there may be a variety of regimes that fit together, but there may
also be discrete sectors in that order where the norms are loosely connected or not clearly articulated and, as a result, no regime exists to
coordinate and harmonize the behavior of states. To emphasize the
heterogeneity of an international normative order is to acknowledge
that

> Even after its emergence, international society remains a historically
> fabricated network of multiple ambiguous themes, concepts, narra-
> tives, and practices that can be recombined, ordered, dispersed, de-
> ferred, and relatively stressed in different ways. Its boundaries are
> inherently problematic. Even the question of its continuity is open to
> controversy. What is historically unique about this anarchical soci-
> ety . . . is how much the commitment to pluralism shared among its

subjects sustains a respect for international society's own historicity, its essential contestedness, its ambiguity, its dependence upon the never quieted play of power. (Ashley, 1990: 47)

Thus the consequence that results when certain rules gain wide acceptance and become formalized as legal rules is important in the analysis of an international normative order. Some rules are likely to promote stability; others may actually cause instability.

What are these rules likely to be? Again, if we conceptualize an international normative order as (1) a core set of norms that define the obligations of the members, and (2) a surrounding set of auxiliary norms that elaborate upon those obligations as they pertain to specific issue areas, then the set we need to examine in terms of their consequences for systemic stability are those core norms that delineate the duties expected of states when they reach agreements with one another (as, for example, when they form alliances).

Norms that define promissory obligations are important because they are developed in a milieu in which there is no automatic harmony. Competition and discord are endemic. Cooperation can occur in this setting, but only if and when states react to the specter of conflict by voluntarily sacrificing some of their autonomy to empower shared injunctions about what constitutes legitimate and illegitimate behavior (Keohane, 1984: 53–54). As Hedley Bull (1977: 19) concludes, "co-operation can take place only on the basis of agreements, and agreements can fulfill their function in social life only on the basis of a presumption that once entered into they will be observed."

To sum up, world politics unfolds under conditions in a bounded anarchy. The web of expectations communicated by prevailing international norms add a degree of predictability to interstate interactions, and thereby reduce the randomness that otherwise would prevail. But norms are subject to erosion and decay. Unless statesmen continually reinforce them, those norms that augur well for international security will be replaced by rules of conduct that may have radically different consequences for the stability of the state system.

2 Promissory Obligation: The Core of the International Normative Order

It would seem that our most serious . . . problems will arise today in situations where one state wants to escape the obligations of a treaty into which it has entered . . . and the other party or parties want to keep the treaty in force and demand continuing performance.

William W. Bishop, Jr.

The binding force of contracts . . . would have almost no sphere in society . . . unless trust could be excited. Trust lies at the basis of society.

Theodore D. Woolsey

An international system lacking a powerful central arbiter is a system of statecraft that invites mistrust and inspires fear. Unanchored by communitarian values or a sense of responsibility to the welfare of the international system as a whole, this self-help system of independent, mutually suspicious units "inhibits mutually advantageous cooperation" (Keohane, 1984: 85). The primary norms on which the international legal system has rested since the Peace of Westphalia (1648) leave states responsible solely for promoting their own advantage; their obligations are restricted to those commitments that they make voluntarily. Sovereign independence is worshipped, as is the right of states to protect and expand their capacity for autonomous action. Not only is politics divorced from morality in such a laissez faire environment, but politics is paramount. "No international moral consensus exists in sufficient depth and strength to sustain a comprehensive and binding international morality" (Schlesinger, 1986: 73).

Where a superior authority is absent, moral principles must be enforced by states independently (Murphy, 1985: 18), thereby leaving the normative obligations of states toward one another undefined. International law reserves for the state the right to judge the propriety of its own actions and permits states to pursue whatever foreign policy goals they wish: "In the last analysis . . . states are still above the law" (Hoffmann, 1971: 47) and are permitted "a complete freedom of action" (Parry, 1968: 2). As Martin Wight (1946: 68) put it, the international political culture enables states "to seek security without reference to justice, and to pursue their vital interest irrespec-

28

tive of common interest." To be sure, an enlarged conception of states' obligations toward one another has occasionally been proposed (see Paskins, 1978). But clearly the view that a government has no "duty vis-a-vis . . . other governments" (George F. Kennan, cited in Hare and Joynt, 1982: 42) has remained dominant since the birth of the modern state system. "[S]overeign states need and want order, but they both exhibit the disposition and claim the freedom to indulge in disorderly behavior" (Claude, 1986: 728).

If neither communitarian values nor a common morality exist, what, if any, are the duties of states? To what higher principles beyond the pursuit of national self-interests are states obligated? It is the purpose of this chapter to explore these perennial questions.

THE UNCERTAIN PLACE OF MORALITY
IN INTERNATIONAL AFFAIRS

There is probably no observer of the contemporary international scene who would not argue that self-interest is both a legitimate and necessary motive for national action. Yet, no observer would argue that international harmony has been achieved by states acting in compliance with that motive. At issue, then, is whether a conception of obligation can create greater order in an anarchic system. In this vein, we might ask with Charles de Visscher (1968: 14) what consequences might result if states embraced "a moral concept that refused to accept the greatness of the State as the sole end of public life?" As Table 2.1 demonstrates, international-relations theorists disagree on whether morality and moral considerations should be empowered to play an influential role in world politics. Let us review the major positions they have taken on this issue.

For purpose of discussion, interpretations of the place of morality in international affairs can be placed along a hypothetical continuum. At one pole are the *nihilists,* who maintain that morality does not, and should not, play a decisive role in relations between nations. At the opposite pole are the *idealists,* who argue that nations, like individuals, are obligated to respond to the commands of high moral principles and to place these commitments above parochial considerations in the calculation of national decisions. In between these two extremes is a wide variety of *realists* who contend that decision makers cannot ignore morality, but that they should also avoid foreign policies guided heavily by those moral absolutes that are divorced from political reality. At the risk of great oversimplification, this trichot-

Table 2.1. Competing Visions of the Place of Morality in International Politics

Examples of Minimalist Views

"The statesman can concern himself with values of justice, fairness and tolerance only to the extent that they contribute to or do not interfere with the power objective."

—Nicholas J. Spykman

"The state has no right to let its moral disapprobation . . . get in the way of successful political action, itself inspired by the moral principle of national survival."

—Hans J. Morgenthau

Examples of Maximalist Views

"No morally responsible person . . . can make national interest supreme whenever it comes into conflict with a broader human interest."

—John C. Bennett

"Power can be invested with a sense of direction only by moral principles. It is the function of morality to command the use of power, to forbid it, to limit it, or, more in general, to define the ends for which it may or must be used."

—John Courtney Murray

omy is employed to classify the contending positions,[1] thus creating categories that represent ideal types of logical possibilities. Most observers, recognizing the limitations of either the maximilist or minimalist extreme, have incorporated ingredients of both in their interpretations.

The Nihilist Interpretation of Morality in World Politics

The first position is represented by the nihilist view. "Nihilism implies a critical negation, not an indifference to values or a refusal to differentiate one idea or image from another" (Newman, 1987: 25).

---

1. The simple typology developed here is not meant to classify the many schools of philosophical thought and the subtle variations within them on the nature of promissory obligations. Debate about the moral nature and obligatory status of promises has been enriched by a lively and complex literature, which should be consulted for a more in-depth analysis of these issues. Representative philosophical writing in this area include Ardal (1968), Atiyah (1979), Locke (1972), MacCormick (1972), MacIntyre (1981), McNeilly (1972), Prichard (1957), Rawls (1955), and Raz (1972).

Nihilists deny the existence of any externally imposed moral standards for international behavior and recognize no justifiable basis for deriving moral precepts. According to this view, "moral discourse is mere cant" (Walzer, 1977: 4) because in international politics lies are not lies and murders are not murders (Croce 1945: 3–4). "To speak of honest diplomacy," Joseph Stalin remarked, "is like speaking of dry water." Like beasts in a jungle, statesmen must fight for survival, unrestrained by rules limiting their sovereign right to choose any self-help action capable of enhancing the prospects for self-preservation.

From this image of a state system doomed to an endless struggle for power, it is a short step to the conclusion that the whole notion of obligations to moral commands (such as virtue and justice) should be abandoned. Any attempt to import morality into the politically autonomous world of international politics would prove self-defeating. Hence, for nihilists, expediency is elevated to the status of a sacred principle paramount to all others. From this, the concise, cynical answer to the question "What is the role of ethics in world affairs?" is that there is no meaningful role for ethics.

This position of moral skepticism is defended by the argument that there are no institutionalized mechanisms for making or interpreting moral precepts at the international level. Given the diversity of value systems throughout the world, and given that we have no accepted basis for choosing between them, those norms that benefit from consensual support are couched in excessively broad terms. Such nebulous platitudes fail to specify clear restrictions on interstate behavior and readily lend themselves to use as propaganda tools. Unprincipled policy actions can be rationalized by citing one or more of the many vague and often contradictory principles available, as is illustrated by the post hoc use of the Brezhnev, Johnson, and Reagan doctrines to justify superpower military intervention in the internal conflicts of other countries. As this illustration suggests, statesmen first select the policy options they prefer, and then invent moral arguments to justify their choices (see Wright, 1953). Ethical evaluation of these choices often becomes a mere academic exercise because there are few if any accepted duties to which a state can hold the behavior of others accountable (Beitz, 1979b).

Asking us to look at the world with candor, adherents of nihilist thought rivet our attention on scenes of malevolence, deceit, cruelty, oppression, and war. They conclude that "the behavior of nations indicates that most of the time interests, judged generally apart from and sometimes in deliberate disregard for moral standards, have been decisive in shaping behavior;'' further, "in making their decisions most statesmen have asked, first, what is needed to be done to preserve the interests of the country, and only second, if ever, what the moral thing might be to do" (Levi, 1969: 193, 197). Resigned to the inevitability of evil and selfishness, nihilists depict diplomacy as a game animated by the practice of deception, fraud, and violence in pursuit of political objectives. Rather than being repudiated, hypocrisy sometimes is forged into a value and "seized on and elaborated into a new doctrine of obligation" (Paskins, 1978: 164). Among the variety of norms that exist in international society, nihilists accept those that support chicanery and sharp practices.[2]

When pressed to its logical resting place (as exemplified by such ancient Chinese Legalists as Han Fei Tzu), the nihilist philosophy argues that national ends always justify the means. All activity is assumed to be fair in war. As Thomas Hobbes articulated this position, "to have all, to do all, is lawful to all." Inasmuch as warfare is perceived to be endemic, natural, and ineradicable, immoral actions are justified if the end of promoting national competitiveness is furthered. The head of state accordingly is exempted from an obligation to comply with any moral precept delimiting a boundary to permissible behavior. For, according to this outlook, lies and crimes are always preferable to political failure.

The separation of morality from power politics is made evident in the interpretation of the duties states assume when they agree to cooperate in pursuing objectives of mutual benefit. Are obligations to honor commitments incurred? To put the nihilist argument succinctly, the amoral climate for diplomacy excuses statesmen from an obligation to carry out their agreements with one another. "Since every obligation of the State," argued Georg Jellinek (1880: 40) "is a fulfillment of the State's object, it subsists only as long as it satisfied that object." Once the state became an absolute mystical entity such as that portrayed by Hegel and idolized by Nietzsche, Meinecke, and strident advocates of the doctrine of *raison d'état*, "it acquired a claim to a different morality or, what is the same, to an absence of

---

2. The *philosophes* of the Age of Reason often described seventeenth-century diplomacy in these terms. According to one observer, national leaders practiced a code of conduct based on the following rules: "Make alliances only in order to sow hatred. . . . Incite war among neighbors and try to keep it going. . . . Have no ambassadors in other countries, but spies. . . . To be neutral means to profit from the difficulties of others in order to improve one's situation" (Diderot, cited in Ruddy, 1975: 39).

morality as understood by individuals'' (Lauterpacht, 1975: 74). Moreover, because it is believed foolish to expect amoral actors to adhere to oaths and promises, compliance with agreements is not a duty and sovereign nations are burdened by no ethical responsibilities to uphold commitments or to adhere to agreements when the exigencies of the moment make their breach rewarding. Expediency is substituted for morality, and the pragmatic use of unprincipled tactics that succeed in realizing the state's goal of maximizing power is condoned. The right of self-defense, for instance, is sometimes extended to and equated with the right to make war. The rejection of ethical obligations is justified by the belief that a state is entitled to be lawless in order to cope effectively.

A good example of the nihilist perspective can be seen in the diplomacy of Shang Yang, an advisor to the ancient Chinese state of Ch'in. In 341 B.C., when a border dispute with the neighboring state of Wei brought the two adversaries to the brink of war, Shang Yang, who had once served under the ruler of Wei, proposed to meet with the prince who was leading Wei's army and peacefully settle their dispute, as befitted old friends. The prince agreed, and was trapped in an ambush Shang Yang had plotted. His army was subsequently destroyed and Ch'in obtained the disputed territory (Creel, 1953: 121).

This event exemplifies a lesson that nihilists classify as a general precept: lying and deception are to be held in high esteem. The calculating ruler who deceives other leaders is to be praised highly for his disingenuous manipulations. Heads of state are encouraged to engage in deceitful and guileful practices to further the welfare of the state and are not to be confined by moral restrictions as to the range of their behavior. As Spinoza once proclaimed, "No holder of state power can adhere to the sanctity of contracts to the detriment of his country without committing a crime." Honesty is regarded as an unrewarding, illusory virtue, while hypocrisy is condoned and often venerated. A classic statement of this position was articulated by Niccoló Machiavelli when he advised that

> A prudent ruler ought not to keep faith when by so doing it would be against his interest and when the reasons which made him bind himself no longer exist. If men were all good, this precept would not be a good one; but as they are bad, and would not observe their faith with you, so you are not bound to keep faith with them. Nor have legitimate grounds ever failed a prince who wished to show colorable excuse for the non-fulfillment of his promise.

The Idealist Interpretation of International Morality

At the other end of the continuum is a set of prescriptions advocating the pursuit of morality in foreign policy. Often characterized as idealism (Carr, 1939), this position challenges the unbridled pursuit of self-interest and recommends substituting for it a duty to engage in principled conduct. This point of view is epitomized by the Gladstonian view that national interests are circumscribed by the rights of other states, and by Immanuel Kant's (1887: 223) conviction that "the violation of public treaties concerns all nations for the reason that it is a menace to their liberty." It was also clearly expressed by a policymaker when American Secretary of State Cordell Hull proclaimed on July 16, 1937: "We advocate faithful observance of international agreements. Upholding the principle of the sanctity of treaties, . . . we believe in respect by all nations for the rights of others and performance by all nations of established obligations."

Idealism also challenges the notion that power politics is all-pervasive. Emphasizing the belief that many of the interests of states converge, idealists argue that not only is respect for moral principles obligatory, but this obligation is largely honored in practice, especially among democratic states. Just as it is accurate to talk about honor among thieves, so, too, is it meaningful to talk about honor among states whose unlimited sovereign rights do not require that they comply with the promises they make.

Few if any observers of international politics would argue that adherence to agreements is universally perceived as obligatory or that states always faithfully honor their commitments. Yet idealists claim that their position is neither naive or utopian because it is inaccurate to describe international politics as occurring without routinized compliance to international obligations. Though not universal, obedience to moral convictions is seen by idealists as widespread: *"almost all nations observe almost all principles of international law and almost all of their obligations almost all of the time"* (Henkin, 1979: 47; Henkin's italics). According to Reinhold Niebuhr (cited in Thompson, 1980: 129), "Hypocrisy is the tribute that vice pays to virtue," an observation that attests to the necessary attention states pay to virtues transcending the quest for power. Summarizing the characteristic pattern of state practice with respect to international regimes across a wide spectrum of issue areas, Robert O. Keohane (1984: 98) notes that "we observe a good deal of compliance even when governments have incentives, on the basis of myopic self-interest, to violate the rules." Even the most ruthless of international actors frequently can be observed proclaiming their intentions to adhere to moral obligations. "If moral statements and standards are irrelevant," Kenneth W. Thompson (1980: 130) asked rhetorically, "why do nations bother to justify themselves as measured by those standards?" Only the total cynic would classify these professions as purely devious stratagems uninspired by a sincere commitment to a moral vision. As John H. E. Fried (1965: 106–107) concludes, it is an "empirical fact" that "by and large international obligations are being honored."

The reason some idealists give for this attention to higher moral principles is that from such observance states obtain what they need—namely order and predictability. The Machiavellian thesis that the few men who seek to be good will be exploited by the many who are not good is challenged by the clear damage that dishonorable behavior will cause to the self-interests of an unrestrained egotist. Violation of moral obligations may allow an actor to take advantage of others in the short run but will injure its long-term reputation and, ultimately, its prestige and power. When these costs are recognized, states have strong incentives to support moral standards. From that support their power can expand instead of diminish; thus, morality pays.

In addition to arguing that morality already plays a role in international politics, idealism holds that in the future morality can be made to play an even larger role. Writing during a time of great mistrust and conflict in world politics that seemed to lend credence to realism's most cynical assumptions, F. S. C. Northrop (1954: 336) proposed that "the cultural values and moral principles of the world in all their living law diversity and also in their unity, rather than . . . power politics, jockeying momentary isolationistic expediency, constitute the realistic basis for resolving the ideological conflicts and disturbances of our world by peaceful means." This proposal recommended reforms based on revision of the thinking underlying realist orthodoxy. It called for courageous choices to be made under the shadow of insecurity, to transform the uncertain moral climate of international politics in order to allow a true ethics of responsibility to take root. But to place international politics on a moral foundation through such a commitment, idealists assume that a fundamental value transformation must first occur:

> It is pure illusion to expect from the mere arrangement of inter-State relations the establishment of a community order; this can find a solid foundation only in the development of a true international spirit of

men. What concerns us is much less the principle of power than the
position taken by the [prevailing] regime with regard to the very notion
of power. What is decisive is the disposition within the State to keep its
actions within the limits assigned to it by a functional conception
which orders power to human ends instead of dedicating it to its own
indefinite extension. (de Visscher, 1968: 34)

International regimes are paragons of rules and norms defined in
terms of rights and duties that institutionalize cooperation in a specific issue area. The "essential rules" of the balance-of-power system
are often cited as an example of a security regime whose success is
predicated on voluntary compliance with its principles of behavior
(see Kaplan, 1957a). Thus, this position holds that it is possible to
create a moral, cosmopolitan society in the global village, and any
absence of moral themes from current diplomatic discourse does not
prove its necessary irrelevance. States can be expected to behave eth-
ically, contingent upon the prior emergence of a moral consensus
among nations about their obligations to practice principled conduct.
The idealist program maintains that moral obligations may not now be
prevalent but ought to be reintroduced into international politics.

The Realist Interpretation of International Morality

Between the nihilist and idealist extremes of our hypothetical continuum of perspectives on international morality, there exists a body
of realist thought which holds that although practical judgment must
be given priority over moral dictates, prudence nonetheless requires
that the definition of national interests be restrained by the development of obligations to moral limitations. Hans J. Morgenthau, perhaps the ultimate modern political realist, maintained that it is a
fundamental mistake to argue that moral principles and the national
interest are opposed forces; instead, he averred that it was appropriate
for foreign policy to be guided by a moral vision. "In order to be
worthy of our lasting sympathy," Morgenthau (1960: 8) wrote, "a
nation must pursue its interests for the sake of a transcendent purpose
that gives meaning to the day-to-day operations of its foreign policy."
Likewise, Herbert Butterfield (1962: 85) attacked the Machiavellian
"invitation to immorality" by observing that because it reduces "the
conduct of good men to the standards of the worst," it was bound to
fail and thus is destined to be rejected. In this context, John H. Herz
(1951) argued that a commitment to moral ideals was a form of realism required to mitigate and moderate the ultimately unrewarding
struggle for power by states.

Even the most opportunistic realists do not subscribe to the vulgar Machiavellianism characterizing the nihilist position. Raymond Aron (1966: 589), for instance, points out that Heinrich von Treitschke, a strong proponent of power politics, recognized that honesty was an effective diplomatic tool and thus there was "no ordinary justification for evoking the contradiction between politics and morality as if it were inevitable." Similarly, D. MacKenzie Brown (1954) argues that even the most ruthless of ancient Indian realists, such as Kautilya, Vyasa, and Shukra, accepted the view that there was a higher moral law to which state policy was subordinate.

An enlightened realist who has internalized moral values should not hope for ethical conduct by others or expect such behavior to be necessarily either forthcoming or beneficial. As Inis L. Claude (1986: 731) points out, "it is clear that having states, great and small, dedicated to the fulfillment of their international moral responsibilities is not a formula guaranteed to produce a more orderly world. A state that is resolutely undertaking to do what it believes to be its [ethical] duty may be more disruptive of international harmony than one frankly devoted to securing its own advantage." Thus for realists, there is an ineradicable tension between two aspirations, one for power and the other for virtue. As Niebuhr (1932) has noted, this tension entails an irresolvable tragedy, because no purely moral solution is available for the ultimate moral issues, but neither does there exist a viable solution which disregards the moral factors.

Former U.S. Secretary of State George P. Shultz is one contemporary policymaker who has expressed this tension between interests and ideals. Speaking before the National Committee on American Foreign Policy during the fall of 1985, he observed:

> A foreign policy based on realism . . . cannot ignore the importance of . . . morality. But realism does require that we avoid foreign policies based exclusively on moral absolutes divorced from political reality.

> Moral posturing is no substitute for effective policies. Nor can we afford to distance ourselves from all the difficult and ambiguous moral choices of the real world.

For Secretary Shultz, then, the challenge faced by realists is to temper moral convictions so they lead us neither to futile crusades nor political paralysis. In this regard, Shultz echoed the repulsion of realists for "the legalistic-moralistic approach to international problems . . .

the carrying over into the affairs of states of the concepts of right and wrong, the belief that state behavior is a fit subject for moral judgment" (Kennan, 1951: 42). But he also echoed acceptance of the conviction that "political expedience itself has to consult the moral sense of those it will affect," and be "softened into prudence, which is a moral virtue" (Wight, 1968: 128).

In this respect, realism displays an ambivalence between the view that states should avoid high moral crusades and the view that their foreign policies must be guided by moral responsibilities that transcend their own selfish interests. Alternatively stated, realists maintain that policy guided by moral absolutes is dangerous and mistaken, although they maintain as well that it is morally necessary to formulate policy in terms of the national interest. For realists such as Morgenthau, "The choice . . . is not between moral principle and the national interest, but between two types of political morality, the one divorced from political reality and taking as its standard the abstract formulation of universal moral principles, and the other intimately concerned with political reality and taking as its standard not only those same moral principles but also the political consequences that may flow from their application" (Robinson, 1969: 186).

Realists criticize the idealist viewpoint on two central points. First, realists consider idealists to be morally naive—idealists believe that moral principles provide easy answers to complex policy problems. Second, idealists are morally pretentious, maintaining that the values guiding one's own country are moral and should be universal. These beliefs lead to a profound realist skepticism about the relevance of morality to international affairs—a doubt for which realists are sometimes accused of cynicism, pessimism, and even nihilism. The general orientation and flavor of realism toward morality is conveyed in Morgenthau's (1951: 34) reluctant acceptance of an unpleasant reality, that "there is a profound . . . truth hidden in Hobbes' dictum that . . . there is neither morality nor law outside the state." As Morgenthau (1951: 35) explained, "above the national societies there exists no international society so integrated so as to be able to define for them the concrete meaning of justice and equality, as national societies do for their individual members. . . . The appeal to moral principles in the international sphere has no concrete universal meaning."

In summary, realpolitik thinking avers that the creation of a legitimate international order is a prerequisite both for a moral consensus to develop in international society and for states to obligate themselves to follow moral standards of conduct. These principles must come through consent. Community is a prerequisite for a shared code of morality. It is not unreasonable to anticipate that this consent will ultimately be forthcoming, these theorists maintain, because, in Arthur M. Schlesinger's (1986: 77) words, the "national interest prescribes its own morality." An enlightened conception of the national interest can lead states to accept voluntarily those norms that set limits to permissible behavior in international conduct. Although they warn that the lust for power and selfishness are entrenched components of an inherently conflictual system, they hold out the possibility, however limited, for "proximate solutions" to policy problems through compromise and cooperation. This, they maintain, can prevent the abuse of moral principles and render useful their application to international conduct. Thus within this tradition can be found expressions of agreement with the view articulated by George Washington that, although nations were not to be trusted farther than they are bound by their interests, national interests would incline them to embrace standards that could civilize relations between states.

In contemplating the various reasons why "an obligatory basis exists for international law, and [why] in substantial measure [international] law is obeyed," Christopher C. Joyner summarizes the thinking of realist theorists by proposing the following reasons.

National governments recognize the utility of the law; they prefer some degree of order and expectation over unpredictable anarchy; obedience is less costly than disobedience; a certain sense of justice may motivate their willingness to obey; or, habit and customary practice in international dealings over many years have operated to promote obedience.

More than any of these explanations, however, is the recognition that reciprocity contributes to . . . more regularized patterns of behavior in the international system. Put simply, states accept and obey international law because governments find it in their national interest to do so. It serves a state's national interest to accept international legal norms if other states also accept these norms, and this reciprocal process can give rise to predictive patterns of interstate conduct in international relations. States, like individual persons, have discovered that consent to be bound by and obligated to certain rules can serve to facilitate, promote and enhance their welfare and opportunities in the society. Contemporary international law consequently has come to embody a consensus of common interests—a consensus which plainly indicates that international law works efficiently and most often when it is in the national interest of states to make it work. (Joyner, 1988: 193–194)

The foregoing review of opinions about the place of morality of international affairs, although nonexhaustive, should be of sufficient breadth to demonstrate the wide diversity of orientations that have been taken toward the question. No single perspective on this issue commands a universal following. Diametrically opposed positions have been voiced throughout history, and between them can be found a variety of intermediary orientations, with still other tensions and contradictions among them. The lack of consensus shows just how uncertain the place of morality is in international politics, and suggests why this uncertainty is unlikely to be easily removed. In anarchy, moral principles are not provided a hospitable environment in which to flourish.

Yet amidst this discord considerable agreement can be found with the Grotian and Kantian beliefs that for peace to exist, relations among nations must be predicated on acceptance of some fundamental principles around which a normative consensus might be built.

The concept of state sovereignty directly undermines the prospects for finding such a principle to which states will agree to obligate themselves. Sovereignty gives to states the opportunity to reject any principle that threatens to reduce their freedom of choice. In order to reconcile the tension between the aspiration for state freedom and the aspiration for international harmony, states must derive rules for behavior from some fundamental moral principle and commit themselves to abide by their strictures. But what moral principle can serve this purpose?

PROMISSORY OBLIGATION AS A THEME
IN DIPLOMATIC DISCOURSE

Is there a sufficient basis for expecting nations to manage their relations by adhering to a common standard of conduct? Is it reasonable to speak, not just of states' rights, but also of their duties? Indeed, is an obligation to "some kind of principle of intermediate order within the chaos of international relations a necessity," as Reinhold Niebuhr (1959: 194) and many others believe?

Perhaps the most fundamental principle applies to those promissory obligations that frame the debate over whether the provisions of the agreements that states negotiate are regarded by them as binding. Do states regard adherence to their commitments as obligatory? Or, conversely, do they feel free to disavow promises when their self-interests can be served by such a violation? At different points in diplomatic history, each of these positions has been embraced, advocated, and

Table 2.2. Contrasting Prescriptions Regarding Promissory Obligations

Obligation Deified

"Kings should be very careful with regard to the treaties they conclude, but having concluded them they should observe them religiously. I know well that many statesmen advise to the contrary, but . . . I maintain that the loss of honor is worse than the loss of life itself. A great prince should sooner put in jeopardy both his own interests and even those of the state than break his word, which he can never violate without losing his reputation and by consequence the greatest instrument of sovereigns."

—Cardinal Richelieu (Armand-Jean du Plessis)

"No one, of ever so corrupt morals, would approve of a prince, who voluntarily, and of his own accord, breaks his word, or violates any treaty."

—David Hume

Obligation Defied

"The practice of politics may be defined by one word—dissimulation."

—Benjamin Disraeli

"A man striving in every way to be good will meet his ruin among the great number who are not good. Hence it is necessary for a prince . . . to learn how not to be good and to use his knowledge or refrain from using it as he may need."

—Niccolo Machiavelli

---

upheld. Sovereignty grants to states the right to obligate themselves to comply with commitments, or to use agreements opportunistically as a clever ruse to exploit others. The dichotomy therefore identifies a division between one normative system based on the inviolability of oaths, and another on the prescription that states are not obligated to keep their promises.

As Table 2.2 demonstrates, the notion of international obligation has sometimes been deified, and sometimes defied. The position toward obligation is one of the most significant boundary lines in international behavior: normative shifts in support or rejection of it have often instigated dramatic changes in prevailing relationships between states. One need only recall the "Munich Syndrome," given birth by Hitler's violation of his pledge not to take advantage of Great Britain's appeasement policy, to see how changes in the orientation of states toward the sanctity of commitments can profoundly alter the moral climate of international interaction. In this context, it is also instructive to recall that this fundamental dimension of the moral climate was seen by Thucydides as a feature that influenced the outbreak of the Peloponnesian War, and that he thought it revealing to observe that at that time "the use of fair phrases to arrive at guilty ends was in high reputation."

Because statesmen during some historical periods have voiced support for a norm stipulating that commitments are binding but have challenged this principle during other periods, their disposition toward this choice has been believed by theorists to be influential in fostering the emergence of either collaborative or discordant relations among nations (although, as we shall see, theorists strongly disagree as to which choice is the more conducive to national and international security). How the climate of opinion in a given historical period has regarded promissory obligations has in turn shaped expectations about state behavior and the standards against which that behavior was judged. As shown in Display 2.1, the failure of the League of Nations to comply with its promise to punish aggressors led Emperor Haile Selassie to point out that the 1935 Italian invasion of Ethiopia raised a host of wider moral issues regarding honesty, loyalty, and trust.

The timeless debate over the issue of keeping promises has pitted the extreme positions of moral nihilism and moral idealism against one another. Whereas the former condones the opportunistic disregard of pledges and the latter proclaims that all promises should be fulfilled, realists join the debate by taking a less absolute position. Although they generally hold that the sanctity of agreements is so fundamental that respect for it should be universal (Niebuhr, 1959: 194), realists also warn against the dangers of making promises and attempting to forge permanent alignments, and they see the violation of agreements as justified when changing conditions reduce the benefits of adhering to a prior promise.

What makes the question of compliance with promises so fundamental is that it lies at the vortex of all relations between states. For David Hume the obligation to keep promises was the foundation of civilized society; for Emeriche de Vattel it was a sacred principle; for Jean Bodin it was the very basis of all justice; and in the twentieth

Display 2.1 ■ Emperor Haile Selassie's Appeal to the Members of the League of Nations

[The] issue before the Assembly to-day is a much wider one. It is not merely a question of a settlement in the matter of Italian aggression. It is a question of collective security; of the very existence of the League; of the trust placed by States in international treaties; of the value of promises made to small States that their integrity and their independence shall be respected and assured. It is a choice between the principle of the equality of States and the imposition upon small Powers of the bonds of vassalage. In a word, it is international morality that is at stake. Have treaty signatures a value only in so far as the signatory Powers have a personal, direct and immediate interest involved?

No subtle reasoning can change the nature of the problem or shift the grounds of the discussion. It is in all sincerity that I submit these considerations to the Assembly. At a time when my people is threatened with extermination, when the support of the League may avert the final blow, I may be allowed to speak with complete frankness, without reticence, in all directness, such as is demanded by the rule of equality between all States Members of the League. Outside the Kingdom of God, there is not on this earth any nation that is higher than any other. If a strong Government finds that it can, with impunity, destroy a weak people, then the hour has struck, for that weak people to appeal to the League of Nations to give its judgment in all freedom. God and history will remember your judgment.

. . . On behalf of the Ethiopian people, a Member of the League of Nations, I ask the Assembly to take all measures proper to secure respect for the Covenant. I renew my protest against the violation of treaties of which the Ethiopian people is the victim. . . .

. . . I ask the great Powers, who have promised the guarantee of collective security to small States—those small States over whom hangs a threat that they may one day suffer the fate of Ethiopia: What measures do they intend to take?

Representatives of the world, I have come to Geneva to discharge in your midst the most painful of the duties of the head of a State. What answer am I to take back to my people?

Source: League of Nations, Assembly, 1936. "Records of the 16th Ordinary Session," *Official Journal* Special Supplement 151, Part II, p. 25.

century for Josiah Royce it was the summum bonum within which
was contained all other virtues. We may presume that throughout history the degree to which states have felt obligated to honor commitments has influenced the kind of relationships that have developed
among them. Therefore the choice between flexible versus binding
conceptions of commitment comprises a fundamental moral issue; the
posture of states toward promissory obligations reflects a normative
preference that relates directly or indirectly to all other rules of international conduct.[3] It is for this reason that it lies at the core of diplomatic discourse. As Paolo Valesio (1980: 21) argues, "every
discourse in its functional aspect is based on a relatively limited set of
mechanisms—whose structure remains essentially the same from text
to text, from language to language, from historical period to historical
period." The theme of promissory obligation is a major part of the
structure of that ongoing diplomatic discourse.

To contend that the way promissory obligations are defined frames
the cultural environment within which states interact is to submit that
it is a universal, temporally invariant aspect of diplomacy. Legal theorists as diverse as Georg Jellinek (1880) and Hans Kelsen (1952)
agree that promissory obligations lie at the core of the international
normative order. They disagree, however, over which specific commitment norms ought to be dominant; Jellinek advocates a flexible
interpretation of obligation, while Kelsen supports a binding interpretation. Before exploring the consequences that may arise from each of
these alternative versions of promissory obligation, it is necessary to
pause and contemplate (1) the nature of the moral climate that exists
when states fail to obligate themselves to the inviolability of oaths,
and (2) the type of environment that exists when they do commit
themselves to such an obligation.

---

3. The proposition that promises are fundamental to international law and society is
consistent with most theories of jurisprudence. The concept of obligation underlies
the law of treaties (Kunz, 1945: 180) and operates as a "meta- or super-norm," from
which all other legal principles are derived (see Allott, 1980: 23, 247). Kelsen's
(1952) description of the place of promissory obligations as a *grundnorm* (basic
norm) emphasizes the dominant role ascribed to norms defining promissory obligations in legal theory. Likewise, to many students of international law promissory
obligations are regarded as a peremptory norm, a *jus cogens* norm that permits no
derogation and which overrides all others. Whatever its jurisprudential status, it is
clearly accurate to characterize commitment as one of the most consequential rules,
creating rights and duties and orienting nearly all exchange.

NORMATIVELY PERMISSIVE VERSUS NORMATIVELY RESTRICTIVE ORDERS

When attention focuses on the norms of obligation that guide statesmen in their dealings with one another, inquiry must proceed with an appreciation of the fact that agreements are not prima facie binding; none are self-enforcing or automatically backed by sanctions external to the parties to them. Thus, states are free to act honorably or dishonorably.

Nonetheless, states often need to reach agreements with one another for a variety of purposes. The agreement to act in concert is a voluntary decision but one frequently reached because states often become convinced that common political objectives can be furthered collaboratively in ways that would not be possible if they were addressed individually. Indeed, despite the political risks involved and the uncertainty of compliance, states throughout history have forged numerous agreements, ranging from tacit bargains to highly formalized treaties. These agreements cover a wide variety of issues, and result from promises to cooperate for many diverse purposes.

Alliances are perhaps the most visible form of interstate agreement, in the sense not only that they exemplify the politics and norms constituting concerted efforts by autonomous actors to commit themselves voluntarily to a particular course of action, but also because they fall into the "high politics" of national security policies and therefore command widespread attention. Agreements to ally are attended by press and public. Moreover, their consequences are far-reaching, involving risks to national survival. As such, they are given primary attention in this book, because of their capacity to illuminate the properties of commitment. It is recognized, however, that the characteristics and consequences of agreements to ally may be different than those governing other types of international agreements. We shall explore the place of promissory obligations in international affairs by examining it in the context primarily of alliances, but in focusing on alliances the applicability of conclusions to all other types of agreements in general cannot be safely assumed.

Still, military alliances, as a special form of agreements between states, exemplify especially well the manner in which, under trying conditions, agreements either bind or break. "Apparently a universal component of relations between political units, irrespective of time and place" (Holsti, 1976: 337), the very concept of alliance "signifies a promise" (Wolfers, 1968: 268). But alliance agreements can vary considerably. Their cohesion is dependent on the motives and

attributes of the consenting parties, the circumstances in which treaties are negotiated, and, of most relevance to our purposes, on the
sense of promissory obligation that the parties assign to their faithful
performance. These characteristics and variations make them a subject worthy of detailed examination.

To conduct inquiry about promissory obligations in international
affairs as revealed in alliance politics, the setting for the formation
and maintenance of agreements is salient. But in this anarchical environment, which invites distrust, it would be inaccurate to imply that
for purely deceitful or exploitive purposes states routinely forge
agreements they do not intend to keep. When states reach agreements,
they usually do so with the expectation of complying with their promises so as to realize the benefits they negotiated. For most states,
most of the time, the intention to honor promises may be assumed to
be sincere at the time the pledges are expressed. "A promise invokes
trust in future actions, not merely in [one's] present sincerity. We
need to isolate an additional element, over and above benefit, reliance, and communication of intention. That additional element must
commit [one], and commit [one] to more than the truth of some statement" (Fried, 1981: 11).

That element of commitment will reveal itself most clearly when
conditions are not stable and when the fulfillment of the promise
comes at a cost. Trust and commitment are "involved only if there is
a possibility that a party [to an agreement] will defect" (Hinde, 1987:
85). It will thus reveal itself when the commitment is severely
tested—when conditions change. Especially in exceptional circumstances, when the conditions that held when a promise was made no
longer exist, the strength of one's commitment will be disclosed. In
those circumstances, the burdens imposed by the promise are likely to
become overwhelming, tempting even honorable men and women to
disavow their pledges. Thus it is not the inclination to act with perfidy
that accounts in some periods for the frequency with which states fail
to observe their oaths (see Garner, 1927: 509). It is the pressure of
substantially changed circumstances that can erode trust. That erosion
is most likely to occur amidst rapid change when prevailing norms
condone the unilateral repudiation of promissory obligations. Conversely, when norms support the sanctity of agreements, trust will
remain an element on which the parties can still rely.

To understand the functional meaning of international agreements,
it is important to ascertain whether after accepting the terms of the
bargain the contractual parties perceived themselves to have been un-

der a common discipline and obligation to honor the bargain even in the event of substantially changed circumstances. The expectations that each party maintains about the duties incurred is critical. If promises are lightly regarded and an obligation to fulfill commitments is not accepted, then the agreements reached can be expected to exert little impact when the costs of their observance mounts. Whether actors believe the agreements they reach incur an obligation under changed circumstances therefore makes an enormous difference for the maintenance of trust and for the continuation of the agreement.

This reality requires attention to be paid to normative dispositions toward fulfilling contracted obligations. The manner through which agreements are terminated, and the expectations of parties to an agreement about the probability of its premature termination, may determine the impact of the agreement and the function it will perform. By their very nature, most agreements between states pledge specific commitments and stipulate duties with respect to a discrete problem or issue. They are formalized, usually in treaties, to make explicit the mutual responsibilities and the conditions under which joint action is to be undertaken. This formalization is designed to reduce uncertainties and to structure expectations. Alliance agreements would not be committed to writing if there were not a perceived need to reduce apprehensions about the reliability of allies in times of crisis. In this sense, treaties represent to some degree an acknowledgment that a verbal promise may not be sufficient to cement mutual obligations. Nonetheless, without normative support for the binding force of contracts, treaties will not enhance confidence that agreements will be observed.

Alliances illustrate the above principle well. Because the breach of alliance agreements prior to the date for which the commitments were scheduled to remain in force is always a feared possibility, alliances are instruments of statecraft influenced by mutual suspicion about the reliability of allies. Neither party can know whether treaty adherence will be practiced when changed circumstances suggest to one of them that the costs of adherence exceed the benefits. We can assume, however, that any calculation of whether an alliance shall be broken will be strongly affected by the kinds of norms prevailing when changed circumstances challenge its durability.

When norms supporting either flexible or binding interpretations of promissory obligations become institutionalized through the customary practice of states, one of two types of normative order are created. When doubts over alliance reliability are pervasive and states

Table 2.3. On Promissory Obligations when Conditions Change: Views of Legal Authorities

Changed Circumstances Permit the Nonperformance of Promises

Legal Authorities

"Treaties expire by their own limitations, unless revived by express agreement, or when their stipulations are fulfilled or when a total change of circumstances renders them no longer obligatory."

—Henry Wheaton

"[International law necessarily presumes the continuing validity of treaties. However, when] the contracting states have entered into the treaty with certain conditions in view, it is not unreasonable to consider the treaty as failing to give expression to their wills when the contemplated circumstances have entirely changed, or have so radically altered that the treaty would evidently not have been signed had the change been contemplated."

—Ellery C. Stowell

International Institutions

"The Assembly of Delegates may from time to time advise the reconsideration by members of the League of treaties which have become inapplicable [through changes in] international conditions whose continuance might endanger the peace of the world."

—Art. 19 of the Covenant of
the League of Nations

Changed Circumstances Prohibit the Nonperformance of Promises

Legal Authorities

"The oldest and doubtless most fundamental rule of international law is that of the sanctity of treaty obligations. That good faith should be kept between states in respect to their contractual agreements has been from the earliest times regarded . . . as a matter of common concern to the whole community of states. . . . Unless the pledged word of a state can be relied upon the entire international community would be imperiled and law itself would disappear."

—Charles G. Fenwick

"Changed conditions are . . . never a ground for refusing to comply with a treaty."

—The International Law Commission

International Institutions

"No State has the right, by itself, to free itself unilaterally from its contractual obligations . . . such a procedure destroys the moral trust between nations which represents one of the foundations of peace."

—Communique of the Atlantic Council,
December 16, 1957

are not expected to uphold their agreements, a *permissive* order arises. Conversely, when the sanctity of agreements is widely embraced, a *restrictive* order emerges. The tension between nihilism and idealism lies at the boundary differentiating these two kinds of order.

The differences in the two contrasting approaches to obligation are illuminated in the policy prescriptions represented in Table 2.2 and by the injunctions of international legal authorities presented in Table 2.3. These differences suggest that no clear consensus on the place of promissory obligation in international politics has endured without eventual challenge. Some see obligations to oaths as a vice that, if pursued, will curse diplomatic practice and bring disruption and destruction by compromising the ability of states to adapt their foreign policies to changes in their external environments. To others, however, it is a virtue that will cure the instabilities afflicting diplomacy. To some, therefore, keeping promises will foster exploitation because there is no authority to ensure the reciprocal compliance necessary for moral behavior; to others, keeping promises is a way of keeping the peace.

It is the purpose of this book to explore the cultural environments that emerge when one of these concepts of international obligation gains force. This investigation is rationalized by Sir Hersch Lauterpacht's (1975: 13) assertion that "the effect of changed circumstances on the continued legal validity of a treaty [is] not only capable of further elucidation and study, [it] is badly in need of it." To discover the global consequences that result when changed circumstances challenge alliance maintenance under different normative climates of opinion requires not conjecture but empirical analysis, which subsequent chapters provide. Here we wish only to illuminate differences of opinion about the likely impact of these diametrically opposed normative orders, and thereby expose the divergent assumptions made by theorists about the advantages and disadvantages ascribed to each.

Table 2.4 summarizes the major differences in the patterns of belief and behavior that have been posited to exist within each of these two normative orders. As this summary should reveal, it is highly unwarranted, in the abstract, to regard either order as inherently positive or negative. Each order entails both costs and benefits, which is why on numerous occasions both have been advocated by statesmen and theoreticians. It therefore would be mistaken to attach a pejorative meaning to these labels by assuming, for instance, that a restrictive normative order necessarily is to be valued whereas a permissive normative order is not.

Table 2.4. Dominant International Characteristics Ascribed to Two Normative Orders

Permissive Order	Restrictive Order
International politics is driven by the quest for power and status	International politics is animated by the quest for order and stability
Power and force are used to settle disputes	Disagreements are peacefully negotiated
The balance of power preserves peace	Great powers use their influence to preserve peace
States are believed to have no obligation beyond their own selfish interests	States are believed to have duties to others, including loyalties that transcend their immediate self-interest
Diplomacy is power- and hierarchy-oriented	Diplomacy is task- and solution-oriented
Expectations are low that agreements will be upheld	Expectations are high that agreements will be upheld
Compliance with negotiated agreements is often violated	Compliance with negotiated agreements is honored
Treaties are infrequently concluded and regularly broken	Treaties are frequently made and seldom breached
Collective problem-solving agreements are infrequently reached	Collective problem-solving agreements are frequently reached
Force and the threat of force are employed to coerce compliance with agreements	Mutual trust and confidence cement alliance ties
Nations realign frequently	Alignments between nations tend to endure
Alignment agreements are perceived to be flexible and the alliances they form are short-lived	Alignment agreements are perceived to be binding and the alliances they create are enduring
Individual responsibility for defense is practiced	Burden-sharing responsibilities for defense are practiced
Foreign policy goals exhibit a high level of discontinuity	Foreign policy goals exhibit a high level of continuity

The challenge for the policymaker and the scholar is to ascertain which order is most promotive of international stability. The proposition that support for binding conceptions of agreements can bring about a more stable international society must be tested empirically, for this view may be mistaken, as nihilists and some realists have argued. Global stability might be fostered more effectively under a permissive order prescribing no obligation other than pursuit of national self-interests, in which a fluid balance-of-power system can best operate. Thus, in a diplomatic environment where keeping one's promises was defined as an obligation, such obligations might either enhance the capacity of states to compete without recourse to war, or make war more probable.

The dilemma posed to international affairs is therefore the timeless problem of both freedom versus authority and individualism versus community. To make promises and to live by a morality that commands that promises be kept is to sacrifice one's freedom and diminish one's independence. Is that obligation a virtue, as Aristotle (*Nichomachean Ethics* V, Chapter 6) believed when he posed the question of whether there can be "any greater evil than discord, plurality and distraction where unity ought to reign, and a greater good than the bond of unity?" Or, in a world of competitive states, is adherence to that command a vice, inviting not order but exploitation?

These questions comprise the primary philosophical problem in international relations. They require that we confront the role of morality in a community lacking consensus about the kind of norms most conducive to national and international security, and to evaluate the blessings and burdens associated respectively with these incompatible norms. It is to this inquiry that we now turn. Specifically, we examine the issues nested within this larger philosophical problem through an examination of how flexibility and commitment influence the formation and maintenance of interstate alliances.

3 Alliances:
Ties that Bind?

True dignity consists in making no declaration which we are not prepared to maintain.

John C. Calhoun

I would rather be an opportunist and float than go to the bottom with my principles round my neck.

Stanley Baldwin

Leaders who forge them are heralded as statesmen; those who breach them are branded as traitors. Because they may increase a state's military strength, their supporters call them indispensible; but because they may tie a state to an unreliable partner, their opponents call them entangling. They are alternately praised for war's prevention and blamed for war's occurrence. Much like the sirens Parthenope, Leucosia, and Ligeia in Greek mythology, they are both desired and feared.

The phenomena these statements describe are, of course, interstate alliances. States *align* themselves with one another when they adopt a common stance toward some shared national security problem (Teune and Synnestvedt, 1965; Skinner and Kegley, 1978). An *alliance* is produced when their tacit agreement to cooperate is made explicit through a written treaty. Alliances, in other words, are formal agreements between sovereign states "for the putative purpose of coordinating their behavior in the event of certain specified contingencies of a military nature" (Bueno de Mesquita and Singer, 1973: 241). The degree of coordination may range from a detailed list of military forces that will be furnished by each party under certain conditions (e.g., the Little Entente of 1920), to a guarantee of neutrality in the event that an alliance member is attacked (e.g., the 1887 Russo–German Reinsurance Treaty), to the broader requirement of consultation should a military conflict erupt (e.g., the *Dreikaiserbund*). The target of the accord may be left implicit, or may be identified as a single country, a group of states, or a geographic region in which the agreement is to take effect. The duration of the accord may be limited to a relatively short period of time, or may be designed to last indefinitely.[1] Designed to serve either convergent or complementary security interests, alliances result from the purposeful choices by two or more states to specify "the conditions under which they will or will not employ military force" (Russett, 1974: 301).

Just as alliances differ according to the scope, target, and duration of their accords, they also differ according to the nature of the commitments that they formalize (Moul, 1988: 252). One way to classify these commitments is to differentiate between *wartime alliances,* whose members join together to fight some third party, and three types of alliances that typically are formed in peacetime: (1) *defense pacts,* where the signatory parties agree to intervene militarily in the event of an attack on one of their numbers; (2) *nonaggression agreements,* in which the parties pledge to remain neutral should one of them become involved in a war; and (3) *ententes,* which merely require consultations if one of the signatories is attacked (Singer and Small, 1966a). Clearly, the nature of each of these commitments varies, as does the prospects for compliance with their treaty provisions. Defense pacts, for example, place more demands on the signatories than do the vague understandings found in ententes. As a result, they are entered into more reluctantly and entail greater incentives for defection when changes occur in the conditions that existed at the time of their formation.

By vowing to adhere to an alliance treaty's provisions, states incur responsibilities. As Michael Walzer (1970: 193) points out, choice through voluntary consent "lies at the very center of our ideas about morality and obligation." Similarly, Sir Henry Sumner Maine (1861) contended that one of the primary characteristics of modern society is the replacement of obligations based on one's position within a rigid hierarchy of ascribed status by obligations based on contractual relationships. In the former, social mores imposed from above give an individual little choice regarding his or her duty; in the latter, duty derives from voluntary agreements that hinge on a binary decision rule: a promise was either made or not made.

---

1. As Charles de Gaulle intimated when he said that "treaties are like the beauty of young women . . . they last while they last," the expected duration of alliances varies widely. International law distinguishes between temporary and perpetual treaty provisions, with pacts *in pertetuiate* referring to the "many such treaties in which the obvious intention is to establish a permanent state of things" (Brierly, 1955: 256). This concept of perpetuity is illustrated by the 1373 Treaty of Friendship and Peace between Portugal and Great Britain, which was invoked by the British Parliament in 1943 as being still in force (DeLupis, 1967: 93).

Despite the apparent simplicity of such a rule, disputes still arise over contractual liability. For instance, consumers may claim that a product was not delivered according to some negotiated schedule, retailers may complain that a franchise was wrongfully terminated by a manufacturer, or national leaders may accuse their allies of not living up to a treaty's provisions. Charges that someone failed to perform as stipulated under the provisions of an agreement may be answered in three ways: (1) the person in question may deny that a transgression occurred; (2) the person may attempt to mitigate responsibility by claiming that the transgression was situationally excusable due to a physical inability to fulfill the agreement; or (3) the person may respond with a demurrer that challenges the applicability of the agreement to the case at hand. Within a hierarchical political system, disputes over contractual liability are adjudicated by a central authority. Within an anarchical political system, they are resolved through reprisals by the betrayed party. It is for this reason that Arthur Lee Burns (1968: 3) sees the key difference between domestic and international politics as residing in the latter's "scarcity or ineffectiveness of fiats meant to bind its agents jointly."

THE NORMATIVE UNDERPINNINGS OF ALLIANCES

Given the lack of fiats to hold states to their contractual agreements, commitment norms arise in world politics to define the extent of state responsibility to promissory obligations. One set of norms may liberate states from their responsibilities when disadvantageous circumstances materialize. In a world where "cheating and deception are endemic" (Axelrod and Keohane, 1986: 226), the ascendance of such norms is understandable. But as pointed out in the previous chapter, during some historical periods norms prescribing faithful adherence to promises have gained widespread support within the diplomatic community. How do these commitment norms take root? Why do states unite with those they have inherent reasons to doubt?

Explanations for why states adhere to purely voluntary agreements in a decentralized, self-help system are often couched in terms of gaining "coldly calculated advantages" (Jordan and Taylor, 1984: 474).[2] On the one hand, alliances reduce the costs associated with foreign-policy undertakings by spreading them among several part-

---

2. Although we have set the discussion of alliance formation and dissolution in the context of a "rational actor" model, this is not to deny that domestic politics, organizational processes, bureaucratic rivalries, and other influences on policymaking will also affect alliance choices.

ners. On the other hand, alliances help a state acquire benefits that could not have been attained by acting unilaterally. Aside from the common benefit of security, which accrues as a "public good" to all members, alliances also bestow private benefits on certain states. One such benefit is increased military capability. By joining the North Atlantic Treaty Organization (NATO), for example, a relatively weak state such as Belgium can supplement its capabilities by gaining access to additional resources, obtaining a steady supply of sophisticated weaponry, and receiving instruction on the use of new technology. Even a powerful state like the United States may enhance its position through NATO membership by sharing the costs of burdensome defense expenditures and by acquiring overseas bases and support facilities from which it may project its power.

Another benefit that flows to some members is increased influence over another country's foreign-policy decisions. Alliances furnish a medium for exerting leverage over partners. Normally we think of this in terms of the alliance leader influencing its smaller partners, as in the case of the United States restraining Great Britain, France, and Israel in the 1956 Suez War. As Christer Jönsson (1981: 256) reminds us, however, "bargaining power accrues not necessarily to the party possessing superior resources generally, but to the party which possesses issue-specific resources, is able to communicate its resolve clearly and convincingly, and is able to exploit asymmetries in its relations" with another state. American television viewers saw an example of this kind of "reverse leverage" in the spring of 1981, when Sheik Ahmed Zaki Yamani, the Saudi Arabian oil minister, stressed the importance of the U.S. sale of AWACS planes in the context of a discussion of Saudi oil policy (Pierre, 1982: 18). Still another private benefit is the opportunity for a national leader to shore up his or her standing at home. Ties with the Soviet Union gave Fidel Castro this kind of opportunity by providing him with a protective shield, economic assistance, and a legitimizing ideology.

In sum, states form alliances for diverse reasons, despite the uneven burdens they necessitate and the inequalities in benefits they provide. Moreover, they do so regardless of the risk that treaty commitments may be repudiated when they are most needed. To borrow a metaphor from Abba Eban, a former Israeli ambassador to the United Nations, states continue to seek refuge under the protective umbrella of a military alliance, even though it may be retracted at the precise moment it begins to rain.

In view of the unequal distribution of costs, benefits, and risks among alliance members, what incentives exist to keep those with a low marginal utility of membership from disavowing their commitments? As Soviet behavior toward its Eastern European allies illustrates, alliance leaders use a variety of means to maintain solidarity within the coalitions that they build (Volgyes, 1988). Perhaps the most common technique is persuasion, wherein a sequence of interconnected claims, grounds, and warrants are advanced to convince a dissatisfied member not to defect from the alliance. At times persuasion may be coupled with a mix of threats and promises in order to dissuade an obstreperous ally from repudiating a prior commitment, or to compel it to retract policies that are thought to violate the original understanding. Finally, some form of physical coercion may be used in an attempt to force an ally to abide by its word. The post-World War II history of Soviet foreign policy contains many instances where Moscow used these techniques to maintain alliance cohesion. When Joseph Stalin chafed at Tito's intransigence in 1948, for example, he used propaganda, covert action, economic sanctions, and pressure from other Eastern bloc members in an unsuccessful effort to hold Yugoslavia within the Soviet orbit. Nikita Khrushchev went a step further when he resorted to military intervention following Imre Nagy's October 1956 announcement that Hungary would withdraw from the Warsaw Pact. Similarly, Leonid Brezhnev turned to force after sending a letter to First Secretary Alexander Dubček on August 19, 1968, which argued that Czechslovakia had violated the agreements their respective countries had reached at earlier meetings in Cierna and Bratislava.

In addition to the above techniques, states also rely on moral appeals to maintain alliance commitments and deter the ever-present potential for breach of treaty. As discussed in the previous chapter, honoring commitments is not, however, a goal that is often valued as an end in itself. Prudence is respected above virtue. The more principled a state's conduct, the more compromised may be its ability to survive and prosper in the bounded anarchy of international affairs, an environment in which subterfuge, suspicion, and betrayal always lurk in the background.

How, then, do norms that oblige states to honor commitments develop, especially when those who abide by their agreements risk harm from states that may be prone to abrogate treaties when changing conditions threaten their perceived interests? The rise and fall of alliance norms may be explained by reference to phenomena observable at two levels of analysis: the national level of foreign-policy decision making, and the systemic level of the international community. Norms defining the extent of promissory obligations emanate from the behavior of states toward one another. These individual actions aggregate to define collective images of acceptable conduct. In order to achieve a better understanding of the dynamics by which changes in behavior at the national level engender alliance norm formation at the systemic level, let us examine the process at each of these two levels of analysis, beginning first with the national level of decision making.

The National Context of Alliance Politics

As noted earlier, given the propensity of most statesmen to believe that their ultimate responsibility is to serve that nebulous standard known as national interest, military partnerships are rarely begotten by high moral principles. Decisions to ally are usually made reluctantly and cautiously, after careful consideration of the costs, benefits, and risks. Although statesmen vary according to the degree to which they are willing to accept risk, they generally only seize an opportunity to form an alliance when (1) the perceived benefits exceed the costs and (2) the costs are politically sustainable. To put it another way, regardless of the risk-taking propensity of its leadership, a nation is likely to "shun alliances if it is believed it is strong enough to hold its own unaided or that the burden of commitment resulting from the alliance is likely to outweigh the advantages to be expected" (Morgenthau, 1985: 201). This pattern is supported by historical evidence showing that "potential alliances which fail to increase both partners' security levels almost never form" (Altfeld, 1984: 538).

The preeminent risk inhibiting the decision to ally resides in the chance that an alliance treaty will bind one's state to a commitment that later ceases to remain in its interest. Alliances are a rudimentary means of "fate control," and many have sown the seeds of undesirable, "fateful" consequences for their members. Ever mindful of this risk, statesmen are understandably wary of entrusting their security to the pledges of others. They know that by doing so, they allow their future foreign policies to be held hostage by previous commitments. Reflecting on this basic inhibition, George F. Kennan summarized the decision calculus of most policymakers with respect to international agreements in the following manner:

> The relations among nations, in this imperfect world, constitute a fluid substance, always in motion, changing subtly from day to day in ways

that are difficult to detect from the myopia of the passing moment, and even difficult to discern from the perspective of the future one. The situation at one particular time is never quite the same as the situation of five years later—indeed it is sometimes very significantly different, even though the stages by which this change came about are seldom visible at the given moment. This is why wise and experienced statesmen usually shy away from commitments likely to constitute limitations on a government's behavior at unknown dates in the future in the face of unpredictable situations. This is also a reason why agreements long in process of negotiations, particularly when negotiated in great secrecy, run the risk of being somewhat out of date before they are ever completed. (Kennan, 1984: 238)

Despite this compelling logic, it is a fact that states frequently overcome their inhibition to form alliances (albeit at different rates in different historical periods). As Arnold Wolfers (1968: 269) points out, "whenever in recorded history a system of multiple sovereignty has existed, some of the sovereign units when involved in conflicts with others have entered into alliances." The incentives to ally for defensive purposes have often proven compelling when two or more states have faced a common threat. Indeed, they can be so strong that states have even found it attractive to make common cause with partners they otherwise find morally repugnant. As Winston Churchill once quipped, "If Hitler invaded Hell, I would make at least a favourable reference to the Devil in the House of Commons."

Necessity, not ideological affinity, is thus the cement of most alliance bonds. In George Liska's (1962: 12) words, "alliances are typically against, and only derivatively for, someone or something." The adages that "alliances are marriages of convenience" and "politics makes strange bedfellows" capture important truths about the conditions that lead states to band together.

Alliances inspire both hopes and fears because they provide opportunities and pose risks. Binding oneself to another entails a serious commitment. Its seriousness stems from three sources. First, an agreement to join forces reduces a state's freedom to maneuver by requiring it to conform with certain contractual stipulations. Second, the agreement also makes the state dependent on each ally's compliance with those stipulations. Third, the agreement may create obligations that are inconsistent with the performance of a commitment to a third state under a previously concluded treaty (Binder, 1988). Moreover, the problem of enforcing an agreement is even more difficult than the problem of bargaining over its terms. Time is destined to test the degree to which allies feel obligated to abide by the provisions of their agreement. Disputes about duties may be expected to arise as new circumstances provoke controversies about the meaning of a treaty's wording. It is for these reasons that the cohesion of any alliance is always in question, and states routinely find it necessary to invest considerable effort in the management of alliance relationships in order to ensure compliance with commitments.

Therefore, even as alliance treaties are signed, the reliability of the parties may be shrouded in suspicion. Though inertia may lengthen the life of an alliance, suspicion will grow when the common threat recedes (Wolfers, 1962: 29). There are, as one foreign policymaker has noted, distinct seasons to the life of every alliance.

> Almost by definition alliances have a limited life cycle. . . . National objectives change, the threat which made it worthwhile to subordinate some national interests to the evolution of a collaborative policy changes also, and the strains of alliance become too great to bear. For though alliance has been an essential device of international politics for nearly three thousand years, it is bound to develop internal strains once the period of clear and present danger is past, since it must involve a relationship between strong and less strong powers, restricting the freedom of both without giving either a decisive influence upon the policy of the other. (Buchan, 1965: 295)

To be sure, many leaders place a positive value on preserving alliances despite the erosion over time of their utility (Rothstein, 1968: 119). But if the costs of honoring the commitment are thought to be increasing due to incompatibilities of interest, the temptation to rescind one's promises will become powerful. As Robert Axelrod and Robert Keohane (1986: 228) put it, "the greater the conflict of interest between the [actors], the greater the likelihood that the [actors] will . . . choose to defect." Obligation conflicts in wartime pose "the ultimate dilemma" (Baker, 1988).

Yet the decision to defect is never easy. A transgressor must be aware that violating an agreement may trigger reprisals. As François de Callières (1963: 130) emphasized, such dishonesty "actually does more harm than good to policy because, though it may confer success today, it will create an atmosphere of suspicion which will make success impossible tomorrow." Moreover, because a former ally's punitive retaliation may cause serious damage, the expedient violation of an alliance commitment is extremely hazardous.

As can be seen in the initial British reaction to the outbreak of

---

Display 3.1. ■ **Alliance Obligations and the British Response to the Outbreak of the First World War**

The policy of Great Britain will not be affected in any way by the announcement that Italy has decided to remain neutral on the ground, as she alleges that no casus foederis has arisen for her Intervention under the precise terms of the Triple Alliance.

This merely proves how brittle an instrument the treaty Is, and Italy will have to settle later on with her own partners as to the justification for her action or inaction.

The French Government has never, directly or indirectly, been led to believe that Great Britain was pledged to any particular method of discharging her obligations to France, although she will remain strictly loyal to the spirit and letter of the understanding.

His Majesty's Government have not decided if they will interfere, or, if so, when they will interfere, in the European war which has now broken out. They have always reserved to themselves the right of determining how we shall play our part in the Triple Entente.

No particular course of action has been decided upon, although both at the Admiralty and the War Office various schemes of action have been worked out to the smallest detail, including the posting of officers commanding-in-chief, their staffs, and their subordinates.

The Cabinet will decide, in the light of events, what course England will pursue, but it may be taken for granted she will be absolutely loyal to her friends.

Source: *The Daily Telegraph,* August 2, 1914 (Special Sunday War Edition).

World War I (see Display 3.1), states are reluctant to assume a generalized policy toward the choices available to them. They prefer instead to reserve the sovereign right to abandon an agreement if and when the costs of adherence become too burdensome. Because future conditions can never be known at the time that the provisions of an agreement are negotiated, all states respect the concept of *raison d'état,* a classic escape clause by which policy reversals can be justified by citing the exigencies of a particular situation. Many theorists and statesmen have claimed that such clauses "are tacitly annexed to every covenant" (see Garner, 1927: 509).[3] Examples abound of states that have tried to escape from alliance agreements by using the justification that national policy interests override international obligations. References to reason of state can be seen in the defense offered by the Ottoman Government for withdrawing from the 1913 Treaty of London and severing its ties with the Allied Balkan Powers. Moreover, "it may also be said that the four major allied Powers that were parties to the inter-allied agreements concerning Germany at the end of the Second World War implicitly recognized the [same] principle . . . in their subsequent political and legal actions" (Friedman, 1964: 301).

Thus it is always uncertain whether an alliance will service the purposes for which it was created; and that uncertainty will increase the longer the alliance remains in force (Lissitzyn, 1967). A treaty of defensive alliance, for example, will normally commit allies to a specified course of action if one of the parties is attacked by a common foe. Since neither party can ever fully anticipate the future, however, the provisions of most treaties are drafted loosely in order to leave each ally room to interpret the nature of the commitment. Yet by writing a treaty with elastic language that diminishes the chance of becoming entangled in a partner's problems, the prospects of being betrayed by that partner at a subsequent point in time are increased. In short, the risks of entrapment and abandonment "tend to vary inversely: reducing one tends to increase the other" (Snyder, 1984: 467).

The International Context of Alliance Politics

Turning from the national to the systemic level of analysis, we find that norms are "transformed when state practice and *opinio juris* change to reflect a new consensus in the international community. . . . In order to effect that change, states interested in a new rule of customary law must take action that violates existing law and they must encourage others to do the same" (Charney, 1986: 914). Consequently, the development of a norm either prescribing or proscribing adherence to alliance commitments derives from the actual conduct of states as reflected in the choices they make in honoring or violating

---

3. "Every treaty," observes Cornelius F. Murphy, Jr. (1985: 88), "as a voluntary limitation upon sovereignty, is written with the implied stipulation that changed conditions liberate a state from its obligations."

their agreements. The more frequent one choice becomes in proportion to the other, the greater the probability that it will culminate in the creation of customary rules of conduct. To put it another way, when a form of behavior becomes widespread, it tends to become obligatory (Kelsen, 1967).

Stanley Hoffmann (1971: 35) captured this relationship between individual behavioral change and collective norm change by noting that rules *of* behavior tend to be converted over time into rules *for* behavior. What most do, others are expected to do (Hoebel, 1954). How individual states behave toward one another in terms of either repudiating or honoring their agreements contributes to the formation of a collective norm that frees states from an obligation to abide by their word, or to the formation of a norm prescribing faithful adherence to commitments. At any given point in time, the international political culture places greater or less stress on flexibility (as opposed to commitment) in its definition of what constitutes an appropriate concept of promissory obligation. In emphasizing one norm rather than the other, a normative order will either facilitate rapid alliance formation and swift realignments or foster alliance longevity by prescribing faithful adherence to treaty guarantees. The former breeds mistrust, the latter helps build trust. Once either of these norms gains wide acceptance throughout international society, the subsequent behavior of states will be shaped by this climate of opinion. As Michael Brecher and Patrick James (1986: 53) have written, "Rule changes may make an alliance more (or less) attractive to one (or more) of its members. Evolving rules also can catalyze the formation of new alliances in response to newly perceived problems. Rule changes affect the way actual and potential alliance partners perceive their objectives, and hence . . . have an impact on alliance dynamics." In fact, the impact of the cultural climate on alliance dynamics may be so great in this area of international politics, that Barbara Tuchman (1984: 5) may be warranted in asserting that "all policy is determined by the mores of its age."

THE STATE OF KNOWLEDGE ABOUT
ALLIANCE RELIABILITY

History is replete with examples of foreign-policy decisions that were influenced by perceptions of whether treaties would be honored by another state. When the Bolsheviks seized power in November 1917, for instance, the British Foreign Office submitted that it was impossible to reach any agreements with the new Soviet government because it was composed of "fanatics" who were "not bound by any ordinary rules" (Little, 1975: 21). Following World War II, White House aides Clark Clifford and George Elsey echoed their British counterparts in reporting to President Harry S Truman that the Soviet Union had violated the Yalta accords, and thus it made little sense to seek new agreements with the Kremlin. Four decades later, similar charges of duplicity and noncompliance were made by U.S. Secretary of Defense Caspar W. Weinberger who, on the eve of the 1985 Geneva summit, urged President Ronald Reagan to resist making any agreements with Moscow that might limit research on the Strategic Defense Initiative (Leffler, 1986). As these three examples illustrate, uppermost in the minds of decision makers contemplating an agreement is a concern about the trustworthiness of the other state, especially in the event of changed circumstances.

Regardless of the importance of trust for decision makers, little research has been done on the reliability of alliance commitments. The research that has been carried out suggests that allies are more likely to assist one another than states that are not allied (Singer and Small, 1966a), but the historical record of assistance is hardly comforting for those considering an alliance agreement. Based on an analysis of 177 alliance war-performance opportunities between 1816 and 1965, Alan Ned Sabrosky (1980a: 177) found that only 27 percent were fulfilled in accordance with treaty commitments, 61 percent were met with abstentions, and 12 percent actually involved allies fighting each other. In short, although alliance members tend to stand together in wartime rather than fight one another, they are most likely to stand aside when a partner becomes embroiled in an armed conflict.

How can we account for variations in the reliability of alliance agreements? Most researchers have sought the answer in the type of commitment, the nature of the relationship between the signatory parties, and the attributes of the nation-states in the alliance. Thus far the results from their work have not converged on a clear answer regarding the importance of these variables. Take, for instance, the effects of alliance class, signatory status, and the juncture at which a commitment is invoked. In their study of alliance reliability during the 1815–1939 period, Ole R. Holsti, P. Terrence Hoppmann, and John D. Sullivan (1973) found that alliances tended to be honored when their specific *casus foederis* is invoked, though no significant differences in performance appeared when controlling for the time period when the treaty stipulations were called into effect. Building upon their work, Sabrosky (1980b) discovered that the degree of reliability appeared instead to be a function of certain classes of alliances that were composed of particular types of states. Specifically, defense pacts and ententes were honored more often than nonaggression agreements, and bilateral alliances composed of states possessing roughly equivalent power were upheld more frequently than those with a major power linked to several minor powers. Using a different research design to extend Sabrosky's research, Randolph M. Siverson and Joel King (1980) found that states in defensive alliances of recent origin tended to assist minor powers in their war efforts. Finally, in a study of thirty-six cases of post-World War II realignment by members of international treaty organizations such as NATO, the Warsaw Pact, and the Arab League, Bruce D. Berkowitz (1983) found that a state is less likely to abrogate alliance commitments when its policy preferences converge with other members, diverge with nonmembers, and its capabilities relative to nonmembers have declined. After adding forty-two cases to a modified version of Berkowitz's data set and replicating his analysis, Michael Altfeld and Won Paik (1986) concluded that changes in a potential realigner's utility for its current allies' issue positions is the most important of the factors identified by Berkowitz in the decision to realign. Thus, although some preliminary research has been done on the question of alliance reliability, the results are sufficiently preliminary to warrant further analysis.

In contrast to the studies reported above, which focus on the type of commitment and the nature of the relationship between the signatory parties, we have argued that reliability is affected by the content of those international norms that bear upon the promissory obligations embedded in alliance treaties. By and large, researchers studying interstate alliances have concentrated their efforts on those properties of alliances that are most amenable to observation and measurement. The number of alliances within the international system, the number of poles around which they are clustered, as well as the tightness and discreteness of the clusters, are examples of these relatively concrete properties. But, as Michael P. Sullivan and Randolph M. Siverson (1981: 18) point out, in order to predict the consequences of those structural configurations generated by alliance bonds, the reliability of alliance commitments must be examined. The same magnitude of alliance commitments, for example, could be associated with different international outcomes if system members held a nihilist attitude toward their obligation to abide by treaty commitments at one time and an idealist view at another. Therefore, if the principles of conduct that are accepted by system members can be determined, we should be able to improve our ability to predict the resultant pattern of alliance behavior and its aggregate consequences.

ALLIANCE RELIABILITY AND INTERNATIONAL ORDER

Of course, as we noted at the conclusion of the preceding chapter, it is still not clear which set of principles are most likely to preserve peace. The relative merits of binding versus flexible interpretations of promissory obligations have been argued since antiquity. Table 3.1 illustrates these contending visions of a state's moral responsibility to honor its alliance commitments.

Uncertainty reduction lies at the core of arguments made on behalf of norms supporting a binding interpretation of commitment. Honoring pledges clarifies expectations and enhances credibility; breaking them causes both friend and foe to question even the most solemn oath. For example, when Nazi troops occupied Bohemia and Moravia despite Hitler's earlier assurances about the territorial integrity of Czechoslovakia, Count Ciano, the Italian Foreign Minister, wondered how much faith could be put in the Führer's word. "What weight," he asked, "can be given in the future to those declarations and promises which concern us more directly" (quoted in Cohen, 1981: 147).

When promises are routinely kept, so this argument goes, uncertainty is reduced because the cultural climate will encourage greater confidence in the behavior of others. Trust in alliance guarantees can strengthen the resolve of partners; doubt makes them insecure. Consider French behavior when Germany warned that its interests in Morocco had been ignored during the formation of the 1904 Anglo-French *Entente Cordiale*. Confident of British support, French Foreign Minister Delcassé recommended resisting Berlin's pressure. As befitted the prevailing cultural climate of mistrust, however, the remainder of the Cabinet lacked confidence in their new ally and therefore acquiesced to German demands for an international conference.

Doubts about the reliability of alliance bonds are also believed to lead to miscalculations, such as those that key officials in Wilhelmian Germany made about the possibility of detaching members from rival alliances. Thinking that states joined alliances by "bandwagoning" with the strong (Walt, 1985), many Germans expected demonstrations

Table 3.1. Are Alliance Obligations Binding?
Some Contending Views of Policymakers

Affirmative Views

"The idea of alliance members choosing when and when not to accept the fruits and duties of membership is dangerous. It creates the conditions for miscalculations and errors in judgment that could ignite conflict."

—David M. Abshire

"Commitment is viewed as an irrevocable pledge."

—Kaiser Wilhelm II

"Around the globe . . . are people whose well-being rests, in part, on the belief that they can count on us. . . . To [desert an ally] would shake the confidence of all these people in the value of an American commitment and in the value of America's word."

—Lyndon B. Johnson

Negative Views

"[A nation has] a right to abrogate a treaty in a solemn and official manner for what she regards as a sufficient cause."

—Theodore Roosevelt

"What we might gain by establishing the steadfastness of our commitments, we could lose by an erosion of confidence in our judgments."

—George W. Ball

"The nation which indulges toward another a habitual hatred or a habitual fondness is in some degree a slave. It is a slave to its animosity or to its affection, either of which is sufficient to lead it astray from its duty and its interest."

—George Washington

---

of power to attract nonaligned states while simultaneously pressuring those aligned with adversaries to abandon their commitments. Gottlieb von Jagow and Alfred von Tirpitz, for instance, assumed that preponderant German strength would force the British to renege on their obligations to France. Similar thinking later led German Chancellor von Bethmann-Hollweg to assume that an Austrian attack on Serbia might shatter Franco-Russian ties by forcing one of them to back out of pledges regarding the Balkans, which each had been voicing since the end of the Bosnia-Herzegovina annexation crisis (Van Evera, 1985: 88).[4]

In sum, arguments that stress the merits of binding promissory obligations contain the following sorites: (1) flexible conceptions of treaty commitments foster uncertainty; (2) uncertainty breeds miscalculation; (3) miscalculation increases the likelihood of war; therefore (4) statesmen should build international legal regimes on a foundation of norms that uphold the sanctity of treaty commitments.

Throughout recorded history, various attempts have been made to ensure that commitments would be upheld. Some cultures have used religious rituals as the Egyptians and the Hittites did in 1285 B.C. when Ramses II and Hattusilius III called upon a thousand of each nation's gods to curse whichever party broke their nonaggression pact.[5] Other cultures have turned to political symbolism, as Athens did in 405 B.C. when it granted citizenship to the Samians in honor of their unswerving loyalty (Quinn, 1981: 23). Still other cultures have sought to guide behavior by emphasizing the actions of moral exemplars (Brinton, 1986: 252–254). Cicero in *De Officiis* (1913: 375–397) and Seneca in *De Providentia* (1935: 17, 22–23) both made appeals of this sort when they praised Marcus Atilius Regulus, consul during the First Punic War, for adhering to an agreement with the Carthaginians, though it had been made under duress. Finally, many cultures, including the Islamic (Khadduri, 1964: 236–237) and the Chinese during the Chou Dynasty (Holsti, 1988: 34), have relied upon an exchange of hostages to strengthen the normative foundations of alliance bonds and guarantee treaty compliance. Although it has been fashionable in recent years to talk about the necessity of confidence-building measures to cement signatory parties to their pledged commitments, these endeavors have been undertaken throughout history whenever states have formalized promises in trea-

---

4. Although von Bethmann-Hollweg held the view that alliances could be broken by military pressure, he did not seem to believe such pressure would affect German calculations. Prior to the Agadir crisis, he told the Kaiser; "If it comes to a war, we must hope that Austria is attacked so that she needs our help and not that we are attacked so that it would depend on Austria's decision whether she will remain faithful to the alliance" (quoted in Joll, 1984: 49).

5. The religious ritual embodied in this treaty can be found in many earlier alliances, including the one between Naram-Sin of Akkad and the King of Elam (ca. 2275 and 2250 B.C.). As a result, Donald L. Magnetti (1978) concludes that appeals to the gods to witness and enforce the promises made in alliance treaties were a common part of the diplomatic ceremonies of the ancient Middle East.

ties and have sought to foster a diplomatic environment that respects the sanctity of contracts.

In contrast to arguments made on behalf of the sanctity of treaty commitments, those that support a more supple interpretation of promissory obligation contend that flexibility engenders restraint. National leaders are assumed to be risk-averse decision makers who will hesitate to engage an opponent when they are unsure about the loyalty of their allies. They will be cautious, acting as if they were aware of the old Italian proverb: *"Fidarsi è bene, non Fidarsi è meglio"* (to trust is good, not to trust is better). Uncertainty, in other words, decreases the probability of war; widespread acceptance of norms promoting elastic definitions of treaty commitment contribute to uncertainty by promoting fluid coalitions, cross-cutting ties, and overlapping interests.

Those who hold this view also claim that a pliant interpretation of promissory obligation helps preserve peace by reducing the probability that states will become entangled in a dispute with their ally's enemies. A norm facilitating the disavowal of commitments is believed to reduce the incidence with which states are pulled into conflicts they could otherwise avoid. For example, this potential danger was avoided in October 1913 when the Russians called upon France to support their protest of General Liman von Sanders' appointment to command the army corps in Constantinople, an appointment that had been made as part of Germany's effort to modernize the Turkish army. Although the French proclaimed loyalty to their alliance with Russia, they avoided becoming involved by making their response contingent on British action, which was unlikely since London had similar connections with the Turkish navy. The alliance norms of the time made this argument more acceptable than would have been the case if rigid adherence to promissory obligations were strenuously supported.

Clearly, a flexible interpretation of obligation gives decision makers considerable latitude in adapting to changing circumstances.[6] It allows them to keep options open, as the Italians did in 1902, when despite membership in the Triple Alliance they secretly assured

---

6. Contemporary advocates of a narrow interpretation of obligation would generally agree with the position forwarded long ago by such individuals as Antiphon, Callicles, and Thrasymachus: binding commitments unnecessarily reduce the chances for powerful states to exploit emerging opportunities. Indeed, Kautilya explicitly sanctioned the breaking of agreements by those states that were rising in the international hierarchy (Bozeman, 1960: 122).

France of their neutrality should the latter find itself in a war with Germany. Moreover, the need for such latitude could be justified by appealing not just to national interest, but also to prevailing diplomatic mores. Thus when Lord Salisbury (quoted in Williamson, 1969: 21) declared "Our treaty obligations will follow from our national inclinations and will not precede them," his pronouncement was not regarded as unacceptably defiant by the standards of the day.

Finally, advocates of a loose conception of promissory obligation point out that flexibility enables third parties to play the role of the "keeper of the balance" between antagonists. Take, for instance, French foreign policy in the mid-seventeenth century. Although Louis XIV had an alliance with the Dutch and provided them with troops, he concluded a secret agreement with Charles II of England in 1667 under which he promised to withhold naval assistance from the Dutch (Friedrich and Blitzer, 1957: 177). In a normative environment condoning rapid alliance formation and dissolution, uncertainties about who is in league with whom, who might unilaterally terminate an alliance treaty prior to its expiration, and who will subsequently join forces with whom, act as a deterrent. So long as the lines between associate and adversary are shifting and unclear, and room is left open for neutrals to maneuver between them, disputes are less apt to escalate to catastrophic wars.

In the final analysis, arguments that promote flexibility converge on the recommendation that leaders should not take a fixed position on things that are not fixed. Prudent statesmen in a decentralized, self-help system should put more faith in their own power than in the good will of others. They should cultivate norms that free their foreign policies from any expectation that alliance agreements must necessarily be upheld under changing conditions. As expressed in the *Mahābhārata,* an ancient Hindu document ascribed to Vyasa (1964: 264), "He who having concluded a treaty with an enemy reposeth at ease as if he hath nothing more to do, is very like a person who awaketh having fallen down from the top of a tree whereon he had slept."

Having surveyed the arguments for and against binding alliance agreements, we are left with the impression that "[f]lexibility and commitment in statecraft offer juxtaposed advantages and drawbacks, and the relative merits of these alternative stances [remain] an issue for several theories of international politics" (Lockhart, 1978: 545). Table 3.2 outlines the main points advanced by both sides in this long-standing debate. In reviewing the thinking behind each of these

Table 3.2. A Comparison of the Ascribed Advantages and Drawbacks of a Binding Conception of Alliance Commitment

Advantages	Disadvantages
Encourages amity between states by fostering a climate of trust	Forecloses options
Provides security through established expectations	Reduces the capacity of states to adapt to changing circumstances
Strengthens the resolve of allies	Weakens a state's influence capability by decreasing the number of additional partners with which it can align
Clarifies national priorities	Eliminates the advantages in bargaining that can be derived from deliberately fostering ambiguity about one's intentions
Increases the credibility of deterrent threats	Provokes the fears of adversaries
Constrains the behavior of the more aggressive members of an alliance	Entraps states in disputes with their ally's enemies
Diminishes the need for others to monitor adherence to treaty provisions	Interferes with the negotiation of disputes involving an ally's enemy by precluding certain issues from being placed on the agenda for debate
Makes explicit otherwise inchoate commonalities of interest among states	Preserves existing rivalries
Cuts communication costs	Stimulates envy and resentment on the part of friends who are outside the alliance and therefore are not beneficiaries of its advantages
Reduces systemic uncertainty	Increases tensions by requiring states to adhere to agreements whose costs over time may have come to exceed their benefits

Table 3.2. (continued)

Advantages	Disadvantages
Cultivates a sense of community among alliance members	Intensifies international conflict by provoking counter-alliances
Establishes the foundations for regional supranational organizations	Confines the range of national roles a state may perform in world affairs
Promotes international security by reducing the fear of attack	Increases the dependence of alliance members on the alliance leader
Extends the form of collaboration among alliance partners beyond military issues	Prevents the effective operation of a balance of power through rapid, ad hoc realignments
Enhances bargaining credibility	Threatens the interests of domestic constituencies who seek ties with states outside the alliance
Reduces erratic behavior by attaching a stigma to it	Expands war by requiring states to become involved in the conflicts of reckless allies
Contributes to a consensus about criteria for differentiating between right and wrong	Provokes fears of hegemonic aspirations by the alliance leader

compelling but incompatible positions, it is important to remember that alliances are simply instruments of foreign policy, not entities whose preservation has intrinsic merit in its own right (Sabrosky, 1980a: 135).

To summarize, we have noted that policymakers face a security dilemma, which they can either address alone or in concert with others. If they choose to act in tandem with another state, they must confront questions about the extent of their obligation to uphold their commitments. One tradition in statecraft counsels that promises should be honored; another teaches that flexibility must be maintained. The interpretations policymakers give to promissory obligations influence the degree to which alliances will continue to shape the behavior of their members once changing conditions alter national objectives.

Alliance reliability, in other words, is contingent on the normative underpinnings of alliance dynamics.

THE ETHICS OF ALLIANCE RESPONSIBILITY

Alliances are agreements to cooperate in security affairs. The right to interpret the commitment formalized by an alliance treaty rests with the signatory parties. Because the conditions that existed at the time of any treaty's initiation eventually will change, each party's sense of obligation is likely to play a decisive role in weighing the option of whether to back out of the agreement. The party who believes commitments should not be broken will act out of an obligation to that value and, in so doing, "he is really keeping faith with himself" (Walzer, 1970).

When the threat that engendered the alliance disappears, trust in an ally's willingness to forgo immediate gain in order to uphold a commitment will diminish. The fulfillment of pledges thus hinges on the capacity of international norms to buttress a particular definition of promissory obligation, one that places a premium on fidelity. Should prevailing norms support anything less when an external threat vanishes, obligations will be dismissed, commitments broken, and the alliance will disintegrate amidst mistrust. As Immanuel Kant once warned, "the universality of a law that everyone believing himself to be in need can make any promise he pleases with the intention of breaking it would make promising, and the very purpose of promising, itself impossible, since no one would believe he was being promised anything, but would laugh at utterances of this kind as empty shams." But while norms permitting the abrogation of treaties might reduce promises to "empty shams," it is not clear from the literature on alliances that this would destabilize the international system. Fluid, shifting partnerships have long been portrayed by balance-of-power theorists as the key to international equilibrium. If they are correct, alliance norms that place a premium on an elastic definition of promissory obligation will be more conducive to preserving peace than those that stress absolute fidelity.

As Robert Axelrod (1986: 1095) reminds us, "an established norm can have tremendous power." If it prescribes faithful fulfillment of commitments, it may be the invisible glue that determines whether treaty ties will bind and alliances will serve the purposes for which they were created. Yet trust among allies may be divisible. The so-called "cod war" between Britain and Iceland indicates that allies in one issue area are not necessarily cooperative in another issue area.

In fact, nonaligned countries are more supportive in many situations than one's own allies. Thus the cause of peace may be advanced by a normative order that allows states the latitude to terminate unilaterally any collective defense treaty that has become anachronistic, to forge new, ad hoc partnerships whenever and wherever they serve national security interests, and to shed those allies that subsequently become an encumbrance.

To evaluate the relative merits of these diametrically opposed positions, a systematic analysis of those norms that support flexibility and binding commitments is required. Empirical evidence can both help us ascertain which theoretical perspective has the most to recommend it and assist us in predicting the ramifications of having either of these positions widely embraced by policymakers. It is the purpose of the next chapter to outline a strategy for generating this required evidence.

Part II

Methodological
Procedures

4 Law, Science, and the Study of Interstate Alliances

Moral facts are facts like any others; they consist of rules of action which can be recognized by some distinctive characteristics; thus, it must be possible to observe them, to describe and classify them.

Emile Durkheim

The social scientist in search of models for the interpretation of world politics, whether he tries to use "new" tools such as those provided by abstract systems analysis, or old concepts such as those of community and society, could do far worse than study the theories presented by writers on international law.

Stanley Hoffmann

For centuries the impact of alliances on world affairs has been vigorously debated. Unfortunately, although the literature generated by this debate is voluminous, the evidence it contains is largely impressionistic. Few studies of alliance meet the "scientific standards of explicitness, visibility, and repeatability" (Burgess and Moore, 1972: 339).

Needless to say, without reproducible evidence any analysis of alliance dynamics is, at best, what Einstein called a *Gedankenexperiment* or, at worst, simply an exercise in naive speculation. In either case, the absence of empirical findings to support either of the rival nihilist, realist, or idealist propositions prevents one from knowing with any degree of confidence whether alliances and peace are related, and if norms supporting treaty compliance enhance or diminish the security of allied states. Despite a long history of intuitive theorizing about these matters, definitive conclusions remain elusive. Hence it is not surprising that a reviewer of the modest body of empirical work on alliances has lamented: "Not only do we face an uncharted sea, as yet no one has succeeded in building a very convincing or watertight ship" (Ward, 1982: 72).

As discussed in the previous chapter, alliances are created to reduce uncertainties by limiting the range of state behavior. To perform this function effectively, allies must be willing to abide by their commitments even at the expense of immediate gain (Lieberman, 1975). Unless treaty commitments are regarded as binding by the signatories,

76

most of the behavioral consequences expected to result from formal alliances are unlikely to be realized. "A problem faced by virtually every alliance is that of ensuring the credibility of its commitments. If adversaries possess serious doubts of this score, the alliance may serve as an invitation to attack. Equally important, if allies themselves have doubts about the assurances of the partners, the alliance is unlikely to survive for very long" (Holsti, Hopmann, and Sullivan, 1973: 22). Formal alliances created in an environment of mistrust will be hollow structures, erected by leaders more for symbolic purposes than to express sincere commitments. When the promises of statesmen are not credible, the behavior of states will be difficult to predict, especially in crises and other periods of rapidly changing circumstances. Therefore, the norms that statesmen embrace with regard to the sanctity of commitments are critical in explaining the consequences that flow from the formation of interstate alliances.

The impact of different types of alliance norms on alliance performance and world politics may be potent, but the evaluation of that impact poses a difficult research challenge. It is the purpose of this chapter to outline the approach to inquiry that will be taken, and identify the assumptions on which it is based.

Even though the importance of the psychocultural underpinnings of alliance dynamics has been recognized for some time (see David, 1975: 12), various methodological obstacles have prevented researchers from analyzing them in a rigorous, empirical fashion. Undoubtedly, the most troublesome of these obstacles is that the decision calculi and motives of leaders are not open to public inspection. Although we can infer the intentions of leaders from biographical material and from the policy pronouncements they use to justify their conduct, we are largely precluded from observing how deeply their feelings about loyalty and honor were held, as well as the extent to which they felt themselves bound by the prevailing norms of their day. If we cannot directly observe the values of decision makers, how can we measure the degree of commitment attached to alliance agreements?

The most advantageous approach to transcending this methodological obstacle is to shift from a national to a systemic level of analysis. This solution has long been advocated but seldom pursued (see Singer, 1968, 1980), even though persuasive arguments have been advanced regarding the impact of macro, ecological variables on micro decisions (e.g., Sprout and Sprout, 1965). Although this shift does not permit us to ascertain the extent to which individual decision

makers feel bound by the alliance agreements they make, it facilitates
the study of change in the psychocultural environment of nations.
Such a perspective allows the systemic effects of aggregated individual choices to be investigated. The shift is warranted because individual behavior is rooted not merely in the unique disposition of a
person, but "it is also markedly influenced by the . . . belief systems
and values current in the culture" (Hinde, 1987: 84).

Any system of entities, including the international system, may be
described in terms of three sets of attributes: physical, structural, and
cultural. Although considerable scholarly effort has been made to obtain reproducible evidence on how the physical and structural attributes of the international system influence state behavior, only very
modest empirical effort has been undertaken on the impact of cultural
attributes.[1] What makes this situation remarkable is that the major
tenets of modern sociological theory proclaim that such attributes
strongly influence the behavioral processes that occur within any
given system (Parsons, 1960: 172).

If the cultural attributes of the international system can serve as a
key point of reference for analyzing the behavioral processes within it,
how might change in these attributes be detected? As noted in Chapter 1, international norms are an expression of those opinions that are
generally held throughout the system about the propriety of specific
kinds of state behavior. Insofar as international law is a medium that
communicates these normative preferences, monitoring changes in the
content of the international legal norms is a particularly useful approach to describing temporal variations in the cultural attributes of
the system. Because alliance "tends to sustain international law . . .
and in turn derives support from it," and because "treaties are employed for formal expression of alliance" (Friedman, 1970: 28), an
examination of changes over time in the law regarding performance of
treaty obligations can serve as an indicator of changes in those international norms that pertain to the sanctity of alliance agreements.
Thus, in order to measure changes in the climate of normative opinion produced by the cultural attributes of the international system, we
shall construct an index that is anchored in the international law of
alliances.

This approach to the observation and measurement of changes in
alliance norms is not, we submit, methodologically unconventional.
To look to international law for evidence of norm transformation is to

1. According to J. David Singer (1971: 18; emphasis added), "the cultural attributes of
   the international system consist of the distribution of personality types, attitudes, and
   opinions among the system's members."

accept a scholarly practice benefitting from a long intellectual history. Indeed, its roots date back to Hugo Grotius, whose *De Jure ac Pacis* (1625) provided the foundation for a positivist approach to public international law that was antithetical to the methodology of the natural law theories that operated from the premise that the universal, peremptory norms of international law were unchangeable (Boyle, 1985: 18). In fact, customary international law is continually evolving (Onuf, 1982a). As Jonathan I. Charney (1986: 914) observes, "customary international law must reflect developments in international society through appropriated changes in the norms. As is true for all legal systems, this law is in flux constantly." Estimating the extent to which these changes occur in alliance norms over time is a prerequisite to the analysis of the impact of alliances in world affairs.

Before proceeding with a discussion of the methodology that will be employed in this approach, a review of the contribution of international law to the study of international norms is warranted.[2] Let us therefore pause to clarify the assumptions justifying our choice among the many available paths to understanding, as well as to evaluate the advantages and limitations of this choice.

ON THE COMPLEMENTARITY OF LEGAL AND SCIENTIFIC SCHOLARSHIP IN INTERNATIONAL RELATIONS

Despite occasional calls for the application of scientific methodology to the analysis of the nexus between international law and behavior (Gould and Barkun, 1970; Falk, 1970: 449, 458–460), investigators operating from both the legal and scientific paradigms have demonstrated a marked reluctance to heed that call. Many sociological and epistemological factors account for this reluctance; however, we submit that the apparent methodological differences separating legal and scientific scholarship are neither necessary nor constructive. The two orientations have more in common with each other than members of either discipline have been willing to acknowledge. For instance, both international law and behavioral science share a common concern with the maintenance of stability; both strive for predictability; both assume that interstate behavior is governed by sufficient regularity to render the search for generalizations a meaningful endeavor. Finally, both seek to account for the patterns that characterize interstate practice. Thus, a symbiotic relation exists between the

---

2. The rationalization for this approach, and the threats to valid inference that it raises, are discussed in further detail in Chapter 5.

two fields: knowledge produced by one contributes to the growth of knowledge in the other.

Given this complementarity of law and science, the gap between the two fields can be bridged by applying the methodology of the latter to the study of the former. To follow this approach is to reintegrate the study of international law into the study of international relations and vice versa. The scientific method increasingly has been perceived to be applicable to the investigation of the international legal order (Lasswell and Arens, 1967; Coplin, 1970), and it has been proposed that legal scholarship advance beyond "the impressionism of earlier approaches" toward the empirical methods of behavioral research. Methods to be considered include cliometric techniques that rely on longitudinal measurement to study historical phenomena (see Falk, 1970: 458, 465; Sheikh, 1974).

Despite these recommendations, research in international law has remained largely detached from scientific analyses of international relations. Many students of the latter have continued to view the work in international law as irrelevant to the task of empirical theory building. This is true even though legal scholarship has contributed to the development of the academic study of international relations, with writers such as Gentilli, Pierino Belli, and Balthasar de Ayala acting as catalysts in the secularization of international relations theory.

In order to bridge this division between legal and scientific research, two basic premises must be accepted. First, it is necessary to assume that legal norms are a social datum that can be treated as "an objective political concept." This is a premise that G. Lowell Field (1949) forcefully argued many years ago but which remains controversial despite supporting arguments by legal scholars (e.g., McDougal and Feliciano, 1961; Kelsen, 1952: 17) and political scientists (e.g., Pye and Verba, 1965). Second, if the international legal order is amenable to observation, then it is also necessary to assume that changes in legal norms are, in principle, measurable. The rationale for this premise is quite simple: measurement is the sine qua non of scientific research.

INTERNATIONAL LAW AS A SOURCE OF DATA OF ALLIANCE NORMS

The goal of creating quantitative indicators in order to measure diachronic changes in the content of commitment norms is also confronted by the controversies surrounding the nature of law. Foremost among these is the view that only "essential" properties of legal phenomena can be measured. This line of reasoning implies that any data gathering effort must begin with a definition of the real essence of the concepts under examination. But those essentialists who seek the true meaning of law face "a question upon which whole libraries have been written, as their very existence shows, without definite results being attained" (Kantorowicz, 1958: 1).

Whatever theoretical problems might have arisen with regard to defining law within states, they are multiplied when the subject of a law among states is contemplated. This task is thus not confined only to defining the nature of law, but also includes determining whether international law is actually law. At least three distinct positions have been taken regarding this question. Monists assert that national and international law are components of a single legal order. Dualists claim that each constitutes a distinct system of law. Finally, a third body of opinion holds that international law is not really law. Although each position is defended vigorously, this great debate has neither clarified the essence of international law nor "wiped out the body of rules that are now accepted for determining the conduct of states" (Williams, 1945: 162).

Tempting as it may be to build theoretical structures on a footing of real definitions, several factors make it unlikely that scholars will ever attain this objective. On the one hand, the question "what is law" is misdirected in that analysts frequently confuse it with queries about the substantive content of law, sources of law, implementation of laws, and obeyance of laws (Kegley, 1970). On the other hand, the quest for the true meaning of law is ill-conceived because it disregards the open texture of terms (Waismann, 1951: 122–123) and the numerous conflicting interpretations given to the notions of truth and meaning (Ogden and Richards, 1938: 186–187). In sum, any attempt to base the scientific study of international legal norms on an essentialist foundation is wrong-headed because "It becomes fairly plain that the attempt to define 'law,' like similar attempts to define 'art' and 'religion' should be abandoned at least if the traditional tight genus-specie kind of definition is attempted. 'Law' simply has no genus . . . [To avoid falling] into the essentialist fallacy, we should ask only how any given word has been used, is used, or, we may propose, ought to be used in a given context. We cease to ask what it 'means'—as if it always and everywhere possessed a certain meaning" (Kegley, 1970: 61–62). Consequently many social scientists no longer struggle to determine the true meaning of law. Instead, like

Laura Nader (1965: 6), they ask how the international legal order might be conceptualized for research purposes.

Our conceptualization does not entail any need to explicate the true meaning of the rules governing alliance performance. Instead, we seek to identify the interpretations made of alliance norms. That is, we are interested in the shared expectations regarding the latitude for noncompliance with alliance promises that existed during different historical periods. This conceptualization of international law as an instrument for creating a climate of opinion about likely behavior accepts the fact that "very many rules of international law were evolved, rather as guidance for statesmen and diplomatists than as guidance for advocates and judges" (McNair, 1961: 687).

Because the rules that make up the international legal order are not amenable to direct visual observation, where might the researcher look in order to classify and monitor international norms? Stanley Hoffmann (1965: 132) has proposed a possible solution by recommending that the interpretation of norms presented by writers on international law be treated as a source of data. Wesley L. Gould and Michael Barkun (1970: 184, 214) agree, arguing that the views expressed by publicists "have traditionally been cited as one of the sources of international law. . . . [In] what ways was international law transformed to fit the world of 1945 and after instead of that of 1939 and before? Was it even transformed significantly?. . . . Even a comparison of textbooks of different periods might prove informative, providing the findings were tabulated and aggregated to present systematic evidence." These recommendations suggest an indirect approach to measuring norm transformation. Evidence on the content of international norms may be derived from what publicists *report* about them in the legal treatises they publish. That is to say, by focusing on what these eminent writers actually *observed* rather than on what norms they thought members of the international community ought to follow, quantitative indicators of alliance norm formation and decay may be constructed by means of content analysis.

The conversion of this source information into quantitative data is not complicated. As Ole R. Holsti (1969: 1) points out, content analysis is a data-making procedure that may be performed upon any communication: "novel, newspaper, love song, diary, diplomatic note, poem, transcribed psychiatric review, and the like." Moreover, it may be used to "draw inferences other than those concerning the characteristics of authors" (North, Holsti, Zanimovich, and Zinnes, 1963: 51). When international legal treatises are subjected to this procedure, the authors are conceived as experts and their descriptions are treated as observations that, when coded, generate data regarding the (1) presence, (2) absence, and (3) intensity with which particular beliefs concerning appropriate interstate behavior were held to prevail at the time of the scholar's writing.

The approach taken to operationalize the content of international norms raises a number of issues, most of which center on problems of construct validity.[3] Although an obvious distance necessarily exists between the concept of an alliance norm and its operational indicator, several considerations suggest that our procedure possesses considerable face validity. Specifically, the procedure may be defended in the following terms.

1. There is a relatively close fit between international norms defined in terms of their communicative function and the information provided by publicists. The information provided by textbook writers describes the assumptions policymakers held about the rules of the system during a particular period of history. We agree with William D. Coplin that the writings of jurists may be seen

> as an institutional device for communicating to the policymakers of various states a consensus on the nature of the international system. It is a "quasi-authoritative" device because the norms of international law represent only an imperfect consensus of the community of states, a consensus which rarely commands complete acceptance but which usually expresses generally held ideas. Given the decentralized nature of law-creation and law-application in the international community, there is no official voice of the states as a collectivity. However, international law taken as a body of generally related norms is the closest thing to such a voice. Therefore, in spite of the degree to uncertainty about the authority of international law, it may still be meaningful to examine international law as a means for expressing the commonly held assumptions about the state system. (Coplin, 1965: 618–619)

Thus, we are not seeking to quantify international law; rather, the concept and indicator relate to the opinions about commitment norms made by those qualified by their expertise and research to summarize the operating rules of the international system.

---

3. As noted in the Preface, this study of alliance norms evolved from a much larger and continuing research project, the Transnational Rules Indicators Project (TRIP). The operational steps by which the contents of these authoritative treatises were screened and coded for a variety of international legal norms are described elsewhere (see Kegley, 1975 and 1982; Raymond 1977 and 1980).

2. The use of textbook writers' opinions as a data source is also recommended because publicists comprise the only professional group dedicated to observing and systematically recording changes in alliance norms and practice. To be sure, the memoirs of policymakers provide information about the "standing rules of procedure" that statesmen perceived to influence their behavior (Snyder, Bruck, and Sapin, 1962). Nevertheless, this information is neither comprehensive nor readily amenable to comparative historical survey because the available information is not representative. Further, it would be misleading to rely on partial accounts to derive impressions about the norms that held sway during particular periods. Hence, international legal texts serve as the best source of publicly available information from which evidence about the norms that have guided state practice may be extracted.

Within international law, the statements of textbook writers are seen as "helping to create the opinion by which the range of consensus is enlarged" (Gould, 1957: 143). As shown in Table 4.1, the writings of eminent publicists have long been considered by judicial tribunals as a source of evidence about the norms operative in the international system. An authoritative statement regarding the propriety of treating the accounts of legal experts as a source of evidence of what international law regards as licit and illicit conduct is provided in Article 38(1)(d) of the *Statute of the International Court of Justice*. It declares "the teachings of the most highly qualified publicists of the various nations" to be a subsidiary means for determining the rules of international law. In Justice Gray's opinion, "where there is no treaty, and no controlling executive or legislative act, or judicial decision, resort must be had to the customs and usages of civilized nations; and, as evidence of these, to the works of jurists and commentators, who by years of labor, research and experience, have made themselves peculiarly well acquainted with the subjects of which they treat. Such works are resorted to by judicial tribunals . . . for trustworthy evidence of what the law really is." (Paquette Habana, Lola, 175 U.S. 677, 700 [1900]).

3. The role of scholars and "opinions of revered writers" in the formation of law possibly has declined in recent years (Onuf, 1982a: 21–22); however, this does not vitiate the use to which their writings are put here. The descriptions provided by these highly qualified scholars remain useful for "the ascertainment of the positive law" (Virally, 1968: 153) and continue to communicate prevailing attitudes

about the nature of international society in general, as well as the extent of promissory obligations in particular. Legal experts perform the task of reporting the crystallized opinion of statesmen about the norms perceived to shape alliance behavior. Moreover, as the conditions of complex interdependence have made the task of summarizing the rules of international law more difficult, the need for publicists to perform this function has increased.

4. Publicists are expert observers of international norms because their writings are explicitly designed to describe the character of the system at a particular point in time. The works of famous scholars have often gone through many editions[4] and increasingly since the 1800s the commentaries of each edition have been revised to reflect changes in norms. For our purposes, these commentaries are especially instructive when publicists took care to characterize the ways in which alliance obligations were undergoing change during the periods in which they were writing. What publicists perceive as the customary practice of states, therefore, may be inventoried to trace the direction and degree of alliance norm transformation.

In sum, if alliance norms are conceptualized as quasi-authoritative statements that communicate prevailing assumptions about the obligations of allies toward one another, then one way to obtain information indirectly on these attitudinal phenomena is to examine publicly observable documents that were explicitly designed to portray the climate of opinion on treaty compliance that existed at the time. By treating legal scholars as expert observers whose role it is to describe the importance attributed to various legal norms, it becomes possible to derive data on changing attitudes toward alliance obligations through both content analysis and the comparison of various legal texts written over an extended period of time. International legal experts articulate shared beliefs about rules for state behavior. Because their writings inculcate awareness about those norms for which there was community support, legal treatises are a viable source from which changes in allies' obligations can be detected.

In order to accomplish this task, 244 authoritative legal treatises were content analyzed under the auspices of the Transnational Rules

---

4. Consider the fact that Oppenheim/Lauterpacht went through eight editions from 1905 to 1955; Hall went through eight editions from 1880 to 1924; von Liszt made eleven revisions of his treatise; and there are twenty-four editions of von Martens' text.

Table 4.1. The Continuity of Opinion Regarding the Importance of Publicists as a Source of Information about International Norms

"Perhaps the most fruitful [source of international law] of all is formed of the works of text-writers of approved authority, showing the usage of nations, or the general opinion respecting their mutual conduct, with the definitions and modifications introduced by general consent. As a general rule, authors of text-books and treatises on international law have risen above the local interests and prejudices which too often influence the writings of diplomatists, and even the decisions of courts, and have treated the subject in a philosophical spirit worthy of all commendation, and which causes their opinions to be referred to as authority on all disputed questions. Of course we cannot expect to find a complete uniformity of opinion in these writers, but there is a very general concurrence of views on all the great and leading principles which they have discussed."

—H. W. Halleck, 1861

"The views expressed by learned writers on international law have done in the past, and will do in the future, valuable service in helping to create the opinion by which the range of consensus of civilized nations is enlarged."

—Lord Alverstone, 1905

"The task of digesting the precedents and transforming suggestions into new rules is mainly the work of the writers on international law."

—Ellery C. Stowell, 1931

"Text-writers . . . may help to create opinion . . . concerning what international law really is."

—James L. Brierly, 1935

"[It] is as evidence of the law . . . that the writings of publicists have been admitted in judicial pronouncements."

—Lassa F. L. Oppenheim, 1955

"Academic works have always played a fundamental and irreplaceable part in making the law known. In our time the increasing complexity of the law makes resort to academic works indispensable . . . as it alone provides a guiding thread in the jungle of statues, regulations and judicial decisions."

—René David, 1984

Indicates Project.[5] The criteria used to select the treatises centered on whether a work had gone through multiple revised editions or had been identified as authoritative by either independent scholarship (e.g., listed in the Association of Law Schools' bibliography of international law texts or included in *The Hague Peace Palace Systematic Catalogue* of classic tomes), or by a recognized legal body such as the World Court or the Institute of International Law.

MEASURING ALTERNATIVE CONCEPTIONS OF ALLIANCE COMMITMENT IN INTERNATIONAL LAW

As noted in Chapter 2, the international legal order has at various times given normative backing to either the sanctity or repudiation of promises. Although support for the binding nature of commitments has been voiced frequently throughout history, so, too, has support for a more flexible interpretation of promissory obligations. Indeed, the number of rationales for the premature abrogation of commitments made to others has been rather extensive. The nihilist mentality that finds the renunciation of alliance promises acceptable assumes that the benefits of flexible, unrestrained sovereign choice outweigh the costs of bad faith, mistrust, and suspicion. This permissive point of view councils against the temptation to expect untrustworthy allies to keep their word. Norms condoning the premature abrogation of treatises facilitate accommodative adjustments in political alignments and allow for allegiances to adapt rapidly to changed circumstances. Norms pertaining to promissory obligation, however, have not remained above reproach because they do not derive from a supreme authority (Murphy, 1985: 15).

Against this ever-present reservation of the sovereign right of states to remain unencumbered by moral edicts, there has been a recognition of the need for faithful performances of treaty obligations. As Emeriche de Vattel noted, "There is no longer any security . . . if [states] did not think themselves obligated to keep faith with one another, and to perform their promises. This obligation is then as necessary, as it is natural and indubitable between nations that live together in a state of nature. . . . Nations, therefore . . . ought inviolably to observe their promises and their treaties" (Vattel, 1916: 196).

Hence we find two opposed injunctions in the thinking of political

---

5. During the first phase of the project, 202 authoritative treatises were analyzed for content. Subsequently the data base has been expanded by coding 42 additional works, to bring the sample to its present size of 244 treatises.

philosophers and legal theorists. Both have informed each other in practice, even as they challenge each other. As a result, the diplomatic discourse on promissory obligations produces a kind of cultural schizophrenia: when one injunction dominates the thinking of the day, the other has always remained haunting in the background. There is an inherent tension between the preference for freedom and that for order, a tension that is perhaps irreconcilable because in any society there is a need and desire for both.

It is revealing that international law reflects the positions of both values. International "legal rules co-exist in complementary pairs, permitting opposing arguments to develop in relations to each complementary norm" (Falk, 1970: 14). An example of the dichotomous nature of many legal rules can be seen in the opposing answers given to the question, "who may interpret a treaty?" On the one hand, the principle *nemo debet esse index in propia sua causa* stipulates that no one may be a judge in his own cause. On the other hand, the principle *ejus est interpretare legem cujus est condere* asserts that he who has the power to make a law has the power to interpret it (see Degan, 1963). As we shall see, a similar antinomy can be found in legal opinions on the question of whether commitments adopted voluntarily by parties to international agreements should be regarded by states as necessarily binding.

For many legal theorists (e.g., Kelsen, 1952, 1967), the most basic obligation of those agreeing to ally is summarized by the norm *pacta sunt servanda* (pacts made in good faith are binding). The roots of this norm can be traced back to the ancient Egyptians, Chinese, and Chaldeans. "To the Greeks the rule of good faith was part of a universal law. To the Romans it was part of the *jus gentium* common to every tribe and people" (Fenwick, 1965: 517–518). By the eighth century it was included by Shaybānī in his *Siyar*, the Islamic law of nations (see Khadduri, 1966). According to C. Wilford Jenks (1958: 143–145), the principle *pacta sunt servanda* is part of every major legal system.

By and large, the primary purpose of *pacta sunt servanda* has been recognized as reducing uncertainty through the promotion of shared expectations that treaty commitments will be honored in good faith. Although supporters of his norm all stress the importance of upholding the irrevocability of promises, some legal theorists qualify their support for an absolute interpretation by acknowledging that there may be contingencies that permit the steadfast adherence to treaties to be relaxed.[6] Writing in 1796, the legal authority Friedrich von Martens agreed that a valid contract created the right for a nation to demand performance of that contract from another party, but only if the former had been discharging its own contractual obligations. For von Martens, inadequate performance by one side releases the other from the agreement.

Qualifications of this sort raise doubts about whether *pacta sunt servanda* is a peremptory norm of general international law, that is, one to which there are no exceptions. *Pacta sunt servanda* ''is frequently reiterated in solemn form,'' but, as William W. Bishop, Jr. (1962: 133–134) points out, it is not always ''well observed.'' Fears about the possibility that ruthless or expedient statesmen will fail to live up to their promises have led many legal theorists to elevate *pacta sunt servanda* to the status of a sacred, inviolable principle in order to create an environment that would deter national leaders from relying upon *raison d'état* as a way of releasing themselves from treaty obligations whenever these obligations ran contrary to perceived interests. These legal theorists would not find it so necessary to take such a posture if the bounded anarchy of world politics was not pregnant with the potential for the doctrine of *pacta sunt servanda* to be eclipsed by a norm liberating states from their promissory obligations.

International law recognizes several grounds for terminating treaties and agreements prior to their originally agreed-upon expiration date. Some justifications, like mutual consent, are noncontroversial,[7]

---

6. The views of those who accept no conditions that justify violating the norm *pacta sunt servanda* are represented by Anthony D'Amato's (1987: 376) claim that ''A treaty is a legal obligation that, under international law, simply cannot be legally violated. There are apparent exceptions to this rule, but they are only apparent.'' Josef L. Kunz (1945: 197) summarized the absolutist interpretation by noting that, ''contrary to the opinion of many writers, . . . *pacta sunt servanda* . . . admits no exceptions.''

7. International law recognizes a variety of legal procedures for the revision and termination of treaties that lie beyond the application of the doctrine *rebus sic stantibus*. Far less controversial because they do not represent a direct challenge to norms prescribing faithful performance of promissory obligations or raise the problem of autonomous abrogation, they include: ''(1) notice by one of the parties pursuant to the terms of the treaty, (2) fulfillment of the provisions of the treaty, (3) expiration of the period of time for which the treaty was concerned, (4) extinguishment of one of the parties in the case of a bilateral treaty, or the subject matter of the treaty, (5) agreement of the parties, (6) conclusion of a new treaty covering the same subject matter or one wholly inconsistent with the earlier treaty, [and] (7) denunciation by one party with acquiescence by the other, and effect of war'' (Nelson, 1958: 879).

while others have been the subject of considerable disagreement. The *clausula rebus sic stantibus* (as matters stand) is the most widely used and hotly contested of these grounds. Indeed, Sir Hersch Lauterpacht (1970: 357) felt so strongly about the vitiating effect of *rebus sic stantibus* that he labeled it a "pseudo-legal doctrine" and chastised the fact that it was "frequently preached by many writers, and some governments." Interpreted in its narrowest sense, it allows a state to terminate an agreement unilaterally if a fundamental change occurs in the circumstances that existed at the signing of the agreement. Thus, for example, when in 1870 Russia declared that it was no longer bound by the provisions of the 1856 Treaty of Paris that related to the neutralization of the Black Sea, its leaders cited the changed circumstances resulting from political events in the Balkans and the development of iron-clad warships as their justification. In contrast, when this rationale is interpreted in its broadest terms, it ostensibly allows unilateral termination if an agreement is considered injurious by one party to the so-called "fundamental rights of necessity" possessed by every state.

Of course, the content of these self-defined rights varies widely and appears to include almost everything. As Table 4.2 shows, some

---

These requirements emphasize the need for a state seeking release from its treaty obligations to first request an ally to agree to the treaty's termination (Oppenheim, 1955: 492–493; McNair, 1961: 493–494). Relatively more controversial are the numerous doctrines that apply to the interpretation of the legality of these procedures, including "unilateral denunciation" in the aftermath of a prior treaty breach (see Tobin, 1933: Sinha, 1966), "frustration of contract," (see McNair, 1948), "affreightment" and "presupposed conditions" (see Ramberg, 1970), "unilateral suspension" (see Sinha, 1966: 206), and "desuetude" and "obsolescence" (see DeLupis, 1967: 93, 96). Although not regarded as *contra legem,* these doctrines challenge the peremptory status of the norm that all contracts are binding *in perpetuite* or for "indefinite duration" (Brierly, 1955: 256). Instead, they provide justifications on which states may draw to release themselves from strict compliance with promises "when changed conditions or an unexpected turn of events have considerably reduced the advantages to be expected from the contract" (Ramberg, 1970: 152). Of course, the existence of these rationales makes the norm *pacta sunt servanda* neither absolute nor impenetrable. They stand in contradiction to the absolute view that a promise is a promise, "a violation of a treaty, irrespective of its effects, does not ipso facto operate to annul the obligations of either the innocent party or the defaulting party" (Sinha, 1966: 206), even in the event that allies rupture their relations or engage in military operations against one another (see DeLupis, 1967). The availability of various legal rationales for treaty abrogation therefore stand in contradiction to, and pull against, the absolute inviolability of the principle *pacta sunt servanda.*

legal theorists "have defined the circumstances under which the rule of *rebus sic stantibus* is applicable in terms so vague and general that the revision or termination of a treaty might be demanded by one party whenever in its opinion the performance of obligations conflicted in any degree with its interests" (Garner, 1927: 512). Hence the doctrine lies at the center of disputes about the duties of states toward the treaties they sign. "There seems to be no recorded case in which its application has been admitted by both parties to a controversy" (Brierly, 1963: 335). For instance, the *clausula* was used by Russia in 1886 to denounce Article 59 in the 1878 Treaty of Berlin with regard to the status of the port of Batoum; it was invoked by Austria-Hungary in 1908 to justify the annexation of Bosnia and Herzegovina; it was conjured up by Germany in 1914 to justify violating the Belgian Neutrality Treaty of 1839; and it was also referred to by Persia in 1918 and China in 1926 during their criticism of "unequal treaties" (see Woolsey, 1926; Briggs, 1949). When applied to alliances, the *clausula rebus sic stantibus* preserves tremendous freedom to maneuver for each state, especially if the broader interpretation is accepted. Alliance agreements under this norm are not inviolable; they can be discounted unilaterally in order to free oneself from their stipulations.

Like the principle of sanctity of treaties, the notion that every treaty has an unwritten clause stating that changes in conditions extant at its signing free the parties from their commitments can be found throughout recorded history. Polybius, for example, describes how Lysicus contended that changed circumstances overrode the obligations of an alliance treaty between Sparta and the Aetolians. Similarly, in 1595, Queen Elizabeth I of England justified her reinterpretation of a treaty with the Netherlands on the grounds of *rebus sic stantibus,* as did King Frederick II of Prussia when he terminated a neutrality treaty with Breslau and occupied the town in 1741. In another exemplary case, Queen Maria Theresa of Austria also invoked the clause when in 1748 she sought to have the territorial settlement of the Treaty of Worms invalidated. Indeed, the abrogation of agreements has been so common that Sinha (1966: 105–192) has identified nearly fifty significant instances during the past century and a half in which the deserted party found it necessary to unilaterally denounce the prior treaty.

Aside from its frequent use in statecraft, *rebus sic stantibus* has also been recognized in many domestic legal systems. The French

**Table 4.2. Examples of Narrow versus Broad Interpretations
of the *Clausula Rebus Sic Stantibus***

Narrow Interpretations

Treaty commitments may be repudiated if (1) extraordinary changes
occur in the circumstances which existed at the time the agreement
was concluded, or (2) performance of the agreement's stipulation becomes impossible:

(1) "when . . . the circumstances essential to the promise, and
without which it certainly would not have been made, happen to
change, the promise falls . . . [and] an exception should be made
to its enforcement."

—Emmeriche de Vattel

(2) "a prince is not bound beyond his capacity to perform the act
promised, and the question of his capacity should be referred to
the decision of a third prince who is to be a man of principle."

—Cornelius van Bynkershoek

Broad Interpretation

Treaty commitments may be repudiated if:

(1) they become "incompatible with . . . [the state's] natural development."

—Johann Kaspar Bluntschi

(2) they prevent "the exercise of . . . natural rights or . . . [of-
fend] in any manner against the principles of absolute justice or the
supreme law of right."

—Pasquale Fiore

(3) they become "essentially burdensome."

—Franz von Liszt

(4) they create "inequality."

—A. Heffler

(5) they become "incompatible with the independence of a state."

—William Edward Hall

---

principle of *imprévision,* the German concept of *Geschäftsgrundlage,*
and the English doctrine of "frustration of contract" accept the logic
of changed circumstances as a grounds for violating previous prom-

ises. In addition, *rebus sic stantibus* has been invoked before the Swiss Federal Tribunal in disputes between cantons (see *Lucerne v. Aaragau,* 1882; and *Thurgau v. St. Gallen,* 1928).

Although the *clausula rebus sic stantibus* possesses a long history, has often been accepted in domestic law, has been referred to in international court decisions (e.g., *Free Zones of Upper Savoy and the District of Gex,* Permanent Court of International Justice [1932] Ser. A/B, No. 46), and has appeared in multilateral covenants (e.g., Article 19 of the Covenant of the League of Nations [1919]), it has been vigorously criticized during periods when statesmen have most craved for stability in international affairs. Defenders of the norm *pacta sunt servanda* have attacked the use of *rebus sic stantibus* by arguing that it is a source of uncertainty that can provoke national fear and, in turn, international conflict. For instance, the 1871 Declaration of London, which opposed Russia's denunciation of the demilitarization of the Black Sea, along with the 1935 Declaration of Stresa, which opposed Germany's repudiation of the military clauses of the Versailles Treaty, implied that uncertainties about the behavior of states would be reduced if they could not unilaterally modify or terminate a valid treaty.

Strictly speaking, *pacta sunt servanda* and *rebus sic stantibus* need not be considered mutually exclusive; the narrow interpretation of the latter may be interpreted as a qualification of the former (Lissitzyn, 1967: 922). Yet, in practice, the two norms conventionally are treated as opposites, both by strident advocates of the broader interpretation of the *clausula* and strict constructionists of the absolutist interpretation of *pacta sunt servanda* (David, 1975: 83). Thus Erich Kaufmann (1911) flatly concluded that unilateral treaty termination was an infraction of *pacta sunt servanda,* Heinrich Lammasch (1918) declared that it was impossible to hold *rebus sic stantibus* as a principle of international law if one accepted *pacta sunt servanda,* and George W. Keeton (1929) proclaimed that a broad interpretation of *rebus sic stantibus* would reduce treaty "bonds" to a "rope of sand." Consequently, during certain periods in the past, international law has drawn a sharp distinction: "Treaties either were binding or were not binding at all" (Gould, 1957: 57). But at other times, the two norms have operated in tandem, albeit with one more widely applied than the other.

An example of an attempt to deal with *pacta sunt servanda* and *rebus sic stantibus* in complementary (rather than mutually exclusive) terms is provided by the Vienna Convention on the Law of Treaties of

1969.[8] Article 26 declares that "Every treaty in force is binding upon the parties to it and must be performed by them in good faith." But Article 62 goes on to qualify this by acknowledging that a fundamental change of circumstances may be invoked as a ground for terminating or withdrawing from the treaty if: "(a) the existence of those circumstances constituted an essential basis of the consent of the parties to be bound by the treaty; and (b) the effect of the change is radically to transform the extent of obligations still to be performed under the treaty." Thus, although both principles were recognized, the norm *pacta sunt servanda* was embraced at that time as the dominant norm.

In the course of the development of international law since the Treaty of Westphalia, these two, largely incompatible norms have uneasily struggled for dominance. The inherent tension between them has never been reconciled, and is further dramatized by the fact that both norms have been assumed implicitly by international law to be part of every treaty. On the one hand, many students of jurisprudence defend the principle *conventio omnis intelligitor rebus sic stantibus* and assert: "Every treaty, as a voluntary limitation upon sovereign power, is written with the implied stipulation of *rebus sic stantibus* (Murphy, 1985: 88). On the other hand, many have proclaimed that *pacta sunt servanda* is tacitly incorporated into every treaty (Wehberg, 1959) because "unless the pledged word of a state can be relied

---

8. For example, the Bulgarian delegate to the Vienna negotiations on the Law of Treaties decried "the trend towards flexibility" he saw developing in 1969 and urged a reassertion of the principle of *pacta sunt servanda* in the norms of international law. The debate between proponents of the norm *pacta sunt servanda* and those subscribing to a norm allowing states to abrogate treaties under changed conditions became a "battleground" (Gormley, 1970: 367, 385). In many other periods unfolding trends have brought the opposition of these contending norms into relief, as exemplified by the debate that emerged between advocates of these contradictory norms at the close of World War I (see Phillimore, 1917), the interwar period more generally (see Kunz, 1945: 187; Garner, 1927: 509), and again with intensity in 1969 (see Gormley, 1970; Lauterpacht, 1970: 355–357). At times this latent struggle over values has surfaced to reveal a vigorous debate in international legal discourse over the nature of promissory obligations. More often, relatively stable international circumstances have permitted a consensus to form that incorporates both contending values into its vision of the duties of allies, thus temporarily masking the pull of these norms against one another. It is the mission of publicists of any period to accurately portray the distribution of opinion regarding the status of treaty norms and to characterize the moral ethos that rendered one norm dominant relative to the other. The images provided by legal authorities of the prevailing norms (not their personal preferences for them) allow the expectations about the permissibility of autonomous treaty abrogation to be reconstructed.

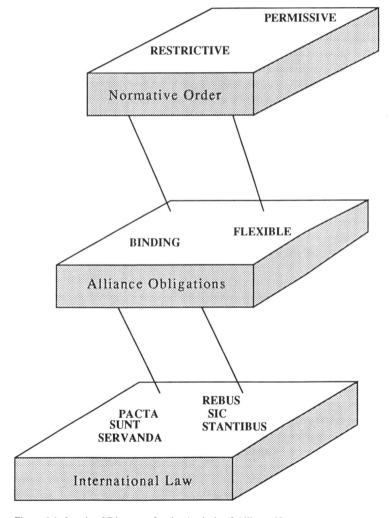

Figure 4.1. Levels of Discourse for the Analysis of Alliance Norms

upon . . . law itself would disappear'' (Fenwick, 1965: 518). In the words of John Eppstein (1984: 14), the first Secretary General of the Atlantic Treaty Association; ''the whole mass of treaties and conventions between them, which constitute the corpus of positive international law, would be waste of paper were it not for the moral rule *pacta sunt servanda.*''

Clearly, stress on one norm entails a rejection of the other; as contending norms, the two concepts of promissory obligations pull against one another, even though both are components of the thinking that underlies all diplomatic and legal discourse. In conjunction the juxtaposed normative categories form a cultural and legal universal: they refer to opposed convictions about the obligatory status of agreements inherent in all social interaction, irrespective of time and place, which require participants to develop expectations about appropriate conduct. As Sir Hersch Lauterpacht (1933: 273) summarized this inherent tension, ''The rule that compacts must be kept is certainly one of the bases of the legal relations between members of any community. But at the same time the notion that in certain cases the law will refuse to continue to give effect to originally valid contracts is common to all systems of jurisprudence.''

Neither binding nor flexible conceptions of agreements between states have survived for any sustained length of time without eventual challenge. Although one conception has tended to prevail in some historical periods, that domination has always receded later, only to regain subsequent support. The ambivalence displayed in the changing posture of international law toward these competing conceptions illuminates the fact that a consensus has not materialized over the issue of which conception of treaty obligation should prevail. Given that each of these norms can potentially alter how treaty obligations are conceived, our index of alliance commitment will focus on diachronic changes in their relative importance within international law.

To identify the kind of commitment norms that the authors perceived as legally permissible at the time they were writing, each treatise was categorized according to whether existing legal norms were seen by the author as supporting or rejecting a binding interpretation of treaty obligations. That is, each text's interpretation was classified in terms of whether *pacta sunt servanda* or a broad interpretation of *rebus sic stantibus* was seen by the author as the dominant norm governing obligations between parties to agreements in general and alliance treaties in particular during the period of history being

described.[9] Once every treatise in a particular half-decade was classified, a summary index of commitment was calculated by means of
the following formula: (the percentage of authors who saw legal
norms supporting a binding interpretation of treaty obligations)–(the
percentage of authors who saw norms supporting a flexible interpretation of treaty obligation)/100. The resulting index ranges from
+1.00 (alliance commitments are binding) to −1.00 (alliance commitments may be terminated unilaterally), with other positions arrayed in
between and a perfect balance (0.00) indicating that neither *pacta sunt
servanda* nor *rebus sic stantibus* was dominant during the half-decade
in question.

By treating these authors as expert observers who attempted to describe and communicate to others what legal norms held sway when
they wrote their treatises, it becomes possible to measure changes in
the relative importance of these norms over time. To be sure, any
given publicist may have been sympathetic to one or the other alliance
norm. But our data-making procedure was designed to record what
this expert observer interpreted as the prevailing alliance norm at that
moment, not which norms he thought ought to be embraced by the
international community. Hence two publicists may both report that
pacta sunt servanda is the dominant norm at a particular time point,
though they might disagree over whether it should be retained as such
in the future. Our coding scheme sought to identify the "is" each
publicist reported, *not* the "ought" advocated.

At this point, the reader has undoubtedly noticed that an analysis
based on these concepts has necessarily referred to phenomena at different levels of discourse. We have used, almost interchangeably, the
words "commitment," "trust," "binding," and "restrictive" to describe one interpretation of promissory obligation (*pacta sunt servanda*); and we have employed the terms "noncompliance,"
"mistrust," "flexible," and "permissive" to describe an alternative
interpretation of promissory obligation (*rebus sic stantibus*). As seen
in Figure 4.1, diplomatic and legal discourse about the place of prom-

---

9. According to Chesney Hill (1934: 17), publicists have been influential in communicating the nature of these doctrines. The following writers have been cited by states
or tribunals: Anzilotti, Fauchille, Brierly, Cattand, Despagnet, Dupuis, Hall, Hatse-
hek, Heffter-Geffeken, Jellinek, Kaufmann, Klüber, Lammesch, Liszt, Oppenheim,
Piédlièvre, Pradier-Fodéré, Rovier, Rolin-Jacquemyns, Schmidt, Triepel, Vattel,
Waldkirch, Werth-Regendanz, Westlake, and Wharton. Although publicists are not
as often cited directly in collective judicial decisions today, they are referred to in the
separate opinions of international judges (Rosenne, 1984: 119).

ises, obligation, and the level of commitment among allies may be linked to different referents. At the most general level, we can distinguish between restrictive and permissive normative orders based on whether their moral values support or reject fidelity, even under burdensome conditions. At another level, we can differentiate between two specific conceptions of promissory obligation governing agreements between allies, one grounded in a binding conception of alliance commitments and the other in a flexible, elastic definition of commitment. Finally, at the most specific level, we can speak about a legal norm that upholds the sanctity of treaties (*pacta sunt servanda*) versus a legal norm that permits the unilateral termination of treaties prior to their expiration date (*rebus sic stantibus*). It is to this third level, international treaty law, that we have turned for an empirical referent for these other, more abstract psychocultural variables.

In conclusion, it is important for the reader to separate these varying levels of discourse when contemplating the interrelated ways in which alliance norms may be discussed in world politics: as the products of moral values from alternative normative orders, as general principles for state conduct, and as specific rules embedded in international law. Although these levels of discourse are required, they imply an auxiliary set of methodological assumptions that must also be rationalized. These shall be illuminated, along with the threats to valid inference they pose, in the chapter that follows.

5 Investigative Principles Underlying the Inquiry

There is no single theory about alliance formation or behavior encompassing all the relevant variables in a manageable and coherent manner.

Amos A. Jordan and William J. Taylor, Jr.

Of particular importance to the study of formal alliances is the relationship between commitment and performance. For instance, it is unknown why nations are led, by some circumstances and by certain associations, to meet their commitments more diligently.

Brian Job

Major epistemological and methodological issues surround the investigation of interstate alliances. The lack of scholarly consensus about the status of the most fundamental propositions regarding the formation, maintenance, and dissolution of alliances may be attributed largely to the difficulties posed by their study. It is the purpose of this chapter to discuss the strategy of inquiry through which we hope to enlarge understanding of alliance norms and world politics. The strategy proposed does not promise to resolve all issues and overcome all barriers to knowledge. Of necessity, a far less ambitious goal is appropriate. We concur with Roger V. Dingman (1979: 245) that "the question of how to study alliances does not lend itself to an easy answer." There is no sure path to knowledge; multiple paths must be simultaneously pursued. We now identify the research principles that guided our investigation of the relationship of alliance norms to international order.

UNCOVERING HISTORICAL REGULARITIES

Relationships among variables often differ across historical contexts. In order to establish generalizations about the effects of alliance norms in which some confidence can be placed, it is necessary to draw upon a research design that controls for those conditions that may influence the effects of alliance norms when global circumstances undergo change. The approach taken to the "level of analysis problem" and to the temporal and the spatial domains is outlined below.

99

The Level of Analysis

A major problem in investigating alliances emanates from the fact that alliance activity manifests itself across different levels. The so-called "levels-of-analysis problem" revolves around the choice of the appropriate level of aggregation for studying alliances (Singer, 1961; 1982: 189). In general, alliances may be investigated by reference to decision making by those who head governments, the attributes of nation-states, or the collective properties of the international system.

Inquiries at the level of decision making in foreign policy typically focus on the perceptions, intentions, beliefs, and values that lead central decision makers to forge alliances and influence their decisions to abide by alliance commitments once made. Analyses at the national level concentrate on such topics as the number of alliance ties that particular nations have, as well as the nation's expectations about the reliability of those to whom they have pledged their allegiance. Finally, studies at the holistic or systemic level investigate such questions as whether the degree of alliance aggregation within the international system bears a relationship to the incidence of war worldwide.

The choice of these levels is important because conclusions about the effects of alliances based on either individual decision makers or national attributes may differ from explanations based on the investigation of properties of the total system. For example, one can look at the question of whether alliance formation promotes or deters war from the perspective of the individual nation state or from the perspective of interactions among all states in the aggregate. Consider the divergent findings on this relationship emanating from the original studies conducted under the auspices of the Correlates of War (COW) project: at the national level, a nation's alliance commitment are not related to the probability of its involvement in war (Singer and Small, 1969b), but at the systemic level the number of alliances existing throughout the international system is related to the frequency of war's occurrence, although not in a consistent manner for all periods of time (Singer and Small, 1968). Thus, the contribution of alliance formation to a single state's national security differs from the contribution of alliance formation to international security in general.

These findings suggest that conclusions about the nature of the relationship between alliance and war must be carefully specified so as to make explicit the level to which inquiry seeks to generalize. It is unsafe to draw conclusions from one level of analysis and assume that they apply at another level. The type of alliance behavior that contributes to a particular state's national security is not the type of behavior that, if practiced by large numbers of states, will contribute to global stability. On the contrary, what promotes peace for an individual state may actually promote war throughout the system of states.[1] Hence the search for patterns must clearly specify the aggregation level. Conclusions revealed for one level cannot be assumed to apply to other levels in the absence of evidence demonstrating that a relationship that holds at the decision-making or national level also holds at the international level.

Our study is restricted to the systemic level of analysis. We shall not investigate the motives that have led individual decision makers to form specific alliances or have influenced their decisions to either abide by or rescind the provisions of the treaties to which they gave consent. Nor shall we inspect how these kinds of choices were influenced by the domestic politics of states. To be sure, the decision to uphold or break a promissory obligation may be rooted in domestic soil.[2] For example, Ronald Reagan's reversal of the Carter administration's grain embargo on the Soviet Union owed much to political pressure from the American agricultural community. Although the actions of individual leaders and domestic political processes are undeniably important in conditioning the normative climate of opinion with the larger international system, any attempt to delineate how these factors within each member of that system aggregated to effect international norm formation or decay would be staggering and far beyond the scope of this study. Fortunately, as Lucian Pye (1971: 89–93) points out, understanding the dynamic processes of the total system does not require that these influences be traced.

---

1. This kind of inconsistency of patterns across levels is not peculiar to alliances. For example, the relationship between the number of international organizations and the incidence of war has been shown to depend on whether membership in international organizations is tabulated for each individual state or aggregated for the entire international system (see Harf, Hoovler and James, 1974).

2. In this context, it is instructive to note that the well-documented cooperative behavior that democratic states are prone to exchange with one another (see Rummel, 1985; Chan, 1984; Weede, 1984; and Small and Singer, 1976) is paralleled by their willingness to incur obligations toward like-minded states. Fellow liberal democratic states, writes Michael Doyle (1986: 1161), "benefit from a presumption of amity; non-liberals suffer from a presumption of enmity." As a result, democratic states have promoted the norms of a restrictive international legal order, particularly when it would be applied to their own interactions.

As discussed in Chapters 3 and 4, the decision to concentrate our evaluation of the effects of alliance norms at the systemic level is rationalized in part by the intractability of investigating the incentives underlying those decisions made by individual policymakers as to whether they should or should not adhere to alliance agreements.[3] Macro processes are not always explained by simple extrapolations from micro phenomena; furthermore, these micro decisions are not easily observable and cannot be aggregated to produce a picture of their distribution. Yet these obstacles are not the primary reasons for our choice to focus on macro processes. The systemic level of analysis is extremely important and worthy of investigation on its own terms. International norms refer to the collective beliefs defining the culture in which individual action takes place. The macro consequences of these operative norms are therefore an appropriate subject of investigation in their own right.

By definition, international norms refer to *macro* phenomena. When we investigate the normative consensus surrounding alliance formation and dissolution, we are examining the *collective* attributes of the international environment within which nations interact. That is, we focus on the "set of attitudes, beliefs, and sentiments which give order and meaning to the political process and which provide the underlying assumptions and rules that govern behavior in the political system" (Pye, 1971: 84–85). When a consensus on alliance obligations crystallizes, international norms specifying principles regarding the sanctity of commitments emerge. In short, norms are "the manifestation in aggregate form of psychological and subjective dimensions of politics" (Pye, 1971: 85). Their consequences can be evaluated without unraveling the complex interface between micro- and macro-level phenomena or tracing the chain of individual decisions and domestic processes that have combined to produce a normative consensus in that culture. Our investigations are therefore restricted to an analysis of the impact of alliance norms on the larger system.

---

3. Subsystemic levels require estimates to be made of such elusive phenomena as individuals' intentions, perceptions and values. This is perhaps why almost all efforts at the national level have sought to analyze alliance commitments through case studies of particular alliances in history (e.g., Kennan, 1984). We are virtually precluded from the study of alliance commitments and their national security consequences for large numbers of states because that endeavor necessitates the prohibitively costly acquisition of detailed information regarding the multiple decisions throughout the life cycle of many alliances.

The Temporal Domain

It is probable that different alliance norms led to divergent consequences during certain phases of recorded history. This possibility inhibits the search for generalizations that apply across epochs. It recommends the search for a theory of alliance norms that is bound to specific temporal circumstances. For the purposes of our study, it is therefore appropriate to compare periods within which differing alliance norms can be said to have gained force, and to confine the comparisons to a clearly demarcated system of international politics.[4]

Accordingly, our analysis will be restricted to alliance activity and norms as they have evolved since the Congress of Vienna. This event is regarded by nearly all diplomatic historians as a critical "turning point" (Oren, 1984) in international affairs. In addition, it is often described as the point at which a true system of international law first began to emerge (Parry, 1968). In fact, the system that arose after 1815 broke the preceding pattern and rested on a unique consensus: "The nation state was the dominant actor and the most relevant form of social organization; world politics were dominated by a handful of European powers . . . [and] the concept of state sovereignty remained relatively unchallenged" (Singer and Small, 1968: 251). Norms pertaining to the obligations of allied states have undergone substantial modification since the Congress of Vienna. To trace this ebb and flow through time and to search for the presence of secular trends as well as cyclical and irregular variations around these trends requires an elongated temporal domain. By extending our span of observations from 1815 to the mid-1970s, we undertake the diachronic comparisons necessary to isolate patterns of relationships according to their specific historical context. In so doing, time-dependent patterns can be identified. Thus, although the writing of such varied theorists as Thucydides, Shang Yang, Kautilya, Machiavelli, and Kant suggest that alliance reliability is a universal concern steeped in a long-standing debate over the respective merits of binding versus flexible interpretations of treaty commitments, our findings are only applica-

---

4. Systems of international history may be differentiated and periodicized according to various criteria. Stanley Hoffmann (1961: 207–208) suggests that a new systemic period arises whenever we witness the emergence of (1) new types of units (e.g., nation-state instead of city-states), (2) new types of predominant foreign policy goals (e.g., deterrence instead of territorial conquest), or (3) significantly different levels of unit military capabilities (e.g., nuclear as opposed conventional weapons systems). Whenever any of these three properties change significantly, the role of alliances tends to change as well (Rosecrance, 1963).

ble to the post-Napoleonic period. Though we have drawn material from across cultures and time in order to illustrate the timeless arguments for and against adherence to the sanctity of alliance agreements, we shall only generalize about the causes and consequences of different kinds of alliance norms within the temporal domain from 1815 to the mid-1970s (and evaluate the implications of the findings to the present).

The Spatial Domain

International norms are not necessarily universal. They may be confined to a particular portion of the globe despite the tendency of cultural values to diffuse over time. This possibility also inhibits the search for generalizations about alliance norms that apply irrespective of location. It suggests the need to build a theory of alliance norms that is bound to specific spatial circumstances.

Geographically, the European "great power system" (Small and Singer, 1982) is arguably the most well-integrated core of active influential states in a cultural setting wherein unprecedented levels of consensus emerged about the system's fundamental alliance rules. Indeed, the European great power system is the locus for the modern state system, the domain from which the entire global system of the contemporary period arises and from which it derives its essential rules (Falk, 1970). For better or worse, the conceptions of commitment embedded in international law have been derived largely from rules created by the major contenders for power within the European system. Thus, we seek to generalize about the consequences of alternate norms regarding agreements among allies only within the major power system that emerged after the Napoleonic wars in Europe and which expanded to a relatively globalized if nonetheless pluralistic (McDougal and Lasswell, 1959) legal system in the present century.

MAXIMIZING GENERALIZABILITY

To uncover the pattern of association between alliance norms and the level of systemic stability, a multi-method strategy of investigation is needed. It will be one that takes an intermediate position between the idiographic and nomological approaches.[5] Specifically,

---

5. Macro-quantitative comparisons of aggregated measures of alliance norms and behavior on which nomothetic statements are based are limited in their capacity to capture idiographic details. Although they can address questions about what is general in the norms and behavior of all states, they cannot capture what is unique. There is a trade-off between richness and rigor, relevance and elegance. The di-

through the use of "focused comparisons" (George, 1979) we can give increased attention to the range of variation around the general patterns uncovered by macro-quantitative analysis, as well as control for the impact of various intervening variables. Where appropriate, case studies provide the opportunity to explore the conditions that surround changes in alliance norms in greater detail so as to avoid missing even small changes that make a critical difference. Such in-depth configurative analysis can illuminate contextually specified relationships and expose the influence of variables that are hidden (and must be treated as exogenous) when aggregate approaches are exclusively utilized (Eckstein, 1975). Thus, we shall seek to investigate the causes and consequences of alliance norms from a position somewhere between the phenomenologists' quest for the ways cultural factors have conditioned the thinking of statesmen when they made decisions regarding alliance compliance and the macro-quantitative researchers' quest for covering laws about global patterns.

It will be our strategy to draw on both a wide spectrum of theory and a substantial stream of empirical evidence in order to develop and refine our understandings of (1) the association between commitment norms and global stability, (2) the factors that modify the nature of these relations, and (3) the reasons why these relationships are exhibited. Indeed, we shall evaluate these associations by using a research strategy that purposely imposes tension between existing theory and available data so that the former is required to be reconstructed in light of the latter. By maximizing the interplay between theory and data, we can illuminate the nature of the relationships being probed in ways that a reliance upon only one of these elements cannot. We therefore ground our inquiry in an approach that combines both theory and data, deduction and induction.[6]

To implement this strategy of investigation, a variety of perspectives are required. Among these is an inspection of the serial relationship through a time-series analysis of changing patterns in alliance norms and the levels of international warfare. Equally inviting and

---

lemma posed for comparative studies is that we cannot maximize generality and complexity at once. But approaches across the level of generality and especially intermediate in the range of analytic possibilities can avoid the disadvantage of either extreme.

6. The dualistic nature of this approach to investigation is actually a form of "retroduction" (see Selltiz et al., 1976: 32–35). By moving back and forth between theory and evidence, we engage in retroductive reasoning by inferring conclusions from evidence and searching for the reasons for these conclusions.

necessary is the use of comparative methods to investigate relationships in different spatial domains and temporal periods since 1815. This is also necessary in order to control for the impact of various intervening variables. In addition, where appropriate, case studies and historical narrative provide the opportunity to explore in greater detail the alliance norms that conditioned the thinking of statesmen as well as the ways the international culture in which statesmen operated molded their conceptions of obligations among allies.

Hypothesized relationships are then tested against multiple streams of available evidence in order to estimate their veracity. When those hypotheses are confronted with evidence drawn from different historical settings, and if our findings converge, then our confidence that revealed relationships are not artifactual products of the methodology that produced them is greater than would be the case had we but relied on a single body of evidence or a single method. The purpose of such scholarship is to reduce the distance between our perceived images of global reality and reality itself. Although that quest is ambitious and never complete,[7] we will come closer to closing the gap if the limitations of the methodologies on which we must rely are appreciated.

This brief introduction to the intellectual traditions out of which this study stems does not, however, exhaust the threats to valid inference that such an approach entails. We conclude our discussion of investigative principles by making explicit these additional problems of historical inference as they apply to the study of alliance norms in world politics.

PERENNIAL PROBLEMS OF HISTORICAL INFERENCE

For purposes of presentation, the obstacles confronting our investigation of alliance norms are broken into two categories: (1) those dealing with questions of adequate evidence, and (2) those dealing with the valid interpretation of that evidence.

---

7. We accept the Platonist conviction that the kind of knowledge that science can uncover is only a portion of what it cannot discover. But this does not mean that we reject the premises underlying scientific, positivist methodologies. To be sure, behavioral science has limitations (see Ferguson and Mansbach, 1988, for a trenchant critique). But it also has clear advantages, particularly in exploring phenomena imbued with myth and cant, on which conventional theories and the folklore of diplomacy advance diametrically opposed conclusions. In order to evaluate these contending points of view, evidence is required. To make an advance in understanding, we need the measurement techniques on which cumulative progress in science has always depended (see Clark, 1971: 109).

Evidential Problems

International norms refer to mental states, namely the conceptions and cognitions embraced collectively by statesmen. They are important because theory must deal with the ways human beings live, act, and see (Will, 1986).

A serious challenge to the investigation of these norms and values is the problem of establishing evidence of their presence and, then, to objectively describe them. We cannot directly observe the faith that statesmen place in allies' professed commitments to one another. We can assume that individuals operate from some subconsciously ordered hierarchy of values regarding the sanctity of commitments between allies. Furthermore, we also can assume that the shared values dominant in the international system exert an impact on the beliefs and behavior of national leaders (Hinde, 1987). Monitoring these phenomena by reference to evidence presents difficulties. Among these, the three most salient are: data validity, data reliability, and sampling.

First, let us examine the threats to accurate assessment posed by the validity of our indicator of alliance norms. Any indicator of normative phenomena taps abstract properties embedded in the thinking of many actors. These "conditions cannot be directly observed because they are too intangible, or because they occurred so long ago or far away as to be out of sight, or are too spread out in time or in space, or comprise too many components to be observed simultaneously" (Singer, 1982: 186). Efforts to measure commitment norms are destined to be imperfect. Our inferences about the direction of change in conceptions of the obligations of parties to agreements over time are contingent upon the degree to which measures derived from international law adequately capture these changes.

As discussed in the previous chapter, the normative conceptions of treaty commitments that prevailed in different historical periods have been operationalized in terms of the changing content of international law as observed by publicists. This approach to indicator construction can only provide a partial representation of the cluster of values that go into the making of norms regarding obligations of parties to alliance agreements.[8] This limitation does not mean that an indicator of

---

8. As noted above, the analysis of "subjective culture" (Triandis, 1972) requires inner meanings to be probed. Our instrument for doing this is publicist summaries of the meanings of international norms. Use of this instrument assumes that publicists are the recorders of the values signified by diplomatic discourse. The approach taken further assumes that international law may be likened to a *verdichtung,* a condensation of the structure of thought and values superimposed on diplomacy (Perelman,

alliance norms grounded in international law is invalid: "There are no
absolute criteria for judging an indicator's validity" (Gurr, 1972: 44).
In choosing to study this kind of macro-cultural phenomena "we often have no choice but to observe those conditions . . . that *are* accessible to our direct senses, and then infer from them the value or
state of the unobserved phenomenon" (Singer, 1982: 186). The body
of commitment norms embedded in international law is, despite its
ambiguities, accessible. The "face validity" of our indicator of
norms surrounding agreements among allies is high because it rests
on what Herbert Blalock (1968) would call an "auxiliary theory" of
jurisprudence. The categorization of obligations made by the most
highly qualified publicists in any period can be claimed to describe
prevailing norms insofar as international law maintains that their writings are designed to communicate states' shared expectations about
the propensity of allies to honor commitments. As Michel Virally
(1968: 153) notes, "International law still remains, in many of its
aspects, difficult to discover and interpret. The research of scholars
continues, therefore, to be useful not only for the ascertainment of the
positive law, but also as guidance for its development."

We can meaningfully investigate the consequences of alliance
norms by reference to this source of evidence on prevailing commitment norms. This is true even without the burden of demonstrating
that every statesman in the international system accepted with the
same enthusiasm the prevailing norms at the time that he or she made
a decision as to whether to adhere to or rescind commitments made to
allies. That is, at the systemic level of analysis we need not depend
upon the existence of an accepted theory of the impact of norms on
the conduct of individual states. This is fortunate, for what Robert O.
Keohane notes about international regimes generally applies to norms
governing international agreements as well: "We know much more

---

1980). International treaty law as summarized by publicists articulates a thought
style and value preference. "Law as a symbol system is a means of conceptualizing
and managing the social environment" (Barkun, 1968: 151). The structure of norms
are given their most direct expression by international law, which communicates a
code of conduct to the participants engaged in diplomatic discourse. This code cannot be said to have been canonized in the sense that all who are involved in the
discourse attach identical meanings and obligate themselves to its strictures in the
same way. But the values underlying the code affect its outcome (Fisher, 1987: 111;
Toulmin, 1950), and thus diplomacy cannot be divorced from the moral climate in
which it takes place (Hare and Joynt, 1982: 41). For this reason the dominant *jurio
opinio* operative within that diplomatic environment can be assumed to exert a powerful influence over the subjective beliefs of statesmen.

about the changes that have taken place in international regimes . . . and about the relationships between shifts in underlying power and these changes, than we know about the effects of the regimes on the behavior of their members'' (Keohane, 1986b: 19). Instead, we can look directly at the norms of the entire system that have found support at various times in state practices.

In conclusion, the validity issue posed by reliance on an indicator of alliance norms rooted in international law is a critical one. Nevertheless, our approach to monitoring these norms is justified by the questions to which this indicator is put. This justification is reinforced, moreover, by the fact that, as the International Law Commission argued in 1982, the law of treaties is the instrument through which such international obligations are expressed (Rosenne, 1985: 4).

A second feature of the information base that affects the kinds of interpretations permitted concerns the reliability of the data. The confidence that can be placed in research findings depends upon the extent to which the evidence on which conclusions are built is reproducible and not biased by misinterpretations made by the collector of data.

In gathering data about alliance norm change through inspection of international legal treatises, precautions have been undertaken at two stages in an effort to assure that the data were as representative as possible. In the data collection phase, statistical tests were conducted to determine the degree to which the picture of alliance norms obtained through content analysis of each text mirrored that derived by the other coders associated with the TRIP project. Our tests suggested that the coders were uniformly in substantial agreement and that the data were not contaminated by coding errors.

To further strengthen the confidence in the reproducibility of the data, textual analyses of the interpretations offered by historians were also conducted. By and large, a high level of concurrence was displayed among the opinions of these expert observers with regard to the alliance norm they reported as dominant at the time they were writing.

Additional precautions were also implemented to safeguard the reliability of the data and to maximize the intertemporal comparability of the index. First, a standardized index summarizing publicist descriptions of alliance commitment for each half decade in the series was calculated according to the formula identified in Chapter 4. Such standardization allows for comparability over successive periods of time. Second, to chart the direction of change in the content of alliance norms, moving averages were calculated so as to smooth the series by reducing the impact of transitory fluctuations as well as random and systematic disturbances in the sample of publicist opinion reviewed.

To reiterate, the question of indicator reliability was approached in two ways. On the one hand, we tested for the possibility that the coders interpreted the legal opinions of publicists differently; intercoder reliability tests demonstrated that the data generated through content analytic procedures were highly reproducible and not dependent on the subjective interpretations of individual coders. On the other hand, we evaluated the internal reliability of the data to assure that legal authorities were in substantial agreement about the type of norms that they perceived to have been supported by the international legal culture at the time they were writing. These inquiries demonstrated that these impressions were reliable across different legal observers. Hence we are confident in the representation of reality provided by our indicator system.

A third issue in the interpretation of evidence regarding alliance norms centers around the question of sampling. In order to generalize beyond the cases studied, we must make the assumption that those treatises selected for content analysis are representative of the larger universe of legal discourse. The fact that fluctuations in the content of alliance norms as shown by our indicator paralleled those described by historians and learned societies such as the Institute of International Law (see Chapter 6) enhances confidence that our sample is indeed representative.

Insofar as we sampled publicists' opinion about alliance norm change within very specific temporal and spatial boundaries, we cannot draw conclusions about alliance norms in other cultural settings. We cannot discover from our data base what happens when promissory obligations erode and trust breaks down in state systems that existed prior to 1815 (such as those in ancient Greece, in the era of Roman domination, in the Middle Ages, or in the multi-state systems of ancient China or ancient India and the like). Inquiry is restricted to a particular setting (post-Napoleonic Europe and the expanding core system of international affairs that developed in the present century). It is only to that sample of recorded history that our research design allows us to make inferences.

Likewise, our conclusions may not apply to the future. Findings based on previous patterns provide a guide to future conditions only if those patterns persist into the future. In the Epilogue we speculate about the implications of the historical lessons for the future, guided by the caution that these prognostications require us to move well beyond the evidence and assume, *certibus partibus,* that the patterns we have discovered will continue to shape world politics in the future.

In conclusion, three potential problems of historical inference surround the kind of evidence produced by this study. The ways in which validity, reliability, and sampling issues are confronted in the generation of evidence affect the analysis of all social phenomena. The problems they pose cannot be transcended in the present study. In acknowledging their existence and dealing with them directly, however, we can recognize the threats they pose to the derivation of unwarranted conclusions. They limit the kinds of conclusions that can be drawn from the research design we employ, and it is important to recognize these unavoidable limitations.

The problems of evidence discussed above do not exhaust the threats of valid inference contained in the research design that shall be utilized. Let us turn to identify briefly another set of issues dealing with the problems of interpreting the gathered evidence.

Problems of Interpretation

What kinds of conclusions are permitted from our data base? Four analytic issues can be identified that will influence the inferences we may safely draw: (1) equivalence, (2) precision, (3) cultural lags, and (4) causality. We now briefly describe each of these and explain our posture toward them.

First, it is important to bear in mind that the study of normative change requires diachronic comparisons. We cannot make dynamic inferences from static data. The study of change therefore requires a method that relies on successive synchronic comparisons with a chronological framework (Thrupp, 1970: 346).

To make intertemporal comparisons from longitudinal indicators of norm change, those indicators must be equivalent. That is, they must represent the same phenomena across the systems or periods that are the object of comparison. "In order to compare something across systems," Henry Teune (1987: 25) notes, "it is necessary to have confidence that the components and their properties being compared are somewhat the same or represent something equivalent."

For our purposes, this requires that the measure of alliance norms presented in Chapter 4 retain its operational meaning throughout the duration of the 1815–1974 period to which we are generalizing. On first impression, this is a difficult requirement to satisfy. "Establishing credible equivalence is difficult as 'meaning' is highly contextual" (Teune, 1987: 25). Alliance norms clearly are subject to varying interpretations in different settings. But this property does not pose an insurmountable obstacle.[9] Our indicator of commitment norms measures a basic dichotomy dividing the two opposed conceptions of promissory obligations, which lends itself operationally to the same meaning in legal discourse across time and space. All statesmen, regardless of their national outlook or historical situation, must make a choice as to whether to honor their promises to allies when changed circumstances reduce the benefits of the commitments they once pledged. Irrespective of who they are, their choice will be influenced by the shared expectations about treaty compliance enshrined in the international law of the age. Those norms will, at any given time, permit or prohibit the non-performance of commitments to allies when changed circumstances make compliance detrimental to the state's perceived interests. Each discrete norm challenges its opposite, and in every epoch one will customarily be given support over the other. Therefore, the type of alliance norms embraced in different contexts can be compared and classified because this fundamental distinction is not temporally or spatially bound for its meaning. The meaning of the choice between flexible and binding promissory obligations is historically and culturally invariant, and thus entails a construction that retains its functional equivalence across time (see Valesio, 1980).

To facilitate further interpretation of macro-trends captured by our quantitative indicator of commitment norms, we shall undertake analyses of the shared meanings of such norms—the "keywords" (R. Williams, 1976) comprising international society's legal culture that frames the diplomatic discourse in particular historical contexts. At any given time, we assume that a permissive or a restrictive conception of treaty obligations will be dominant in the legal dialogue, determining which type of alliance norm will be accepted by statesmen (Fisher, 1987: 111). Because these discrete contexts are potentially "discourse-specific" (Felperin, 1985: 18), a "contextual" (Frey, 1970: 234) interpretation of publicists' observations allows their pictures of alliance norms to be compared. It also discloses their image

---

9. "What is absolutely vital," observes Fredrick W. Frey (1970: 232), "is for the researcher to understand the full meaning of his operations, not for these operations to be totally equivalent."

of the direction in which alliance norms were changing, as well as the significance that publicists ascribed to these observed changes. The appearances of repetitive phrases and constructions in their legal discourse inform us about the degree to which the particular culture at the time rested on a consensus. The data quality control[10] accruing from this kind of supplemental analysis enables an estimate to be made of whether the proscriptions and prescriptions regarding alliance commitments observed in legal treatises paralleled the secular trends exhibited in the aggregate index of alliance norms.

A second question of data interpretation pertains to the amount of precision in the measurements of change in alliance norms. Diachronic comparisons must also be judged against the degree to which it is possible to measure meaningfully changes in the support that alternate alliance norms have received over time. At issue is the extent to which inferences can be made about precise variations in the level of support registered for each competing norm across different time periods. Though our indicator allows us to measure the relative degree with which different conceptions of alliance obligations have been accepted within different periods, contextual, configurative comparisons can strengthen the basis for conclusions about changes in alliance norms. This is especially true when descriptions of unfolding trends were provided by historians. Such comparisons permit changes to be traced chronologically in order to validate our conclusions about the *direction* in which the winds of normative change were blowing at different points in time.

A third issue surrounding the interpretation of changes in commitment norms relates to the manner in which those changes unfold. It is commonplace in cross-cultural research to note that cultural change tends to develop very slowly, perhaps cyclically (Namenwirth and Weber, 1987). For that reason, it is also appropriate to control for the potential presence of cultural lags.

Delays are customarily involved in the transformation of international norms. A substantial lag may exist between the time statesmen alter their definition of obligation and the time those norm changes are recognized and incorporated into the treatises of publicists. These intervals, moreover, are unlikely to be either fixed or regular (Burklin, 1987). The correspondence between alliance norms and alliance performance will never be congruent. Only when support for binding

---

10. This kind of textual analysis conforms to an accepted research strategy (Kuechler, 1986) for evaluating equivalent properties by adopting them to different contexts.

as opposed to flexible conceptions of alliance commitments became widespread, intense and prolonged, can a stretch of history be categorized in terms of its predominant orientation. Thus, although the temporal variations exhibited in our data reveal inflection points and trends, they do not disclose the precise dates at which alliance norms shifted direction from support for one (*rebus sic stantibus*) as opposed to the other (*pacta sunt servanda*) norm of treaty compliance.

Similarly, relationships between alliance norms and war may be influenced by time lags. Norm change may have a delayed effect on the extent of war occurring. Therefore, various methods will be employed in order to determine whether changes in trends were affected when (1) time differences between measures are introduced or (2) dramatic events or random shocks (e.g., a world war or the advent of nuclear weapons) altered the prevailing pattern. By using lags of differing duration and chronological ordering, we can render the results from our time-series data more interpretable.

Finally, but not exhaustively, we return to the troublesome threat to inference posed by the issue of causation. Neither correlation nor chronology are causation. However, these associations and orderings provide clues from which conjectures about causal connections might be drawn. For instance, if changes in commitment norms regularly precede changes in the level of global stability, the former may very well be a cause of the latter. Nonetheless, to build a cogent case for a causal relationship between the content of commitment norms and systemic conditions, a theory is required which can explain the pattern exhibited by the evidence.[11] That is, the relationship between variables can provide clues as to causal connections between them, but a theory showing how and why norms impact upon global circumstances is required for causal linkages to be demonstrated. Such an explanatory theory has yet to be constructed.

Given this limitation, we shall test the theoretical proposition that when alternate commitment norms are accepted at the international level, the prospects for global stability will either be improved or diminished. "We cannot statistically demonstrate the accuracy of [such] a . . . causal theory," notes Ted Robert Gurr (1972: 161), but "we *can* use these conventions to determine whether such a theory is consistent with the patterns in our data, and hence to weed out inaccurate theories." Because we are bringing evidence to bear on two

---

11. For our purposes, we mean by theory a statement of relationships between two or more variables, specification of the conditions under which these relationships are expected to hold, and an explanation of why they take a particular functional form.

rival hypotheses regarding the impact of flexibility versus commitment in alliance dissolution, we shall be building a theory by determining which of these two equally plausible but incompatible hypotheses is more consistent with the evidence. The discoveries made will pave the way for the construction of a more complete theory of the causal relationship between belief and behavior in the international system.

No such theory specifying how norms influence behavior currently exists: "Although rules, norms and principles are distinguished from another, it is not clear on what basis their prescriptive force—which obviously unites all these concepts—rests" (Kratochwil, 1987: 148–149). We must therefore proceed on the assumption that when certain values are commonly accepted, that consensus serves as a background factor influencing decisions regarding choices between compliance and nonadherence with alliance commitments. Indeed, we adopt the position that the cultural context shapes the kinds of alliance norms and behaviors that are likely to be exhibited (see Isard and Smith, 1980 and 1982).

The search for a causal theory of the relationship between alliance norms and global stability therefore can be informed by evidence about the nature of that relationship and changes in it over time. If we can uncover a pattern of association between these two properties of the international system, we will have generated clues as to where the basis for a causal theory might be found. In so doing, we shall also have derived a clearer recognition of the limits of our ability to generalize about the existence of such a relationship. In fact, should the evidence produced by such an empirical investigation fail to disclose a clear pattern of association, then the incentive for developing a general theory that links international order to its normative foundations will have been weakened considerably. If that is the case, we may question the utility of explaining cooperation, communication, and order in international affairs by reference to international norms. Conversely, if a strong association is exhibited, then this knowledge will justify the search for a theory of international order that traces the condition to the impact of normative values.

The foregoing summary of the epistemological principles and methodological approaches that underlie this study are designed to expand the reader's awareness of the problems in drawing conclusions about systemic relationships from historical evidence. We have sought to make explicit the threats to valid inference posed by both the kinds of evidence employed and the problems of interpretation that accrue from examination of that evidence. From awareness of these limitations we have a better basis for judging the contribution that such inquiry can make to understanding the relationship between alliance norms and world politics.

With these caveats in mind, let us turn from a discussion of investigative principles to the analysis of alliance norms in world politics. We shall begin the analysis by first examining the sources of their transformation.

Part III

The Sources of
Alliance Norm
Transformation

6 War and the Transformation of Alliance Norms

War forces men to make moral choices.

James Michener

Moral codes adjust themselves to environmental conditions.

Will Durant

International norms emerge in response to changes in the international system. The factors that precipitate the modification of international norms in general, and alliance norms in particular, are multiple. Such norms are difficult to trace because of their complexity, the diverse wellsprings that shape their evolution, and the obstacles presented to their observation. It is for these reasons that "the manner in which normative ideas are generated and diffused, legitimated and delegitimated, within the international system remains little understood" (Ikenberry, 1987: 5).

As a point of analytical departure, we can operate from the premise that within the bounded anarchy that characterizes the international system, changes in state practice can be assumed to exert a particularly powerful influence over the kinds of customs condoned by its members. As discussed in Chapter 1, when these customs are prescribed by the most powerful states in the system, the rules that derive from their prescriptions have tended to become dominant. This propensity suggests that alliance norms have been conditioned by periods of systemic transformation that occurred during transitions between periods when a single hegemonic state was unambiguously predominate and those in which power was highly diffused among many centers of power. During such periods of transition alliance norms are prone to adaptation and adjustment. "Reigning ideas or norms . . . become discredited and fade away. . . . [T]he spread of new norms or ideas and the discrediting of old ones are related. . . . When one set of norms are exhausted or lose their legitimacy, opportunities for the spread of new norms open up" (Ikenberry, 1987: 1–2). To discover how we can best account for shifts in the degree of emphasis placed on binding as opposed to flexible commitment norms, and to ascertain what systemic influences have historically given rise to the ascendance of either a permissive or restrictive normative order for the performance of alliance commitments, we need to examine the historical processes that surround the rise and fall of hegemonic states, and their linkages to the kinds of alliance norms that are supported.

We begin by focusing on the most brutal of these processes: the recurrent onset of interstate war. It is axiomatic that war comprises the essential reality underlying politics among nations. Although there is an ingredient of hyperbole in the characterization, Hans J. Morgenthau (1985: 52) captured an element of truth in his observation that "all history shows that nations active in international politics are continuously preparing for, actively involved in, or recovering from organized violence in the form of war."

Given the ubiquity of this activity, it is appropriate to first inquire how variations in the magnitude and severity of warfare have given shape to the kinds of alliance norms that have been embraced. That is, we need to explore the sources of norm formation and decay by treating norms as a dependent variable.[1] For an analysis of the causes of alliance norm transformation, a multi-method approach is required. Hence, in order to determine whether those international norms that pertain to the reliability of alliance commitments have been transformed by global wars, we shall undertake (1) a trend analysis, (2) focused comparisons, and (3) a statistical analysis of aggregate data. These inquiries shall pave the way for a subsequent inquiry in the chapter that follows of a related proposition: that changes in the distribution of power unleashed by global wars condition the type of alliance norms that gain acceptance.

THE LONG CYCLE OF WORLD LEADERSHIP AND THE EVOLUTION OF ALLIANCE NORMS SINCE 1815

The concept of an international hierarchy has been at the core of many systemic theories about world politics. For the past five centuries, those at the apex of this pyramid have formed alliances with weaker powers to protect their status, just as those at its base have

---

1. Those studies that have analyzed the relationship between alliances and war have heretofore given almost exclusive attention to war as a dependent variable. Almost without exception, various properties of alliances have been treated as factors that either inhibit or deter the outbreak of wars. As Arthur A. Stein and Bruce M. Russett (1980: 399) have pointed out, war's "role as an independent variable has been curiously ignored." As a result, the effect of war on system change has been "addressed only in passing rather than in systematic comparative studies" (Siverson, 1980: 211). This chapter seeks to rectify this imbalance.

formed counteralliances to protect themselves from exploitation. Periodically, the relentless struggle for position within this highly stratified environment has resulted in system-transforming wars. These are cataclysms through which a coalition of challengers to the prevailing hegemonic power has overturned the preexisting rank order of states. These wars and the hierarchical reorderings that follow in their aftermath have occurred at fairly regular intervals. Thus many theorists speak of a "long cycle" of global war that has unfolded within the history of the modern world system (see Rosecrance, 1987; Goldstein, 1988).

Are these long cycles associated with the transformation of alliance norms? In particular, have global wars led to support for a binding conception of commitment norms—of the rules underlying international agreements in general and agreements to ally in particular? Or, following these systemic conflagrations, have statesmen instead been prone to jettison a binding conception of commitment in favor of a nihilistic conception that rationalizes a flexible, elastic notion of compliance with treaty provisions? The primary reason for asking whether global wars have precipitated norm transformation is quite simple.

> The great turning points in world history have been provided by these hegemonic struggles among political rivals; these periodic conflicts have reordered the international system and propelled history in new and unchartered directions. They resolve the question of which state will govern the system, as well as *what ideas and values will predominate,* thereby determining the ethos of succeeding ages. The outcomes of these wars affect the economic, social, and ideological structures of individual societies as well as the structure of the larger international system (Gilpin, 1981: 203; emphasis added).

In short, major normative and institutional transformations have followed in the aftermath of global wars. In their wake, statesmen have generally recognized the need to replace chaos with order, and this climate has created unique opportunities for reconsidering prevailing practices and reevaluating those norms that were created to sustain them. Global wars exert pressure on statesmen to examine values, redefine moral positions, and create new rules for the international system. It is at such times that "macro-decisions" reached through the "struggle for laying down the rules of the game" tend to be made (Perroux, 1948).

All major attempts to reorganize international society for purposes of war prevention have been undertaken during the aftermath of a war widely perceived as the cause of intolerable damage: Westphalia after the Thirty Years' War, the Congress of Vienna after the Napoleonic wars, the League of Nations after World War I, and the United Nations after World War II. Only after such a total breakdown has the international situation been sufficiently fluid to induce leaders and supporting publics of dominant nations to join seriously in the task of reorganizing international society to avoid a repetition of the terrible events just experienced. (Falk, 1970: 500)

Victorious states habitually have seized the opportunities created by the turmoil following general wars to promote new rules, which, if implemented into a revised security regime, could preserve their dominant position and prevent the recurrence of catastrophic destruction in the future. "The struggle over rules," notes George Modelski (1986: 5) "is prejudged by the prior selection to global leadership" of a successor, which can be expected to press for new rules of alliance designed to cement the new international order. Its preferences will be for rules conducive to an "environment where the alliance leader is safe, secure, and indeed a leader" (Russett and Starr, 1989: 94).

Long cycle theories reject both linear conceptions of historical development and models of relationship between systemic variables that assume that such relationships are temporally invariant. They contend instead that characteristic behaviors and norms will be specific to particular phases of the global long cycle. A pattern of alliance activity and the norms reinforcing it will take hold in one historical context, only to change in another, in a repetitive cycle of erosion and accretion. Associations between variables may actually reverse themselves as the system moves through these phases. For our purposes, long cycle theory provides an inviting foundation from which to explore the relationship between general war and the content of alliance norms.

This interpretation of system transformation is represented most directly by George Modelski's theory of the long cycle of world leadership, as tested and developed further by William R. Thompson (1988) and others (e.g., Rasler and Thompson, 1989; Thompson and Zuk, 1986). According to Modelski (1978), the most important structural periodicity within the modern world system involves the distribution of global reach capabilities. Ever since 1494, when Charles VIII's march to Naples ended the era of Renaissance diplomacy and the Treaty of Tordesillas inaugurated a new era of global politics, the world system has experienced a succession of four-phased cycles of capability concentration and deconcentration. The first of these phases, *global war,* occurs at intervals of approximately a century in length. When these devastating struggles between the system's major actors conclude, a single dominant state emerges as the provider of the public good of security and manager of international economic relations. It possesses the capacity to restructure rules in its own interests. During the subsequent *world power* phase, the system's distribution of military and economic capabilities becomes highly concentrated. Over time, however, memories of war and reconstruction fade, rivals arise, and the policies and position of the dominant state come under attack. This *delegitimation* phase is followed by a phase of *deconcentration* wherein the dominant state loses its preponderant position and the distribution of capabilities within the system gradually becomes more diffused. Finally, as this shift from unipolarity to multipolarity continues, rivalries intensify and eventually erupt into another global war to determine the next successor to the role of world power. The cycle is therein completed, and the new cycle commences.

Another way to conceptualize the long cycle is in terms of a lack of adjustment between the demand for, and the supply of, global order (Modelski and Thompson, 1987). Two factors engender this imbalance. On the one hand, the "production conditions" of the goal in question (order) are such that a long period of time lapses between the decision to begin production and the onset of the production process. On the other hand, because the normative consensus that underlies the world system is minimal, lengthy "production information" gaps arise between the decision by world leaders to produce order and the final act of consumption by nonleaders. Given the continual push and pull between what are termed production and information conditions, the amount of order in the world system will tend toward the periodicities that economists call cobweb processes.

To summarize the precepts of long cycle theory, Modelski (1987a, 1987b) purports that the world system of the past half-millennium has had two sets of characteristics: (1) evolutionary development whereby increasingly wealthy, more powerful states have initiated significant political innovations while they were at the summit of power, and (2) a recurrent pattern of global wars followed by leadership succession and, eventually, leadership erosion. These characteristics of development and recurrence can be thought of as representing positive and

Table 6.1. The Linkage between Long Cycle Processes and the Transformation of Alliance Norms

Long Cycle Phase	Cobweb Processes		Feedback Processes		Hypothesized Content of Alliance Norms
	Supply of Order	*Demand for Order*	*Stages in the Developmental Loop*	*Stages in the Regulatory Loop*	
Global War	Deficit: leadership succession	Preference for order rises to maximum level	Macro-decision	Macro-decision	Increasingly binding commitments
World Power	Maximum output of order under condition of unipolar preponderance	Preference for order begins to decline	Innovations diffused	Postwar peace settlement	Maximum level of binding commitments
Delegitimation	Deficit: nationalist challenges to status quo	Preference for order falls to minimum level	Problem recognition	Perceived threat to global stability	Increasingly flexible conception of commitments
Deconcentration	Increased output of order under condition of multipolar balance of power	Revival in preference for order	Innovations proposed	Coalition formation	Maximum level of flexibility in commitments

negative feedback. The positive, or developmental, loop begins with agenda setting in the face of new systemic problems. This is followed by the cultivation of alignments by innovators, and the ratification of those innovations by global war. In the wake of global war, the innovations are more widely diffused as one power assumes the role of world leader and promotes new rules for international practice. The negative, or regulatory, loop begins when a challenge to the status quo is perceived as a threat. This is followed by the formation of rival coalitions that, in turn, beget another global war. Taken together, these two processes form a double feedback loop animated by a macro-decision process that selects world leaders, produces new challengers, and culminates recidivistically in global war.

Long cycle theory thus contains an account of the use world leaders make of alliances and, of equal importance, which types of norms governing commitments between allies are embraced during each discrete phase of the long cycle. As outlined in Table 6.1, two distinct hypotheses can be derived from this account: (1) an alliance norm prescribing the irrevocability of commitments will enjoy consensual support during the world power and global war phases, and (2) during the delegitimation and deconcentration phases an alliance norm accepting the permissibility of unilaterally terminating a commitment will receive support from the international legal culture.

The reasoning that leads to these expectations stems from some compelling assumptions. In the first instance, global leaders are satisfied, status quo powers; understandably, they are prone to define their mission as the preservation of the system of world politics they dominate in order to protect their advantaged position. One way of fulfilling this objective is to align themselves with other states, thereby aggregating capabilities and deterring threats to their supremacy without taking on additional territorial burdens through conquest or excessively burdensome expenditures for arms. Perhaps for this reason "all world powers have been adept at creating coalitions" (Rosecrance, 1987: 289). For the alliance to serve these purposes, its members must consider their commitments binding. World leaders therefore will tend to support norms prohibiting the renunciation of alliance commitments prior to their scheduled termination date. A norm requiring alliance oaths to be honored will serve the interests of the preponderant state. As a general rule, norms that advance the interests of the powerful tend to gain acceptance (Axelrod, 1986).

The dynamics underlying the preferences for norms binding alliance members to commitments during the world power phase draw attention to the incentives for this norm from the perspective of a world leader. But the same preference can also be found among challengers: during this phase their interests, too, are served by a regime encouraging members of a counteralliance to be bound by the provisions to which they gave their consent. "Presiding over an alliance," Inis L. Claude (1986: 7) notes, "is *de rigueur* for great powers." This includes great powers cast in the role of challengers, who are in need of alliances tightly bound by a sense of obligation. Such binding norms enhance a great power's ability to manage, lead, and dominate those allies that join it in pursuit of common power and security objectives. In fact, support for obligatory conceptions of alliance commitments may be even more essential for hegemonic aspirants, for their need for faithful allies is perhaps stronger than is the need of reigning world powers. "The challengers do attract allies," William R. Thompson (1988: 256–257) observes, but the "problem is that the allies that are essential to victory in the long run are likely to see their position directly or indirectly threatened by continental expansion. Either they are globally oriented states that have the opportunity to retain, to regain, or to succeed to the system leader position without pursuing the challenger's high overhead strategy. Or they are regionally oriented land powers that find themselves in the way of the challenger's expansion."[2] For challengers and their potential partners, norms obligating firm commitments are indispensable; therefore alliances during the global war and world power phases will tend to be rigid, and defections from alliance ties will not be condoned.[3]

As the demand for global leadership decreases (delegitimation) and power in the international system becomes increasingly diffused (deconcentration), however, alliance formation becomes rapid and global

---

2. Note that world leaders have sometimes forged alliances with leading contenders (The Netherlands with Great Britain in the seventeenth century, and Great Britain with the United States in the nineteenth and twentieth centuries). The benefits of a bond were presumably mutual: for the leader, to ally with and thereby exercise control of a potential competitor aspiring to hegemonic status; for the challenger, to deter preemptive attack by the leader. In either case, a restrictive order prohibiting the severance of alliance obligations served the interests of both parties during this phase of the cycle.

3. As the case of the special relationship between Great Britain and the United States illustrates, binding alliance norms may also cement a world leader and a potential rival in a firm alliance and thereby deter the onset of a costly struggle for domination. Because this norm may serve the interests of great powers in this way, in the world power and delegitimation phases it is not uncommon for both leaders and challengers to support a restrictive order prescribing the faithful performance of promises in order to prevent an unrestrained contest for domination.

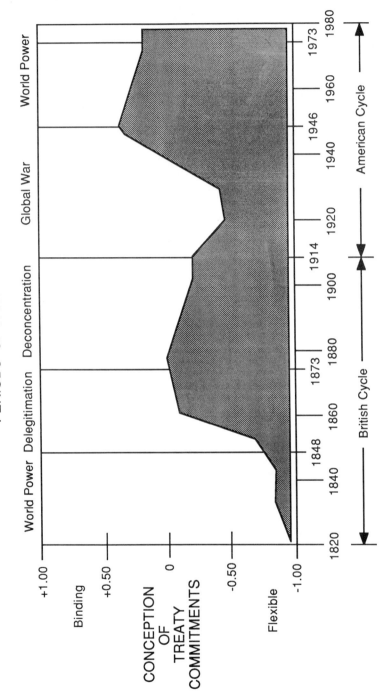

Figure 6.1. The Transformation of Alliance Norms Following the Napoleonic Wars (ten-year moving average)

stability tends to rest precariously on the maintenance of a fluid balance of power (Gulick, 1955). Within such a system, coalitions of short duration and limited purposes are required in order for swift realignments to occur. These coalitions rest on norms permitting a state to renege on its commitments when national self-interest so warrants. Rigid alliances are eschewed, and treaties are not forged to tie allies into permanent bonds. As a result, during these phases of the long cycle, elastic, flexible conceptions of the commitments alliance partners make with one another are to be expected. Indeed, they will be advocated, for flexible alignments are required as an "essential rule" of behavior by actors in a multipolar balance-of-power system (Kaplan, 1957b).

A FIRST PROBE OF THE DATA: HISTORICAL TRENDS AND CYCLICAL PATTERNS IN ALLIANCE NORMS

To what extent are the hypotheses about changes in the content of alliance norms deduced from the long cycle theory upheld by historical evidence? In order to determine whether support exists for the hypotheses about the ebb and flow of alliance conceptions derived from long cycle theory, the temporal boundaries of each phase in the long cycle of world leadership needs to be specified. According to Modelski (1982: 111), the modern world system has undergone five cycles of capability concentration and deconcentration since the Italian Wars of 1494–1516. Because the data base available when this book was undertaken begins at the end of the Napoleonic Wars, we shall limit ourselves to the cycles that have occurred since the Congress of Vienna, the British cycle and the American cycle. Within these two cycles are five phases: *world power* (United Kingdom), 1815–1848; *delegitimation,* 1848–1873; *deconcentration,* 1873–1913; *global war,* 1914–1946; *world power* (United States), 1946–1973; and *delegitimation,* 1973–1980. Figure 6.1 plots our indicator of alliance obligation against each of these phases so that the direction of its diachronic path can be compared to the theoretical expectations of long cycle theory.

The trend line shows that in the aftermath of the Napoleonic Wars considerable emphasis was placed on norms stressing flexible conceptions of state obligations with respect to the interpretation of treaty commitments. Similar to the laissez-faire ideology of political economy that gained strength, the general faith placed in free-wheeling equilibrium as a source of stability at the time (Kennedy, 1987: 152–153) made states reluctant to permanently commit to allies. The doctrine in international law stating that an essential change in the conditions under which a treaty was concluded would free a state from its treaty obligations was highly emphasized during the Concert of Europe (1816–1848). The perceived importance of binding conceptions, however, gained strength prior to the outbreak of the wars of European unification (1848–1870). It subsequently underwent a very gradual erosion as flexible alliance norms received support once again throughout the Bismarckian era of European diplomacy (1871–1890) and the wave of imperialism (1891–1914) preceding the First World War. Following the end of that cataclysmic war, intense debate about the functions of alliances and the duties of allies erupted. During this interregnum the perceived importance of flexible alliance commitments momentarily increased. Beginning in the 1920s, however, a vigorous emphasis on binding alliance obligations began to take root and eventually accelerated rapidly. Support for the rule that treaties are binding contracts between signatory states remained intense and stabilized at the conclusion of World War II (although, as discussed in the Epilogue, normative support for the sanctity of treaties began to show signs of incipient decay in the 1970s, and the support for this norm has eroded at an accelerating pace since then).

It is revealing that the trends derived from our indicator, based on publicists' interpretations of the changes in commitment norms occurring at the time they were writing, conform to the descriptions given by historical studies of treaty law. These studies generally assert that the doctrine of *rebus sic stantibus* received its greatest support during the early nineteenth century (Walker, 1980: 1040) and experienced renewed emphasis at the end of the First World War (Huang, 1935: 7). In addition, they portray the interwar period as a time of transition during which *rebus sic stantibus* was criticized (Vamvoukos, 1985: 21) and ultimately superseded by the doctrine *pacta sunt servanda* (DeLupis, 1986: 482). The unusual level of attention that was paid to the kind of alliance norms that were perceived to provide a framework for a durable peace was reflected in both scholarly writings and diplomatic discourse. Of the various doctoral dissertations written on *rebus sic stantibus* since the turn of the century, 56 percent were completed between the two world wars.[4] The diplomatic mood and

---

4. The following individuals authored dissertations on the role of *rebus sic stantibus* in public international law: Petrus Johannes Abram Idenburg, Amsterdam (1923); Georges Cattand, Paris (1929); Hans Leonhard Hertschik, Coburg (1931); Ekkehard Schesemer, Marburg (1934); Ting-Young Huang, Johns Hopkins (1933); Chesney

Table 6.2. Landmarks in the Changing Status of Binding Obligations in Treaty Law

"It is an essential principle of the Law of Nations that no power can free itself from the engagements of a treaty, nor modify its terms except with the assent of the contracting parties."

—The Treaty of London, 1919

"The Assembly of Delegates may from time to time advise the reconsideration by Member of the League of Treaties which have become inapplicable and the consideration of international conditions whose continuance might endanger the peace of the world."

—Article 19 of the Covenant of
the League of Nations, 1919

"All members . . . shall fulfill in good faith the obligations assumed by them."

—Article 2(2) of the United
Nations Charter, 1945

"Every treaty in force is binding upon the parties and must be performed in good faith."

—Article 26 of the Vienna Convention
on the Law of Treaties, 1969

tenor of the times are reflected in the policy debate over the Covenant of the League of Nations. As President Woodrow Wilson summarized the issue,

> [Rejection of the Covenant of the League of Nations proposes] that we should make no general promise, but leave the nations associated with us to guess in each instance what we were going to consider ourselves bound to do and what we were not going to consider ourselves bound to do. . . . This . . . proposes that we should not acknowledge any moral obligation . . . ; that we should stand off and say, "We will see, from time to time; consult us when you get into trouble, and then we will have a debate, and . . . we will tell you what we are going to do" (cited in Link, 1965: 148).

Hill, Harvard (1934); Walter Schuchmann, Giessen (1936); Irene Bremer, Leipzig (1937); and Richard Fiessler, Heidelberg (1937). Several others were written on the role of *rebus sic stantibus* in private international law.

In summary, the interwar period was a time of transition that tested the wisdom of prevailing practices. Out of the contest for the supremacy of contending norms there emerged a renewed and revigorated rejection of secret diplomacy, permissive definitions of obligations, and flexible standards of treaty adherence.

Inspection of this historical trend reveals the presence of several cycles in alliance norms, though not entirely consistent with the direction predicted by long-cycle theory.[5] The overall picture is one of three quite distinct shifts: (1) movement away from flexibility from 1815–1860; (2) a very gradual return to flexibility in the 1860–1914 period, which gathers momentum with the outbreak of the First World War; and (3) dramatic movement from 1919 toward binding commitments, which leveled off at an unprecedented high level precisely at the conclusion of the Second World War and underwent a very modest decline thereafter. The institutionalization of these general normative trends in customary international law is exhibited in the major statements on these opposed norms in law-making conventions and treaties (see Table 6.2).

The fact that the periods for these cycles are somewhat irregular suggests that the degree of emphasis paid to these norms at any point in time has tended to be modified somewhat by the peculiar environmental circumstances enveloping each successive phase of the long cycle. The phases of the cycle do not repeat on the same schedule. Having lain dormant, a commitment norm will tend to regain attention, only to once again recede in emphasis before another cycle of these phases commences. These fluctuations clearly appear to be associated with the outbreak of war. But the pattern is not consistent; although several major turning points in the norm indicator are observable, only one was clearly associated with a global war (World War I). The others were more modest, occurring in the wake of World War II and in a lesser set of conflicts (the wars of European unification). The evidence shows that the magnitude and direction of alliance norms did shift, but that the magnitude and direction depended on the unique attributes of the war in question. Moreover, the normative response to global wars was strikingly different in the two centuries under examination: in the nineteenth century flexible commitment norms were embraced, whereas in the twentieth century

---

5. In the vocabulary of the statistician, these cycles are more accurately classified as "fluctuations" as opposed to "periodic series," inasmuch as the intervals between changes in the direction of these trends are not regular and the periodicities are not uniform.

binding norms predominated. Thus, the impact of war on the transformation of alliance norms is not as uniform as long-cycle theory predicts.

A SECOND PROBE OF THE DATA: FOCUSED COMPARISONS OF NORM CHANGE IN THE WAKE OF HEGEMONIC WAR

To uncover the factors that have influenced the rise and fall of alliance norms since the Congress of Vienna, it is necessary to delve into the specific historical periods in which these changes occurred. That is, we need to inspect the micro decisions that led to macro norm transformations. For that purpose, "focused comparisons" (George, 1979) of these periods are required. Let us inspect the factors and circumstances that stimulated alliance norm modification more closely in order to better illuminate the influences that conditioned these periodicities. In so doing, the impact of global war as a catalyst to alliance norm revision warrants emphasis.

Global wars comprise a special case of interstate wars. Although debate surrounds their definitional criteria (see Thompson, 1988), virtually all scholars would include the Napoleonic Wars in the nineteenth century and World Wars I and II in this century as such wars.[6] Each of these wars might be likened metaphorically to an earthquake. Following a buildup of enormous pressure, massive structural changes occur. Consequently, the post-Napoleonic period of the Concert of Europe (1815–1848) and the so-called century of total war in the 1900s are attractive for a focused comparison.

In addition to comparing these two periods, however, it is also very useful for our purposes to compare them to the great power wars that occurred during the period of European unification (1848–1870). It is during this period that profound and rapid transformations in alliance norms occurred, and this epoch thus deserves more detailed contextual scrutiny. Moreover, this period was system-disrupting in its effects. Just as an earthquake is followed by aftershocks of varying magnitude and duration, global wars are also followed by wars that

---

6. According to Jack S. Levy, "the following defining characteristics of hegemonic war are individually necessary and jointly sufficient. First, the conflict must at some point involve the leading military power in the system. Hegemony over the system is conceivable only through a major victory by the leading power or its decisive defeat by a rising challenger. Second, the war must involve the active participation of most of the great powers in the system. . . . A third criterion for general war is that it must be substantial war involving sustained and intense combat" (Levy, 1985b: 365).

can affect the rate and direction of norm change. This occurred in the turbulent period between 1848 and 1870. Within the period of European unification, four wars between great powers were fought: the Crimean (1854), Austro-Italian/Sardinian (1859), Austro-Prussian (1866), and Franco-Prussian (1870). These wars drastically altered the European balance of power. Ties between the Habsburg and Romanovs were severely strained by rivalry over the Danubian Principalities; Austria's defeats at Magenta, Solferino, and Königgrätz ended its influence over German and Italian affairs; and the newly unified German Empire emerged as the dominant military power on the continent. By including this period in our analysis, we gain a broader inferential base from which additional conclusions about cyclic transformations and historical turning points can be made.

Post-Napoleonic Europe

Napoleon's quest for empire challenged not just the existing distribution of power on the European continent, but it also threatened the fundamental principles underlying the Westphalian conception of order (see Murphy, 1982; Coplin, 1966; and Gross, 1969). The decentralized, laissez-faire system of legitimized competition among sovereign equals came under direct attack as Napoleon sought to replace the Westphalian system with an imposed, hierarchical organization that would place authority for the management of interstate relations under centralized rule. By challenging the Westphalian order, he endeavored to resurrect and recreate the quasi-world government that had operated throughout the medieval system. But with the defeat of Napoleon came the defeat of his vision. "Napoleon seized upon a pre-Westphalian, imperial vision of European order with himself at the apex of authority, but what is notable is that Napoleon did not succeed. When the Congress of Vienna cleaned up after the Napoleonic wars in 1815, its participants were careful to restore the pre-Napoleonic map of Europe so that the game of nation-state coexistence in accordance with laissez-faire rules could be played again" (Miller, 1985: 31).

As Paul Kennedy (1987: 143) notes, "The turbulence and costs of the 1793–1815 struggle—known to the nineteenth century as 'the Great War'—caused conservatives and liberals alike to opt as far as possible for peace and security, underpinned by devices as varied as the Concert of Europe or free-trade treaties." Conspicuously prominent among the rules the statesmen of Europe sought to restore in a revived Westphalian regime was reliance upon self-help measures for the redress of grievances between states. The new normative order accepted conflict as a natural condition; incompatibilities of interests between states were seen as inevitable. Disputes were expected to arise, just as friction was expected to result from bodies in contact. States defended the right to serve their own interests by competing and struggling with one another (see Kegley and Raymond, 1986). In order to compete, wide latitude in the interpretation of agreements to ally was permitted. Indeed, references to the *clausula rebus sic stantibus* increased in international treaties in order to give allies room to maneuver and to allow them to rationalize the unilateral denunciation of a treaty commitment. By providing the most powerful states freedom to sever their bonds with allies when conditions changed, the new regime sought to reduce the incentives for initiating war and, most importantly, to contain its spread so that it would not once again engulf all members of the system. The key to this system—the lubricant that would allow a homeostatic equilibrium to materialize—was a flexible conception of alliance commitments. A norm permitting the desertion of a coalition was required so that a countercoalition could readily materialize in order to meet the threat posed by a new alliance that threatened to consume the system.

A review of the use made by states of unilateral denunciation to amend or breach treaties lends support to the contention that a flexible system of alliance norms existed during this epoch of balance of power diplomacy. One survey (Sinha, 1966) of the use of this doctrine between 1793 and 1963 demonstrates that the vast proportion of unilateral denunciations were congregated in the nineteenth and early twentieth centuries, a period during which a permissive legal order with respect to performance of treaty obligations was dominant.

As Henry Kissinger (1973) has observed, the world that was restored in the aftermath of the Napoleonic Wars was a world with a clarity of purpose and a consistency of vision. Highly obsessed with the preservation of peace and the management of great power relations, the conservative outlook that dominated the Concert of Europe was motivated by the intense desire to avoid another system-wide war of devastation. That outlook was forcefully advocated by Great Britain, the world leader during this phase of the long cycle. To succeed in this goal, a set of rules for the preservation of the balance of power was required. These rules, if followed, were presumed to reduce the incidence of war by facilitating coalition adjustments and flexibility in alignments and by permitting Great Britain to play the foreign policy role of a "balancer" within this system. Therefore, a binding alliance norm was rejected in the aftermath of the Napoleonic Wars in favor of a norm that enabled rapid realignments to offset any threat to gain preponderance by a powerful coalition.

The Wars During the Period of European Unification

If the fragile consensus of normative opinion underlying the Vienna settlement managed to persist with important adaptations for three decades, that regime nonetheless underwent challenge and ultimately eroded. The revolutions that swept across Europe in 1848 undermined both governments and the rules for international conduct advocated by those governments and the system's world power (Great Britain). Indeed, 1848 marked the advent of the "delegitimation phase" of the long cycle, during which the world leader and the rules for behavior it prescribed were increasingly challenged. The erosion of consensus left the system without a coherent security regime, and in the midst of this upheaval the concept of treaty obligations expressed in international law underwent a period of challenge and ambiguity.

Crises exert pressure for legal innovation, and the events sweeping Europe in 1848 prompted reinvigorated efforts to formulate new rules to regulate the violence that had been unleashed. Renewed consideration was directed at rules designed to create systemic stability following the outbreak of the Crimean War (1854). Discussion of the conditions under which states should abide by their alliance commitments began to increase, and this questioning amidst pervasive suspicions and fears led to renewed great power support for a code of behavior that interpreted treaty commitments as relatively more binding. In sum, despite the apparent harmony at the 1856 Congress of Paris and the conferences in London (1850, 1864, 1967), Paris (1858, 1860, 1869), and Vienna (1853, 1855), statesmen now challenged the underpinnings of the old normative order. The diplomatic dialogue delineated a new ethos.

It is important to remember that this period differs qualitatively from the others we are comparing, as we are not speaking about a singular, systemic conflagration, but about a series of wars of lesser scope and magnitude. This was a period of normative readjustment, to be sure, but the nature of norm change displayed in Figure 6.1 also suggests that as the position and leadership of Great Britain began to wane and new rivals such as Prussia began to challenge Britain's supremacy, statesmen increasingly questioned the wisdom of encouraging flexible conceptions of alliance obligations. The norm *pacta sunt servanda* received increasing support (although it was not unanimously embraced).

The rise in support for a binding interpretation of treaty obligations that began in the 1840s was followed after 1870 by a reversal toward a relatively more flexible concept. The balance of power necessitated support for relaxed rules regarding treaty compliance to facilitate rapid alliance formation and ad hoc realignments. At this time, therefore, the frequency with which states invoked the doctrine of *rebus sic stantibus* in order to release themselves from treaty obligations increased (Friedman, 1964: 301).

No doubt the rapidly changing diplomatic circumstances during this period increased the incentives for creating a permissive normative order and intensified pressure for norms that did not hold states rigidly accountable for their interallied agreements. As always, the changes in the normative climate were influenced by rapid changes in the distribution of power. With the decline of Russian power after the Crimean War and the rise of German influence, the new situation called for the revision of rules. "Both at the time and even more in retrospect, the year 1870 was viewed as a decisive watershed in European history. On the other hand, perhaps because most countries felt the need to draw breadth after the turbulences of the 1860s, and because statesmen operated cautiously under the new order, the *diplomatic* history of the Great Powers for the decade or so after 1871 was one of a search for stability" (Kennedy, 1987: 188).

Yet, as always, the need for allies and reliable alliance partners did not recede during this turbulent period. Accordingly, great effort was put into the construction of a number of alliance systems and the creation of norms to back them with the expectation that breaches of agreements would not be tolerated. Bismarck's ability to weld together a "conservative triple alliance" of the monarchies in Eastern Europe with the formation of the Three Emperor's League in 1873 and the Dual Alliance between Germany and Austria in 1879 were indicative of the faith that some statesmen continued to place in loyalty among coalition members. Effort was invested in creating alliances built on the principle that pacts were binding and resting on the expectation that if attacked timely assistance from allies would be received.

The cooperation expected to result from the alliances did not endure, however, and particularly after 1885 a number of them underwent rapid disintegration. The treaty system that had been developed and the norms that served as the foundation of the alliances did not persist (see Kennan, 1979), even though alliance activity accelerated. But the alliances that came into place in this volatile environment were neither rigid nor permanent. They were designed to maintain the balance of power by creating criss-crossing coalitions and flexible alignments. As alliances broke up they were replaced by a series of secret agreements between the conflicting parties (such as the secret promise of both Germany and Austria-Hungary to assist Rumania against a Russian attack, and Bismarck's celebrated "Reinsurance Treaty" with Russia in 1887) that rationalized acceptance of a far more flexible and fluid system of alignment and realignment.

At the root of this growing fear of entangling alliances was a concern that such commitments would entrap an actor in the conflicts of an ally rather than protect it from attack by others. The evolving mood toward flexible alliance norms was captured in Bismarck's memoirs, when in 1898 he reflected "Count Shuvaloff (the Russian foreign minister) was right when he said the idea of coalitions gave me nightmares" (McDonald and Rosecrance, 1985: 75). Perhaps as a consequence, he advocated short-term alignments, and concluded a number of public and secret treaties designed for rather limited ends—reassuring nervous friends, isolating enemies, and avoiding Germany's own exclusion from a predominate coalition (such as the dreaded Franco-Russian alliance). Britain's practice of "splendid isolation" arguably was inspired by the same concerns.

In summation, during the deconcentration phase commencing in 1873 great ambivalence toward binding concepts of alliances was characteristic. Prior to and through the early stages of this span of the long cycle, binding alliances were pursued as a way of limiting the range of choice among numerous antagonists. But as antagonism escalated to war, a turn in fear toward more fluid conceptions of alliance permitting rapid adjustments of relationships among contending parties arose. As a result of this experience, by the 1880s there was a movement toward renewed acceptance of flexibility as a principle to govern relations among states joined in alliance. Evidence on the alliance norms among these states in the 1870s and the 1880s suggest that "In wartime or in anticipation of war [i.e., the 1870s] bipolarity and consistent obligations [were] the order of the day. [But in the 1880s] in peace and to prevent war, inconsistent ties [proved] more appropriate. . . . [R]elations among the feuding powers were nonetheless held together by a pattern of inconsistent ties and obligations. The system did not degenerate into chaos perhaps because the enemy of a friend was often a friend'' (McDonald and Rosecrance, 1985: 80; see also Healy and Stein, 1973).

Thus, the years of the wars of European unification were followed by a prolonged period of growing acceptance of elastic definitions of treaty obligations. The deconcentration phase of the long cycle (1873–1914) was a period in which the renunciation of alliance agreements prior to their scheduled termination date was increasingly (if ambivalently) regarded as permissive. The invocation by Bulgaria of the *clausula rebus sic stantibus* in the Bulgarian Declaration of 1908, through which the Treaty of Berlin (1878) was defied, epitomized the normative climate and was followed by other challenges to the binding stature of prior agreements. Indeed, during this period the *clausula rebus sic stantibus* began to receive increased expression in the international law of alliances. Despite the hope—and promises— of aid from allies, which indicated a level of trust in the performance of commitments, trends in the diplomatic record and legal order speak to another reality, namely, the mounting suspicion that in the event of war alliances might not guarantee the needed protection and assistance that were pledged. That trend toward acceptance of flexible interpretations of alliance obligations persisted until the First World War—an unanticipated and catastrophic war that threw into question the wisdom of the prevailing norms for international conduct.

The Century of Total War

The twentieth century has often been characterized as a period of "total" war. This characterization rests on the fact that in the 1900s the world experienced truly globalized wars for the first time. In addition, during this century the magnitude and intensity of warfare increased as the number of participants in them grew and as the destructiveness of their weapons expanded exponentially.

Conceptions of international legal norms underwent substantial modification in response to the grim realities of global war. The period immediately following the outbreak of the First World War was one in which the costs and benefits of flexible versus binding norms of alliance commitment were critically and intensely evaluated. Indeed, alliance commitments, whether buttressed by insistence on compliance or not, were alternately chastised as a source of war or praised as an instrument for its prevention. As revealed by the emphasis given to the themes of balance of power and secret diplomacy within the diplomatic discourse of the day, the interwar period witnessed great effort to reconcile these contending propositions. "The problem of the invalidity of treaties on account of the immorality of their *pacta contra bonos mores,''* noted Josef Kunz (1945: 187), became, like that of duress, "prominent again in the inter-war period."

During the closing days of the First World War flexible conceptions of alliance obligations received increasing support. As noted above, this was consistent with the view prevailing that fluid alliances were necessary to enable one side to build a winning coalition and therein bring the war to a successful conclusion. This support intensified as the war was fought, and thus facilitated Italy's shift in alliance partners.

That proposition was subsequently challenged by the perceived failure of the balance of power to keep the peace and the contribution it was believed to have made to the war's advent. It was primarily the expansion of a European conflict into a global war that threw into question the contribution of alliances to stability, as well as the validity of international norms that permitted secret, flexible, and allegedly amoral alliances. The atmosphere was pregnant with fears of alliance diplomacy in general and alliance default in particular, and these fears motivated the victors to advocate rules for faithful adherence to security pacts. At Versailles, statesmen undertook a major reassessment of the principles that had governed international conduct and reached the conclusion that a fundamental reorientation was necessary. Led by Woodrow Wilson, the political idealists framed a philosophy of international relations that attributed the cause of the world war in a large part to the operation of the balance-of-power system and the shifting alliances alleged to keep it in equilibrium that, in their opinion, had encouraged rather than deterred warfare. They sought to replace the balance of power with a system that would rest on collective security and a rule of law. Damning secret diplomacy and uncertain alliance commitments, the reformers prescribed a new regime of "open covenants, openly arrived at" along with a conception of obligation between states that stressed the propriety of honoring commitments. In many respects, the year 1919 represented a cultural watershed—a turning point in the rules that were to subsequently govern alliance politics. The creation of the League of Nations, depicted by Sir Edward Grey as an institution of members "binding themselves to side against any Power which broke a treaty" (Link, 1965: 94), marked a fundamental departure in customary state practice.

The interwar period proved to be one in which the edict *lex semper dabit remedium* (the law will always furnish a remedy) was embraced. As a corollary to the emphasis placed on international organization, legal means to the control of warfare were stridently advocated. Article 8 of the League of Nations Covenant, for example, advocated that "the maintenance of peace requires . . . the enforcement by common action of international obligations." The growing emphasis placed on the binding nature of promissory obligations applied directly to the bonds that were forged in this period between states in alliance. Hence, rather than fleeing from alliances perceived to be potentially entangling, during the period between the two world wars states joined them with increasing alacrity. That renewed enthusiasm was inspired by the growing confidence in agreements within the emergent normative order; the expectation was shared that promises should and would be honored. Alliance formation became frenetic and, possibly, of unprecedented proportions. The frequency with which states entered into formal alliance led Walter Consuello Langsam (1954: 79) to label the 1923–1933 period "the era of pacts." A review of the conspicuous treaties and alliances forged (see Figure 6.2) between the wars reveals a strong preference by states at that time to protect their security through the recruitment of allies, and to insure their assistance in the event of an attack by advocacy of faithful performance of treaty stipulations. Although the magnitude of cross-cutting alliances in this period is impressive, it potentially may underrepresent the actual frequency of alliance formation. It is important not to overlook the unknown number of secret alliances that undoubtedly were given birth during this phase, contrary to Article 18 of the League Covenant, which required all treaties of alliance to be publicly announced and registered. Regardless of the measure used, the rate at which states formed formal alliances with one another rose steadily between 1920 and 1940, with the percentage of nations in the international system involved in alliances expanding from 10 percent in 1920 to nearly 80 percent in 1940 (Singer and Small, 1966a: 13; Gurr, 1972: 144).

It may be conjectured that the increasing stress placed on faithful performance of allies' pledged obligations contributed in part to the rise of this alliance activity. At the same time, the inclination of states to actively forge alliances and cement their stipulations in formal treaties also stimulated support for the norm *pacta sunt servanda*. Regardless of the problem of recursiveness in this causal connection, it is evident that the pattern of covariation was strong: the formation of binding alliance norms moved in monotonic conjunction with the formation of alliances among states. The era of pacts

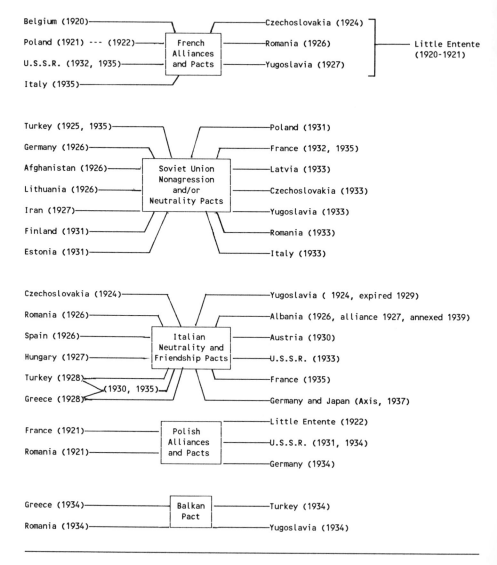

Figure 6.2. Alliances and Pacts between 1920 and 1940
Note: Dates in parentheses identify the year in which treaties were signed.
Source: Derived from Langsam (1954: 92)

was the beginning of a new era of *pacta sunt servanda*. Presumably, states sought to reduce uncertainty during the interwar period by engaging in the first and promoting the second, for in diplomacy both alliances and norms prescribing faithful performance of promises have at times been perceived as vehicles for the reduction of uncertainty as well as for the creation of order and predictability in the relations of nations.

Although the interwar period represented an age of alliance politics, it did not represent an age in which the struggle between flexible and binding alliance commitments was resolved. It merely signalled the hesitant emergence of a culture in which the latter gradually dominated the former. Indeed, the normative climate was punctuated throughout this period with frequent episodes during which the norm *pacta sunt servanda* was directly challenged (which perhaps explains why statesmen at the time attacked so vigorously these challenges to the precept that pacts are binding). It was the "increasing number of instances in defense of claims for the revision or termination of treaties which were entered into when such changes were unforeseen" that led one observer (Garner, 1927: 509) to reflect that the doctrine *rebus sic stantibus* was far from extinct as a principle governing alliance agreements. Noting at the time that "the world has been and is now passing through a era of remarkable change," he predicted that "it is not improbable that there will be further demands . . . for the revision or termination of treaties." and that "the rule *rebus sic stantibus* is likely to be invoked with increasing frequency in the near future" (Garner, 1927: 510–511, 514). This prophecy was partially fulfilled by "the successive revisions of the Treaty of Versailles and the Treaty between Britain and Egypt of 1936" (Friedman, 1964: 301). As World War II neared, the binding character of promises underwent renewed attack and was undercut dramatically by the German violation of its Non-Aggression Pact with the Soviet Union, its betrayal of its pledges to Czechoslovakia, and its abrupt disregard for its promises regarding Poland. However strongly advocated in the international legal culture, the history of international relations between the world wars reveals in stark relief that the norm prescribing the solemn performance of promises is likely to yield when states encounter basic changes in their circumstances and turn to *Staatsraison* to service national interests rather than previous commitments. If rapidly changing and threatening circumstances test the strength of bonds between allies, the outbreak of war creates conditions that tend to break them. In war, trust breaks and old norms erode, only to be replaced by new ones.

Although the outbreak of the Second World War cast substantial doubt on the path to peace that was outlined in the idealist program, the realpolitik program that replaced it in 1945 continued to stress the notion that commitments between states should be regarded as binding. World War II and the atomic weapons that brought it to conclusion ushered in a new era. As John F. Kennedy remarked, those weapons changed all the questions and all the answers. But among the old questions that remained were the policy choices available to states regarding alliances and the sanctity of the commitments on which they rested. Here the alternatives that were selected reinforced rather than rejected the answers diplomatists had previously embraced, and the era of alliance politics continued with renewed enthusiasm. As the cohesion of the Allied powers' wartime coalition dissipated with its defeat of its common enemy and the Cold War ignited, new stress was placed on the construction of alliance systems to conduct the emergent new contest for global leadership (for elaboration, see the case study of this period in Chapter 8). As rivals, Washington and the Kremlin now found themselves in great need of allies in order to maximize their power relative to one another. Accordingly, rather than fleeing from entangling alliances, allies constructed alliances with abandonment. The perceived necessity of allies enabled the superpowers to overcome any lingering fears of entrapment or over-extension (Deibel, 1987a: 102).

The globalization of the great powers' security commitments generated by this new "pactomania" produced a series of Western multilateral alliances, among them the Rio Pact in 1947; the Organization of American States (OAS) in 1948; the North Atlantic Treaty Organization (NATO) in 1949; the Southeast Asia Treaty Organization (SEATO) in 1955; the ANZUS Pact of 1951, which tied Australia, New Zealand, and the United States to each other; and the Central Treaty Organization (CENTO), to which the United States was a tacit partner. Likewise, the Warsaw Pact (1955) solidified Soviet bloc countries in a binding security arrangement.

In addition, a large number of bilateral systems reinforced the interlocking alliance systems created by the United States; the U.S. defense treaties with the Philippines (1951), South Korea (1953), the Republic of China (1954), and Japan (1960) stand out as the most important and costly of the more than forty agreements forged. The security treaties between the Soviet Union and the People's Republic of China (1950) and Cuba (1961) represented the Soviet Union's search for security through bilateral agreements during this time. Few obstacles to the formation and maintenance of alliances deterred their creation in this era of pacts in the first two decades after World War II. Like the interwar period, the 1945–1965 period can also be labeled an era of pacts, given the strong preference exhibited by states at that time to protect their security through the recruitment of allies, and to insure their assistance in the event of an attack by the formalization of agreements to aid one another in treaty stipulations.

This activity is consistent with the expectations predicted by long-cycle theory. The post-World War II period marked the beginning of a "world power" phase of the long cycle as the United States emerged as the new world leader. From that hegemonic position, the United States acted as predicted: it built a network of alliances, backed by norms obligating allies to abide by their treaty commitments religiously. No room was left for neutrals, and desertion from the constructed "free world" was not tolerated. Similarly, the primary challenger for the global leadership role, the Soviet Union, also energetically sought to attract and bind allies by promoting rules that proscribed desertion from alliance commitments and prescribed punishment for any member, such as Hungary or Czechoslovakia, seeking to remove itself from its commitments. Neither superpower was tolerant of defection. Thus, the alliance rules that emerged were the rules advocated by the superpowers, whose interests they served. Those interests placed a premium on loyal allies. Coalition cohesion within the blocs called for norms prohibiting abandonment of commitments. This norm was also embedded in international law, which placed even greater emphasis on the sanctity of treaty commitments in the wake of the Second World War. As a result, the continuing growth of support for the sanctity of alliance obligations during the 1946–1973 world power phase of the long cycle is understandable.

Long-cycle theory maintains that the power and position of the world leader would decay by the early 1970s and new norms of alliance obligation would receive emphasis to facilitate this challenge to the legitimacy of the global power's reign. Events occurring since 1973 do suggest that support for the sanctity of alliance commitments did begin to erode at about that time. American supremacy was thrown into doubt with the failure of U.S. policy in Vietnam, and in the early 1970s the incipient stages of the delegitimation phase commenced, and with it support for alliances began to collapse.

To many legal authorities and students of international law, the symptoms of decay for support of the norm *pacta sunt servanda* in the 1970s were met by surprise. The conventional view at the time maintained that support for the norm *pacta sunt servanda* was sacrosanct (see Gormley, 1970: 372). The emphasis on the binding character of agreements among allies had been so prolonged that it was widely regarded as deeply entrenched, even institutionalized. But when the Vienna Conference on the Law of Treaties convened, the sanctity of oaths and the irrevocability of treaties became the focal point of discussion and debate. *Pacta sunt servanda* was made a target of attack by certain participants (recall the discussion in Chapter 4), as new enthusiasm was expressed for a less restrictive interpretation of the obligations of parties to international agreements to one another. "The main battle-ground, surprisingly, was the traditionally accepted norm of pacta sunt servanda. . . . [The] attempt by the International Law Commission over a period of sixteen years to codify this classical norm in the simplest possible language" noted one publicist at the time, "so seriously split the two U.N. conferences that there was a strong possibility that the final Plenary Session in May 1969 might not be able to muster the two-thirds vote required to adopt the Draft Convention" (Gormley, 1970: 367–368). Stated differently, there emerged increasing support for the view that "the norm pacta sunt servanda is not absolute and impregnable" (Sinha, 1966: 76). Although, predictably, the states at the apex of power in the international hierarchy mounted an intense effort to combat the growth in acceptance by others of this interpretative principle, and though they succeeded in securing language that at least paid lip service to the binding status of international agreements (Gormley, 1970), the Vienna Convention presaged the challenge to the inviolability of agreements that future state practice would later help to grow in strength.

It is uncertain whether this erosion signified a new turning point at which a flexible conception of alliance commitments once again began to gain the status of the more dominant norm. But the fragmentation and disintegration evident in many multilateral institutions and bloc structures in the 1970s and 1980s suggest that central decision makers then began to distance themselves from the lessons that their predecessors drew from the First and Second World Wars. It may be that the impact of these global wars on alliance norms waned with the advent of a new delegitimation phase. If so, long cycle theory would prognosticate that a permissive normative order promoting flexible alliance norms accommodative to the needs of the emergent new international environment of dispersed power can be expected to arise as the twentieth century draws to a close. (The implications of this possibility for global stability are explored in the Epilogue.)

Inferring Historical Linkages Between War Termination and the Transformation of Alliance Norms

The preceding outline of the historical development of alliance norms since 1815 does not speak with a single voice. The linkages between system-disrupting wars and changes in the content of alliance norms display complex variations across epochs. Not only does the magnitude, duration, and destructiveness of each of the wars in our observation period vary, but the rate and direction of change in alliance norms is also subject to somewhat differing patterns of variation. Further exacerbating the detection of consistent patterns of covariation is the fact that the rate of change of these cultural macro-phenomena is governed by lag effects of uncertain duration.

We must resist the temptation to engage in *post hoc propter hoc* reasoning that would invite the conclusion that because a pattern of norm modification has followed a particular path in the past the former caused the latter. Chronology does not reveal casualty, but some propositions can be extracted from observing these temporal patterns:

1. The long-term movement in the conception of treaty obligations since 1815 exhibits a secular trend in the direction of repudiation of the sovereign right of states to unilaterally terminate alliance commitments; the obvious periodicities around this trend imply that the movement toward acceptance of binding, obligatory commitments has been interrupted by temporary reversals.
2. Alliance norms differed in content in the nineteenth versus the twentieth centuries at the end of system-transforming wars. In the nineteenth century, system transforming wars precipitated an acceptance of norms which supported flexible conceptions of commitment. In the twentieth century, these global wars have given rise to norms that supported binding commitments.
3. Regardless of the content of alliance norms during the world power phase of the long cycle, they will be challenging during the delegitimation phase.

In sum, the historical record revealed by our indicator of alliance norms leads to a conclusion that two largely incompatible norms regarding alliance commitments have struggled with each other for dominance throughout the history of the post-Napoleonic system. The data show that neither binding nor flexible conceptions of treaty obligations have persisted without eventual challenge. Although one has tended to prevail to the exclusion of the other in some historical periods, that domination has always receded at a later point in time. The temporal ambivalence displayed in legal opinion about these competing conceptions suggests that a permanent consensus has not been reached on which conception best serves the national interests of states in the international community.

The analysis provided above also suggests that nineteenth-century statesmen generally perceived their interests to be served by acceptance of flexibility in the commitments they made to their alliance partners.[7] In the twentieth century, however, statesmen deduced the opposite conclusion, namely, that their interests were served best by support for a regime that prescribed that commitments be faithfully honored. Unlike the British "world power" phase of the long cycle, during the American phase alliance structures became highly institutionalized due to the rigid, bipolar division of the world into two well-defined, internally cohesive coalitions. The stability of these alignment configurations was reinforced by the preference of their members to join allies together into binding association that gave no latitude for realignment, nor permission to desert from the commitments so formed. Backed by fear of adversaries and strengthened by perceived threats from rival coalitions, in the aftermath of World War I, and more so in the wake of World War II, alliance networks became highly bureaucraticized and institutionalized, taking on a "permanence" unprecedented in modern history. Such norms and practices precluded the operation of a balance-of-power system along the Westphalian conception that the drafters of those treaties prescribed in the mid-seventeenth century.

---

7. Included among these statesmen were several important British officials. For example, George Canning, who became foreign secretary after Viscount Castlereagh's suicide in 1822, supported an independent course based on "every nation for itself and God for us all." Similarly, Lord Palmerston, foreshadowing the famous 1907 memorandum by Eyre Crow, proclaimed in 1848 that Great Britain had no eternal allies and no perpetual enemies.

A THIRD PROBE OF THE DATA: STATISTICAL ASSOCIATIONS BETWEEN WAR TERMINATION AND ALLIANCE NORM TRANSFORMATION

Any decision as to whether an alliance commitment should be honored becomes more fateful "as the international environment moves from a condition of peace to war and back again" (Dingman, 1979: 252). Since many theorists agree with Hedley Bull's (1977: 187) observation that war is "a basic determinant" of the structure of the international system and since our examination of general war failed to produce uniform results across the periods compared, we can extend our analysis by examining the combined impact of all forms of war on alliance norms.

More specifically, to ascertain whether war has had an impact on the content of alliance norms, we shall now examine the association between our commitment index and the amount of major power war *ending* in each half-decade between 1816 and 1974. Because it is commonly held that international law reflects the normative orientation of the most active and influential states, we shall focus on those wars in which at least one major power was an active participant and in which each side sustained at least a thousand battle-connected fatalities. Two measures of the level of wars ended by major powers were taken from data generated by the Correlates of War projects (Singer and Small, 1972; and Small and Singer, 1982); these were *magnitude* (the number of nation-months normalized by system size) and *severity* (the number of battle deaths).

Table 6.3 presents the results from a time-series regression analysis of the association between the magnitude and severity of major power war ending and the degree to which alliance treaty obligations were considered binding over the duration of the 1816–1974 period. The analysis was performed with the Cochrane-Orcutt technique of generalized least-squares. Each independent variable was lagged one time unit and transformed with a log + 1 transformation.

As predicted by our hypotheses, the results show moderate positive relationships. In general, the greater the number of participants in war and the more destructive those wars become, the greater will be the support that develops for norms requiring allies to adhere to their commitments. Although the F statistics reveal that these relationships are significant at the .05 level, the t statistics do not permit us to reject the null hypothesis that the regression coefficients are not significantly greater than zero. Hence we need to undertake further anal-

Table 6.3. Bivariate Relationships Between the Amount of War Terminating and Norms Regarding the Extent of Treaty Commitments, 1816–1974

Dimension of War	Degree to Which Obligations Considered Binding			
	r	b	F	DW
Magnitude	.42	.13	6.53	2.08
		(1.61)		(.27)
Severity	.37	.05	4.69	2.09
		(.96)		(.28)

Note: The entries in parentheses below each regression coefficient contain *t* statistics. The value of ρ is given in parentheses below the Durbin-Watson statistic.

ysis before drawing any conclusions about the relationship between war termination and treaty commitment.

Another step that we should take in analyzing the data is to investigate whether the above relationship changes when intervening variables are controlled. Perhaps the most plausible intervening variable is the amount of alliance activity within the major power system. It is conceivable that the relationships reported in Table 6.3 are spurious, with the correlations between war and commitment norms occurring because alliance activity is mutually related to both variables. In order to determine whether this is actually the case, we calculated the first-order partial correlation coefficients between each dimension of war ending and alliance commitment, controlling for two indicators of alliance activity: *scope* (the percentage of major powers in alliances) and the *rate* of change in that percentage. As can be seen in Table 6.4, the results sustain our previous finding: the relationships between the magnitude and severity of major power war ending and the degree of support for binding commitments remain positive in direction and increase in strength. In other words, irrespective of the proportion of states in alliances or the amount of change in that figure, increased emphasis tends to be given to the binding character of allies' commitments at the conclusion of wars.

One further step we should take in attempting to sort out the effects of possible intervening variables is to utilize spatial and temporal controls. That is, we can compare the major power and central systems during the nineteenth century, as well as the major power and interstate systems during the twentieth century. In so doing, we can

Table 6.4. First-order Partial Correlations Between the Amount
of War Terminating and Norms Regarding the Extent of Treaty
Commitments, Controlling for Alliance Activity, 1816–1974

Degree to Which Obligations Considered Binding

Dimension of War	Controlling for Scope	Controlling for Rate
Magnitude	.86 (.74)	.40 (.16)
Severity	.79 (.62)	.47 (.22)

Note: The entries in parentheses next to the first-order partials are squared partial correlation coefficients.

see if the original bivariate relationships change as we move through time and across space.

World War I was used as the temporal boundary between the centuries for both theoretical and empirical reasons. In the first place, as noted above, many world system theorists, from Modelski (1978) to Wallerstein (1984), have convincingly argued that 1914, not 1899, marks the end of nineteenth-century diplomatic behavior. In the second place, data-based studies (e.g., Job, 1976; Siverson and Duncan, 1976) have demonstrated that alliance initiation activity was characterized by different processes before and after the First World War.

Our choice of 1914 as the temporal boundary between the nineteenth and twentieth centuries affected our choice of spatial controls. Given that international law is alleged to exert its greatest influence over those states that play a fairly vigorous role in world politics, the "central system" provided the most appropriate comparison for the nineteenth-century major power system. On the other hand, the interstate system provided the best comparison for the major power system of the twentieth century, because the growth of interdependence after World War I and the system's concomitant geographical expansion made it difficult to draw a sharp distinction between central and peripheral system membership (for the operational definitions of the major power, central, and interstate systems, see Singer and Small, 1972: 22–30).

As Table 6.5 reveals, the introduction of spatial and temporal controls produces a refining effect: regardless of the spatial domain, the original bivariate relationship is weakened in the nineteenth century, but strengthened in the twentieth. These findings show that the mag-

Table 6.5. A Comparison of the War Termination and Commitment Norm Relationship by Century and System Level, 1816–1914 and 1915–1974

Degree to Which Obligations Considered Binding During the Nineteenth Century

Dimension of War	Major Power System				Central Power System			
	r	b	F	DW	r	b	F	DW
Magnitude	.17	.09	.51	2.05	.26	.18	1.28	2.13
		(.63)		(.08)		(1.09)		(.07)
Severity	.10	.01	.11	1.97	.10	.00	.10	1.97
		(.07)		(.07)		(.02)		(.09)

Degree to Which Obligations Considered Binding During the Twentieth Century

Dimension of War	Major Power System				Interstate System			
	r	b	F	DW	r	b	F	DW
Magnitude	.62	.12	5.57	2.06	.49	.14	2.88	2.23
		(2.10)		(.29)		(1.46)		(.36)
Severity	.51	.05	3.09	2.31	.52	.08	3.39	2.29
		(1.42)		(.25)		(1.56)		(.32)

Note: The entries in parentheses below each regression coefficient contain *t* statistics. The value of ρ is given in parentheses below the Durbin-Watson statistic.

nitude and severity of war termination in the twentieth century had a direct, statistically significant impact on the rise of binding interpretations of alliance obligations; for the nineteenth century, the correlations are negligible (as we would expect based on our previous case study of the immediate post-Napoleonic period).

How can we account for this intercentury difference? The most cogent answer seems to lie in the character of wars that were fought during each century. Both the nineteenth and twentieth centuries experienced war. But following the end of the Napoleonic Wars, a century passed before another cataclysmic war erupted. In contrast, a subsequent catastrophic war broke out only twenty years after World War I. Arguably, the impact of certain types of wars on the international system are different than others. Variously called general (Toynbee, 1954), global (Modelski, 1978), hegemonic (Gilpin, 1981), or world war (Wallerstein, 1984), this form of intense struggle appears to exert a substantial influence on alliance norm transformation (as well as the tendency of states to form and rely on alliances). Indeed, this interpretation is consistent with J. David Singer and Michael Wallace's (1970: 36) finding of "really dramatic increases" in the creation of new intergovernmental organizations "on the heels of the most severe and drawn-out wars."

WAR TERMINATION AS A SOURCE OF CHANGE IN THE CONTENT OF ALLIANCE NORMS

After the destruction has been surveyed and the losses tallied, national leaders often reflect on the causes and consequences of the bloodshed they have witnessed. Sometimes they experience deep, personal changes. Following the outbreak of the Nez Perce War in 1877, for example, Chief Joseph distinguished himself as a military strategist in a series of epic battles. But at the end of the war, when he reflected upon the suffering of his people, he proclaimed: "From where the sun now stands I shall fight no more forever." Having lost faith in warfare as an instrument of influence, he reached the conclusion that trust must be placed in the promises pledged in treaties to preserve security. The subsequent violation by the U.S. government of its many treaties with the nations of native Americans may illustrate the danger that resides in reliance on the words of treaty framers. But the example illustrates the capacity of wars to fundamentally alter beliefs about alternative paths to peace in an anarchic world.

The evidence surveyed in this chapter does not explain what specific conclusions about alliance commitment any given statesman will draw at the end of a particular war (or about the wisdom or foolishness of the conclusions reached). Hypotheses linking war termination to an increase in support for the sanctity of agreements received mixed support. Nevertheless, the findings demonstrate that the twentieth-century interpretation of promissory obligations has been substantially shaped by war. Since the Second World War, alliance structures were made rigid by the bipolar division of the globe into two tight bloc coalitions. The stability of these politico-military configurations was reinforced by a preference of their members to join together into binding associations that did not provide much latitude for realignment. The alliances built in the immediate aftermath of World War II were products, in part, of leaders' experiences prior to and during that global war.

In general, whereas the pattern of association between the outbreak and termination of global war and the type of alliance norm gaining dominance has been different in the present century from that in the preceding century, the impact of war on alliance transformation has been somewhat similar. In both periods, wars have precipitated changes in the mores of the age (although the directionality of change has been inconsistent). The demand for moral relativism and flexible alliance norms in the wake of war in the nineteenth century gave way to the demand for rigid adherence to alliance commitments in the wake of twentieth-century wars. The general historical movement of these normative modifications have followed a cyclical path, though not in strict conformity to the phases predicted by long cycle theory.

At all times, statesmen face an inevitable clash between the need for the faithful execution of promises between allies and the need for the preservation of options in the event of changed circumstances. This irreconcilable conflict between opposed values led to the creation of a permissive normative order in the nineteenth century and a restrictive order in the twentieth. Thus, war only provides a partial and incomplete explanation of alliance norm transformation. Left out of the equation is the distribution of power in the system. Are changes in the concentration and diffusion of global power also related to transformations in alliance norms? If so, in what ways? We turn our attention to these questions in the next chapter.

7 System Structure and the Transformation of Alliance Norms

[H]umanity corresponds to the universe itself . . . simply through one only principle, namely, the submission to a single Prince. We conclude from this that Monarchy is necessary to the world for its well-being.

Dante Alighieri

No sane man could really believe . . . one individual could rule the whole world as a temporal monarch, with all men obeying him as their superior. If a tendency in this direction did appear, there would be wars and revolutions without end.

Pierre Dubois

Turbulent times prompt questions. When rapid change erodes the moral underpinnings of international life, those affected by the turmoil frequently ask if the state system can be restructured in such a way as to provide a new, more stable normative order. As can be seen in the reactions of Dante (1957) and Dubois (1956) to the turmoil in Europe during the last quarter of the thirteenth century, however, no consensus exists on which type of governing structure or organizing principles are most likely to create such an order.

Dante and Dubois wrote at a time when the medieval idea of a Christian commonwealth was being challenged by the concept of secular sovereignty. The cosmopolitanism of St. Thomas Aquinas and Pope Innocent III had given way to a constellation of territorial states. So rapid was this change that those in their youth who had witnessed the pious death of the crusading St. Louis or the defeat of Manfred were hardly more than middle-aged when St. Louis's grandson attacked a pope and Manfred's grandson reconquered Sicily from the papal champion (Strayer, 1955: 189). Whereas canon law had once provided a system of norms to guide the relations between Christian governments, Church authority was now declining as Europe seethed with unrest. For Dante, the solution to this turmoil was centralizing power in the hands of a universal monarch. Dubois, on the other hand, favored dispersing power among a community of separate nations. In their opposing views about the merits of different ways to structure the state system we can find the origins of a debate that has been of continuing interest to students of world politics.

At the heart of this debate is a question that remains unanswered: Do certain structural conditions lead to the formation of international norms that help to preserve peace? The goal of this chapter is to examine whether the structure of the state system is associated with the content of alliance norms. Does a concentration of power engender support for the sanctity of agreements? Or, conversely, does a dispersion of power produce such support? By treating the structural attributes of polarity and polarization as independent variables that affect the way in which alliance treaties are interpreted, we seek to determine when prevailing norms will consider agreements binding and when they will condone the opportunistic renunciation of commitments. Once we know when each of these rival interpretations of promissory obligation tends to gain system-wide acceptance, we can to turn our attention in Chapters 8 and 9 to how they are related to crisis management and war prevention.

THEORIES ON THE IMPACT OF SYSTEM STRUCTURE ON ALLIANCE NORMS

What structural features promote the rise of a restrictive legal order, one that places a premium on upholding promissory agreements? Perhaps the greatest difficulty in answering this question lies in the variety of ways scholars, journalists, and policymakers use the term "structure." As Joseph L. Nogee's (1975: 1204) literature survey demonstrates, "There is no agreement within the discipline on what kind of international structure prevails, when that structure came into existence, or what preceded it."

Much of the disagreement over how to describe the structure of the international system is attributable to general confusion surrounding the concepts of polarity and polarization (Rapkin and Thompson, with Christopherson, 1979). Some writers contend that the "structure of a system changes with changes in the distribution of capabilities across a system's units" (Waltz, 1979: 97). From this perspective, unipolar systems are those containing a single dominant power center, bipolar systems contain two centers, and multipolar systems possess more than two such centers.[1] Other writers focus on alignment patterns rather than power centers (Jackson, 1977: 90). For them, the structure of the system changes as shifts occur in the degree to which

---

1. Although most theorists use the term multipolarity to describe any international system containing more than two great powers, George Modelski (1974: 2) restricts the term to "a Three-to-Seven Great Power system, where each holds at least 5

lesser powers cluster around the great powers. Thus a system with two dominant power centers can be said to be moving toward a greater degree of bipolarization as its members form two separate blocs whose external interactions are characterized by increasing levels of conflict while their internal interactions become more cooperative (Rapkin and Thompson, 1980: 378–379). In summary, much of the literature on the international system discusses two distinctly separate structural phenomena: the distribution of power (*polarity*) and the propensity of actors to cluster around the most powerful states (*polarization*).

How might changes in polarity and polarization affect the transformation of international legal norms? Does system structure matter? And if it does matter, does it do so in predictable ways? As can be seen in Table 7.1, conflicting schools of thought exist. On the one hand, the Lauterpacht-Oppenheim tradition in legal theory holds that international law flourishes when there is a diffusion of military capabilities within the state system, and when alliances are flexible enough to permit the power of any given state or group of states to be counterbalanced by equivalent power elsewhere in the system. On the other hand, William R. Thompson (1983: 143) has pointed out that scholars from several different traditions share the opinion that the ''rules of the system . . . tend to be established during period[s] of high capability concentration and the leadership/dominance of a single state.''[2] At first glance, both schools of thought appear plausible; and while both could be wrong,[3] it would seem that they cannot both be

---

percent of available military power, but no more than 25 percent, and all together hold at least 50 percent of such power.'' When power centers are greater in number and smaller in magnitude, he classifies the international system as dispersed rather than multipolar.

2. Specifically, he identifies Wallerstein's world-economy perspective, Modelski's theory of the long cycle of world leadership, Organski's power transition model, and Gilpin's conceptualization of hegemonic war and change. Although important differences exist among these four bodies of scholarship, Thompson observes that they reach similar conclusions about the relationship between system structure and norm formation.

3. Ian Clark's (1980: 175) contention that the basic norms of the international system have not changed even though there have been changes in the structure of the system suggests a null alternative to the two schools of thought portrayed in Table 7.1: the amount of polarity and polarization within the state system are unrelated to the degree of support that prevailing norms give to a binding interpretation of alliance treaties. According to this line of reasoning, a variety of nonstructural factors affect alliance norms. One frequently cited factor is social learning. Changes in the way statesmen interpret promissory obligations are said to be the result of a learning

right. But a second look is needed here, for certain types of norms may arise during periods of power parity while others may surface during periods of preponderance.

Which of these two schools of thought most accurately describes when alliance norms will support binding versus elastic interpretations of promissory obligations? Given our findings in the previous chapter on the relationship between war termination and norm formation, a possible answer to this question can be found in hegemonic stability/leadership theory, a diverse body of literature that "posits that changes in the relative power resources available to major states will explain changes in international regimes" (Keohane, 1980: 132). An example of the reasoning behind this kind of explanation can be found in the field of international political economy.[4] Here various theorists have argued that a relationship obtains between global political structures and the openness of international trade regimes. Without a single leader to use economic and political clout to create and maintain an open international economy, the free exchange of goods, capital, and services would at least be inhibited by protectionist policies. At worst, the regimes would be replaced by complete autarky. It is for this reason that these theorists maintain that a relative decline in the capability of the world leader will reduce the ability and willingness of that state to continue playing the leadership role. The diffusion of power during hegemonic decline is thus expected to lead to

---

cess, not the product of any given configuration of international power. Sometimes social learning unfolds gradually out of the reciprocal exchanges that evolve during long-term sequential interaction; and at other times it occurs rapidly following set-piece test cases that serve as precedents for conduct in similar future situations (Cohen, 1981: 100). Once reigning alliance norms are discredited and a different interpretation of promissory obligations emerges, emulation will stimulate the diffusion of this new perspective, regardless of the existing levels of polarity and polarization.

4. Actually, two forms of hegemonic leadership/stability theory can be found within the field of international political economy. The first form, represented by the work of Charles P. Kindleberger (1981: 247), contains the assumption of altruism: because of the economic benefits they obtain, the privilege of leading, and an interest in providing the public good of world stability, hegemons furnish an open market for distress goods, a steady flow of capital for long-term lending, and a rediscount mechanism to provide liquidity when the monetary system is locked in crisis. The second form of the theory can be seen in the work of Stephen D. Krasner (1976). In contrast to Kindleberger's benevolent hegemon, the leadership of which benefits all, Krasner portrays hegemonic leaders in a more coercive light. According to his interpretation, hegemons use their superior strength to establish and enforce regimes that increase their own growth and aggregate income, but such regimes may not be to the advantage of other states (Snidal, 1985).

Table 7.1. Divergent Opinions on the Relationship between the Distribution of Power among Nations and the Growth of International Legal Norms

Power Parity as a Condition Fostering Norm Formation

"A law of nations can only exist if there be an equilibrium, a balance of power, between the members of the family of nations."

—Lassa F. L. Oppenheim

"An equilibrium of forces inherently unstable, always shifting, always changing . . . encourages cooperation, conciliation, and the growth of law."

—Nicholas J. Spykman

"It is in balance-of-power systems that the authority of international law has been greatest."

—Stanley Hoffmann

"A world balance of power is a precarious security, but it is the best there is, and it is the only road to law."

—John A. Perkins

Power Preponderance as a Condition Fostering Norm Formation

"Questions of authority and even right have been resolved by global wars . . . because they resolve the question of who is the strongest in the system. A system leader emerges with some amount of authority and with some ability to declare what is right and what is wrong by establishing or modifying the rules of the system."

—William R. Thompson

"It is easier to get a norm started if it serves the interests of the powerful few."

—Robert Axelrod

"Where no clear preponderance of power is concentrated in the hands of one or a few enforcing organizations . . . at best only laws of behavior, corresponding more or less closely to the actually existing probabilities of behavior patterns, can be used as imperfect guidelines for coordination."

—Karl W. Deutsch

"The evolution of any system has been characterized by successive rises of powerful states that have governed the system and have determined the pattern of international interactions and have established the rules of the system."

—Robert Gilpin

systemic uncertainty and conflict. As Charles P. Kindleberger (1973: 305) put it, "for the world economy to be stabilized, there has to be a stabilizer, one stabilizer."[5]

Efforts also have been made to extend hegemonic stability/leadership theory beyond the confines of international political economy (e.g., Bonanate, 1976, 1979). When applying a variant of the theory to the rise and decay of international norms, Robert Gilpin (1981: 36) proposes that the dominant states "impose rules on lesser members [of the international system] in order to advance their particular interests." Yet to aver that prevailing international norms will reflect the interests of the powerful, Gilpin admits, is not to reveal much about the content of those norms, for as new states rise to the summit of global power, they often have different perceived interests than their predecessors.

One possible exception lies in those rules pertaining to promissory obligations. Regardless of the different ideologies and forms of governance between a *Pax Romana* and a *Pax Americana,* hegemonic states such as Rome and the United States tend to have a common interest in maintaining bonds that bind (Senghaas, 1983: 123). As states who generally have arrived at the apex of the international hierarchy after grueling wars, one of their primary goals is to preserve that privileged position. We may predict, therefore, that preponderant powers will tend to support norms prohibiting the repudiation of commitments, for their interest in upholding the status quo will be served by norms that stabilize the alliances and international organizations that they create.[6] Their security interests will also be served by norms

---

5. The evidence pertaining to this assertion is mixed. A growing number of studies report findings that challenge the predictions of the hegemonic stability/leadership theory in foreign economic policy (see Cowhey and Long, 1983; Lawson, 1983; Mc-Keown, 1983; Lake, 1984; Stein, 1984). Similarly, although some empirical support can be found for the more general proposition that global warfare is less prevalent when capabilities are highly concentrated in a unipolar system (Haas, 1970; Thompson, 1986), Jack S. Levy's studies (1985a) suggest that unipolar periods are unstable.

6. The norm *pacta sunt servanda* has been acknowledged by many students of international politics as a bulwark of the status quo, invoked primarily by those states who are satisfied with their position in the international pecking order (e.g., see Schuman, 1969: 274–276; Van Dyke, 1966: 270–271). Indeed, as Anthony Carty (1986: 67) reminds us, representatives of these states historically have seen individual treaties "as part of a framework of treaties which were to reflect as well as maintain a material distribution of power." By way of contrast, the representatives of powerful, dissatisfied states have been prone to challenge the notion that treaties are inviolable, for such a challenge advances their efforts to "redraft the rules by which relations among nations work" (Organski and Kugler, 1980: 23). In his examination of

that prohibit the unilateral renunciation of prior arrangements for foreign bases, stationing troops abroad, and an integrated defense (Beres, 1972: 705).

On the other hand, when power in the international system becomes increasingly diffused and alliances are less polarized, norms upholding the sanctity of alliance treaties are likely to erode. As Glenn Snyder and Paul Diesing (1977: 428) have pointed out, the interests of allies in multipolar systems are heterogeneous. When this is combined with a condition of approximate parity, the probable result will be for members of the state system to favor alliance norms that allow them to keep their options open and shift allegiances in response to changing circumstances, even if that means breaking a treaty and changing partners during a crisis.

Based on these considerations, what we shall label as the hegemonic stability/leadership thesis on commitment norm formation can be stated as follows: high, stable levels of capability concentration are associated with the emergence of a restrictive legal order, whereas the diffusion of national capabilities among relatively equal major powers is associated with the rise of a permissive order. Therefore, the degree of support that international norms give to binding interpretations of alliance commitment is likely to increase as the structure of the international system moves away from a fluid, multipolar distribution of power.

In order to ascertain whether this thesis is warranted, we shall examine it in greater detail with a case study.

A CASE STUDY OF THE RELATIONSHIP BETWEEN SYSTEM STRUCTURE AND ALLIANCE COHESION

Over time, nation-states come to occupy roles within the international system that are enmeshed in complex networks of obligations and mutual expectations. Among the roles that policymakers in lesser powers may perceive as appropriate for their situation is that of the "faithful ally" who declares a willingness to support fraternal states with all means possible. K. J. Holsti (1970) has argued that the foreign policy actions of a given nation-state generally will be consistent

---

the 1958 and 1960 United Nations Conferences on the Law of the Sea, Robert L. Friedheim (1968: 76) found that delegates from weak, dissatisfied states also insisted that "existing rules might no longer be practical because of changed conditions." In other words, individuals from "have not" states were inclined to see advantages in a permissive legal order, and thus frequently took positions based on the norm *rebus sic stantibus.*

with its national role conceptions, and the opportunity for changing roles will be influenced by the structure of the international system. More specifically, he suggests that the greater the concentration of power in the international system and the more polarized the configuration of alliances, the less the opportunities for foreign policy restructuring, particularly with regard to shifting from the role of a faithful ally to one emphasizing diversity in diplomatic contacts and flexibility in political commitments.[7]

Post-World War II French foreign policy is cited by K. J. Holsti (1982: 6) as an example of such restructuring during a period when the international system began to move away from rigid bipolarity. Therefore it provides us with an inviting opportunity to conduct a "plausibility probe" (Eckstein, 1975) of our thesis that high levels of systemic polarity and alliance polarization are associated with support for binding interpretations of alliance treaty commitments.

At the center of French foreign policy during this period was Charles de Gaulle, an individual who accepted the realist maxim that "international life, like life in general, is a battle" (de Gaulle, 1964: 78). Consistent with this Hobbesean outlook were his corollary beliefs that military force is a natural part of international life, and that the nation-state, as the primary actor in world affairs, needs force capability in order to guarantee its security. "Only if children cease to be born," claimed de Gaulle (1960: 2), "only if minds are sterilized, feelings frozen, men's minds anesthetized, only if the world is reduced to immobility, can [force] be banished."

For de Gaulle, there were two ways to increase security in a world where nation-states constantly battle for hegemony. The first, or elemental guarantee, is through armaments; the second, or supplemental guarantee, is through alliances. Of the two, the latter is more problematic because an alliance commitment may infringe on what de Gaulle called "the free disposition of oneself." Due to this potential restriction on a leader's decision latitude, de Gaulle (1964: 216) saw military alliances as an expedient with "no absolute virtue, whatever may be the sentiments on which they are based."

Nowhere did this point of view have a greater impact on alliance

---

7. Strictly speaking, K. J. Holsti (1988: 315–316) uses the terms polar (two power centers) and hierarchical (one power center) to describe systemic structures characterized by a high degree of capability concentration. Furthermore, he refers to the degree of cohesion in the system when describing the propensity of smaller states to cluster around these power centers.

cohesion than it did with respect to the French posture toward the North Atlantic Treaty Organization (NATO). Reflecting on his nation's humiliating defeat in the Second World War, de Gaulle (1959: 276) lamented "But how short France found her sword to be, at the moment the Allies launched their attack on Europe." When that long, grinding war ended, France needed supplemental security guarantees. "France had been materially and morally destroyed by the collapse of 1940 and by the capitulation of the Vichy people. . . . France came out of the ordeal greatly weakened in every respect" (de Gaulle, 1964: 233).

Though excluded from the Yalta Conference, various French leaders still hoped to forge a prominent role for their nation in the postwar world. Echoing the Comte de Vergennes, they believed in *la politique du grandeur,* according to which France was destined by virtue of history, culture, and geography to hold a position of supremacy in Western Europe and continue her so-called civilizing mission throughout a vast colonial empire. One way for a war-weary France to acquire increased diplomatic leverage would be to act as an arbiter between the Anglo-Saxon powers (Britain and the United States) and the Soviet Union. Moreover, such as position could be enhanced if France also led a new, third force in world politics composed of those states that bordered the Alps, the Rhine, and the Pyrenees. It was in this spirit that Louis Saillant, president of the *Conseil National de la Résistance* saw France "the hyphen between nations;" and Maurice Schumann, the leader of the Catholic *Mouvement Républicain Populaire,* portrayed France as "the wedding ring of the great marriage" (DePorte, 1968: 72–73). To be sure, France did enjoy some success in restoring her international position, as can be seen by the acquisition of an occupation zone in Germany and a permanent seat on the United Nations Security Council. Nevertheless, France was frustrated in the attempt to be an arbiter among the great powers: the United States became displeased with French actions on the Allied Control Council; Britain could not be wooed away from its "special relationship" with Washington; and the Soviet Union remained unwilling to support French proposals for an autonomous Rhineland. As Emile Giraud summarized the situation, France lacked the wherewithal to play Talleyrand's game once more. "[It was] a weak country, physically and morally very tired, politically divided, without financial power or economic capacity, without resources, without appreciable military force, incapable of meeting its most pressing needs" (cited in Furniss,

1960: 23). The balance of power had shifted, and the changed conditions which materialized left France exposed to unparalleled vulnerabilities.

Largely out of necessity, therefore, France turned to NATO to compensate for its lack of elemental security guarantees. With a tradition of seeking security through alliances extending back to Francis I in the sixteenth century, there was nothing novel about this decision. What gave participation in NATO its distinctive flavor was the magnitude of French dependence upon the United States for national defense and economic reconstruction. While episodes such as the rejection of Washington's plan to station Jupiter and Thor missiles on French territory symbolized the Fourth Republic's quest for independence and refusal to acquiesce to American supremacy within the Atlantic Alliance, serious concerns were voiced along the Seine over the depth of the American commitment to defend the Continent. The French National Assembly, for example, criticized the lack of automaticity in Article 5 of the North Atlantic Treaty. In the words of Foreign Minister Georges Bidault (quoted in Serfaty, 1968: 33), the North Atlantic Pact was "not the result of enthusiasm . . . but the fruit of a very grave disappointment [the failure of the Moscow Conference of 1947] and . . . a very heavy fear" (the intensification of the Cold War following the fall of the Benes regime in Czechoslovakia). Indeed, Theodore Draper (1988: 151) argues that the transition from a broad verbal commitment to a full-fledged integrated military organization was especially welcomed by the French since they had little faith in the binding force of words. Similarly, Wolfram F. Hanrieder and Graeme P. Auton (1980: 102) portray one of the original aspirations behind Premier René Pleven's plan for a European Defense Community as gaining a greater American commitment to Continental defense. Yet several events led the French to question the sanctity of the American security commitment, even after the communist invasion of South Korea prompted the NATO allies to establish a more formal decision-making apparatus to coordinate their actions if a similar attack occurred in Europe. Among these events were the perceived lack of American support for France in Dien Bien Phu (1954), the Suez Crisis (1956), and the Algerian civil war (1954–1962).

The lack of U.S. support for French interests in North Africa combined with France's weakness in strategic forces to give officials in the Fourth Republic two unpalatable options: France could either bring its colonial policies in line with Washington's desires, or forgo the American nuclear guarantee. Once U.S. territory became vulnerable to attack from Soviet intercontinental ballistic missiles, the credibility of the American retaliatory threat to punish the Soviets for an invasion of Western Europe was called into question. To shore up the American guarantee and obtain a veto right over the use of the American nuclear arsenal, de Gaulle proposed that Britain, France, and the United States establish a tripartite organization within NATO that would develop a common strategy for the alliance and reach joint decisions on the use of nuclear weapons. The failure of his triumvirate proposal, together with de Gaulle's objections to a multilateral nuclear force and his outright rejection of extending the Nassau Agreement to France, set the stage for the development of an independent nuclear force and withdrawal from the integrated military structure of NATO.

French misgivings about the United States had arisen before the birth of the Fifth Republic. Irritation with Washington's reluctance to assist the French nuclear program and frustration over American domination of NATO led Premier Gaillard to publicly criticize NATO's organization and privately explore the possibility of cooperating with Italy and other European states on the common production of nuclear weapons (Kohl, 1971: 25–27).[8] Nor was de Gaulle the only major political figure following the collapse of the Fourth Republic who held reservations about the American position in NATO. Prominent opposition leaders such as Gaston Defferre and Jean Lecanuet also expressed concerns about dependence on the United States and the credibility of its commitment to the defense of Europe. But it was Charles de Gaulle who orchestrated the clamor for a European Europe existing "by itself for itself," and he went so far as to invoke the spectre of superpower collusion in an effort to instigate doubts about the value of American promises. The unpalatable position that France held within the global distribution of power prompted the Fifth Republic to reassess the value of those alliance commitments that had previously been made out of perceived necessity. Trust in the

---

8. Although France entered the nuclear club by detonating an atomic bomb in the Sahara on February 13, 1960, a nuclear weapons program had emerged during the Fourth Republic. According to Lawrence Scheinman (1965), feasibility studies and preparations for the fabrication of nuclear weapons were begun by the *Commissariat à l'energie atomique* (CEA) in 1954. Within a few months, the CEA began to receive financial support from the Ministry of Defense, and, by May 1955, the *Bureau d'études générales* was established within the CEA for the purpose of designing a bomb. Eighteen months later, a secret military program was begun with the aim of having CEA produce an atomic bomb.

American willingness to adhere to its promises had broken down; accordingly, French policymakers concluded that prior agreements with NATO no longer served French national interests.

In a series of memoranda (March 11, March 29, and April 22, 1966) the French government communicated its decision to withdraw from NATO on July 1, 1966, and demanded the removal of all NATO personnel and equipment from French soil by April 1, 1967. Under Article 13 of the North Atlantic Treaty, once the treaty had been in force for twenty years, any party could withdraw one year after it delivered a notice of denunciation. Since the treaty had come into force on August 24, 1949, no move by the Elysée was expected until 1969. But de Gaulle insisted that he was not denouncing the North Atlantic Treaty; he was disengaging from NATO's integrated multinational military structure.[9] Regardless of the fine line that he wished to draw between the treaty and NATO, subsequent statements by the French government indicated that the treaty itself had been repudiated. According to Article 5, an armed attack against one party "shall be considered an attack against them all." Yet Premier Georges Pompidou declared in a television interview on March 28, 1966, and again in a speech before the National Assembly on April 20, that leaving NATO would make it possible to maintain a free hand and keep out of a war between the United States and the Soviet Union (Goodman, 1975: 102).

What accounts for this shift in French foreign policy from an emphasis on commitment through upholding alliance guarantees to one stressing flexibility through the unilateral repudiation of an agreement prior to its agreed-upon expiration date? On numerous occasions de Gaulle pointed to changed international conditions. By the early 1960s, France was "in sharp ascendance" (de Gaulle, 1964: 223) and the United States was thought to be declining relative to its rivals. Speaking at a press conference on July 23, 1964, de Gaulle expressed

---

9. De Gaulle's loose interpretation of promissory obligations was not unique in French diplomatic history. An earlier example of an elastic definition of duty to one's allies can be found in the following passage taken from the memoirs of Louis XIV, the Sun King of France.

> If one shall speak the truth quite frankly, treaties are concluded from the beginning with this mental reservation. All the beautiful provisions about alliances, affirmations of friendship and the promises to great advantages, do only mean according to the experience of centuries, as understood by the two signatories, that they want to abstain from armed encroachments and from public enmities. Secret violation of the treaties which are not visible to the public are expected (cited in Bernholz, 1985: 173).

the view that tremors were shaking the diplomatic landscape. The international system was moving toward multipolarity, a change that called for a new foreign policy and the repudiation of commitments that did not jibe with emerging global realities. "It is clear," de Gaulle insisted, that "things have changed" since the end of the Second World War:

> The Western States of our old continent have rebuilt their economies. They are rebuilding their military forces. . . . On the other hand, the monolithic nature of the totalitarian world is in the process of dislocation. . . . Lastly, great aspirations and difficulties are deeply agitating the developing countries. The result of all these new factors, complicated and interrelated, is that the division of the world into two camps led by Washington and Moscow respectively corresponds less and less to the real situation. (cited in Kulski, 1966: 156)

According to de Gaulle (1971: 201), NATO had ceased to guarantee the survival of Western Europeans. As a result, the commitment embodied in NATO's military apparatus must be reinterpreted in the light of changed conditions. "Nothing can make a law enforceable," he proclaimed, "when it no longer agrees with the ways of the times. Nothing can make a treaty wholly valid when its object has changed. Nothing can make an alliance remain as such when the conditions in which it was concluded have changed. It is therefore necessary to adapt the law, the treaty and the alliance to the new factors" (de Gaulle, 1966: 20).

France now possessed a modest countervalue nuclear capability (the *force de frappe*), which was justified by Pierre Gallois's (1961: 22) concept of proportional deterrence. France allegedly would be able to deter a larger adversary by having the capability to inflict enough damage to offset any gains that might be achieved through a first strike on France. The Soviet Union, for example, could destroy France, but French Mirage IV bombers could tear off a Soviet arm (*arracher un bras*), a price thought too dear to pay for attacking France. Thus at a time when NATO came to be seen as unresponsive to French interests, France turned to a national deterrent to guarantee its territorial integrity.

The Gaullist notion of an independent security policy reached its zenith in 1967 with the "fortress France" ideas of total sanctuary (*sanctuarisation totale*) and all horizon targeting (*la défense tous-azimuts*). As outlined by the Chief of Staff of the French Armed Forces, General Charles Ailleret (1968), future threats in a multipolar world could come from any point on the compass; therefore France should be prepared to stand alone and retaliate against any part of the globe rather than remain integrated within an a priori alliance. This argument rationalized the disavowal of a collective defense treaty that had seemed so compelling under different circumstances and therefore had been voiced with such assurance.

To summarize, French behavior in the aftermath of World War II fits K. J. Holsti's (1982) conceptualization of foreign policy restructuring. During the Fourth Republic, when military power within the international system was highly concentrated and alliances were bipolarized, government officials in Paris stressed the norm *pacta sunt servanda* in their dealings with allied governments. But as the contours of the international system became more fluid with the diffusion of power toward an incipient multipolar structure, members of President de Gaulle's Fifth Republic used the norm *rebus sic stantibus* to justify their efforts at foreign policy restructuring.

As Benjamin A. Most and Harvey Starr (1989: 133) have argued, system structure is empirically important when accounting for international outcomes, even though it may not be logically sufficient. It is important because decision makers such as Gaillard and de Gaulle operate within systemic structures that delimit opportunities for behavior. "The Fourth Republic," writes Alfred Grosser (1965: 2), "was preoccupied by foreign policy out of necessity, while General de Gaulle's preoccupation was one of taste." Whereas the menu for choice in the immediate post-war environment was constrained by the structure of the international system, more selections were available two decades later, and de Gaulle was willing to avail himself of these opportunities.

If this case is viewed as an illustration of the claim that the structure of the international system is related to the content of alliance norms, then the record of French foreign policy from 1945 to 1968 can be interpreted as sustaining the hegemonic stability/leadership thesis. High levels of capability concentration and alliance polarization were associated with support for a binding definition of promissory obligations, while the diffusion of power and the erosion of what Richard A. Falk (1971) calls "the bipolarity of allegiance" gave rise to protestations that alliance treaties could be modified unilaterally when circumstances changed. But a single case, however suggestive, does not provide enough evidence to establish a general historical pattern. Additional corroboration is required for nomothetic generalizations to be accepted. It is to a broader base of information that we now turn.

TESTING THE RELATIONSHIP BETWEEN SYSTEM STRUCTURE AND ALLIANCE NORMS

Plausibility probes are at best a "form of hypothesis assessment that falls short of rigorous hypothesis testing" (George, 1979: 52). In order to give the hegemonic stability/leadership thesis a more thorough test, let us shift from a contextualized case study to a time-series regression analysis of the relationship between system structure and alliance norms.

Measurement and Model Building

As in the previous chapter, the *dependent* variable used in our time-series analysis is the relative importance attributed by the international legal order to the norms *pacta sunt servanda* and *rebus sic stantibus*. Once again, we measured this by means of the index described in Chapter 4 (hereafter labeled COMMITMENT).

Polarity and polarization are the two *independent* variables employed to account for the variance in the dependent variable. We based the strategy for operationalizing them on four assumptions. First, polarity and polarization are two separate structural dimensions of the international system. Second, any observed movement back and forth between multipolarity, bipolarity, and unipolarity is a manifestation of the more general process of capability concentration and deconcentration (Thompson, 1986: 614). Third, given that our ultimate concern is with the reliability of military alliances, an index linked directly to variations in the amount of military capability concentration is more relevant for hypothesis testing than some omnibus indicator of gross potential power. Finally, because vertical nuclear proliferation makes it difficult to derive and interpret equivalent measures of military capability concentration over time, it is appropriate to restrict our temporal domain to the period prior to the development of major improvements in missile and warhead accuracy, and the deployment of multiple independently targetable reentry vehicles, cruise missiles, antisatellite weapons, and other exotic technology.

As a result of these assumptions, indicators of polarity and polarization were aggregated by half-decade over the 1820–1969 time span.[10] To measure polarity, data were obtained from Alan Ned Sabrosky's (1985a: 161) reformulation of the Correlates of War (COW) project indices of national capabilities. His index of the concentration of military capabilities (MILPOL) is derived from the standard

---

10. To avoid the potentially distorting effects of the First and Second World Wars, these measurement intervals were modified, with readings taken in 1913 rather than 1915, in 1938 rather than 1940, and in 1946 rather than 1945.

deviation of the actual percentage shares of military expenditures and personnel held by major powers divided by the maximum possible standard deviation of the percentage shares. To measure polarization, data were drawn from Frank Wayman's (1985: 129) study of coalition configurations. His index of alliance polarization (POLAR) is based on the ratio of actual to potential poles in the major power system, where actual poles equal the number of blocs formed by major powers in defense pacts plus the number of nonbloc major powers, and potential poles equal the number of major powers.

When taken together, COMMITMENT, MILPOL, and POLAR can be used to model the hegemonic stability/leadership thesis. The model posits that normative support for a binding interpretation of treaty commitments tends to increase as military capabilities become concentrated in the hands of fewer major powers and as alliance configurations become more polarized. Stated formally,

$$COMMITMENT = f\ (MILCON + POLAR) + u$$

where the strength of support for the norm *pacta sunt servanda* is seen as a function of the additive impact of MILCON and POLAR plus a stochastic error term (u), which includes any unspecified variables affecting COMMITMENT, as well as any random measurement errors.

Given that we have thirty quinquennial observations on three continuous variables covering the 1820–1969 period, the statistical procedure most appropriate for testing the model is time-series regression analysis. In order to determine whether the assumptions of regression analysis were violated by our data, several diagnostic tests were performed. First, to check for non-normal disturbances we compared the observed and expected distributions of the residuals using Chi-square to test the null hypothesis that the errors were normally distributed.[11] Given that the value of Chi-square was not significant (1.52 with df = 1), we concluded that the errors were normal.

Second, to check for autocorrelated disturbances the serial correlation coefficient and the Durbin-Watson statistic were calculated. In addition, student's *t* was used to test the null hypothesis that the er-

11. Although regression analysis is based on the assumption of constant error variance, our original test of the model showed evidence of variance nonstationarity, which was attributable to the variable POLAR. Several procedures are available to correct for variance nonstationarity, but the most common is to log-transform the time series (Pindyck and Rubinfeld, 1975). As a result, we used the natural log of the POLAR time series in the analysis that follows.

rors in one time period were not correlated with errors in the ensuing time period. Because the serial correlation coefficient was close to zero (*rho* = $-.015$), the Durbin-Watson statistic was 2.02, and the value of the *t*-test was not significant ($-.076$ with df = 26), autocorrelation did not pose a problem and ordinary least squares regression could be used instead of generalized least squares.

Third, to check for heteroskedastic disturbances we calculated the Bartlett test of the null hypothesis that the errors had a constant variance. Since the test result was not significant (4.16 with *df* = 2), we concluded that the model contained constant residual variance.

Finally, based on Klein's rule, multicollinearity did not appear to present a problem since the pairwise predictor correlation ($-.23$) was neither statistically significant nor did it exceed the overall multiple correlation coefficient.

Having thus shown that the model does not violate the major assumptions of regression analysis, let us now examine the results that emanated from the application of this statistical procedure to our data:

$$\text{COMMITMENT} = -.98 + .56 \text{ MILCON} + .50 \log \text{POLAR}$$
$$(3.46) \qquad\qquad (1.80)$$

$$R = .57 \ R^2 = .33 \ F = 6.53, \ p < .01 \ DW = 2.02.$$

Looking first at the standardized regression coefficients, we see that both independent variables are positively related to the rise of international legal norms supportive of binding treaty commitments, although MILCON is the more potent predictor. According to the *t*-statistics reported in the parentheses below each standardized regression coefficient, the coefficients are significantly greater than zero and cannot be attributed to chance.[12] Furthermore, the *F* statistic indicates that the model as a whole is significant at the .01 level. To

---

12. Caution should be used when interpreting the results pertaining to POLAR. Based on an a priori belief that the sign of the coefficient for POLAR would be positive, in a right-tail test the value of the *t* ratio exceeds the *t* distribution value of 1.703, using *df* = 27. Taking the more conservative approach of assuming that direction had not been predicted in advance, however, for a two-tailed test at the .05 level we would need a *t* ratio of 2.052 or larger to reject the null hypothesis that the regression coefficient for POLAR is not significantly greater than zero. Throughout this book, we report the results from such significance tests even though the data are not derived from a random sample. These tests are reported to provide a general benchmark for the threshold of importance. Our theoretical interpretations rely most heavily on the measures of association that are calculated.

put all of this another way, the results indicate that the greater the concentration of military capabilities and the greater the degree of alliance polarization, the greater the support for binding alliance commitments. As a general rule, therefore, when military capabilities gravitate toward fewer and fewer powers and become aggregated through the formation of alliances around them, support for the norm that allies are obligated to abide by the promises they make tends to increase. Conversely, when military power becomes more diffused and alliances fragment into a kaleidoscope of shifting loyalties (as throughout most of the nineteenth century), a permissive legal order arises, which upholds the view that promises may be repudiated to facilitate adaptation to changing international circumstances.

These results notwithstanding, the multiple coefficient of determination suggests that there is still considerable room for improvement when accounting for the variance in the dependent variable. Perhaps the model could be strengthened through an alternative specification. Thus far we have treated the effects of polarity and polarization as independent and additive. It may be that these two variables have an interactive effect similar to that between acceleration and time in Galileo's theory of free fall. If, for example, Galileo had postulated that the distance through which any freely falling body that starts from rest will move in a given time is equal to 1/2 (gravitational acceleration) + (time)^2, empirical tests would have shown him to be wrong, even though he had identified the correct independent variables. Thus, to investigate the possibility of an interaction effect between our independent variables, we reformulated the model to specify a multiplicative relationship between MILCON and POLAR.[13] Nevertheless, the reformulation added nothing to our understanding of alliance norms. Not only was the product of MILCON and POLAR unrelated to our commitment index ($r^2 = .01$), but when this new interaction variable was inserted into the original model, its estimated coefficient was not significantly greater than zero ($t = -.48$).

Another reformulation of the model involves a more dynamic specification. Rather than focusing on the existing structure of the state system, we can examine the impact that changes in the levels of polarity and polarization have upon alliance norms by using delta values ($X_t - X_{t-1}$) of MILCON and POLAR as independent variables. Upon

---

13. The two alternative specifications that we tested were:

COMMITMENT = a + b1 (MILCON) (POLAR)

and COMMITMENT = a + b1 MILCON + b2 POLAR
+ b3 (MILCON)(POLAR).

testing this version of the model, however, we found that it accounted for very little of the variance in our commitment index ($R^2 = .07$). Moreover, the regression coefficients for MILCON ($t = .17$) and POLAR ($t = -1.47$) were not statistically significant, nor was the model as a whole significant ($F = 1.09$).

In summary, static levels of polarity and polarization exhibit an independent, additive impact on alliance norms. The model we constructed from these two analytically distinct structural variables performs better than any alternative specification of the hegemonic stability/leadership thesis.

It also performs better than the more common practice of predicting system-level phenomena merely on the basis of the number of existing poles. When we treated our dependent variable as a trichotomy (*pacta sunt servanda* was the dominant norm / *rebus sic stantibus* was dominant / neither norm dominated), the number of poles described by Rosecrance (1963) and Levy (1985a) as a trichotomy (unipolar / bipolar / multipolar), and then used the Guttman coefficient of predictability as our proportional-reduction-in-error measure in analyzing the resulting contingency tables, we found that we had little ability to predict the category of the dependent variable by knowing the category of the independent variable (Rosecrance classification, lambda = .14; Levy classification, lambda = .35). That is to say, a simple cross-classification of the number of poles and the prevailing interpretation of treaty commitment within each half-decade in the temporal domain produced results that were weaker than those from our model. Although this is encouraging, we still need to examine how well the model performs once we control for possible intervening variables.

Refining and Extending the Model

One plausible refinement in the analysis would be to control for the characteristics of the alliance commitments within the international system at a particular point in time. It is highly probable that both the number of commitments made (*alliance aggregation*) and the tightness in the clusters of nations that result from these treaty agreements (*alliance cohesion*) will affect the content of alliance norms. High levels of alliance aggregation, for example, could be connected with normative support for binding commitments owing to a loss of interaction opportunities (Deutsch and Singer, 1964). Each alliance commitment reduces, to some degree, the interaction opportunities available in the international system, and the loss of these

Table 7.2. The Impact of Capability Concentration and
Alliance Polarization on Commitment Norms, Controlling
for Alliance Aggregation

	Degree of Alliance Aggregation	
	High	Low
b1 MILCON	.71 (3.49)	−.19 (−.76)
b2 log POLAR	.27 (1.34)	.28 (1.04)
R	.72	.35
R^2	.52	.13
F	6.57, p < .05	.86
DW	2.11	2.35

Note: The entries in parentheses after each standardized regression coefficient contain
t statistics.

opportunities is likely to diminish the freedom of states to maneuver.
Alternatively, when the magnitude of alliance commitments within
the system is low, the aggregate amount of interaction opportunities
will be far greater, thereby encouraging the rise of fluid, amoral alliances and the advent of a permissive legal order. It is in this latter
environment, where alliances are crafted without regard to ideology,
cultural affinities, or personal ties, that we would expect to find
strong support for the norm *rebus sic stantibus,* since it facilitates
swift realignments by allowing states to terminate a treaty of alliance
unilaterally if a fundamental change occurs in those circumstances
that existed at the signing of the agreement.

In order to control for the degree of alliance aggregation, Alan Ned
Sabrosky's (1985a: 161) data on the percentage of all states in an
alliance of any class was used to create high and low subgroups, according to whether a given half-decade was above or below the median level of alliance aggregation for the entire 1820–1969 period.
Table 7.2 presents the results derived from controlling for high versus
low levels of alliance aggregation. As can be seen, the model does
not perform well when the amount of alliance commitments within
the system is low. When the amount of alliance commitments is high,
however, the model does much better, with MILCON being a far
more potent predictor of the content of alliance norms than POLAR.
In other words, at high levels of alliance aggregation, the greater the
degree of concentration in military capabilities, the greater the support for binding commitments by prevailing international norms.

Another intervening variable that has the potential to affect the climate of opinion regarding promissory obligations is the amount of systemic tightness created by alliance agreements. Several factors may produce tight blocs: marginally committed members may withdraw from alliances; new, highly committed states may join; or existing members may choose to upgrade the nature of the commitment (Bueno de Mesquita, 1978: 250). When describing bloc cohesion, most observers refer to the attributes of hierarchy and sectorial scope (Holsti and Sullivan, 1969: 163). The more hierarchically organized a bloc and the wider the range of issue areas in which it operates, the tighter the composition. While all bloc leaders attempt to assimilate the goals of the bloc within their own national goals, Morton A. Kaplan (1957b: 117) asserts that those at the helm of tight blocs are more successful. The primary reason is that within these blocs "everything is political, including trade, culture, and the like; no area of activity is permitted to remain autonomous from political relationships" (Holsti, Hopmann, and Sullivan, 1973: 166–167). Thus any deviation by an ally from its bloc-sanctioned role would constitute a potential challenge to the political order established by the bloc leader; and unlike its counterpart at the head of a loose bloc, a tight bloc leader would not hesitate to use its superior military strength to repress an obstreperous ally since it is not committed to a tradition of bargaining with subordinates (Dinnerstein, 1965: 589–601; Rothgeb, 1981: 494). In short, those countries that belong to tight blocs experience high levels of external penetration and consequently have little decision latitude over whether they may terminate an agreement unilaterally prior to its agreed-upon expiration. Regardless of the degree of capability concentration within the system, tighter alliances are expected to lead to fewer ambiguities in mutual security commitments (Brown, 1987: 72–73) and more support for the norm *pacta sunt servanda*.

In order to control for the degree of alliance cohesion, each half-decade of our temporal domain was classified as tight or loose, depending upon whether it was above or below the median score on Bruce Bueno de Mesquita's (1975: 210–216) index of systemic tightness. Once the time series was partitioned, we found it necessary to use the Cochrane-Orcutt technique of generalized least-squares in our analysis because autocorrelation appeared in the residuals. The results are displayed in Table 7.3.

Contrary to our expectations, controlling for high versus low levels of systemic tightness did not yield impressive results. Although we

Table 7.3. The Impact of Capability Concentration and Alliance Polarization on Commitment Norms, Controlling for Alliance Cohesion

	Degree of Alliance Cohesion	
	Tight	*Loose*
b1 MILCON	.71 (2.75)	−.20 (−.85)
b2 log POLAR	.13 (.54)	.50 (2.15)
R	.66	.63
R^2	.43	.40
F	3.79	3.38
DW	2.19	2.13

Note: The entries in parentheses after each standardized regression coefficient contain *t* statistics.

have accounted for a moderate amount of the variance in the commitment index, the model as a whole was not significant when applied to either subgroup. At high levels of cohesion, MILCON is the only independent variable with a regression coefficient that is significantly greater than zero. Since the coefficient is positive, the results converge with our previous finding that a binding interpretation of promissory obligations tends to surface when military capabilities are highly concentrated in the hands of a few great powers. At low levels of systemic tightness, however, the impact of polarity is less noteworthy. Instead, when the existing blocs of states are loose, the greater the degree of polarization in the configuration of alliances, the greater the support for the sanctity of agreements.

In summary, our refinement of the model (based primarily on controlling for alliance aggregation as an intervening variable) gives moderate support to the hegemonic stability/leadership thesis. Such an interpretation of the data requires that we briefly return to our findings in the previous chapter regarding post-Napoleonic support for a flexible interpretation of promissory obligations, especially given the hegemonic status that long cycle theorists ascribe to Great Britain during the early part of the nineteenth century. Although naval supremacy and vast financial resources provided decision makers in London with unparalleled global reach, Britain did not of itself possess an overwhelming preponderance of capability with which it could orchestrate events on the European continent. In comparison to the other major powers, its average percentage share from 1816 to 1839 of demographic, industrial, and military capabilities (as measured by the Correlates of War composite index) was only 28 percent of the aggregate major power total. Certainly Great Britain was the global leader in the strict sense used by long cycle theorists, but it was not the preponderant state in a unipolar European great power system. Indeed, the level of systemic polarity in the wake of the Napoleonic Wars was considerably less than that which characterized the immediate post-World War II environment. Whereas the average level of military capability concentration (MILCON) was .189 between 1820 and 1839, it stood at .342 between 1946 and 1965 (with scores of .137 and .373 marking respectively the low and high values on this index that were attained during the entire 1820–1969 time span). Thus, unlike after the Second World War, the structure of the great power system following the Napoleonic Wars encouraged the emergence of norms promoting flexibility, which facilitated Great Britain's role as a balancer which often shifted its marginal disposable capabilities from one side of the diplomatic scales to the other in an effort to maintain a European equilibrium.

STRUCTURAL SHIFTS AS A SOURCE OF CHANGE IN THE CONTENT OF ALLIANCE NORMS

Centuries ago, the early Rennaissance Italian city-state system suffered from turmoil born of civil strife between feuding Guelph and Ghibelline parties, imperial competition between rival families, and a broader intellectual conflict between piety and secularism. As a participant in the political life of that era, Dante Alighieri was ultimately swept up by the turbulence of his native Florence and banished under the threat that if he returned he would be burned alive. Casting an admiring glance back to the Rome of Augustus, he advocated centralizing power as a means bringing order to a chaotic world.

In the spirit of Dante, the major conclusion reached from the evidence examined in this chapter is that a restrictive legal order that contains international norms supportive of strict adherence to promissory obligations is most likely to emerge when military capabilities are highly concentrated and the level of alliance aggregation is high. In contrast, when the international system swings into a phase during which military capabilities become more dispersed and interstate amities and enmities are not clustered into clear, antagonistic blocs, we find that the international legal order contains far greater support for the norm *rebus sic stantibus*.

These results provide an empirical underpinning for the long-standing but untested theoretical argument that system structure is one of the main sources of international norms (e.g., see Brown, 1988: 14). They also prompt speculation about how alliance treaty norms interact with system structure to affect the stability of the international system, a topic that will be explored in greater detail in Chapters 8 and 9.

One of the topics about which such speculation often occurs pertains to the consequences of different polarity configurations. Advocates of bipolarity assert that a world containing two centers of power that are militarily preponderant relative to the next tier of states will be stable because the heightened tension accompanying a great power duopoly encourages the bloc leaders to exercise caution, to assume greater responsibility for their actions, and to restrain the crisis-provoking, aggressive actions of their subordinate allies. Conversely, those favoring multipolarity believe that the parity of a great power oligopoly will be stable because a rise in interaction opportunities increases the chances of cross-cutting rather than overlapping cleavages, and because a diminution in the share of attention that can be allocated among many potential adversaries reduces the rigidity of conflicts. In rebuttal, the former submit that owing to this lack of clarity, multipolarity will promote war through miscalculation. The latter retort that lacking suppleness, bipolarity will deteriorate into a struggle for supremacy.[14]

Initial research on the relationship between power distributions and war unearthed a perplexing finding, one that exacerbated the debate

---

14. Advocates of bipolarity include Riker (1962), Waltz (1964), and Zoppo (1966); while Wright (1965), Gulick (1955), Kaplan (1957b), and Deutsch and Singer (1964) back the argument in favor of multipolarity. These disagreements at the systemic level of analysis over whether the onset of war is affected by the distribution of capabilities are paralleled by similar debates at the dyadic level. Some theorists argue that "mistrust and even status create a compulsion to war" (Pfister, 1974: 61), while others reply that equality between the members of a dyad promotes peace (Kahn, 1960: 759). Although most of the empirical research supports the contention that preponderance deters war (e.g., see Garnham 1976a, 1976b; Weede, 1976), some researchers maintain that "few wars result between states that are closely balanced in power capabilities" (Ferris, 1973: 123; also see Smith, 1982: 74). In an effort to reconcile these seemingly antithetical findings, Benjamin A. Most and Harvey Starr (1987) demonstrate that neither dyadic preponderance nor dyadic parity is logically sufficient for conflict initiation. Certain types of dyadic power distributions, whether they are preponderant or balanced, may have greater potentials for conflict, but this potential may not be actualized if national leaders lack the necessary willingness to exploit the opportunities they encounter. According to Henk Hou-

over the relative merits of different polarity configurations. The diffusion of capabilities toward approximate parity among many states seemed to preserve peace in the nineteenth century, and a high, stable concentration of capabilities among very few states looked as if it safeguarded peace in the twentieth century (Singer, Bremer, and Stuckey, 1972). More recently, however, Bruce Bueno de Mesquita (1981) has accounted for this puzzling finding by showing that any given configuration of power could produce either war or peace depending on the risk-taking propensities of national leaders.[15] Both peace through parity and peace through preponderance can be supported in isolated instances, contingent upon the extent to which leaders are risk-acceptant or risk-averse.

Nevertheless, even if the distribution of capability does not determine whether war will occur, apparently it does affect the form a war will take if it is fought (Vasquez, 1986: 315). Polarized alliances, a multipolar distribution of capability, and relatively equal strength on both sides all play important roles in shaping the type of war that occurs. According to John A. Vasquez (1987b: 132), "increasing polarization of blocs makes for longer wars, multipolar distribution of power makes for wars of greater magnitude, and equal capability between blocs increases the severity of wars" (see Levy, 1985a; Levy and Morgan, 1984; Wayman, 1984; and Thompson, 1983). This conclusion, combined with the finding in this chapter that a deconcentration of military capabilities is associated with support for *rebus sic stantibus,* leads us to infer that the international system will probably experience greater conflict when statesmen interpret promissory obligations in a way that allows them considerable leeway to opt in or out of alliances on an ad hoc basis.

Such an inference is obviously unsettling given that the global community is now facing what Raimo Väyrynen (1988: 7) calls the pro-

---

weling and Jan G. Siccama (1988), the type of dyadic power distribution that has the greatest potential for war is a distribution characterized by rough equality but one side rapidly overtaking the other.

15. In a related study, Charles W. Ostrom and John H. Aldrich (1978) did not find support for any of the leading hypotheses that link the number of prominent, independent actors in the major power system to the probability of war. Regardless of the size of the major power system and the distribution of power within it, the potential initiation of war may be not only conditional on whether national leaders are risk-acceptant or risk-averse, but also on prevailing attitudes within the international system toward war *qua* war (Lebow, 1981: 247–254) and the extent to which normative rules have been developed to control the use of force (Wallensteen, 1984; Kegley and Raymond, 1986).

cess of devolution. As military and economic capabilities have diffused from the major powers to secondary and peripheral states, and as the divisions within the U.S.- and Soviet-led blocs have widened, disagreements about alliance duties and responsibilities have become commonplace within both NATO and the Warsaw Pact. Simply put, the international system has become bipolycentric (Spanier, 1975). Although the United States and the Soviet Union still possess military superiority over the remaining members of the state system, multiple centers of political decision now exist. Pressures for dealignment within this hybrid structure may not result in a dismantling of the formal institutions of either alliance, but it will mean changing the scope of alliance commitments (Kaldor and Falk, 1987). In the words of Silviu Brucan (1984: 103), "We are witnessing a crucial conflict in world politics: the old thrust toward centralization of power is now clashing with the drive to decentralize power."

Insofar as the process of devolution has been associated historically with a shift in the prevailing interpretation given by statesmen to promissory obligations, let us redirect our attention from the sources of alliance norm transformation to its consequences. Are shifts in the content of alliance norms related to the onset of crises and war? If so, are we correct in our earlier inference that movement away from the sanctity of agreements is destablizing? Or, is Anthony Carty (1986: 77) correct in proposing that an increasing insistence on the obligatory character of treaties may be an indication that the system is about to disintegrate? Eminently reasonable arguments can be made for the validity of both positions. Because "the relevance of law to conflict," as Richard A. Falk (1968a: 42) reminds us, "is a matter to be settled by systematic empirical inquiry" rather than by conjecture, it is to such an inquiry that we turn in the next chapter.

Part IV

The Consequences of Alliance Norm Transformation

8 Alliance Norms and the Control of International Crises

Policy options may . . . be reduced materially by initiating or increasing alliance commitments during a crisis, especially with partners who cannot be depended upon to view the resulting obligations as reciprocal. Such pledges may ultimately force a choice between two unpalatable alternatives: reducing the commitment under threat, thereby seriously eroding one's credibility in the future; or backing the promise to the hilt, with the possibility of becoming a prisoner to the ally's policies.

Ole R. Holsti

The structure of any international crisis is organic rather than artificial; it is the result of gradual growth; and however much one may seek to detach and mount the specimens for purposes of exposition, it must never be forgotten that at the time they were part of the thought, feeling, and action of sentient human beings, exposed to all the impulses and fallibility of human nature.

Harold Nicolson

Throughout history disagreements between states have escalated into military confrontations. To reduce the threat of war, these confrontations must be managed, a task that requires policymakers to weigh the trade-offs between a variety of complex alternatives and make choices under stress. Among the factors that policymakers must consider are the expectations each side has of the other and the forms of behavior generally regarded as permissible by members of the international community. International norms delineate the range of acceptable policy choice and thereby limit the options considered. Even in situations of extreme threat and reduced decision time, which liberate policymaking processes from the customary constraints on decisions, statesmen are likely to frame the policy choices available to them in terms of prevailing practices and norms (Scheinman and Wilkinson, 1968). Indeed, respect for prevailing norms may increase rather than diminish during a crisis.

Confronted with a state of emergency demanding immediate action, leaders are forced to give consideration to choices they can otherwise largely ignore. During such times, they are required to address three interrelated questions: (1) What position should they take on their state's commitments? (2) What principles of conduct are likely to guide the response of adversaries and allies? and (3) What attitudes regarding the irrevocability of commitments do they wish to see held by other members of the international system? These questions are important, a decision is unavoidable, and the results that flow from the actions undertaken are consequential. Leaders must live with the consequences of their choices, whether they decide to honor their commitments or to renege on them when changed circumstances increase the costs of compliance. Their choices will not only determine whether others will be willing to trust their word in future encounters, but will also affect the normative climate within which other states subsequently interact. Moreover, during a crisis the shared expectations about the probability of allies coming to the aid of the threatened state, and of the aggressor's ability to count on the assistance of its allies, will affect the number of parties to the dispute and, undoubtedly, its ultimate outcome. Thus, those normative principles that define the extent of one's obligation to fulfill commitments to allies have a direct impact on the prospects for resolving disputes peacefully.

The relationship between the reliability of alliance commitments and the occurrence of international crises has had a prominent place in theoretical discussions of world politics. In particular, this relationship has received special attention in the *realpolitik* literature that stresses the endemic nature of international conflict, the insatiable struggle among states for power, and the repetitive tests of states' resolve provoked by this competition. Confrontations fostered by rivalry and suspicion encourage states to turn to allies for defense assistance. It is during crises, when a state's security and survival are threatened, that reliable allies are most required, and when the capacity of treaties to couple the hesitant will be most needed. Not only do enemies probe each other's resistance and strength, but states also challenge the resolve of each other's allies during such times. Intense fear of foes increases the need for faithful friends. In this atmosphere where trust in others is minimal, the degree to which international norms sanction the opportunistic disavowal of commitments may be crucial in determining if an alliance treaty actually binds its signatory parties and thereby makes a given pact meaningful. For at the brink of war, allies' commitments to one another will receive their ultimate test: ties will either bind or break.

For example, when the Vietnam conflict escalated, the guarantees contained in the SEATO alliance were put to the test. In response, Australia, New Zealand, Thailand, the Philippines, and the United States adhered to the SEATO treaty, whereas certain other signatories, such as Britain, France, and Pakistan, failed to abide by the spirit if not the letter of their prior agreement. During this crisis, the norms were not strong enough to bind all signatories, with the result that the alliance failed to achieve the purposes for which it had been designed. Thus, in an international crisis prevailing alliance norms may influence decisions as to whether to honor commitments and thereby determine whether alliances make the expected contribution to mutual security.

The nature of crises bring into focus some empirical questions that contain very pragmatic policy implications. Have changes in the content of commitment norms been associated with fluctuations in the frequency, scope, or intensity of serious disputes among states? If so, what is the nature of these associations? What do they tell us about the norms that policymakers should embrace in order to more often succeed in peacefully reconciling their differences? What do they imply about the uses in diplomacy to which alliances and promises can most effectively be put?

This chapter focuses on these questions, the crux of the nihilist-idealist debate discussed in Chapter 2. Historical evidence is probed to ascertain whether changes in those normative principles that bear upon the reliability of commitments among allies have been associated with changes in the frequency, scope, or intensity of crises between major powers.

THE NATURE OF INTERNATIONAL CRISES

Although the concept of international crisis is frequently referred to, it is an ambiguous term. Sometimes it is used at the national level of analysis; at other times it is used at the systemic level (Brecher and Wilkenfeld, 1989). In order to clarify the meaning that we shall attach to the concept, we shall define and conceptualize it at the international level in accordance with the logic outlined in Chapter 5.

International crises represent departures from the usual volume of international events, ''a 'change of state' in the flow of international political actions'' (McClelland, 1968: 160). Indeed, one of the primary distinguishing features of international crises is that, while they are attended by dramatic increases in hostile interactions between at least two conflicting members of the international system (Zinnes,

Zinnes, and McClure, 1972), they have system-disrupting consequences whose impact extends far beyond the security of the immediate participants. "A crisis," Oran R. Young (1968b: 19) notes, "is a situation which disrupts the system or some part of the system." Thus if not managed successfully a crisis may potentially transform the system. "In any given international system, critical variables must be maintained within certain limits or the instability of the system will be greatly increased—perhaps to the point where a new system will be formed" (Hermann, 1972b: 10).

By their very nature, then, international crises are both norm-reinforcing and norm-transforming events. They occur when conditions change rapidly and when states are confronted with threat, that is, when their trust of others and their own confidence in the best approach to security is most suspended. Crises shape the climate of opinion that will dominate the future conduct of diplomacy, for they will either strengthen the prevalent principles of conduct or set precedents for the inauguration of a new pattern of expected behavior.

> Although crises are not always distinct turning points in international politics, at a minimum they tend to strengthen pre-existing trends. Furthermore, the behaviour of the participants in a crisis will affect not only their images of each other—and thereby their future attitude and behaviour towards one another—but also the image that other states hold of them. Once conceived, these images may be difficult to change. Even when a crisis is resolved without open hostilities, therefore, its repercussions will usually be persuasive if not immediately dramatic. (P. Williams, 1976: 13)

Uppermost among all the repercussions that result from the ways policymakers manage the crises they encounter is the image they create about the credibility and reliability of their pledged word. Their conduct during a crisis will inspire either confidence or distrust in their subsequent promises to others. For when threatened by aggression, doubt and distrust in the motives of others, accompanied by a loss of control and confidence, combine to increase incentives to practice deceit and renege on prior promises. It is therefore at times of crisis, more so than any other, that a state's core values about the sanctity of oaths are most revealed. Prevailing norms regarding promissory obligations will be thrown into sharp focus by diplomatic practice in situations where national interests are most threatened, and where unusual opportunities are created to cite *raison d'état* as a rationale for abandoning treaty obligations. As "a situation requiring a choice between mutually incompatible but highly valued objectives'' (Morse, 1973: 127), a crisis is an occasion when values must be clarified and prioritized. Like times of rapid change in general, so also to a greater degree ''A time of crisis . . . creates receptivity to new ideas . . . and it generates a willingness to take risks'' (Falk, 1980: 42). The feelings of uncertainty and anxiety accompanying a crisis result in part from this disagreeable attribute of crisis situations.

A foreign policy crisis refers to the situation experienced by a state threatened with aggression by another. Charles F. Hermann's (1972b: 6–8) definition is widely accepted as authoritative: ''a crisis is a situation that (1) threatens the high-priority goals of the decision-making units, (2) restricts the amount of time available for response before the decision is transformed, and (3) surprises the members of the decision-making unit by its occurrence.'' When viewed from the perspective of the system, ''the main features of international crises are: (1) acute and rapid changes in the variety of intensity of interaction patterns among states, (2) decreased systemic stability, (3) increased probability of violence in the system, and (4) short duration'' (Maoz, 1982: 16).

As summarized in Table 8.1, crises at the national level create pressures that upset existing decision-making structures and routines, and they affect the kinds of options that states might seize by opening the door to new policy initiatives. At the international level, they heighten system tension and call into question states' commitments and intentions; they comprise the ultimate security issue because ''an international crisis is a sequence of interactions between the governments of two or more sovereign states in severe conflict, short of actual war, but involving the perception of a dangerously high probability of war'' (Snyder and Diesing, 1988: 87; emphasis deleted). At both levels, crisis conditions provoke reconsideration of prior pledges by others and challenge the reliability of previous commitments to allies.

As hostile forms of competitive bargaining, it is important to accentuate the fact that crises often perform one of the primary functions for which war traditionally has been used, namely, to force an enemy to comply with one's wishes. They are a means of resolving with minimal violence those disputes that are too intense to be settled by routinized procedures. A crisis is appropriately regarded as something that lies in an intermediate zone between peace and war

Table 8.1. Attributes of International Crises

Definitional Characteristics and Precipitant Causes
- circumstances change rapidly, therein surprising policymakers
- environmental change conveys a message of direct threat to the nation's core values
- pressure exists for prompt decisions in the absence of full information
- the amount of time available for formulating a policy response is greatly constricted
- decisions must be reached when feelings of uncertainty and unpredictability are accompanied by fear and urgency
- the expectation of armed conflict increases
- the threat of escalation to war is regarded as high

Policymaking Consequences
- interrupts the processes by which foreign policy decisions are routinely made
- concentrates decision-making power in the hands of leaders and their immediate advisers
- intensifies the search for policy options and evaluation of available alternatives
- precipitates rigorous reconsideration of national interests
- focuses great attention on the intentions of adversaries and allies
- increases dependence on allies' commitments while diminishing confidence in their reliability
- raises uncertainty about the probable outcomes of various policy choices
- expands the capacity of decisionmakers to depart from established policy and chart innovative new directions and relations with others
- increases the amount of communication via adversaries and allies

Systemic Impact
- intensifies the level of hostility with enemies and the level of conflict and/or cooperation between allies

Table 8.1. Attributes of International Crises (continued)

Systemic Impact (continued)

- affects and potentially modifies the essential structural variables of the international system, including the possible delegitimation of existing norms and their replacement with new ones
- either increases the cohesion of alliance systems or leads to their fragmentation

---

(Lebow, 1981).[1] How decision makers manage these threatening situations largely determines whether a war will in fact result, because "almost all wars are preceded by a crisis of sort, although of course not all crises eventuate in war" (Snyder and Diesing, 1988: 90).

Given the definition of international crisis as a situation characterized by an increase in the intensity of conflictual interactions between adversaries and a high probability of military hostilities, to what indicator can we turn to monitor changes in their frequency and intensity? For this purpose, the construct serious interstate disputes (SIDs) is useful. International crises are invariably products of militarized disputes, in that they result from situations where one state confronts another with a military threat. SIDs refer to "state actions involving threats to use military force, displays of military force, or actual uses of military force." Operationally, SIDs are explicit, overt, nonaccidental, and government-directed or sanctioned actions (see Gochman and Maoz, 1984).

Figure 8.1 shows the number of "militarized interstate disputes," as defined by these criteria, that occurred from 1816 to 1976.[2] These

---

1. According to this conception, crises that culminate in violence cease to be crises and become wars. Examples of wars that were preceded by a crisis include World War I, Suez (1956), and Kashmir (1948). Conversely, some situations popularly termed crises in fact do not meet these criteria. The "oil shock" that characterized the global energy situation during the OPEC decade of the 1970s is an example. Surely the situation involved threat, but neither surprise nor, somewhat less so, time pressure could be appropriately used to describe it, and the potential use of force to resolve the dispute was not perceived to be high.

2. For additional empirical evidence on the historical frequency of international crises, see Abolfathi, Hayes, and Hayes (1979), Hopple, Rossa, and Wilkenfeld (1980), Mahoney and Clayberg (1980), Brecher and James (1986), and Brecher, Wilkenfeld, and Moser (1988). For a systematic analysis of the determinants of crisis outcomes, see Brecher and Wilkenfeld (1982).

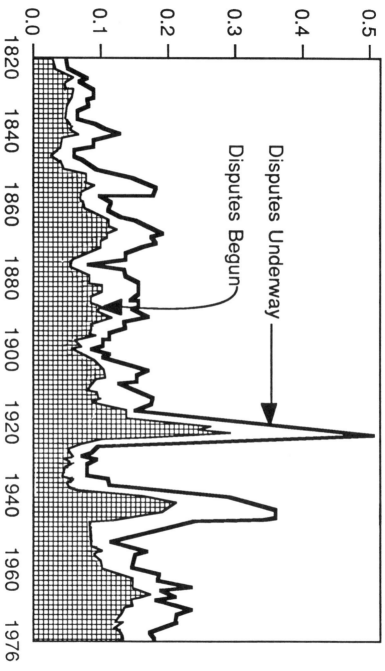

Figure 8.1. Fluctuations in the Number of Serious Interstate Disputes, 1816–1976.
Note: The data on serious disputes are normalized for system size and are derived from
Gochman and Maoz (1984).

data suggest several conclusions: the number of SIDs has moderately increased over time; the average number of SIDs under way has risen in the twentieth century in comparison to the nineteenth; the era surrounding both world wars has been the most crisis-ridden; and the nuclear era has experienced a consistently high level of such confrontations. Over 40 percent of all the crises between 1816 and 1976 are estimated to have arisen in the three decades following World War II.[3] Between 1946 and 1976 an average of 12.7 military disputes began each year, and an average of 18.2 were under way annually (Gochman and Maoz, 1984: 592). (The fact that the more recent periods have experienced relatively greater numbers of militarized disputes lies behind the widespread impression that contemporary world politics is in a state of perpetual crises.) To these conclusions can be added the observations that the duration of interstate crises has increased and that the superpowers have been the most active participants in postwar crisis events.[4]

What impact, if any, have alliance norms had on this pattern? Our intent in this chapter is to determine whether changes in the incidence of international crises have been historically associated with changes

---

3. Additional data on international crises between 1928 and 1979 confirm this pattern (Brecher, Wilkenfeld, and Moser, 1988). This evidence demonstrates that the incidence of international crises concentrated around the major war in the system during this time frame (World War II), with the years 1936–1941 and 1945–1950 being periods of particular instability. Moreover, this evidence reveals that the global atmosphere has been charged with the threat of war especially between roughly 1960 and 1963, which represents the transition from a bipolar to a bipolycentric power distribution. This "turning point" in international affairs that witnessed important shifts in the strategic balance toward parity (see Chapter 7) and an accompanying shift in strategic thinking about the role of nuclear weapons away from offense and toward deterrence and defense (see Goldberg, 1989). Finally, this evidence shows that the most recent years covered by these data (1975–1979) have been among the most crisis-prone, suggesting a general increase over time in the incidence with which threats to global peace under conditions of crisis have been prevalent.

4. According to two studies by the Brookings Institution, the United States and the Soviet Union have been especially apt to use or threaten to use force to achieve their foreign policy objectives, often in conflicts within other nations. According to these studies, "gunboat diplomacy" was used 215 times by the United States (an average of 7.2 incidents per year over a thirty-year period since the end of World War II) (Blechman and Kaplan, 1978: 547–553); in contrast, there were 156 recorded instances of Soviet attempts to use or threaten to use force to achieve foreign political objectives (Kaplan, 1981: 689–693). For further documentation of this pattern of superpower behavior, see Zelikow (1987).

in the content of commitment norms among allies. To introduce this inquiry, let us examine more closely the cultural conditions under which crisis decision making unfolds.

THE NORMATIVE SETTING FOR CRISIS DECISION MAKING

Crises are situations of danger that can produce either disaster and destruction or success and survival. A multiplicity of demands, cross-pressures, and uncertainties face a decision maker when crises erupt. Apprehension increases due to the lack of information. For all policy-makers, the "essence of crisis is its unpredictability" (Schelling, 1966: 97). Yet "cognitive research suggests that people are simple information processors during both routine and crisis decision periods" (Powell, Purkitt, and Dyson 1987: 213). To reduce uncertainty and fears when feelings of a loss of control and confidence are evoked, people are prone to rely on their expectations and for this purpose to heighten the attention paid to established practices and normatively approved principles of conduct. During crises policymakers are inclined to manage the decision-making task by placing it within a set of rules. Normally statesmen accomplish this by relying on norms for guidance about the feasible, legal, and politically acceptable options available.

> [D]ecision-makers do not approach a crisis with a mind that is a *tabula rasa*. Their view of events will always be structured by their beliefs, perceptions, and values and their own *internal* political calculation of the costs, benefits, and risks of any given course of action. If the domestic political atmosphere in which the crisis erupts is already menacing and key values held by the decision-maker are threatened, the definition, evaluation of, and solution to the problem will be structured largely by those values which are at risk. In such situations, the decision-maker will feel enormous constraints. . . .

> [D]uring a crisis when supreme political values are at stake, the prevailing political climate at the time the crisis breaks . . . can exert a decisive influence on the policy choices of the decision-maker to the detriment of the national interest. (Hampson, 1988: 246)

"Statesmen," Donald J. Puchala and Raymond Hopkins (1983: 86) have observed, "nearly always perceive themselves to be constrained by pinciples, norms, and rules that prescribe and proscribe varieties of behavior." Those perceptions are likely to be especially prevalent in stressful situations where crises encourage serious consideration of the range of acceptable choice defined by prevailing norms. In comparison with other situations, the force of normative expectations may either decrease or increase in crises; nevertheless decision makers remain confined by them. Among the primary constraints under which they operate are existing policy goals, which consist of the commitments, practices, and orientations of their predecessors. In fact, faced with the perceived need to do something, decision makers in crises will be especially sensitive to prior commitments, practices, and orientations, if for no reason other than that the high-priority interests threatened by crisis situations are embedded within existing policy goals. The tendency to equate successful crisis management with the restoration of precrisis conditions may also be operative.

What factors are likely to weigh heavily on national leaders when circumstances require immediate decisions whose consequences are far-reaching and fateful? Foremost among these factors is the leader's beliefs about the intentions, perceptions, and code of conduct of the enemy, as well as those of allies on whose reactions the disputants may have to depend in order to resolve the conflict without loss of face, power, or life. To succeed, realistic estimates of adversaries and allies must be obtained. For this, decision makers must rely on their images of the norms that they assume will most influence the choices others will select. Thus the outcome may depend on their capability to accurately judge the posture toward promissory obligations lodged in the minds of others.

As noted about international norms generally (Chapters 1, 2, and 5), the extent to which policymakers have assimilated the values and norms of the international culture at the times they face crisis decisions are not amenable to direct observation.

> It is difficult to analyze the impact of background considerations upon crisis policy because of the problems involved in reconstructing policy-makers' understanding of them. Policy-makers rarely articulate their assessment of the relative importance of the host of environmental conditions which influence any particular decision. They are more likely to acknowledge the importance of these conditions obliquely, in ways that are difficult to translate into useful analytical categories. Policy-makers are themselves often unaware of the complex motivations that underlie their behavior. James Joll writes: "When political leaders are faced with the necessity of making decisions the outcome of which they cannot foresee, in crises which they do not wholly understand, they fall back on their own instinctive reactions, traditions and modes of behavior. Each of them has certain beliefs, rules or objectives which

are taken for granted; and one of the limitations of documentary evidence is that few people bother to write down, especially in moments of crisis, things which they take for granted. But if we are to understand their motives, we must somehow try to find out what, as we say, 'goes without saying.' '' (Lebow, 1981: 229–230)

Thus, although it can be assumed that policymakers will depend on prevailing norms to predict the likely reactions of allies and adversaries during times of crisis, the extent of that reliance cannot be estimated precisely. We cannot ascertain the degree to which policymakers felt confined by prevailing normative constraints at the time they were forced by the situation to define the range of policy options.

Nonetheless, this epistemological difficulty does not diminish the importance of psychocultural factors as determinants of conduct. One of the ironies of crisis situations is that although they remove many of the customary impediments to policy innovation, the limited time frame within which decisions must be reached precludes long-range planning and an exhaustive deliberation of all available alternatives. Under duress of threat, and in the absence of adequate time and information, decision makers are prone to reason by analogy and to defer to precedents (May, 1973). For this, they tend to rely on their historical recollections and normative beliefs about what is accepted as permissible (Neustadt and May, 1986). In other words, it is reasonable to assume that norms help to define in the minds of policymakers the range of permissible foreign policy goals and alternatives, although in ways the decision maker himself may not be fully aware. The influence of norms "lies in [the] power to set reasonably fixed limits to political behavior and provide subliminal direction for political action . . . ; limits and direction all the more effective because of their antiquity and subtlety whereby those limited are unaware of the limitations placed upon them" (Elazar, 1970: 257).

This impact is illustrated in many crisis episodes. For example, during the Cuban missile crisis Robert Kennedy's argument against using an air strike to destroy the Soviet missiles in Cuba illustrates how norms may govern the ways choices are often made.

Whatever validity the military and political arguments were for an attack in preference to a blockade, America's traditions and history would not permit such a course of action. Whatever military reasons [former Secretary of State Dean Acheson] and others could marshal, they were nevertheless, in the last analysis, advocating a surprise attack by a very large nation against a very small one. This, I said, could not be undertaken by the U.S. if we were to maintain our moral position at home and around the globe. Our struggle against Communism throughout the world was far more than physical survival—it had as its essence our heritage and our ideals, and these we must not destroy. (Kennedy, 1971: 16–17)

Although it is warranted to assume that decision making during a crisis will inevitably be influenced by the norms and expectations of the leaders making those decisions, that influence is neither direct nor easy to document. As noted in Chapter 5, we cannot observe those thoughts, feelings, and normative values that guided the choices made by decision makers in a crisis.

In addition to the other reasons for conceiving of norms as attributes of the international system at large, this obstacle to analysis requires exploration of the systemic consequences of alternate norms during crisis situations. The assumption underlying this treatment is that it is through policymakers' perceptions of the "unspoken rules of diplomacy" that the linkage between actor and system is established. "Although a crisis is catalyzed by behavioral actions, these actions, the trigger to a unit-level crisis, can always be traced to their perceptual origin. Here lies the organic link between the two levels of crisis [the system level and unit levels of analysis]" (Brecher and James, 1986: 30).

Our focus, therefore, is on systemic rather than national properties. It does not investigate crises from the standpoint of the individual statesmen experiencing them, but instead follows the approach taken by Michael Brecher and Patrick James (1986: 22) by specifying "change in the system components, process, and structure [through an examination of] system attributes, stability and equilibrium." This conception is consistent with the macro-level, historical inquiry of alliance norms discussed in Chapters 4 and 5. Our inquiry seeks to examine the relationship between alliance norms and international security, rather than focusing on the effects of a particular state's posture toward its alliance commitments and its impact on the state's subsequent national security. Because "we can distinguish between system-related definitions and decision-related definitions of international crises" (Maoz, 1982: 16), it is important to keep the distinction in mind and to emphasize that it is with respect to the former level of analysis that this investigation is appropriately confined.

FLEXIBILITY AND COMMITMENT AS FACTORS INFLUENCING THE ONSET OF INTERNATIONAL CRISIS

Do certain types of alliance norms reduce the frequency of crises and lower the probability that serious disputes will escalate to war? Which culture is more conducive to the successful management of international crisis: one with a restrictive climate that prescribes the faithful performance of treaty obligations, or a permissive climate that condones the violation of pledges between allies when changed conditions make compliance costly? Conflict theory as well as conventional diplomatic wisdom are divided on the answers: "Though steeped in war preparations, modern alliances . . . have also been rated as instruments of peace in the precarious conditions of these times. Alliances have in fact shown this duality of personality—war promotion and peace-seeking—throughout the ages" (Friedman, 1970: 3).

As stated in Chapter 3, a substantial portion of the literature on this problem as well as the beliefs embedded in diplomatic practice operate from the inviting assumption that the willingness of states to honor treaty commitments when crises erupt adds stability to the international system. From this point of view, norms that support compliance with treaty commitments limit conflict and increase predictability. During a crisis, uncertainty increases; therefore, support for the norm that agreements between allies are binding facilitates the management of these militarized disputes by adding greater predictability, order, and mutual confidence to the relations among nations.[5]

On the other hand, theory and diplomatic experience are equally cogent in suggesting that there are many problems associated with binding commitments. The crises that preceded World War I are the preeminent illustration; to some, the lesson of 1914 was that disputes between smaller states allied to the major powers contributed to the onset of a global war. To those historians, World War I was sparked by the crises and expanded into a general war when the great powers exceeded the obligations required of them (see Richardson, 1988). According to this point of view, unwarranted support for smaller al-

---

5. The advent of the Korean War is often cited to illustrate this principle because this episode is generally regarded as having been precipitated by the uncertainty created by Secretary of State Dean Acheson's ambiguous signals about the willingness of the United States to abide by its commitment to come to the aid of South Korea in the event of an external attack upon it.

lies locked in a serious dispute may be dangerous in an atmosphere of crisis because of the probability that other powers will become ensnarled. During periods when the inviolability of oaths are dominant, it is more difficult for national leaders to preserve room to maneuver: they find it hard to escape obligations and sever ties with allies, with the result that they may become entrapped in their allies' disputes. To put it another way, systemic uncertainty may not be altogether destabilizing, insofar as it may inhibit the risk taking from which crises emerge and which tends to accompany the behavior of those most involved in them. A permissive environment thus may reduce the frequency of interstate disputes by deterring countries from responding to emergent conflicts with the threat of force, and by decoupling others from those that arise. Conversely, as commitments come to be regarded as more binding in a restrictive environment, the number of parties of disputes may actually increase and antagonisms may grow more, not less, intense. The prescription that follows is that leaders should not promote the binding norms of a restrictive legal order. The international system would be less crisis-prone in the absence of norms that insist alliance commitments be steadfastly respected.

Thus, diplomatic and theoretical discourse point to contradictory conclusions. Some individuals hypothesize that binding agreements dampen the sparks of international crises, while others hypothesize that they will lead them to engulf allies in the flames of war. To evaluate the relative merits of these arguments and thereby help resolve this controversy, the consequences that result when either of these antithetical norms gain force must be analyzed. To ascertain which perspective has the most to recommend it and better predict the effects that will result when either binding or flexible norms receive support in the international community, we now turn to examine the available historical evidence.

First a statistical test of these rival hypotheses with the available data from the post-Napoleonic era is presented. This is followed by a case study of the origins of the Cold War—a protracted series of international crises emerging between former allies that was profoundly influenced by the failure of both great powers to comply with the agreements they reached with one another during and in the immediate aftermath of World War II. The findings from that case of crisis decision making during very rapidly changing conditions serve to illustrate as well as refine the findings from the preceding macro-quantitative historical analysis.

STATISTICAL TESTS OF THE INFLUENCE
OF ALLIANCE NORMS

We first address the question of whether binding conceptions of alliance commitments increase or decrease the extent to which serious disputes occur among the major powers. This is approached in three ways: we begin with a bivariate analysis of the 1820–1914 time period, followed with a replication using different data and an enlarged spatial domain, and conclude with a multivariate analysis that controls for possible intervening variables.

The rationale for selecting the 1820–1914 time period can be summarized as follows. First, studies by Patrick J. McGowan and Robert M. Rood (1975), Brian Job (1976), Randolph Siverson and George Duncan (1976), Richard Li and William Thompson (1978), and George Duncan and Randolph Siverson (1982) have demonstrated that this was a period when the balance of power was multipolar and temporal and spatial distribution of alliance formation was random. Second, various researchers (e.g., Chi, 1968: 424; Franke, 1968: 454–456) have pointed to the scarcity of reliable alliance commitments as a key factor in producing the serious disputes that led to the breakdown of other balance-of-power systems. Third, many legal theorists postulate that authoritative international law flourishes during balance-of-power periods (Hoffmann, 1961: 214–215). Finally, this period was one in which decision makers expended considerable effort in developing "rules of the game" to regulate competition and thereby prevent crises (Lauren, 1983: 35). In sum, the 1820–1914 time frame constitutes a crucial historical test: we expect that changes in the reliability of alliance commitments will be related to the incidence of serious disputes during this "golden age for international law" (Hoffmann, 1968: xvii).

As noted above, international crises have been defined operationally as serious militarized disputes (SID). The raw data on these events have been collected by the Correlates of War (COW) project (Wallace, 1979: 9–11), and these data have been used to create three outcome variables, which have been aggregated by five-year intervals: *frequency* (the number of serious disputes normalized by major power sub-system size); *scope* (the percentage of major powers involved in serious disputes); and *intensity* (the percentage of major power disputes that escalated to war).[6]

---

6. See Singer and Small (1972: 23) for a discussion of the membership criteria used by the Correlates of War project to define the "major power subsystem." Our analysis is restricted to the European major powers.

Table 8.2 presents the results from a simple bivariate analysis of the relationship between the macro indicator of alliance treaty commitment described in Chapter 4 and the frequency, scope, and intensity of serious major power disputes. Insofar as the existence of autocorrelated disturbances in our time series data would make least-squares estimators inefficient, we used generalized least squares (GLS) regression analysis.

Although the magnitude of the correlations is modest at best, their negative direction indicates that serious major power disputes decreased as alliance commitments came to be seen as binding. That is, international crises were less frequent, involved fewer parties, and escalated to war less often when the legal order placed emphasis on the principle that states are obligated to fulfill their commitments to allies.

To strengthen the grounds for our inference that binding alliance norms are inversely related to international crises, a second body of evidence can be examined. For purposes of convergent validation, we shall now extend our analysis to include dependent variables derived from the data set assembled by Randolph Siverson and Michael Tennefoss (1982). This supplementary data set consists of conflict events that involve one or more major powers. These events are categorized into the following three levels of hostility.

I. *Threat:* either an explicit verbal statement threatening overt military mobilization, or mobilization itself directed at a target state or states but with no actual use of force;

II. *Unreciprocated Military Action:* direct military force taken by one state against a non-responding target state;

III. *Reciprocated Military Action:* military force taken by one state which provokes the target state to engage the initiator in military combat. (Siverson and Tennefoss, 1982: 152–153)

Since our index of alliance commitment gives a composite score for each half-decade we observe, three dependent variables were created by aggregating the number of each type of conflict event at five-year intervals, and then normalizing the data to control for the size of the interstate system. Additionally, because the coding procedure used by Siverson and Tennefoss constitutes a three-point hostility scale, a fourth dependent variable was created by weighing and summing each event that occurred during a particular half-decade.

**Table 8.2. Bivariate Relationships Between Norms Regarding
the Extent of Treaty Commitments and Serious Major
Power Disputes, 1820–1914**

Extent to Which Commitments are Considered Binding

Outcome Variable	r	b	ρ	DW
Frequency	−.42	−.71	−.43	1.49
Scope	−.37	−.98	−.34	2.01
Intensity	−.20	−.12	−.21	1.94

Table 8.3 presents the results from a GLS analysis of the relationship between alliance commitment and the four outcome variables
taken from the Siverson and Tennefoss conflict-event data set. Unlike
the previous table, which concentrated on disputes between major
powers, in Table 8.3 the spatial domain has been expanded to include
those disputes in which at least one major power participated. The
results of the GLS analysis reveal, again, only a modest relationship,
but the negative directions of the slopes and correlation coefficients
support the inference that interstate conflict tends to decrease as alliance commitments come to be seen as binding.

Controlling for Intervening Variables

Obviously, bivariate analyses of this kind provide a preliminary investigation into the relationship between international norms and serious major power disputes. Therefore we need to find additional ways
to acquire evidence that will strengthen the grounds for inference
about the nature of the association.

One possibility would be to examine the relationship between alliance commitment and serious disputes while controlling for the dynamic movement of states in and out of alliance with one another.
Traditionally, studies of alliance dynamics have conceptualized this
kind of flexibility in a structural sense, that is, in terms of the degree
to which alliances are equiprobable and time-independent. It is conceivable that the relationships reported in Tables 8.2 and 8.3 are spurious, with the correlations between commitment norms and serious
disputes being due to the fact that changes in structural flexibility
were mutually related to both variables. Thus we need to determine
whether the rate of alliance formation was a hidden intervening vari-

Table 8.3. Bivariate Relationships Between Norms Regarding the Extent of Treaty Commitments and Interstate Conflict, 1820–1914

Outcome Variable	Extent to Which Commitments are Considered Binding			
	r	b	ρ	DW
Level I Conflict	−.40	−.01	.37	2.19
Level II Conflict	−.40	−.01	−.28	1.97
Level III Conflict	−.44	−.01	−.28	1.89
Scaled Hostility	−.66	−.03	−.41	2.37

able that accounted for the correlations we discovered. Toward that end, we have relied on the Poisson-based measurement technique that Robert M. Rood and Patrick J. McGowan (1974: 6, 11) developed in their study of alliance flexibility. To measure this flexibility, they calculated the average rate of alliance formation by five-year intervals (m), and then determined the cumulative probability that the observed number of alliances formed in each period (x) was less than m. These probabilities were a measure of changes in the rate of alliance formation: the higher the probability score, the greater the structural flexibility during the half-decade under study.

Upon incorporating these data into our analysis of the COW data from the 1820–1914 period, we found that the first-order partial correlations between alliance commitment and serious disputes, controlling for structural flexibility, indicate that the relationships involving frequency (−.39), scope (−.34), and intensity (−.16) remain negative in direction, though they become slightly weaker than the zero-order correlations displayed in Table 8.2. Regardless of the extent of actual activity in the formation alliances, the previously observed pattern remains: increases in support for strict fidelity to alliance commitments lead to reductions in the frequency, scope, and intensity of militarized disputes among major powers.

Similar results were obtained when we incorporated the Rood and McGowan data into our analysis of the Siverson and Tennefoss data. The first-order partial correlations between the commitment norm index and interstate conflict, while controlling for structural flexibility, show that the associations involving Levels I (−.44), II (−.45), and III (−.44) conflict remained negative in direction, as did the association involving scaled hostility (−.69). In summary, the same magnitude and distribution of alliances will tend to be associated with different amounts of conflict, depending upon the reliability of the commitments underlying those alliances. Although flexible alliances are lubricants that facilitate the maintenance of a balance of power between rivals, the findings indicate that that balance will more likely remain stable if states adhere to their treaty commitments.

Introducing Time Lags

Still another way to strengthen the grounds for our inferences is to introduce time lags into the statistical analyses. Rather than assuming a contemporaneous relationship between serious disputes and those norms governing the sanctity of alliance commitments, we can take precedent into account by distributing the impact of legal norms over time. To incorporate time lags, we assume that our outcome variables at time point *t* are affected by the content of legal norms from several preceding points in time. However, to avoid multicollinearity between the measures of alliance commitment at *t, t-1, t-2, . . . , t-n*, we must specify a priori some conditions about the form of the distributed lags. In accordance with the Almon method, we have posited that the lag weights can be approximated by a polynomial function (Dhrymes, 1971; Ostrom and Hoole, 1978: 228).[7]

Table 8.4 shows the results of a multivariate analysis of the combined impact of both structural flexibility and alliance commitment norms upon the frequency, scope, and intensity of serious major power disputes as measured by the COW data, with time lags introduced between the commitment index and the outcome variables. Although, as we would expect, structural flexibility is inversely related to the extent to which alliance obligations are considered binding (*r* = −.18), legal theory suggests that each variable exerts an *independent* influence on the occurrence of serious disputes. It is one thing, according to this line of reasoning, to be able to switch alliance partners regardless of ideology, cultural affinities, or personal ties; it is quite another to do so prior to the expiration of one's current alliance agreements. Either action would increase systemic uncertainty, but the possibility of the latter does so exponentially. For example, de-

---

7. More specifically, in the analysis that follows we have utilized a four-period lag structure where:

$$w_i = c_o + c_1i + c_2i^2 + c_3i^3$$

where $i = 0, 1, 2, 3, 4$, and $w_i = 0$ for i less than 0 and greater than 4. This specifies that the lag weights follow a third-degree polynomial for the first four lagged values and 0 otherwise.

Table 8.4. Multivariate Relationships between Structural Flexibility, Treaty Commitments, and Serious Major Power Disputes, 1820–1914

$$\text{Frequency}_t = .76 - 2.57 \text{ FLEXIBILITY}_t + 2.49 \text{ FLEXIBILITY}_t^2$$
$$- \sum_{i=0}^{4} a_i \text{ COMMITMENT}_{t-1}$$

Almon lag coefficients:

$a_o = -.27$	$a_3 = -.04$
$a_1 = -.10$	$a_4 = -.07$
$a_2 = -.03$	$a_i = -.51$

Mean lag = 1.11

$R = .71$ $R^2 = .51$ SER = .31   DW = 2.10 $(-.22)$

$$\text{Scope}_t = 1.17 - 1.16 \, (\log_e \text{ FLEXIBILITY})_t$$
$$- \sum_{i=0}^{4} a_i \text{ COMMITMENT}_{t-1}$$

Almon lag coefficients:

$a_o = -.16$	$a_3 = -.04$
$a_1 = -.10$	$a_4 = -.14$
$a_2 = -.04$	$a_i = -.48$

Mean lag = 1.79

$R = .79$ $R^2 = .63$ SER = .22   DW = 2.40 $(-.82)$

$$\text{Intensity}_t = .27 - .26 \text{ FLEXIBILITY}_t$$
$$- \sum_{i=0}^{4} a_i \text{ COMMITMENT}_{t-1}$$

Almon lag coefficients:

$a_o = .01$	$a_3 = -.05$
$a_1 = -.21$	$a_4 = -.05$
$a_2 = -.16$	$a_i = -.46$

Mean lag = 1.94

$R = .42$ $R^2 = .18$ SER = .39   DW = 2.00 $(-.02)$

Note: The value of ρ is given in parentheses following the Durbin-Watson statistic.

spite signing a twenty-five-year defensive alliance at Venice in 1454, the acceptability of repudiating commitments made the leaders of those Italian city-states that joined the Most Holy League uncertain about the future behavior of their new allies. As Garrett Mattingly (1971: 90) described their concerns: "Most of them believed that if the lamb had to lie down with the lion, or even if one wolf lay down with another, a wise animal kept one eye open." Due to this reasoning we have included both predictor variables in our multivariate GLS equations.

Each equation portrays the best fit that could be made to the data. A comparison of the multiple coefficients of determination for the three equations reveal that we can account fairly well for the frequency and scope of serious major power disputes, but we cannot account very well for their intensity. In other words, our indicators permit us to predict the incipience of interstate disputes and the number of parties to them better than they allow us to predict the escalation of serious disputes into war.

According to the regression coefficients in the frequency equation, there is a curvilinear relationship between structural flexibility and the number of serious disputes between major powers. The sequence of a negative followed by a positive coefficient indicates that the curve is a parabola with the shape of an inverted U. Hence we can infer that the number of serious major power disputes that occurred between 1820 and 1914 was high whenever prior alliance structures were either extremely rigid or extremely fluid. Combining this finding with the negative lag coefficients that appear in the equation for our alliance commitment index, we conclude that dangerous disputes occur less often when there is a moderate degree of structural flexibility and treaty obligations are interpreted as binding.

The negative coefficients in the scope equation reveal that the number of major powers engaged in serious disputes decreases as alliance memberships become more fluid and treaty obligations become more binding. As in the frequency equation, the relationship between structural flexibility and disputes was curvilinear, although an examination of the scatterplot for this relationship showed that the shape of the curve was not parabolic, and thus could be modeled by transforming each flexibility score into its natural logarithm.[8] The implication of this model is that the scope of dangerous disputes declines at a de-

---

8. Because the natural logarithm of zero does not exist, we added 1 to each flexibility score prior to transformation.

creasing (rather than constant) rate as structural flexibility increases. Thus, the parameters of the first two GLS equations indicate that serious disputes happen less frequently and tend to involve fewer great powers when system members perceive all other states as equally eligible as potential allies, but also perceive that once an alliance treaty is signed, it will not be unilaterally abrogated prior to its scheduled termination date.

Turning finally to the intensity equation, it is clear from the multiple coefficient of determination that here we are unable to obtain a predictive power commensurate with that obtained for the first two equations, although the coefficients for both of our independent variables are once again negative.

In summary, three regularities have been uncovered in these analyses of the relationship between serious disputes and those legal norms that define the nature of alliance commitments in the 1820–1914 time period. First, the evidence suggests that the number of serious disputes between great powers decreases when international norms support a binding conception of treaty commitments. Second, it indicates that the percentage of major powers involved in serious disputes also decreases when norms of this type prevail. And third, it suggests that the magnitude of threat and degree of destruction will be limited when agreements are widely regarded as binding. These findings warn us that in periods when the opportunistic renunciation of commitments to allies is widely condoned, the number of great power disputes, the number of parties to them, and the severity of destruction can be expected to increase.

THE CONTEMPORARY SETTING FOR
CRISIS MANAGEMENT

The basis for inference about the role of alliance norms in the management of international crises can be strengthened by moving beyond the pre-World War I classical balance-of-power period and inspecting the pattern of association exhibited in the post-World War II period. In contrast to the 1820–1914 time span in which flexible norms of promissory obligation were emphasized, this subsequent period was an era marked by increasing support for binding commitments and the concomitant rise of a restrictive legal order (recall Figure 6.1). The differences between these two periods make them useful for a focused comparison. If we obtain the same findings about the association between alliance norms and crisis management when using the case study method on this latter period, then we have more confidence in the conclusions we drew from our macro-quantitative study of the pre-World War I period.

As previously noted, the post-World War II era may be characterized as uniquely crisis-prone. Because the use of war as an instrument of policy has been severely restricted in the nuclear age, the threat of force may have become more important than its actual use (P. Williams, 1976). The military challenge of an enemy short of the use of war has become a common substitute for the actual use of armed conflict, and the frequent willingness of great powers to bargain competitively by flexing their military muscles for the purpose of intimidation and coercion has contributed to the recurrence of international crises. The frequency with which states have threatened warfare in order to induce compliance by others has heightened tension, especially in the post-World War II international system.[9] This has been one of the reasons why the contemporary period is often seen as an age of crisis.[10]

But the era since World War II has also been one in which support for binding conceptions of promissory obligations has been intense. A restrictive legal environment has co-existed with a system in which the incidence of crisis has been endemic. How do we account for this anomaly, which seems to run counter to the general historical pattern between 1820 and 1914? What does the contemporary pattern illuminate about the relationship between alliance norms and crisis management?

To begin, let us recall that at the advent of the post-World War II period the international system rested on very weak and ambivalent consensual foundations. It is not hyperbole to characterize world politics at the conclusion of World War II as a system in which trust in

---

9. Additionally, although international crises are hardly peculiar to the post-World War II system, the propensity for crises to escalate to war has been relatively pronounced since 1945 (see Gochman and Maoz, 1984: 600). The frequency of militarized disputes between great powers has led to the perception of nearly continual threat and system instability. This atmosphere has provoked widespread fear, massive military expenditures for purposes of deterrence, and repeated episodes of threat and counterthreat.

10. The cliche that we live in an age of crisis has assumed particular relevance in the twentieth century. President Dwight D. Eisenhower, for instance, reflected in his memoirs that he could not "remember a day that had not brought its major or minor crisis." But what "makes all of our crises more dangerous," observes John Platt (1969: 1116), "is that they are now coming on top of each other." This global trend is similar to what happened prior to World War I when the length of time between the outbreak of international crises decreased (see Hartmann, 1983: 347–352).

adversaries' restraint in using force was minimal. With the breakdown of trust between the superpowers in 1945, these former comrades in arms threatened each other militarily and repeatedly tested the reliability of their allies. Thrown into suspense by the resulting chaotic atmosphere was the status of promissory obligations.

This interregnum did not last for long. A consensus soon crystallized to instill renewed support for binding alliance norms. Chaos bred increased need for order, and vigorous support for the norms of a restrictive legal order brought into being widespread enthusiasm for a regime that prescribed the sanctity of commitments.

What factors permit the high incidence of crises in this restrictive environment to be explained? A clue is provided by the fact that whereas the incidence of interstate crises was high in this period, the proportion of these crises escalating to war between the *great powers* actually fell. As previously suggested, one plausible explanation for this might be found in the inhibiting influence of nuclear weapons. The human and material costs of warfare may have curtailed its frequency among the great powers. Many crises may have arisen, but most of those involving nuclear armed states have been managed successfully. This change may result from the fear that a war may get out of hand. "The widespread recognition that military force has become dangerously volatile and potentially uncontrollable ensures that many states resort to it only in the face of serious provocation and after the most careful consideration. Faith in victory at an acceptable cost is far less well entrenched than in the past. Consequently, in some circumstances that previously might have led to hostilities, force has been replaced by a more amicable—or at least, less violent—means of settling disputes" (P. Williams, 1976: 46).

A corollary explanation of this association resides in the probability that the virtual absence of war between the great powers (Gaddis, 1986; Kegley, 1990), amidst frequent crises between them, may be due to the high regard with which the sanctity of commitments between allies has been held throughout the 1945–1975 period. Alliance ties did bind, in part because commitments between allies received wide support and were backed by a strong normative consensus throughout the post-World War II era.

Now consider in this context as well the high incidence with which foreign overt military interventions[11] have occurred since the conclu-

---

11. Herbert K. Tillema's (1989: 190–196) data delineate the frequency of this type of military activity between September 1945 and December 1985. We follow his

sion of the Second World War. These threats to international peace involving primarily weak states in the system's periphery[12] have repeatedly disrupted systemic stability. But remarkably few of these militarized interventions were actually internationalized through escalation by the involvement of rival great powers. This is particularly surprising in light of the number of these conflicts that have involved the superpowers' allies, who routinely have called on their great power patrons for military assistance in accordance with the provisions of existing defense treaties. Such situations have tested the reliability of the patron, inasmuch as these disputes have often been met with displeasure by the superpowers, whose fear of escalation to war has made them reluctant allies. Nonetheless, despite the challenge posed to the superpowers to "manage" their allies, the record attests to the ability of the superpowers to abide by their treaty commitments while successfully restraining their allies from the use of force (Stein, 1988: 173). Alliance bonds have not broken, even though the disputes encountered by the superpowers' allies have made for an environment fraught with crises.

definition:

> Foreign overt military intervention is operationally defined as direct combatant or combat-preparatory military operations conducted upon foreign territory by units of a state's regular military forces. It includes conventional deployments of ground combat units that include such actions as alert patrol, offensive maneuver, riot quelling, armed occupation of territory, and battle. It also includes other, usually less intense, combatant military actions such as: commando or other small unit raids; aerial bombing, strafing and rocketry; ground-based artillery or rocketry; and naval gunnery and rocketry. Overt military intervention includes all such operations within territories subject to other's jurisdiction, and also within distinct non-self-governing territories such as colonies, protectorates, mandated or occupied lands not fully integrated within the generally recognized boundaries of a state. It excludes operations conducted by a state within its own integral territory. Overt military intervention excludes less blatant forms of international interference such as covert operations, military alerts, shows of force, garrison deployments or deployments of other forces not immediately prepared for combat, incursions across international borders that do not involve occupation of territory or other overt military actions, military assistance, and activities of police units, irregular forces, multinational peace forces and international observer groups that do not directly involve the overt military intervention as defined above. Overt military intervention also excludes incidents confined to small arms border fire, engagements among vessels at sea, or encounters among aircraft in flight. (Tillema, 1989: 187–189)

12. This pattern is even more pronounced when the frequency of the internationalization of civil wars in the postwar period is compared with earlier periods, a comparison that demonstrates the extent to which the contemporary period has witnessed the confinement of local wars and prevention of their expansion into wars between larger numbers of participants (see Raymond and Kegley, 1987, and Kegley and Raymond, 1983).

The other side of this patron-client relationship entails the question of whether superpower interventions in the Third World would drag allies along. Whereas binding notions of promissory obligations might have required allies to become involved in the interventions of their great power allies, most treaties of alliance since World War II have in fact protected the weaker party without demanding from them reciprocal support in the event a superpower ally intervened in the internal conflict of a third party (see Pearson, 1981). Those treaties, backed by binding commitments, therefore, have not entangled states in the interventions of the superpowers with which they were allied. On the contrary, relatively weak states have not been bound to provide military support for the militarized conflicts of their patrons.

Thus, regardless of how the obligations of allies have been spelled out in treaties since 1945, the product has been a prolonged great power peace of unprecedented duration since the advent of the nation-state system in 1648 (Kegley, 1991). This period has been one populated by many militarized disputes that have threatened to spill over to major power war, but all these threats were met. The sanctity of oaths may be assumed to have contributed to this success: "Successful crisis management is . . . a function of cultural, organizational, and personal behavioral patterns established long before the onset of any crisis" (Lebow, 1981: 335). The institutionalization of the norm *pacta sunt servanda* in international treaty law set in place a restrictive legal order that reduced uncertainties about the conduct of states when these unanticipated threats to peace arose, and thereby made the task of crisis decision making relatively less burdensome than in periods where a permissive order was dominant. Binding promissory obligations tied allies together, facilitated communication, enhanced their ability to coordinate their foreign policies, and increased the credibility of deterrent threats. In short, the binding nature of these obligations has served to confine the scope of warfare, not broaden it.

Greater insight into the linkage between alliance norms and the control of international crises in the contemporary international system can be obtained by examining more closely the conditions that gave rise to the series of crises known collectively as the Cold War. The history of the Cold War dramatizes the manner in which changes in alliance norms bring in their wake changes in the capacity of states to manage threats to peace.

THE COLD WAR: PERPETUAL CRISIS, PERPETUAL PEACE

The Cold War is a classic case of the breakdown of trust, in which the loss of faith by each great power in the ability of its former ally to keep its promises contributed to the rupture of the grand wartime coalition and to the advent of a conflict that frequently threatened to become a "hot" war (Barnet, 1988). In the context of crisis management, its evolutionary course can be broken into three phases.

The first phase of this evolutionary course, the *wartime alliance* between the United States and the Soviet Union, illustrates how politics makes strange bedfellows and why the existence of a powerful common enemy can unite very dissimilar states into a binding coalition. In order to defeat their common enemy, both states were able to suspend their initial distrust of each other and subordinate their ideological differences to their mutual national interest in collaborating for self-preservation (Miner, 1988). As the disagreement over when the Western powers should have opened a "second front" in Europe demonstrates, the wartime collaboration operated in spite of latent doubts by both states about the other's intentions. Although this collaboration reached its zenith at the Tehran summit of December 1943, both powers largely continued to conduct themselves in conformity with the agreements they struck, as shown by initial adherence to the principles of the 1941 Atlantic Charter, the 1943 Moscow Declaration, and nearly $11 billion of U.S. lend-lease supplies sent to the Soviet Union.[13]

The ability of the United States and the Soviet Union to pursue common wartime interests suggests that a Cold War in the immediate aftermath of World War II was neither inevitable nor predetermined and that the continued collaboration of these states was by no means precluded. Indeed, continued cooperation was envisioned by Soviet and American leaders, at least in their official discourse in the early phases of postwar negotiations (see Gaddis, 1972). Speaking to Senator Claude Pepper in September 1945, Joseph Stalin pointed out that with the defeat of Hitler the two wartime allies would "have to find a

---

13. The actual record of U.S.-U.S.S.R. wartime collaboration is ambiguous and does not lend itself to clear interpretation. It appears that both powers maintained suspicions and harbored fears of betrayal (see Kegley and Wittkopf, 1989: 62–70). Despite the controversial nature of this diplomatic record, it is not unreasonable to trace the origins of the Cold War to the misperceptions and apprehensions that resulted from the allies' difficulties in resolving their disagreements during the Second World War.

new basis for our close relations in the future" (cited in Yergin, 1977: 4). Similarly, President Franklin D. Roosevelt expressed the hope that the wartime collaboration between the two powers would continue after the war. As Presidential adviser Harry Hopkins described the thinking of the Roosevelt administration: "The Russians had proved that they could be reasonable and farseeing and there wasn't any doubt in the minds of the President or any of us that we could live with them and get along with them peacefully for as far into the future as any of us could imagine" (cited in Ekirch, 1966). Roosevelt believed that the United States and the Soviet Union would honor their agreements and resolve their differences through negotiation, a belief based on the wartime experience of both allies meeting their obligations. The Russians "are friendly people," the president observed. "They haven't got any crazy ideas of conquest . . . and now that they have got to know us, they are much more willing to accept us" (cited in Gaddis, 1982: 9).

The second phase of this transition from trust to distrust, a *crisis of confidence,* commenced with the conclusion of the Second World War. A cardinal principle of balance-of-power theory is that alliances formed prior to or during wartime to combat a common adversary will disintegrate when the common enemy is defeated. The victory by the Soviet, American, and British allies over Hitler's Germany and Imperial Japan produced not only peace for a system that had been devastated by the ravages of total war, but also a world fraught with uncertainty. Political agreements that had been carefully arranged and maintained in order to survive in the common struggle against the Axis powers were quickly suspended. In their place, a rapidly changing, chaotic international environment of ill-defined borders, states without sovereign governments, power vacuums, and economic disarray emerged. New issues such as the disposition of Poland surfaced to provoke fears and erode trust. The wartime consensus regarding goals, standards of behavior, and mutual obligations that had typified the allied efforts to defeat the common enemy deteriorated. With victory came a loss of faith in the allies' willingness to abide by their agreement to construct a new, more peaceful, world order. Trust among the allies broke when the enemy's resistance was broken. The wartime alliance was an alliance in name but not in fact.

The adversarial relationship that became the Cold War found its origin in the misunderstanding and mistrust that was bred in the waning days of the war and in its immediate aftermath. Conditions were changing dramatically, and these changes exerted pressure for the reassessment of previous understandings, agreements, and definitions of national interests. For example, the liberation of Italy by British and American troops led Washington to keep the Soviet Union off the Control Commission and to erect a Western-style parliamentary democracy in that country, while the Soviets denied the Western allies a place on the Bulgarian Control Commission and subsequently created "people's democracies" across Eastern Europe in the wake of the Red Army's drive toward Berlin. Rapidly changing conditions also diminished the value of observing promises and eroded support for the sanctity of treaties. The geostrategic situation had shifted overnight as the United States and the Soviet Union became increasingly aware that they stood alone at the apex of global power and had been cast by historical circumstances into the role of contestants for hegemonic status. They had more to fear from each other than they had reason to place confidence in each other's motives. They became rivals, as Alexis de Tocqueville had prophesied more than a century earlier. Throughout history, where there has been rivalry between great powers, there has also been mistrust and misperception. The two giants' manifest and latent power fueled their fears of each other. These fears were compounded by cognizance of the new areas in which their interests came into conflict, and were animated by the suspicions that inevitably accompany the withering away of old arrangements in the face of new realities.

These dramatically changing global circumstances ushered in a period in which the rationale for reevaluating the wisdom of previous promises became compelling. Changed circumstances called for a new (if temporary) enthusiasm for a flexible interpretation of treaty obligations, based on the logic of *rebus sic stantibus,* which would allow the straitjacket of unwelcome agreements with a rival to be jettisoned. It is instructive that in the aftermath of World War II a large number of treaties were denunciated and breached prior to their scheduled date of termination (Sinha, 1966). Most notably, concerns about compliance with the wartime accords and with the agreements reached at Yalta and Potsdam rose rapidly to the top of the superpower bargaining agenda. The issues surrounding adherence to agreements came to symbolize the growing distrust that both superpowers felt of their rivals' willingness to abide by the terms of those treaties they wished to see remain in force. President Truman publicly warned the Soviets, for instance, that the continuation of cooperation was contingent upon the Soviets' faithful performance of their obligations. In a meeting with Soviet Foreign Minister Molotov on April 23,

1945, Truman went one step further by berating the U.S.S.R. for breaking the Yalta agreements. When Molotov protested that he had never been spoken to like that in his life, Truman replied, ''Carry out your agreements and you won't get talked to like that'' (cited in LaFeber, 1985: 17). Similarly, the Kremlin accused the United States of repeated duplicity in disregarding the agreements to which the United States had pledged itself.

The history of this contested interregnum is replete with examples of both superpowers' efforts to violate, ignore, or redefine the nature of their own treaty obligations while sanctimoniously berating the rival for its alleged opportunistic nonperformance of its agreements (Leffler, 1986). The focus of both was selective, as each concentrated attention and critique on only those provisions that served their parochial national interests while ignoring those agreements that benefitted the interests of the other. The tendency for states to equate their own interests with morality was displayed in the exchange of attacks and counterattacks.

What made the temptation to selectively repudiate previous agreements so irresistible for the superpowers was the fact that the international strategic situation had changed so remarkably. These changes undermined the ostensible wisdom on which the prior promises had been predicated and appeared to make many of these understandings conflict with perceived national interests. A permissive interpretation of obligations thus rationalized the selective abrogation of commitments that were no longer attractive. In particular, the shifting balance of conventional power and Soviet occupation of liberated territories in Eastern Europe led to radically different interpretations by the Kremlin and Washington about the meaning of the Yalta accords. Understandably, the Soviets were most reluctant to withdraw from any part of their sphere of influence, a refusal that was branded by the United States as a clear violation of the Declaration on Liberated Europe (see Schlesinger, 1967). The Soviets made the same charge in response to the American refusal to evacuate U.S. military forces from bases abroad (Iceland, Portugal, Denmark, Panama, and elsewhere), even though the United States previously had committed itself to this withdrawal once the Axis powers were defeated. The Soviet refusal to remove its forces from northern Iran in 1946, in defiance of its pledge to withdraw, symbolized the willingness by the superpowers to expediently renege on prior promises and, alongside developments in Greece and Turkey, provoked the crisis that rapidly expanded into a Cold War.[14]

Further complicating the willingness of the superpowers to remain faithful to their previously negotiated accords was the Soviet complaint that the United States expected the U.S.S.R. to accept voluntary limitations on its behavior in line with the spirit of an agreement. But as Edward Luttwak (1980: 133) points out, "Soviet leaders have been frank in stating that only the actual language of treaties is binding. . . . It has been *Western* statesmen who have insisted that this or that . . . treaty has generated a binding 'spirit' of cooperation."

Sole possession of the atomic bomb by the United States and the intoxicating sense of power conveyed by this circumstance revolutionized the postwar environment for Americans. Overnight, the new situation destroyed many of the American incentives for preserving the grand alliance (Sherwin, 1973) and led, some allege (e.g., Alperovitz, 1985; Herkin, 1980), to U.S. acceptance of the threat of use of atomic weapons as instruments of influence against the "next enemy," the Soviet Union (Sherry, 1977). This new military factor in the geostrategic equation weakened considerably the arguments made on behalf of American compliance with agreements that now appeared to run counter to U.S. interests. In such an environment, a less restrictive and more elastic interpretation of commitments received growing emphasis in the United States, at least with regard to dealing

---

14. It is difficult to balance the blame for this rupture of faith that resulted from noncompliance with treaty agreements. It is important to recall that violations were committed by both states (for sometimes very similar reasons, rationalized by similar reasoning). Melvyn P. Leffler concludes:

> By citing Soviet violations. . . . American officials excused their own departure from wartime accords and rationalized their adoption of unilateral measures to safeguard American national security interests. But these American initiatives were not simply responses to Soviet transgressions; for the most part Soviet violations did not trigger and cannot be said to have legitimated America's own record of non-compliance. Most Soviet actions in Eastern Europe during the winter and spring of 1945, for example, were legally permissible under the armistice agreements and were compatible with a host of Anglo-Soviet understandings. . . . The Kremlin's pattern of compliance with wartime agreements in the immediate aftermath of World War II appears no better or worse than the American record. . . . The experiences of the early Cold War reveal that wartime agreements were violated not by the Soviets alone but by all the signatories and not necessarily because of evil intent but because of apprehension and expediency. (Leffler, 1986: 116, 121, 123)

with the Soviet Union. Promissory obligations, in other words, were seen as divisible: they should be upheld with friends, but could be broken with rivals.

This brief but critical phase of the transformation of relations between former wartime allies was one in which the sanctity of oaths came under extreme pressure from both superstates. The history of this period attests to the many ways the wartime and postwar accords between the United States and the Soviet Union were reinterpreted, abrogated, and violated. The repeated record of noncompliance led to the unraveling of the alliance, the erosion of trust, and ultimately, the advent of the Cold War (see, for example, Theoharis, 1970; Snell, 1956; Clemens, 1970; Gaddis, 1972; Yergin, 1977; Messer, 1982; and Rose, 1973). The superpowers acted opportunistically in response to changing circumstances. They embraced a realpolitik interpretation of oaths and put narrow self-interests above principle. The end of honor meant the end of alliance and the beginning of antagonism.

The lesson derived from this phase of the evolving Soviet-American relationship is that bad faith leads to bad relations and creates a crisis atmosphere. Mistrust resides in the conviction that others are duplicitous, and antagonism is produced when that conviction is joined by the belief in one's self-righteousness. This orientation overlooks beneficial aspects of international agreements and the undesirable diplomatic consequences that result when an expediential posture toward promissory obligations is assumed. This was illustrated during the period immediately following the end of the Second World War.

> By their very nature, great power agreements demand compromise and are wrapped in ambiguities. Pressures to interpret provisions, even unambiguous ones, to comport with national self-interest are relentless on both American and Soviet officials. Leaders of both countries tend to act opportunistically yet demand punctilious behavior from their adversaries. Their sense of expediency and self-righteous hypocrisy endanger efforts to regulate competition through international agreement. If competition is to be channeled into constructive avenues and conflict contained, both great powers must abandon the temptation to use the issue of adherence to agreements as a morality play or a propaganda ploy; both sides must wish to define their security in terms of compliance and accommodation rather than in terms of other priorities that compete with and may take ascendancy over a cooperative relationship. (Leffler, 1986: 90)

Promptly brought into existence by the mounting mutual suspicions that the great powers harbored about each other's intentions to comply with commitments was a new, more threatening period of Soviet-American rivalry: "a war called peace" (Crozier, Middleton, and Murray-Brown, 1985). By placing greater emphasis on restricting the adversary's power while projecting one's own, a third phase in alliance dynamics commenced. This era is truly one of endemic international crises. Within it has occurred "some of the most bitter and persistent antagonisms short of war in modern history" (Gaddis, 1986: 100), a fact that renders the post-1947 era an age of *perpetual crisis.*

Among other characteristics, what distinguishes a brief crisis of confidence period from a protracted period of perpetual crisis is a difference in the normative climates of each period. When trust broke down between the United States and the Soviet Union after the Second World War, standards for the performance of duties by allies were first relaxed and then broken. Treaty violation became common, and what was condoned by the superpowers defined the permissible for others, which similarly had incentives for freeing themselves from prior alignments. (The Yugoslav attempt to break away from the Soviet bloc was exemplary.) But support for flexible definitions of commitment norms never gained sufficient force to crystalize into a permissive legal order. The momentary crisis of confidence in adherence to agreements was soon replaced, with renewed vigor, by norms prescribing strict adherence to agreements and faithful compliance with their provisions as the restrictive order that had taken root prior to the war was given renewed support. Still, occasions did arise where the norm *pacta sunt servanda* was broken. For example, when justifying the 1952 effort to stop all U.S. aid-receiving nations from shipping embargoed goods to communist countries, Congressman Laurie C. Battle proclaimed that when the United States takes emergency action for its national defense, it does so "without regard to prior commitments" (cited in Adler-Karlsson, 1968: 44).

Ironically, the changed circumstances that eroded the wartime coalition subsequently served to transform unaligned states into allies whose cohesion was backed by commitments to the new alliances. The emergent bipolar world, with the United States and its allies making up one pole and the Soviet Union and its allies the other, called for a different normative structure. Washington and Moscow now found themselves in great need for allies in order to maximize their power relative to one another. With the emergence of the Cold War, there commenced an intense, almost predatory competition for allies who could assist in the superpower struggle, with a premium placed on the acquisition of loyal allies. The two superpowers found their interests served by promotion of a regime that prohibited the desertion of an ally from its commitments and which tolerated little room for neutrals. Able to pay high prices to attract allies, they were both willing to pay even greater prices for keeping them.

Conversely, instances of perceived disloyalty elicited the wrath of the superpowers. For example, although in 1957 Canada's Progressive Conservative government had accepted the stationing of U.S. nuclear forces on Canadian soil, when the delivery systems were entered into service five years later, Prime Minister John Diefenbaker outraged President Kennedy by refusing to accept the nuclear warheads. Later, when Diefenbaker did not render the allied support expected by the Kennedy administration during the Cuban missile crisis, the United States drew attention to his reneging on alliance commitments.

The changed strategic situation, symbolized by the advent of a tight bipolar world, required support for alliance norms far different from those norms that received acceptance during the classical period of the multipolar balance of power. Out of this situation the norm *pacta sunt servanda* was given enthusiastic acclamation by the superpowers and elevated to a sacred principle to be respected by clients and patrons alike. The viability and cohesion of NATO and the Warsaw Pact were perceived to rest on the principle that agreements were binding. Peace was proclaimed contingent upon the inviolability of commitments among allies. Dean Rusk (cited in Weinstein, 1969: 52) captured the new preference when he declared "American alliances are at the heart of the maintenance of peace, and if it should be discovered that the pledge of America was worthless, the structure of peace would crumble and we would be well on our way to a terrible catastrophe." He might have added that the United States, committing itself to honor its commitments, hereafter would not tolerate defection of its allies from their pledge to honor their commitments. The Soviet Union adopted the same position and set out to enforce, somewhat ruthlessly, a regime prohibiting the disavowal of commitments by its allies (see Volyges, 1988).[15]

---

15. Instructively, one of the major themes of the propaganda campaigns from both Washington and Moscow on violations of agreements in the late 1980s was the need for the other side to live up to the norm *pacta sunt servanda*. When complaining about the Krasnoyarsk radar station, the Reagan administration's 1987 report to the Congress on "Soviet Noncompliance with Arms Control Agreements" portrayed *pacta sunt servanda* as the cornerstone of international law: "states are to observe and comply with obligations they have freely undertaken" (U.S. Department of

To turn this discussion full circle, we find in the Cold War support for the conclusion suggested by the macro-quantitative statistical analyses performed above. There it was demonstrated that when binding conceptions of alliance commitments have prevailed, a reduction in the frequency of international crises has occurred. The converse of this was also suggested: historically, periods in which the inviolability of oaths have not been embraced as a norm for alliance behavior have also been periods in which the frequency of serious disputes among great powers have increased. This relationship is also displayed in the changing dyadic relationship between the United States and the Soviet Union. As wartime allies largely abiding by their agreements, trust was preserved and serious disputes between them were relatively infrequent. As the common enemy was defeated, however, the two states confronted each other in a struggle for power and opportunistically violated many of the agreements they had previously forged. Permitting themselves to step outside the terms of the accords they had pledged to honor as allies, they found themselves victims of their own hand as the breakdown of trust led to the rupture of their relationship. Their ongoing dispute threatened repeatedly to spill over into war, as the practice of "brinkmanship" continually took the contestants to the precipice.

This crisis atmosphere has persisted through the 1980s. Yet paradoxically, in order to compete for allies and contain their competition with each other at a level short of war, the superpowers once again advocated a norm prohibiting the violation of agreements among allies. And throughout the duration of this seemingly perpetual crisis, peace nonetheless was preserved, superpower threats to each other were successfully managed, and tacit rules for strategic bargaining were constructed and respected.[16] Moreover, when the general incidence of militarized disputes reached unprecedented levels for the system as a whole, it is instructive that under the rules of this regime

State, 1987). Likewise, Major General Obinyakov's (1987) complaints about the American Thule (Greenland) and Fylimgdales (Britain) radar stations also identified the conscientious discharge of international obligations as the core of international law.

16. As Christer Jönsson (1984: 191) concludes, "the superpowers seem to have arrived at a tacit understanding of principles guiding their crisis interaction. Between crises they may be willing to play poker; but once the crisis comes to a head they play chess. According to one observer [P. Williams, 1976: 200], 'one of the most remarkable features of superpower crises is the extent to which the proprieties, conventions and norms have been adhered to without deviation'. " For another account of this compliance, see Alexander George (1986).

most of these crises did not escalate to war, and war between the great powers did not occur once throughout the course of this "long peace" (Gaddis, 1987; Kegley, 1991).

The convergence of findings emanating from aggregate data analysis with lessons extracted from the case of the U.S.-U.S.S.R. experience lends support to the proposition that a correlation between binding alliance norms and the control of international crises is not artifactual. What applies to the international system as a whole applies as well to the superpowers since 1945: when the binding stature of agreements are respected widely, crises emerging from militarized disputes tend to be managed successfully.

THE BENEFITS OF A RESTRICTIVE LEGAL ORDER IN THE MANAGEMENT OF INTERSTATE CRISES

The purpose of this chapter has been to probe the relationship between alliance norms and the frequency, scope, and intensity of serious major power disputes. Whether allies can be counted on to comply with the treaty obligations they swear to execute is a policy-making concern whenever crises erupt. It is when allies are most needed that the fear of abandonment becomes more pronounced. States sign treaties of alliance to communicate information to friends and foes alike. The ability of such treaties to signal others receives its ultimate test during the advent of serious militarized disputes. An alliance pact will be reduced to a meaningless piece of paper if, when tested by suddenly threatening situations, the parties to them fail to respect the sanctity of oaths.

The advent of international crises also have direct systemic consequences. As threats to international security generally, a militarized dispute has the capacity to spill over national boundaries and encompass a large number of countries in a costly, destructive general war. Crises, therefore, affect far more than the immediate interests of those whose antagonism and threats initially provoked them. All allies are, of course, immediately affected; in addition, neutrals and third parties—many of whom find themselves locked in bilateral defense agreements with one another—cannot look with indifference at a threat to peace that ultimately can undermine their own national security. In an interdependent world, a crisis anywhere is a crisis everywhere.

International crises take the members of the international system into uncharted waters. Order, predictability, confidence, and control are diminished, as an uncertain future casts its shadow over states' collective fate. When crises erupt, states find themselves untethered, unsure of the conduct of others. At such times, the prevailing norms of commitment among allies provide a compass to which they instinctively turn to reduce uncertainties. Those norms serve as Weberian (1958) "cultural tracks," channelling actions along either a predictable or an unpredictable path. In a restrictive environment where the sanctity of promises are held in high regard, the former results. In a permissive legal order sanctioning the repudiation of commitments, however, the freedom exists for an unpredictable realignment of allegiances.

Which of these normative climates has been the more conducive to the preservation of peace? According to the meaning of a crisis defined by the Chinese ideogram, crises entail both danger and opportunity. At the international level, the danger is war, and the opportunity is for the strengthening or severing of commitments. Our results demonstrate that the type of commitment norms accepted by allies at the time a crisis erupts affects the process of determining how the danger will be met and the kinds of opportunities that will be seized. In conclusion, the evidence assembled in this chapter provides an important clue as to how states might better cope with the uncertainties of a turbulent international environment. On balance it suggests that the prospects for the successful management of disputes among states will be enhanced when countries feel themselves obligated to adhere to the commitments that they pledge, and when they promote principles of conduct that prescribe the faithful performance of commitments to allies. Adherence to commitments augurs well for harmony among states; the inclination to disregard them does not.

9 Alliance Norms and the Escalation of Crises to War

Boys . . . [are] cheated with dice, but an enemy with oaths.
Lysander

I had little confidence in the value of written treaties of alliance generally. I had seen too many instances in which they had been forgotten, or disregarded, or found to be irrelevant, or distorted for ulterior purposes when the chips were down.
George Kennan

When we think of the consequences of international norms, we ordinarily imagine their role in resolving disputes. Historically, statesmen have attempted to resolve disputes in three ways: through war, through use of force short of war, and through peaceful means. Because the international system lacks an ultimate authority to which statesmen can turn for the peaceful resolution of their disputes, they often feel compelled to rely on coercive self-help. Aside from going to war, acts of self-help include military occupations, blockades, embargoes, boycotts, and other uses of force. In the short run these procedures provide a way to redress one's grievances, but in the long run they may influence the course of a conflict without ever settling the underlying disagreement.

In the preceding chapter, we examined the impact of alliance norms on the uses of force short of war, and found that normative support for binding promissory obligations dampens serious interstate disputes. The goal of this chapter is to extend our analysis beyond the study of crises by determining whether those norms that support the sanctity of alliance commitments also have been related to decreases in the use of war as an instrument of self-help.

THE PUZZLING RELATIONSHIP BETWEEN ALLIANCES AND THE ONSET OF WAR

For centuries the impact of alliances on world affairs has been debated vigorously. As shown in Table 9.1, much of the debate centers on whether alliances promote or inhibit global stability. Those who contend that alliances promote stability draw inspiration from the famous maxim attributed to Vegetius, a fourth-century Roman general:

218

Table 9.1. Alliances and Global Stability: Curse or Cure?

Alliances as a Source of Stability

"Whenever an aggressor arises, alliances are indispensible to avoid war."

—Robert Strauss-Hupé and Stephen Possony

"Alliances may be regarded as essential methods in the regulatory process of international politics. . . . They help fill the gap between the ideals of organization and the realities of quasi-anarchy in the international system."

—Charles O. Lerche and Abdul A. Said

"If the states system . . . is to exist and be maintained by common exertions, no one of its members must ever become so powerful as to be able to coerce all the rest put together."

—Friedrich von Gentz

Alliance Aggregation as a Source of Instability

"The grouping of states in permanent alliances . . . would tend to . . . decrease stability."

—Quincy Wright

"Alliances increase tensions rather than promote security."

—John Burton

"Alliances are related to general international instability. Alliance races occur when the international environment appears likely to change. Leaders of international coalitions and particular nations may see the opportunity to mold the international system in a way favorable to their interests. Or they may fear that others may try to change it in an unfavorable way. In either case, they attempt to surround themselves with friendly allies, who may help them if the need arises. The alliance races themselves may add to international instability because they may threaten additional groups."

—Francis A. Beer

---

si vis pacem, para bellum (if you want peace, prepare for war). Possessing allies, it is argued, enhances military preparedness and can make a nation sufficiently strong to deter an attack. An example of this line of thought can be found in the work of Francesco Guicciardini, the Florentine statesman and author, who wrote that the mutual jealousy, unremitting scrutiny of rivals, and elaborate strategic calculations behind the formation of alliances among the Renaissance Italian city-states "did not make the peace any less stable, but rather made the powers more alert and more ready to bring about the immediate extinction of all those sparks that might start a fire" (cited in Butterfield, 1968: 137). The same point was made later by Francis Bacon, who viewed the alliances forged by King Henry VIII of England, Francis I of France, and Charles V of the Habsburg Empire as a bulwark of international security because they encouraged their members to be watchful and to parry expansionistic thrusts at vulnerable areas. Similarly, the Göttingen historian, A. H. L. Heeren, pronounced that the alliances and counteralliances of the eighteenth-century European balance-of-power system resulted in "a constantly wakeful attention of the states to one another . . . and, in general, the preservation of a feeling of the value of independence, and the elevation of politics above gross selfishness" (cited in Craig and George, 1983: 18). In sum, exponents of peace through preparedness declare that alliances promote global stability by fostering vigilance and enhancing deterrence.

On the other hand, those who believe that alliances contribute to instability argue that even a large number of allies may not be sufficient to deter an aggressor, particularly when the coalition consists of minor powers. Wars, they insist, could still occur under a variety of conditions: an irrational leader might strike because of his utter contempt for the opposing alliance's capabilities and resolve; a desperate leader might see preemption as the only solution to a costly, protracted conflict; or a risk-acceptant leader might use surprise as a force multiplier to create a fait accompli before the victims could mobilize and deploy their military forces. As Virgil quipped, "It never troubles a wolf how many the sheep be."

But even if a state possesses military partners of considerable strength, there are several reasons why critics of alliance building consider it destabilizing. First, alliances look menacing; hence it is likely that they will reinforce existing cleavages, cause states outside the alliance to scramble for allies of their own,[1] and thus raise tensions to a new, more dangerous level. "[W]hat is defensive to one party," observes George F. Kennan (1984: 117), "is offensive to the other; and it has never been the custom of the envisaged opponent . . . to place much confidence in such professions of defensive

---

1. Presumably the scramble for allies is motivated by a desire to offset the military might of an adversary by adding a new ally's power to one's own or by denying the addition of that power to the enemy.

intent on the part of those who are banding together for military purposes directed against him." Second, alliances are entangling; they can drag members into conflicts that do not affect their vital interests. Finally, alliances are sanguineous; their very existence means that even if a state can see that its resources are inadequate to sustain further combat, it would be encouraged to continue fighting in the hope of gaining aid from its allies (Kennedy, 1984: 11). It was for these reasons that Jawaharlal Nehru (cited in Singham and Hune, 1986: 306), a founder of the nonaligned movement, expressed a determination to "keep [India] away from the power blocs or groups, aligned against one another, which have led in the past to world wars and which may again lead to disasters on an even greater scale."

To sum up, whereas some scholars and policymakers advance the proposition that alliances sustain peace, others echo Sir John Frederick Maurice who lamented that "if you prepare thoroughly for war you will get it." Unfortunately, although the literature generated by the debate between advocates of these two positions has been voluminous, the evidence it contains on the systemic effects of alliance aggregation is largely impressionistic. J. David Singer and Melvin Small (1968) attempted to remedy the situation by bringing the scientific method to bear on the possible connection between alliances and war. Rather than resolving this long-standing debate over the relationship between war and alliance, however, their research actually aroused further controversy by revealing that alliance aggregation and the onset of war were positively related in the twentieth century but negatively related in the nineteenth. Once again, as in so many instances in the past, awareness of the extent of our ignorance increased with the growth of scientific knowledge.

The search for solutions to puzzles has been portrayed as the driving force behind scientific research (Kuhn, 1970). Clearly the Singer and Small discovery was puzzling: it inspired various replicative studies based on different data sets (e.g., Rood and McGowan, 1974; Levy, 1981), measurement techniques (e.g., Wallace, 1973; Bueno de Mesquita, 1978), and statistical tests (e.g., Ostrom and Hoole, 1978; Thompson et al., 1980). But despite this additional research, the relationship between alliances and war remains a puzzle, for the results of these replications have not converged on a single set of conclusions.

To solve a puzzle, we must possess clues to make an inference about the whole based on what we know from an often incomplete and seemingly disjointed collection of parts. In effect, this obliges us to think like detectives and, as Dina Zinnes (1980a: 318) points out, "Thinking like detectives makes us look for the not necessarily obvious or even visible operating principles." Indeed, as Brother William of Baskerville explained to Adson, the Benedictine novice in Umberto Eco's (1980: 304) *The Name of the Rose*: "solving a mystery is not the same as deducing from first principles. Nor does it amount simply to collecting a number of particular data from which to infer a general law. It means, rather, facing one or two or three particular data apparently with nothing in common, and trying to imagine whether they could represent so many instances of a general law you don't yet know, and which perhaps has never been pronounced." Given that the relationship between alliance and war is a puzzle for which we lack enough clues, where should we now search? Operating like detectives, can a new piece, previously overlooked, be uncovered to add to this mysterious, old puzzle? And if so, how can we tie all of the clues together in a way that accounts for the divergent results emanating from earlier studies?

Embedded in our description of the international system as a bounded anarchy is a conviction that norms have been neglected for too long in the search for clues about the relationship between alliance and war. We believe that research on alliance norms will not compete with the findings of previous studies; rather they will complement them and yield a more adequate, multicausal explanation of the relationship.

ALLIANCE NORMS: A NEW PIECE IN AN OLD PUZZLE

When Demosthenes instructed his fellow Athenians in 371 B.C. that our actions "should always be just; but we must also be careful, that they are attended with advantage," he revealed one of the chief difficulties of statecraft, namely, balancing ethical responsibilities with pragmatic interests. Seldom if ever do foreign policy choices lack moral ramifications, and one of the most common of these choices pertains to the extent to which an ally ought to sacrifice the opportunity for an immediate gain in order to uphold a treaty commitment. Loyalty sometimes collides with perceived national interests.[2] As we

---

2. It is important to bear in mind that not every breach of the rules contained in a treaty annuls the agreement. Many breaches are the result of "misinterpretations of instructions by lower ranking officials without serious political overtones, and are often easily rectified through the diplomatic channel" (Rosenne, 1985: 8). Indeed, Friedrich Kratochwil (1987: 154) notes that "a violation of a rule, when admitted by the perpetrator, might actually strengthen the future adherence to the rule by the

have argued throughout this book, the attitudes that national leaders hold toward the sanctity of agreements will determine whether alliances are the artifacts of insincere promises, or whether they are truly ties that bind.

Stephen Van Evera (1984: 97) illustrates this point when he contrasts the Triple Alliance and the Triple Entente with Bismarck's alliances of the 1880s. It was not the mere existence of the alliances of 1914 that caused and spread the first World War; it was their unconditional nature. Bismarck's network of alliances, he claims, "would have lowered the risk of war by facing aggressors with many enemies, and by making status quo powers secure in the knowledge that they had many allies. Wars also would have tended to remain localized, because the allies of an aggressor would have stood aside from any war that aggressor had provoked."

Inherent in the foregoing argument is the proposition that fluid alignments are less dangerous than rigid coalitions where allies back one another unreservedly, regardless of whether their behavior is defensive or provocative (Van Evera, 1984: 96). The experiences of the Swiss "urban leagues" of the thirteenth century (e.g., Basle with Rhine towns, Berne with the Burgundian Confederation, and Zurich with Swabian towns) and similar combinations formed by Italian cities in the late fourteenth century (e.g., the League of Bologna) lend support to the view that flexible, short-term alliances aimed at warding off expansionary threats tend to stabilize decentralized, self-help systems. Furthermore, the experience of World War I supports the view that alliances that provide unconditional support for their members may prevent a war from being swiftly decided. France, for example, "could hardly have kept going after the disastrous Nivelle offensive and the 1917 mutinies, Italy could hardly have avoided collapse after its defeat at Caporetto in 1917, and the Austro-Hungarian Empire could hardly have continued after the dreadful losses of 1916 (or even the 1914 failures in Galicia and Serbia) had not each of them received timely support from its allies" (Kennedy, 1987: 256).

Yet counter examples abound. Perhaps the most famous is the failure of flexible, short-term alliances to deter Frederick the Great from his quest to acquire Silesia, a quest that ultimately entailed three wars and succeeded despite the Great Diplomatic Revolution of 1756, engineered by Count Kaunitz, the Austrian foreign minister.

trespasser and others alike." In contrast to these minor breaches, recall that we are concerned with deliberate repudiations that possess sufficient gravity to violate a provision central to the accomplishment of the purpose of the treaty.

What these examples and counterexamples imply is that no configuration of alliances can guarantee global stability. Certain configurations may, however, be less war-prone than others. If, as suggested above, the flexibility and reliability of alliance commitments are more important to the stability of the state system than the number of alliances that are formed, then the following questions rise to the top of our research agenda: How much flexibility should ideally exist in alliance formation rates and partner choice? How much faith can alliance members place in the reliability of their partners given prevailing norms regarding promissory obligatons?

As discussed in Chapter 3, different answers have been given to these questions. According to one school of thought (e.g., Waltz, 1967), rigidly maintained alliance structures such as those exhibited in the bipolar world after World War II help prevent war by clarifying the positions of potential friends and foes. With freedom of action thus reduced, wars are less likely to result from miscalculation or erroneous perceptions. Another school of thought (e.g., Deutsch and Singer, 1964) contends that fluid, pluralistic configurations help prevent war by increasing unpredictability. The cross-cutting ties, overlapping interests, and competing loyalties intrinsic to this kind of structure make it unclear how much external opposition belligerents would face in the event of hostilities, leading states to act with caution whenever war seems imminent. Whereas the former school associates international stability with uncertainty reduction; the latter school claims that stability is increased by maximizing uncertainty.

These divergent answers show that our picture of the relationship between alliance and war is "blurred and sketchy" (Zinnes, 1980b: 359). There is little agreement as to whether alliances contribute to the onset and expansion of war, or to its containment and prevention. Conceivably, this is because there is an element of truth in each school of thought (Rosecrance, 1966). That is to say, the relationship between alliance flexibility and war may not simply be positive or negative as the above views intimate. Instead, based on Michael Wallace's (1973) research, there is some evidence that the relationship may actually be curvilinear. If one looks only at data that show when the system initially moves away from a low level of polarization, the relationship would appear to be negative. Alternatively, if one looks only at data that show the latter phases of movement toward a highly polarized system, the relationship would appear to be positive. Like a parabola, the relationship reverses direction beyond a certain point, therein suggesting that very loose and very rigid alliance structures both cause war (Wallace, 1973: 597). We submit that although this finding helps clarify how the research results that we already have fit together, it is also necessary to determine if an important piece is still missing from the puzzle, namely, the role of prevailing alliance norms.

EMPIRICAL TESTS OF THE HYPOTHESIZED CONNECTION BETWEEN ALLIANCE NORMS AND WAR

Having made the argument that alliance norms are a missing piece in the alliance and war puzzle, it now remains for us to determine whether we can account for the onset and expansion of war by referring to changes in their content. On the face of it, such a claim would appear warranted since many scholars assert that although international norms do not necessarily prevent violence, they do reduce the amount of war that occurs within the state system (Castren, 1954: 5–6; Jacobini, 1962: 242; Padelford and Lincoln, 1967: 435).

A Research Design for Testing the Relationship Between Alliance Norms and War

The correlational design we have chosen for investigating the linkage between alliance norms and war contains four features. First, it addresses whether war broke out within a given period and, if so, how much war occurred. The former is measured in dichotomous terms (war or no war), while the latter is measured by three indicators: *magnitude* (the number of nation-months of war normalized by system size), *severity* (the number of battle deaths), and *intensity* (a ratio of severity to magnitude). As in Chapter 6, the operational definitions and raw data are taken from the Correlates of War (COW) project (see Singer and Small, 1972).

Second, because many individuals charge that international law only reflects the normative orientations of the most active and influential states, we have restricted our tests to two spatial-temporal domains: the European great power system of 1820–1914, and the central power system of 1820–1939.[3] Threats to valid inference about

---

3. Our objective here was to strengthen the design by comparing different spatial-temporal domains that contained "active and influential" states. Following Robert M. Rood and Patrick J. McGowan (1974), we selected World War I as the breakpoint for our first domain and used their membership criteria to define Great Britain, France, Prussia/Germany, Austria-Hungary, and Russia as the European great powers. In our second domain, we selected World War II as the breakpoint and adopted

the impact of alliance norms on interstate behavior are reduced by this procedure, since both domains were unaffected by the existence of nuclear weapons, a factor that could alter the capacity of alliances to combine military capabilities in any meaningfully additive way.

Third, with regard to measuring the content of prevailing alliance norms we have used the commitment index described in Chapter 4 as an independent variable. The higher the score on the index, the greater the support within the legal order for the norm *pacta sunt servanda;* the lower the score, the greater the support for *rebus sic stantibus.* Consistent with the methodological practices employed in preceding chapters, the data were aggregated by five-year intervals.

Finally, in order to add controls to our tests of the association between alliance norms and war we have included two indicators of structural flexibility. In our great power tests, we rely upon the Poisson-based measurement technique proposed by Richard E. Hays (1973) and adopted by Robert M. Rood and Patrick J. McGowan (1974: 6) in their study of alliance flexibility during the nineteenth century. As described in Chapter 8, they calculated the average rate of alliance formation by half-decade (m), and then determined the cumulative probability that the observed number of alliances formed in each period (x) was less than m. The higher the probability score, the greater the flexibility within a given five-year interval. By way of contrast, in our central power tests, we rely on an indicator that Manus L. Midlarsky (1975: 83) borrowed from information theory. The indicator, which is based on finding

$$\sum_{i=1}^{N} - P(x_i)\log_b P(x_i),$$

was originally developed to measure the variety of patterns in signals that were transmitted at a given period in time. By focusing on the probabilities (P) of the occurrence of specific alliances rather than signals (x_i), we sought to make an inference about flexibility from the changes in the variety of alliance patterns between half-decades.

Results of Data Analyses

The theoretical argument that alliance norms and war are related can be examined empirically in two basic ways. We begin with the

---

the Correlates of War project central system membership criteria. Simply put, the central system includes those states in addition to the European great powers that play vigorous parts in interstate politics (see Singer and Small, 1972: 22–30).

question of whether the type of alliance norm that exists during a given period is related to the *outbreak* of war. Subsequently, we turn our attention to whether the type of alliance norm is related to the *amount* of war that breaks out.

To determine whether we can predict the outbreak of war by knowing the type of alliance norm that dominated the international legal order during a particular period, we treated our dependent variable as a dichotomy (war/no war) and our independent variable as a trichotomy (*pacta sunt servanda* dominated/ *rebus sic stantibus* dominated/ neither norm dominated). The two most common approaches to analyzing nominal-level cross-classifications of this kind are by measures based on chi-square and by proportional-reduction-in-error (PRE) measures.[4] Cramer's *V*, the chi-square-based measure we employed, revealed a strong association between alliance norms and war among the great powers ($V = .66$, $X^2 = 8.38$, $p = .02$) and a moderate association among the central powers ($V = .44$, $X^2 = 4.54$, $p = .10$). Chi-square-based measures, like Cramer's *V*, are both sensitive to marginal distributions and difficult to interpret. Therefore, we also calculated Goodman and Kruskal's tau, a PRE measure that usually gives smaller values than *V*. Once again we found our ability to predict the category of the dependent variable based on knowing the category of the independent variable greater for the major powers ($\tau_b = .44$) than for the central powers ($\tau_b = .19$). Between 1820 and 1914, war among the great powers occurred in every half-decade during which *rebus sic stantibus* was the dominant norm, and in 50 percent of the half-decades when *pacta sunt servanda* dominated. Between 1820 and 1939, war occurred among the central powers in 93 percent of the periods when *rebus sic stantibus* dominated, and in 60 percent of the periods when *pacta sunt servanda* dominated.

Although these results generally support the contention that war is less likely to occur when international norms uphold the sanctity of treaty commitments, it is clear that wars still occurred with alarming

---

4. A brief statistical note is in order here. We have used Cramer's *V* for our chi-square-based measure of association rather than either Tschuprow's *T* or the contingency coefficient because *V* has a value of 0.00 whenever the independent and dependent variables are statistically independent, and because *V* can attain unity even in contingency tables that are not square. On the other hand, we have used Goodman and Kruskal's tau for our PRE measure rather than the more common Guttman coefficient of predictability (λ) because lambda is inappropriate in situations in which modal frequencies of the independent variable are concentrated in one category of the dependent variable. In our data, this occurred in the war category of the war/no war dichotomy.

frequency in both these spatial-temporal domains regardless of whether promissory obligations were viewed as binding or elastic. Thus we need to take up the second of our two questions about the systemic impact of alliance norms, that is, whether the type of alliance norm that exists during a given period affects the level of war that occurs.

Table 9.2 presents the results from a simple bivariate analysis of the relationship between our index of alliance commitment and the magnitude, severity, and intensity of war.[5] The direction of the correlations supports the hypothesis that the level of war decreases as alliance conceptions become more binding, but the moderate to weak strength of the correlations limits the amount of causal impact that can be imputed. Moreover, before we can advance even modest claims about the nature of the relationship, we need to conduct more stringent tests to ascertain if the preceding correlations are in fact spurious.

**Table 9.2. Bivariate Relationships between Treaty
Commitments and the Level of War**

	Degree to Which Obligations were Considered Binding					
	Great Power System (1820–1914)			*Central Power System (1820–1939)*		
Dimension of War	r	ρ	DW	r	ρ	DW
Magnitude	−.42	−.68	1.52	−.34	−.13	1.92
Severity	−.37	.58	1.16	−.24	−.08	1.78
Intensity	−.37	.35	1.68	−.28	−.03	1.93

In order to see if the relationships reported in Table 9.2 were spurious, we calculated the first-order partial correlations between alliance commitment and each dimension of war, controlling for structural flexibility. As mentioned earlier, we used the Poisson-based measure of flexibility developed by Rood and McGowan as a control in the great power domain, and Midlarsky's information theory measure in the central power domain. Our intent was to find if the results from two different spatial-temporal domains would lead us to the

---

5. As in those previous chapters where the existence of autocorrelated disturbances in our time-series data made ordinary least squares estimators inefficient, we used the Cochrane-Orcutt technique of generalized least squares regression (GLS) analysis.

same conclusions. For the great powers, we found that the partials remained negative, but larger in size over the zero-order correlations for magnitude $(-.63)$, severity $(-.53)$, and intensity $(-.47)$ of war begun. For the central powers, the partials were also negative, though they did not show much change in size over the zero-order correlations involving magnitude $(-.33)$, severity $(-.21)$, or intensity $(-.28)$. Although these results are preliminary in every sense of the word, they nonetheless suggest that commitment norms may indeed be a missing piece in the alliance and war puzzle.

If international norms regarding the nature of one's treaty obligations are a missing piece, then we should be able to account for changes in the *amount* of war fairly well by combining our alliance commitment index with our measures of structural flexibility. This would allow the relationship between alliance and war to be illuminated more fully. Although both measures of structural flexibility are inversely related to the degree to which treaty obligations are considered binding $(r = -.18)$, the weakness of the relationship is somewhat surprising and leads us to hypothesize that the degree of structural flexibility within the system and the content of prevailing commitment norms may exert an additive influence on the amount of war that occurs. It is one thing (as we have argued in Chapter 8) to be able to switch alliance partners regardless of ideological affinities or personal ties; it is quite another to do so prior to the expiration of one's current alliance agreements. Therefore, given the likelihood that these two predictor variables are independently related to war, we included both of them in a set of multivariate, time-series regression equations.

Table 9.3 gives the results from the regression analysis for the great powers. Overall, they fit our theoretical expectations fairly well. Taking both independent variables together, we can account for roughly two-thirds of the variance in the magnitude and severity of war. A comparison of the betas shows that structural flexibility is the most potent of the two independent variables. Further examination reveals that binding alliance commitments were inversely related to the amount of war, while structural flexibility exhibited a curvilinear relationship that took the form of a second-degree polynomial.[6] Insofar as the parabolic shape of this curve indicates that the amount of war

---

6. Based on a visual inspection of our scatterplots and the theoretical proposition mentioned earlier (that there is a curvilinear relationship between alliance polarization and war) we attempted to fit several different types of curves to the data. Of these, a second-degree polynomial gave us the best fit.

Table 9.3. Multivariate Relationships between Treaty Commitments, Alliance Flexibility, and the Level of War: Great Power System, 1820–1914

Dimension of War	Degree to Which Treaty Obligations Considered Binding (Beta)	Degree of Structural Flexibility (Betas)	R	R^2	F	DW
Magnitude	−.37 (−2.44)	−2.79 (−4.09) +2.15 (+3.15)	.81	.65	8.79	2.23 (.32)
Severity	−.43 (−2.99)	−2.52 (−4.06) +2.04 (+3.26)	.82	.67	9.48	1.66 (.49)
Intensity	−.34 (−1.73)	−1.80 (−2.05) +1.52 (+1.72)	.61	.37	2.79	1.73 (.43)

Note: The entries in parentheses below each standardized regression coefficient contain *t* statistics. The value of ρ is given in parentheses below the Durbin-Watson statistic.

begun is high whenever alliance configurations are either extremely flexible or extremely rigid, we postulate that peace is best preserved when there is a moderate degree of flexibility in alliances, and when those alliances that are formed are considered binding by their parties.

Does this postulate hold up when we change our spatial-temporal domain and our measure of structural flexibility? Table 9.4 contains the results from the central power analysis. In essence, the findings parallel those displayed in the previous table. First of all, the beta weights disclosed that the relative potency of the independent variables was the same: changes in the flexibility of alliances had a greater impact on war than changes in those norms regarding the extent of a nation's treaty obligations. Second, the direction of the betas supported the postulate that less war occurs when there is a moderate amount of fluidity in the structure of alliances, and the content of

Table 9.4. Multivariate Relationships between Treaty Commitments, Alliance Flexibility, and the Level of War: Central Power System, 1820–1939

Dimension of War	Degree to Which Treaty Obligations Considered Binding (Beta)	Degree of Structural Flexibility (Betas)	R	R^2	F	DW
Magnitude	−.40 (−2.10)	−1.28 (−2.04) +1.29 (+2.11)	.52	.27	2.29	2.00 (.31)
Severity	−.22 (−1.24)	−1.21 (−1.83) +1.39 (+2.14)	.51	.26	2.21	1.73 (.12)
Intensity	−.31 (−1.40)	−.76 (−1.05) +.73 (+1.04)	.36	.13	.95	1.92 (−.01)

Note: The entries in parentheses below each standardized regression coefficient contain *t* statistics. The value of ρ is given in parentheses below the Durbin-Watson statistic.

existing international norms upholds the inviolability of alliance commitments. But in spite of the convergence of both analyses in these areas, the multiple coefficients of determination were not as robust in the case of the central powers as they had been for the great powers. Nevertheless, these findings provide evidence that it is unwise to restrict ourselves solely to the international system's structural attributes when attempting to solve the alliance and war puzzle. Behind the formalities of treaty signings lurk important psychocultural variables that have behavioral consequences. To the leaders forging them, the reliability of an alliance is critical; and here, expectations of credibility, commitment, and loyalty may matter as much as the words appearing in either the documents they endorse or in the speeches they deliver at the signing ceremonies.

In summary, studies of alliance dynamics have traditionally conceptualized flexibility in terms of the ability of a given state to form new alliances with any other state in the international system, even its ideological enemies. As expressed by Morton A. Kaplan (1957b: xiv–xv), "any alignment is as probable as any other alignment. . . . [and] any particular alignment should not predispose the same nations to align themselves with each other at the next opportunity." Alliance formation, in other words, is depicted as a stochastic process; any combination of states is as probable at the upper boundary of flexibility as any other combination. Deviations from this degree of flexibility are often explained by referring to the personal idiosyncracies of particular leaders, their domestic political constraints, or bureaucratic inertia (Lockhart, 1978: 553–559). Throughout this book we have argued that flexibility can and should be conceptualized in still another sense: besides investigating the degree of structural flexibility that occurs within different alliance configurations, we also need to look at the flexibility afforded states by international norms to break existing alliance treaties.[7]

When international norms are added to the other pieces of the alliance and war puzzle, it is possible to draw several conclusions about the sources of global instability, conclusions that often are overlooked by those who only pay attention to the more tangible, concrete properties of alliances. To begin with, despite the praise often given to such leaders as King Hiero of Syracuse (270–216 B.C.) for the diplomatic acumen to disregard promises and switch allies whenever considerations of power and interest dictate, our findings indicate that the state system tends to become unstable when allegiance is ruled by expedience. But beyond this, our findings also indicate that it is destabilizing for alliance configurations to become so polarized and rigid that allies back one another unreservedly regardless of whether their behavior is provocative. Peace, we conclude, is best preserved when there is a moderate amount of flexibility in alliance initiations and partner choices, when commitments are made judiciously and not left open-ended, and when promissory obligations are considered binding by prevailing international norms.

TREATIES, TRUST, AND THE RACE TO RUIN

At this point, it might be helpful to take stock of the results discussed in this and the previous three chapters, as there are a number

---

7. See Bilder (1981) for a survey of techniques used by states to protect themselves against the possibility that their alliance partners may not uphold their treaty obligations.

of points that merit special attention when considered in conjunction with the results from other research projects.

Systemic Trajectories and War

The manner in which international norms arise and spread throughout the state system is not well understood. Yet it is clear that planned rule making usually follows in the aftermath of destructive wars. These periodic conflicts present unique opportunities to evaluate past practices and promote new rules to replace those that have become discredited. At times, these revised rules have supported the sanctity of promissory obligations; but at other times, they have legitimized the opportunistic renunciation of promissory obligations. Prevailing international norms of this sort are one of the main factors that determine whether the state system will move along a stable or unstable trajectory in the wake of war.

The foundation for the *stable trajectory* lies in capability concentration. During periods when military strength lies in the hands of one or very few major powers, a restrictive legal order upholding the inviolability of treaty commitments tends to emerge. When subsequently combined with a moderate amount of flexibility in the configuration of alliances, this norm enhances the prospects for managing crises, lowers the probability of war, and reduces the magnitude and severity of violence if war does erupt.

Although an *unstable trajectory* may also unfold after a system-transforming war, it is more typically grounded in the diffusion of power among many, relatively equal states. A welter of causes have been proposed by scholars working out of different paradigms to explain this process of capability deconcentration. Uneven economic growth within the world-economy (Chase-Dunn, 1981: 36), the transfer of new strategic technologies from advanced to less advanced societies (Gilpin, 1981: 180), and the success of some states in rapidly developing a more efficient means for extracting and pooling human and material resources (Organski and Kugler, 1980: 20) are just a few of the causes that have been hypothesized. But regardless of the source of capability deconcentration, the consequence has customarily been the rise of a permissive legal order that accepts an elastic interpretation of treaty commitment. "If the leading actors [within the state system] directly control a sufficient fraction of the total relevant capability," observes Charles F. Doran (1983a: 171), "[international] law will have an oligarchic rather than a pluralistic . . . bias." However, "[as] the disparity of power between the leading actors and others in the system declines, far more flexibility results."

An environment where promissory obligations are not honored breeds mistrust, alarm, and an upswing in serious disputes. The bitter rivalry between Rome and Sassanid Persia between A.D. 363 and 502 is one example from an early period that demonstrates war can be avoided in such an environment (see Bullough, 1957: 66). The general historical pattern indicates, however, that the odds are not high for this outcome, especially considering Manus Midlarsky's (1984) finding that the accumulation of serious disputes has often been a progenitor of war.

One way the build-up of such disputes leads to war is through the tendency of leaders in successive crises to employ more coercive bargaining techniques in each subsequent encounter (Leng, 1983). The problem with relying on coercive diplomacy to communicate resolve is that bullying tactics and physical threats to vital interests have been found to be associated with the escalation of crises into wars (Gochman and Leng, 1983; Leng and Wheeler, 1979; also see Leng, 1984).

Another way that the build-up of serious disputes can raise the probability of war is through the tendency of those involved in confrontations to seek allies and acquire additional arms. Richard W. Mansbach and John A. Vasquez (1981) have shown that during a series of disputes, numerous distinct political stakes become linked into a single over-arching issue. This tends to increase the intractibility of the conflict and lessens the prospects for an amicable settlement, so the disputants are inclined to search for assistance through the formation of alliances. According to Bruce Bueno de Mesquita (1981: 152), alliances increase the chances of victory by 7 percent for the initiating side in a war, and by twice that amount for the target nation. In view of these statistics, the search for allies is not surprising. This strategy ultimately may prove to be destabilizing, however, because alliance aggregation has been found to be related to subsequent increases in arms expenditures (Wallace, 1972), perhaps as a hedge against the ever-present possibility that in a permissive normative order one's partners may defect when they are most needed.

The difficulties posed by alliance acquisition are twofold. In the first place, serious disputes that take place during arms races tend to escalate into wars (Wallace, 1979, 1980, 1982). In the second place, if war occurs, the effect of alliances will be to spread the hostilities and create a larger, more complex conflict (Siverson and King, 1979).

Thus, as the state system moves farther along this unstable trajectory, it becomes increasingly difficult to preserve peace. The search for allies will grow intense, and states will tie their fate to the promises of those with whom they align; but eventually this system will break down if these alliance commitments are not buttressed by norms that support the faithful observation of promissory obligations. It is then that alliances will fail to perform their primary function: deterring aggression by others.

Let us pursue the implications of these historical patterns by turning to a case study that reveals the ruinous nature of the unstable trajectory that the state system followed in the aftermath of World War I.

Moral and Material Disarmament in the Interwar Period: A Case Study

The disarmament negotiations between the first and second world wars are instructive of the difficulties inherent in efforts to preserve peace amidst a climate of mistrust. The peacemakers of 1919 declared that the purpose of the severe limitations placed by the Treaty of Versailles on the size and composition of Germany's armed forces was "to render possible the initiation of a general limitation of the armaments of all nations." They went on, in Article 8 of the Covenant of the League of Nations, to proclaim that "the maintenance of peace requires the reduction of national armaments to the lowest point consistent with national safety." Of course, these ambitious plans could easily collapse if states felt insecure. Thus, in its effort to alleviate insecurity, the League was forced to wrestle with the larger question of whether "moral disarmament" [trust] should precede "material disarmament" [weapons reductions], or vice versa.

What made this question both urgent and vexing was the turbulent environment of the period. Attitudes toward promissory obligations were undergoing a profound transformation at this time. World War I had shaken the moral consensus of a state system whose leading members had once been linked by familial and cultural ties. As C. A. W. Manning (1962: 101–113) points out, international law functions like a language game that sets the rules for diplomatic communication. With the coming to power of the Bolsheviks in Russia (1917), the Fascists in Italy (1922), and the National Socialists in Germany (1933), the old rules of diplomatic discourse and behavior broke down. "It is difficult to play chess with someone who insists upon moving his bishops like rooks," observe Gordon A. Craig and Alexander L. George (1983: 58), and it was equally difficult to reach agreement with a Bolshevik or National Socialist negotiator "who employed all of his diplomatic guile to make agreement impossible."

Further complicating a situation in which revisionist powers attempted to gain advantages over others by breaking the rules of the diplomatic game was the frequency with which the status quo powers worked at cross-purposes. France, having lost its bid to control the left bank of the Rhine River as a physical guarantee against future German aggression, sought security through a combination of alliances with Belgium, Poland, and the Little Entente (Czechoslovakia, Rumania, and Yugoslavia). But neither these alliances nor the collective security provisions of the League satisfied French Foreign Minister Raymond Poincaré. He tried in vain to secure a precise, binding military commitment from the British, who preferred instead to establish a more flexible relationship. Differences in their respective definitions of security also led these wartime partners to disagree over French and Belgian occupation of the Ruhr in 1923 and the wisdom of having an autonomous government in the Palatinate. Salvador de Madariaga, a participant in many of the interwar arms control negotiations, summarized the Franco-British dialogue on disarmament and security in the following terms:

> The Frenchman said: "We are all agreed about principles; therefore, please sign this paper in which our agreed principles are set forth and developed to their logical conclusions." And the Englishman answered: "True, we are agreed about principles, there is no need to sign anything at all. When the time comes to apply them, we shall do so in the light of the circumstances, and since we are agreed on principles, there is no doubt but that we shall agree as to their application." Then the Frenchman was taken aback and went home full of misgivings: "He does not want to sign, therefore he does not really believe in the principles," he suspected. While the Englishman went home muttering: "He wanted to pin me down forever. I wonder what he had up his sleeve." (de Madariaga, 1929: 25)

The Franco-British dialogue revealed the extent to which expectations about the intentions of others concerned those who participated in the disarmament negotiations. Presumptions about the strength of another party's commitment were critical to the crafting of treaties, and, more importantly, to their ultimate effects.

Despite the welter of uncertainties in the postwar diplomatic atmosphere, a naval arms limitation regime was crafted at the 1921– 1922 Washington Conference.[8] Its principal feature was a 5 : 5 : 3 : 1.67 : 1.67 ratio in battleship tonnage for the British, American, Japanese, French, and Italian navies, with a ceiling of 525,000 tons standard displacement, and individual vessel tonnage set at 35,000. Outside the category of battleships, a 5 : 5 : 3 ratio was established for aircraft carriers, with a ceiling of 135,000 tons, and individual vessels limited to 27,000 tons displacement. The conference was applauded as a great success, but soon thereafter the signatories began exploring ways to circumvent the limitations in the regime. Fleets were expanded in fields not constrained by the Five Power Treaty (e.g., cruisers, destroyers, and submarines), and qualitative improvements that enhanced combat effectiveness were made on those vessels that were quantitatively restricted (e.g., utilizing new alloys to construct stronger, lighter hulls, building higher-efficiency engines, raising gun turrets, and using a different type of propellant to increase firing range and accuracy, as well as adding deck armor to protect against air attacks). In short, by the mid-1920s it was clear that the Washington Conference had not stopped the naval arms race; it had merely rechanneled competition into unregulated areas.

If the process of material disarmament had stalled, many individuals believed that it was because a shroud of suspicion hung over the state system. Consequently they called for moral disarmament to build mutual confidence and nurture international goodwill. Echoing that same sentiment, John G. Stoessinger (1986: 371) notes that "the problem of disarmament is not disarmament at all, but is in essence the problem of forging the bonds of political community."

---

8. Three major treaties were negotiated at the Washington Conference: (1) the Four Power Treaty (December 13, 1921) established American, British, French, and Japanese spheres of influence in the Pacific; (2) the Nine Power Treaty (February 6, 1922) endorsed the maintenance of an "open door" for commerce throughout China, while calling upon the signatories "to respect the sovereignty, the independence, and the territorial integrity of China;" and (3) the Five Power Treaty (February 6, 1922) limited the naval araments of Great Britain, the United States, Japan, France, and Italy. In addition to these major treaties, several minor agreements emerged from the Washington Conference, including an informal understanding between Japan and the Soviet Union regarding the withdrawal of Japanese troops from Siberia and northern Sakhalin, and formal treaties between China and Japan (February 4, 1922) and the United States and Japan (February 11, 1922) concerning various disputed issues in the Pacific.

In 1925, in order to encourage moral disarmament, a series of agreements were reached at Locarno, Switzerland. According to the final protocol of the conference, the participants hoped that by guaranteeing the frontiers between Germany and her western neighbors, and by providing a mechanism to resolve any future disputes, suspicion would dissipate and League members could hasten the material disarmament promised in Article 8 of the Covenant.

But progress was slow. The League's Preparatory Commission for the Disarmament Conference began meeting in 1926, but quickly became paralyzed by disagreements over what types of weapons should be limited and how deep to make any cuts. Similarly, the Geneva Naval Conference of 1927 was unsuccessful in its attempt to extend the Washington ratio to auxiliary ships. Heartened by advances made at the 1930 London Naval Conference, representatives from 61 countries came together in Geneva during 1932 under the auspices of the World Disarmament Conference. Unfortunately, this effort failed because conference participants could not reach any agreement, underscoring the difficulties that arise when trust breaks. From the perspective of E. H. Carr (1948: 190), ''The failure of the Allied Powers to carry out their promise to disarm justified, or at any rate explained, the rearmament of Germany. This rearmament necessarily led to increased apprehension and increased armaments in other countries; and the vicious circle which the statesmen of 1919 had hoped to break was once more complete.''

As this experience indicates, peace is difficult to preserve when the state system moves along an unstable trajectory. In a climate of mistrust, where the repudiation of promissory agreements is accepted by prevailing international norms, states are less likely to find security in alliances. One powerful and trustworthy ally may be worth more than a dozen feeble and fickle allies (Schuman, 1969: 277), but the scarcity of reliable partners may tempt states to seek security in arms. Yet the very normative environment that evokes this behavior may thwart efforts to control arms races. The demise of the Washington naval arms limitation regime in the 1930s underscores why a modicum of trust is crucial for the success of an arms control agreement. Continued war preparation by members of the regime contributed to the perception that commitment to the regime was less than firm (Hoover, 1980: 107). Nor could verification substitute for trust. Allan S. Krass (1985) points out that information from even the best monitoring systems is often incomplete and ambiguous. Without a minimum of trust, garbled information could lead one to assume the worst about an adversary, draw sinister conclusions, and embark upon the fatal leg of a race to ruin. As Mikhail Gorbachev put it in his December 7, 1988, speech to the United Nations, without trust "it is difficult to make headway in politics."

BRINGING THE EVIDENCE TOGETHER

The rules of the international legal order, embodied in diplomatic discourse, rest on what C. A. W. Manning (1962) has called an allegiance to shared myths. Foremost among these deeply held beliefs are the ideas of the sovereign territorial state and the "billiard ball" model of how such states interact. According to these beliefs, each state is a closed, impermeable unit in full control of all land, people, and resources within the hard shell of its fortified boundaries (Wolfers, 1962: 19). When national interests collide, the outcome is determined by the relative mass and velocity of those states involved in the collision. From this point of view, national leaders continually face the problem of weathering the impact of forces beyond their control.

Under these circumstances, what standard of conduct should guide foreign policy? How can states best cope with those external forces that seem to threaten their security?

By presenting an image of reality, a myth assigns significance to certain ostensibly historical events and instructs us about their meaning. Because myths often teach by allegorization, their instructions are ambiguous and subject to alternative interpretations. Nowhere is this more evident than in the rules pertaining to "state necessity" that derive from shared myths about a world where sovereign territorial units collide with one another like balls on a billiard table. Owing to the alleged exigencies of necessity, one rule defends the right of states to renounce commitments when changed circumstances render them burdensome. Another rule assumes that necessity is merely a subterfuge for expediency, and proclaims that commitments are binding. The former rule lies at the core of a permissive normative order; the latter, at the core of a restrictive order.

Although wars have occurred within both types of order, the prospects for peace have been enhanced when a restrictive normative order has existed together with a moderate amount of flexibility in the pattern of alliance formation. From the vantage point of the systemic level of analysis, the most stable architecture of alliances is one in which commitments are limited, specific, and backed by international norms that support a binding interpretation of promissory obligations.

Part V

A World Without Honor: Conclusions

10 Trust and International Order

But why is it not possible for the properly-understood interest of the States themselves, co-operating by reason of ethical motives, to induce them to unite and freely restrict the methods of their power politics, to abide by law and morality, and to develop the institution of International Law . . . to a full and satisfactory efficiency? Because none of them will trust another round the corner.

Friedrich Meinecke

Treaties are the bones and sinew of the global body politic, making it possible for states to move from talk through compromise to solemn commitment. They are also its moral fiber, the evidence that governments and people have pledged their "full faith and credit" to one another. . . . A nation that deliberately sets out to debase its treaty-worthiness, quite simply, is in danger of becoming a global street person: self-destructive and heedless of its own best interests.

Thomas M. Franck

The primary task of statecraft in an endemically insecure state system is to increase national security. Nations can do this either by building up their own military and economic strength, or by joining with other nations in some form of collective defense. Every state must confront the difficult choice of whether to go it alone or to go it with others. The choice is difficult because "joining a military alliance can either increase or decrease a country's security, depending on the behavior of the other alliance members" (Fischer, 1984: 136). In large measure, whether security is increased will depend on the confidence that can be placed in the likelihood that one's allies will abide by their promises when an occasion arises that requires them to fulfill their obligations.

Throughout diplomatic history, many theorists and statesmen have interpreted binding alliance commitments as a mistake because they compromise a state's ability to adapt to changes in the flow of threats and opportunities. But many others have depicted faithful compliance with promises as a stabilizing element. To some, therefore, making

242

promises jeopardizes national safety and erodes international security; to others, keeping promises is a way of keeping the peace.

Our goal has been to uncover the causes and consequences in world politics of the espousal of two conflicting views of promissory obligations. The first view holds that states in alliance should feel free to release themselves from treaty responsibilities when compliance with their provisions would undermine national interests, and the second contends that international agreements between allies should be regarded as binding. These norms are rooted in opposed international legal principles, captured in the *clausula rebus sic stantibus* and the doctrine *pacta sunt servanda*. Each principle addresses the fundamental question on which the axiology of the international legal order hinges: can international agreements be altered without the consent of all the parties to them?

Underlying the entire spectrum of diplomatic discourse on this topic is the subjective concept of trust. As Bernhardt Lieberman (1968: 359) has written, embedded within most debates on foreign policy lies a concern whether it is "important, possible, or sensible to trust a nation, or group of nations, in the conduct of international affairs, [and, once] a treaty is signed . . . can or should a nation or group of nations be trusted?" He defined the positions taken to these timeless questions in the following terms:

> Without doing lethal damage to the essence of the arguments, it is possible to dichotomize the various views about these questions. One group argues it is irrelevant, and possibly dangerous, to consider the notion of trust in the conduct of international relations. Nations, it is said, will act in their own self-interest and abrogate treaties, agreements, or their word informally given, whenever it is believed to be necessary to do so. It is said that a nation that does not act in its own self-interest is difficult to deal with; trustworthy behavior contrary to national interests is irresponsible and dangerous. Therefore there is no point in concerning oneself with such a value-laden notion as trust. Trust is irrelevant in the conduct of international affairs, it is said, and if we seek to resolve conflicts among nations rationally, before they become harmful and mutually destructive, we must not trust our opponents at all; we must not even consider such a notion seriously.
>
> A second group believes that at the root of the difficulty in international affairs is the fact that nations cannot and do not trust each other. Aggressive behavior and conflicts arise not so much from genuinely irreconcilable conflicts, but more from mistrust, suspicion, and untrustworthy acts. They believe that one should impress upon one's op-

ponent one's good intentions. One should take actions that do not endanger one's own security, but that promote trust and demonstrate
good will. One should sign arms control and disarmament agreements,
small ones at first, but agreements that will build mutual trust and positive feelings. (Lieberman, 1968: 360)

These juxtaposed views are represented by the nihilist and idealist
philosophies about the place of promissory obligations in world
politics.[1] Let us recall the differences separating these views of statecraft. At one extreme is the nihilist view, which regards promises as a
mere guise designed to enhance the power of those making them;
breaking promises and the practice of treachery are to be expected
when advantages can be gained by a betrayal. The aphorism that de-
fines a diplomat as "a man sent abroad to lie in the interest of the
state" captures the cynical world view held by exponents of the nihilist philosophy. Treaties entrap and are dangerous. States should
never permit themselves to become entangled in agreements from
which they cannot retreat without destroying credibility and cannot
transcend without substantial risks. The security of all will be jeopar-
dized under a regime that restricts states to the steadfast performance
of their commitments.

In contrast to this view, idealists proclaim that sincerity is a virtue
and that a state's interests are served by maintenance of its commitments. A central tenet of this philosophy is that the capacity of governments to resolve their disputes peacefully will be enhanced if they
act honorably and operate from the expectation that others will recip-
rocate. According to idealism, the prospects for cooperation and
peace are improved when suspicion and uncertainty are reduced, and
for this normative support must be given to a restrictive definition of
promissory obligations.

Finally, lying between nihilism and idealism is the so-called realist
philosophy that assumes that statesmen think in terms of national in-

1. As discussed in Chapter 2, these positions represent the logical extremes on a hypothetical continuum; they describe polar positions on promissory obligations, which in
the real world are rarely adopted unreservedly. Moreover, they may be classified in
alternate ways. For example, Franklin B. Weinstein (1969: 41) conceives of the debate as a struggle between two conceptions of commitment: "a situational concept of
commitment [focusing] on the rationality of the specified course of action in light of
the requirements of the situation, [in contrast to] a nonsituational view [which] sees
mainly the need to keep commitments in order to serve interests outside the immediate situation. A situational commitment is merely a statement of a country's
present view of its interests; a nonsituational commitment is a binding and permanent
pledge."

terest defined as power, and proscribes that they act, not in terms of promises about intentions, but in terms of prudence defined as weighing the consequences of alternative policies. Although the realist is aware of the ethical significance of a foreign policy choice, the yardstick of success against which that choice must be measured is national survival. What counts is not whether the choice meshes with some principle of justice, liberty, or the like, but whether it succeeds in advancing the security of the state. Thus classical realists subscribe neither to gross expediency nor to moral universalism; and as such, they tend to respond to abstract questions about the sanctity of agreements by deferring to the concrete circumstances of a given time and place.

The key issue on which these conflicting philosophies diverge is a fundamental element shaping world politics: the capacity for the building of trust between nations. Irrespective of whether one holds that a faith in others' good will is responsible for the world's afflictions, or, instead, is the route to the solution of the problems besetting international politics, trust is the key.[2] "No matter how amoral the conduct of international affairs may appear to some," underscores Lieberman (1968: 361), "a notion of trust, or some similar notion, is involved." All international exchanges are influenced by the sense of trust that parties to an exchange bring to it; every relationship between states is shaped by the expectations the parties maintain about each other's credibility, reliability, and capacity to adhere to promises. Therefore, the political functions and consequences of trust and mistrust, and the relationship of trust to the security dilemma facing nations (Gralnick, 1988), are topics deserving of careful analysis. The fact that "the systematic analysis of trust and distrust in social relationships" has been neglected (Barber, 1983: 5) underscores the need that this book has attempted to meet.

Our point of departure for this inquiry has derived from Richard Falk's (1970: 609) thesis that "trends in loyalty patterns are one of the important determinants of the future quality of world legal order" (and, we add by extension, global stability). Our objective, like that of Bernard Barber's (1983: 5) philosophical account of *The Logic and Limits of Trust,* has been "to try and show how broad social changes

---

2. Trust is a universal concept, which explains why "whenever philosophers, poets, statesmen, or theologians have written about man's relationship to his fellow man, to nature, or to animals, the phenomena of trust and betrayal, faith and suspicion, responsibility and irresponsibility, have been discussed" (Deutsch, 1958: 265).

have affected the different meanings of trust and how changes in particular social institutions [and diplomatic practices] can be understood as responses to varying degrees and meanings of trust.''

Trust ''can be regarded as the correct and appropriate starting point for the derivation of rules of proper conduct'' (Luhmann, 1979: 4). The rules of proper international conduct have not always placed a binding moral obligation on states to adhere to promises; instead, the opportunistic violation of commitments has often been regarded as a viable and proper policy choice. The bounded anarchy in which world politics unfolds makes the matter of trust a prominent concern for all who are engaged in interstate intercourse.

Mistrust is endemic in world politics and suspicion, pervasive. The absence of a higher authority to enforce international law exacerbates the insecurity of nations and requires them to compete for survival with actors unrestrained by rules of proper conduct. Trust is undermined in such a setting since there is little basis for confidence in others' honorable intentions and consistent conduct. Yet precisely because of this and ''the lack of agreement about what it means to be committed'' (Weinstein, 1969: 40), trust plays an important role in diplomacy.

Part of the reason stems from the paradox that interdependence among states requires a degree of cooperation, yet reliance on others enhances states' vulnerability to exploitation. Nation-states exist in inherently ''mixed-motive'' circumstances: mutually beneficial collaboration based on trust is the sine qua non for security under precisely those conditions where the temptation to exploit is great and the immediate cost of exploitation of others is minimal. Interaction within the state system is thus shaped powerfully by conditions where the need for trust is great but the basis for its creation is most lacking.

Under even relatively stable conditions all members of the international community face great uncertainty. ''Even among close allies, solidarity usually has proved perishable as time has brought changing conditions'' (Weinstein, 1969: 42). When conditions change rapidly and interests subsequently diverge, the basis for confidence diminishes further and uncertainty increases, thus compromising the ability to act on predictions about the behavior of others. It is then that trust in others' willingness to abide by their agreed course of action will be suspended, since predictability is a prerequisite for trust (Lewis and Weigert, 1985: 976). Furthermore, when the pace of change accelerates, the force of norms will be tested. Changing circumstances will reveal whether norms can serve the function for which they were de-

signed: structuring expectations and guiding behavior within restricted boundaries.

Alliance norms operate as a cultural template, communicating
awareness of the conduct to be expected in particular circumstances.
All norms thus condition behavior. In certain circumstances a consensus may emerge prescribing the faithful performance of oaths, and
when this kind of treaty regime materializes actors who depart from
the rules embedded in the regime are likely to suffer unacceptable
costs for their violation. Trust, therefore, is a situational condition
that can and sometimes does arise, even in a system of self-
adjudicating obligations where law is reduced to politics. There is
strong evidence that trustworthy behavior between nations in the past
has on occasion been built, in a system inhibiting its construction.
Thus both possibilities—a system predicated on mistrust and a system underpinned by trust—are available as alternatives, inasmuch as
there are historical counterparts for both (Lindskold, 1978).

Before reviewing and interpreting the global conditions that are associated with these possibilites, a closer inspection of the concept of
trust and its intimate relationship to alliance norms is warranted.

TRUST IN WORLD POLITICS

To illuminate the consequences which result when trust is built and
when it erodes, we have sought to discover the empirical relationship
between alliance norms and global stability. We have not explored
the motives individual nations ascribe to themselves and to others regarding commitments, or the processes through which norms are internalized; instead, we have examined the intersubjectively shared
expectations about promissory obligations that will develop when a
consensus on alliance norms crystallizes. This orientation concurs
with the view that "trust must be conceived as a property of *collective* units (ongoing dyads, groups, and collectivities), not of isolated
individuals. Being a collective attribute, trust is applicable to the relations among [national units] rather than to their psychological states
taken individually" (Lewis and Weigert, 1985: 968). Trust and distrust, in other words, are cultural phenomena conceived at the macro
level rather than at the micro level of individual actors (see Chapter
5). They are inherently social-psychological concepts "since individuals would have no occasion or need to trust apart from social relationships" (Lewis and Weigert, 1985: 969). A modicum of trust in
others, therefore, is endemic to the functioning of relations between
members of all alliances, and the performance of all alliances are af-

fected by the shared expectations held about the behavior of actors in contingent circumstances.

The perceived credibility and reliability of allies is influenced by the intersubjectively transmittted set of beliefs generally held about promissory obligations. These expectations are "social constructions" (Weigert, 1981); "the cognitive content of trust is a collective cognitive reality" (Lewis and Weigert, 1985: 970). By communicating images about the probable and permissible conduct among parties to alliance treaties, these norms shape the behavior of states by connecting the normative consensus at the systemic level to the reactions of states to allies and adversaries at the national level. International norms thus link the micro and macro levels of analysis, with perceptions providing the connecting tissue. They derive from voluntary support, and are preserved through voluntary compliance, for states are sovereign actors with few if any sanctioned obligations. A "norm represents a special form of social control in which the [actor] controlled typically agrees with and supports the legitimacy of the constraints imposed on him" (Carson, 1969: 174).

Moreover, international norms about the performance of promissory obligations are situational. They accrue power and exert an impact on outcomes whenever a normative consensus crystallizes around either *pacta sunt servanda* or *rebus sic stantibus* as principles of conduct. The moral context in which alliance formation occurs—whether inspired by an idealist vision stressing the inviolability of promises or a nihilist vision stressing the right of states to revise or terminate treaties unilaterally—will affect the capacity of treaties to cement relationships between allies when they are most needed: when changed circumstances reduce the advantages of a treaty for one or more of the parties.

Captured by the tension between these two opposed policy prescriptions is the critical element of trust. Indeed, as Emile Durkheim and others have stressed, trust is the ingredient that underwrites the capacity of a system to function peacefully and to bond its members in agreements. However, as a core component of all social systems, trust is a highly subjective cultural variable with which many meanings are associated (see Table 10.1). As J. David Lewis and Andrew Weigert observe, "trust is a highly complex and multidimensional phenomenon, having distinct cognitive, affective, behavioral, and situational manifestations which may not be co-present at any particular point in time. . . . One may trust in some respects and contexts but not others" (Lewis and Weigert, 1985: 976).

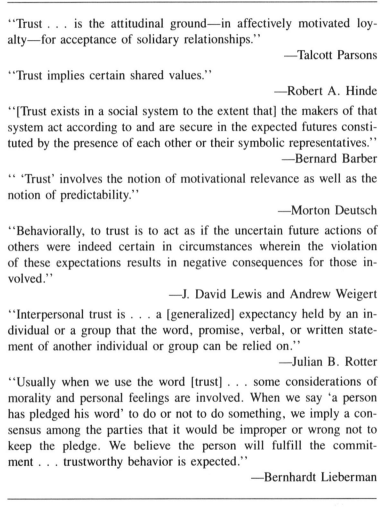

**Table 10.1. Common Attributes Associated with
the Concept of Trust**

"Trust . . . is the attitudinal ground—in affectively motivated loyalty—for acceptance of solidary relationships."

—Talcott Parsons

"Trust implies certain shared values."

—Robert A. Hinde

"[Trust exists in a social system to the extent that] the makers of that system act according to and are secure in the expected futures constituted by the presence of each other or their symbolic representatives."

—Bernard Barber

" 'Trust' involves the notion of motivational relevance as well as the notion of predictability."

—Morton Deutsch

"Behaviorally, to trust is to act as if the uncertain future actions of others were indeed certain in circumstances wherein the violation of these expectations results in negative consequences for those involved."

—J. David Lewis and Andrew Weigert

"Interpersonal trust is . . . a [generalized] expectancy held by an individual or a group that the word, promise, verbal, or written statement of another individual or group can be relied on."

—Julian B. Rotter

"Usually when we use the word [trust] . . . some considerations of morality and personal feelings are involved. When we say 'a person has pledged his word' to do or not to do something, we imply a consensus among the parties that it would be improper or wrong not to keep the pledge. We believe the person will fulfill the commitment . . . trustworthy behavior is expected."

—Bernhardt Lieberman

The influence of the level of trust on relations among nations is illuminated by the practices that become prevalent when either a nihilist or an idealist philosophy has governed diplomacy. When one as opposed to the other of these contrasting views has gained support, a normative climate of opinion has been created, leading to different kinds of systems with different cultural properties. When doubts about reliability become pervasive and the expectation gathers momentum that states are unlikely to uphold their agreements, a culture of mistrust has arisen. Conversely, when demonstrations of integrity become recurrent and a norm prescribing honesty in statecraft gains strength, the result is a political culture grounded in trust.

It is said that states, as autonomous actors, are free to choose, but they are not free to determine the consequences of their choices. Different consequences result when either of these opposed approaches to promissory obligations gains force. When mistrust is ubiquitous, certain patterns of behavior are observable, patterns that do not occur when trust is pervasive. We shall now examine those historical patterns uncovered by the empirical analyses conducted in preceding chapters.

CHANGING CONDITIONS AND DIVERGING INTERESTS

Various facets of the linkage between trust, mistrust, and norms pertaining to promissory obligations have been examined in this volume through both comparative case studies and macro-quantitative analyses. A multi-method approach was used to examine the available evidence in a variety of ways in order to lessen the possibility that our findings were dependent on, and specific to, a particular set of treatments. As a consequence, we can state with considerable confidence that the patterns observed hold across the cases explored. The findings for which support was strongest are summarized in Table 10.2.

The results disclose a number of characteristics about the role of alliance norms in world politics. Specifically, the findings inform us about the nature of the environment that will emerge when states fail to embrace the sanctity of agreements, and the type of environment that materializes when they do commit themselves to such an obligation.

Turning first to the evolutionary path of the transformation of alliance norms, the findings indicate that, historically, reconceptions of the sanctity of oaths regularly have both preceded and followed the outbreak of general (or system-transforming) wars. In the previous century, the advent of severe violence between the major powers led the statesmen of that period to see their interests served best by acceptance of flexibility in the alliance commitments they pledged to others. In the mid-twentieth century, general wars led statesmen to deduce the opposite conclusion, namely, that their interests were served best by support for a regime prescribing that commitments be faithfully honored.

These historical patterns throw into perspective some dynamic properties of the international system. In general, the nature of the normative climate of opinion is most severely strained when the international system is disrupted by fundamental changes. This tends to occur in the aftermath of general wars (Chapter 6) or in periods when the global distribution of power undergoes dramatic transformation (Chapter 7). In both instances, changed circumstances provide crucial tests of moral philosophies regarding the obligations of states toward the commitments they make. Such changes foment a reconsideration of basic national values and interests, which, in turn, leads to a reassessment of whether allies will "carry out their fiduciary obligations and responsibilities, that is, their duties in certain situations to place others' interests before their own" (Barber, 1983: 9). Whereas the fundamental changes wrought by general war may give support to the normative premises underlying either *pacta sunt servanda* or *rebus sic stantibus,* those changes produced by increases in the degree of capability concentration and alliance polarization tend to result in an increase in support for the norm *pacta sunt servanda.*

As Figure 10.1 summarizes, when global conditions change, the interests of states tend to diverge, alliance agreements are reevaluated, and the norms addressing adherence to commitments are either weakened or strengthened. When the former transpires, the state system is likely to experience greater turbulence; when the latter occurs, stability usually follows.

These findings illuminate the consequences that result when a permissive versus a restrictive interpretation is given to promissory obligations. Whether actors believe the agreements they reach incur an obligation makes a critical difference for the maintenance of the agreement and for the kind of normative atmosphere in which subsequent agreements will be negotiated. Support for the belief that pacts between allies are binding has enabled alliances to perform the function for which they were created, namely, to enhance the security of its members. Contrary to the pessimistic prophecies of nihilists, the formation of alliances underwritten by binding commitments has not increased the incidence of war; nor has it automatically widened the scope of conflicts when they erupted by drawing allies into them.

This reality underscores the importance of normative dispositions toward fulfilling contracted obligations. The manner through which international agreements are terminated and the expectations of parties to an agreement about the probability of its premature termination determine the impact of the agreement and the function it will per-

Table 10.2. The Causes and Consequences of Alliance Norm Transformation: A Summary of Findings

Proposition	Qualification	Evidence
Causes		
The greater the magnitude and severity of war termination, the greater the support for binding promissory obligations.	The relationship is stronger in the twentieth century than in the nineteenth century.	Comparative case studies, trend analysis of 1816–1974, and time-series regression analysis of 1816–1974, controlling for century, great power vis-à-vis central system, and alliance activity.
The greater the concentration of military capabilities (polarity) within the state system, the greater the support for binding promissory obligations.	The relationship is strongest at high levels of alliance aggregation and cohesion.	Case study, contingency table analysis, and time-series regression analysis of 1820–1969, controlling for the number and tightness of alliances.
The greater the polarization of alliances, the greater the support for binding promissory obligations.	The relationship is strongest at low levels of alliance cohesion.	Case study and time-series regression analysis of 1820–1969, controlling for the number and tightness of alliances.

The greater the support for binding promissory obligations, the less the frequency, scope, and intensity of serious interstate disputes.	The relationship is stronger with regard to the frequency and scope of serious disputes.	Case study, trend analysis of 1816–1976, and time-series regression analysis of 1820–1914, controlling for alliance flexibility and time lags.
The greater the support for binding promissory obligations, the less the incidence of threats, unreciprocated military action, and reciprocated military action.	The relationship is strongest when all conflict events are combined and weighted.	Case study and time-series regression analysis of 1820–1914, controlling for alliance flexibility.
The greater the support for binding promissory obligations, the less the probability of war.	The relationship is stronger among major powers than within the central power system.	Case study and contingency table analysis of 1820–1939, controlling for system level.
The greater the support for binding promissory obligations, the less the magnitude, severity, and intensity of war begun.	The relationships are stronger among major powers than within the central power system.	Case study and time-series regression analysis of 1820–1939, controlling for system level and alliance flexibility.

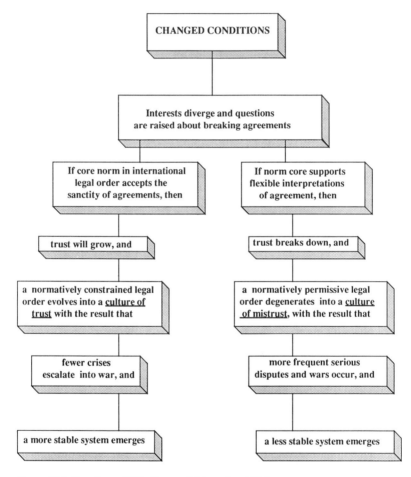

Figure 10.1. Promissory Obligations and International Order

form. Because they have such clear costs and risks associated with them, every alliance is forged with acute awareness and fear of the possibility that a grave violation of the central purpose of a treaty might occur, and parties to alliances have often joined them with apprehension and disparate interpretations of the obligations implied by the commitments pledged. The potential that agreements might be breached undermines trust. Alliances are an instrument of statecraft seldom undertaken without some mutual suspicions about the trustworthiness of allies. And yet, no agreement to ally can be struck without some modicum of trust in others' intentions. No party can know *a priori* whether treaty adherence will be practiced or whether the agreement will be used to exploit the faith of those abiding by its terms. This makes trust—confidence in the credibility of others—the cornerstone of every alliance, the fundamental factor that will determine the alliance's viability and efficacy.

To extrapolate beyond the empirical regularities disclosed in our data, we now explore the major difference in the patterns of belief and behavior that occur within two divergent cultures: one founded on mistrust, the other on trust. In so doing, we seek to delineate the social constructions of international reality that are likely to be associated with these two cultures, and summarize the probable international behavior that will occur in these different systems. In reviewing these postulated differences, we should keep in mind that the diplomatic discourse has proceeded largely in the absence of attention to these empirical regularities—a neglect with dangerous policy implications for the future.

THE CULTURE OF MISTRUST AND THE CULTURE OF TRUST

Heinrich Harrer (1959), a member of the first party to climb the notorious Eiger Nordwand, stressed the importance of loyalty and reliability as qualities in a rope-mate. Allies, like mountaineers tied together during a perilous climb, depend on their partners for security in a hostile environment. When doubts about the loyalty and reliability of allies spread throughout the state system, however, they can produce a cultural climate that raises tension and stifles cooperation.

A Culture of Mistrust

Within a culture of mistrust, statesmen accept Montaigne's dictum that "the public good requires us to betray and to lie." Deceit is justified as a tactic of statecraft because competition between states is believed to be zero-sum, and unscrupulous practices allow one to take advantage of others to accrue power. Hortatory proclamations of principled conduct and observance of commitments are greeted with Caliclean incredulity. Trust is virtually absent within such purely competitive relationships (Kohn, 1986: 150). The quest for exploitation, and the expectation that others are driven to do the same, inspires intense feelings of suspicion.

When states feel that their counterparts have no sense of obligation to treaty commitments, they will prize self-sufficiency and pursue isolationist, unilateral foreign policies. Trusting states are able to rely on others, but mistrustful states rely on themselves. In such an environment, alliances will be temporary, ad hoc arrangements, and alliance disintegration will be rapid and frequent. As David Hume wrote in his *Treatise of Human Nature*, "Where promises are not observed, there can be no leagues nor alliance." Whenever a conflict is thought to exist between self-interest and duty to others, the latter will be disregarded.

A culture of mistrust is dominated by multiple fears: the fear that trusting will open oneself to exploitation; the fear that tying one's fate to others will create expectations that cannot be fulfilled; and the fear that commitments will create an entangling position from which it will be impossible to extricate oneself without prohibitively high costs and risks. These fears encourage the belief that all states are destined to deal with inherently unreliable international actors. The chronic suspicion casting its shadow over the history of post-World War II Soviet-American arms control negotiations illustrates how mutual distrust can undermine the prospects for treaty making, even where both adversaries clearly have common interests in reaching arms control agreements. Entrenched doubts about treaty compliance leads to a preoccupation with verification procedures. As Lord Carrington told the authors in an interview in Brussels at NATO Headquarters (June 16, 1987), "in today's world it is better to reach no arms agreements than to reach one which is not verifiable." Such doubts also fuel continued arms racing, as Ronald Reagan seemed to acknowledge when he observed on November 5, 1985, "Nations do not distrust each other because they are armed. They arm themselves because they distrust each other."

Within this cultural atmosphere, "whatever the leaders and spokesmen of a country say, they must always be judged as insincere unless they talk in terms of the struggle of power" (Hare and Joynt, 1982: 37). Inherent bad faith in the intentions of others promotes suspicion. The belief that others cannot be trusted is maintained especially by unprincipled actors, who are well described by the ancient Greek maxim "He who mistrusts should be trusted least." As Machiavelli argued, "force, favor, and fraud" are three weapons of power; and those without scruples are likely to use fraud in order to obtain the ends they seek. Not wishing to be duped again, these gullible states who have been previously victimized by false promises will be hesitant to trust others. Hence mistrust is contagious: it breeds behaviors that accelerate its diffusion.

Ironically, the fulfillment of promises may reduce a state's bargaining power in future negotiations, because favors extended tend to become defined as rights and are often regarded as implying further obligations. In addition, promises may create indebtedness and dependence on those with whom one makes agreements; and they may engender the expectation that further agreements enlarging those commitments will be forthcoming.

It is for these reasons that in a culture of mistrust, the concept of irrevocable commitments is regarded as sacrificial, dangerous, and damaging. It is foolhardy to accept a binding interpretation of promissory obligations given the probability that the circumstances that prevailed when agreements were reached will someday be altered, thereby removing the basis for an agreement's original justification. When security promises are pledged, the future is likely to present each side with the necessity of choosing between two unpalatable alternatives: reneging on the promise and thereby sacrificing credibility, or standing by the commitment and thereby becoming entangled in an ally's conflicts. Thus the prudent statesmen would do better to avoid making commitments, and would be advised not to entrust his state's security to the commitments of others. As Charles de Gaulle once put it: "Over any extended period of time, it is inevitable that the situation will change, and when that happens . . . alliance commitments will collapse" (cited in Weinstein, 1969: 50).

This position creates a paradox in that it is precisely in uncertain situations where order and predictability are most needed, and for this faith in the willingness of others to abide by their agreements is required. But within a culture of mistrust, the normative underpinnings for this faith do not exist. States are left with no alternative but to rely on themselves and remain restlessly vigilant. Consequently, their insecurities increase, even while their need to depend on others also increases.

Unfortunately, the lack of trust underlying alliance politics may lead not only to the deterioration and ultimate rupture of bloc cohesion. More than the durability of coalitions may be at stake. Mistrust may contribute to the general "security dilemma" in world politics. Glenn H. Snyder has stated this thesis lucidly:

the primary alliance dilemma among the major states follows the logic of an N-person prisoner's dilemma. Each state has two options: seek allies or abstain from alliances. If all states are about equally strong and are interested only in security, all are fairly well off if all abstain, since each has moderate security against individual others, while alliances involve various costs, such as reduced freedom of action, commitments to defend the interests of others, and so forth. Alliances will form, however, for two reasons: (1) some states may not be satisfied with only moderate security, and they can increase it substantially by allying if others abstain; (2) some states, fearing that others will not abstain, will ally in order to avoid isolation or to preclude the partner from allying against them. Once an alliance forms, a counter-alliance necessarily follows, since there is no way of knowing that the first alliance is intended only for defensive purposes. The eventual result is the division of the system into two rival coalitions. This outcome is worse than all-around abstention because each state has incurred the risks and burdens of alliances with little improvement in its security. (Snyder, 1984: 462)

This self-defeating outcome can be traced to an absence of trust. By worshipping unrestrained sovereign autonomy above the voluntary respect for contract on which fiduciary relationships depend, a cycle of apprehension is created that destroys the foundation for orderly and predictable behavior. In this spiral of distrust, the security dilemma facing the international community is created, not resolved.

To summarize, we theorize that the results of the breakdown of trust at the international level parallel the results found at the interpersonal level (see Lewis and Weigert, 1985: 980). When trust breaks down, interaction between parties declines, as does the level of cooperation. The probability of terminating relationships and agreements increases, as does both the threat of force and its overt use. An atomized, insecure existence is thus created, colored by feelings of suspicion. The erosion of trust also tends to occur in the context of rapid change, especially in large, complex systems comprised of heterogenous members lacking an institutionalized network for collective problem-solving. The paradox is that the trust required to reduce complexities, encourage reliability, and enhance predictability is most fragile in the very system where it is most needed.

A Culture of Trust

The assumptions that rationalize behaviors leading to creation of a culture of trust seem obvious. Yet it is not self-evident that one should put blind faith in the word of others or refrain from taking some action that might bring immediate gain, especially if the international system is populated with states that are likely to act dishonorably. Consider, for example, the episode described by Xenophon in his *Anabasis*, an account of a Greek mercenary expedition that occurred twenty-four hundred years ago in Asia Minor. Given mutual suspicion between the Greeks and Persians, and given the conclusion that neither side had a reason to harm the other, the Greek commander proposed personal contact as a way to prevent any misunderstandings from escalating into combat. When the Persians offered to host a banquet, the Greeks trusted that it was a sincere gesture of goodwill, not an act of deception. They were wrong. The banquet was a ruse designed to catch the Greek officers off guard and eliminate them so that a leaderless Greek army would become easy prey for the Persians. Clearly, trusting the unscrupulous is dangerous. For this reason it is useful to examine the kinds of practices—constructive and destructive—that are exhibited when the belief becomes widespread that commitments must be kept.

We have argued that trust builds in an environment where agreements are honored. Information is easily exchanged in a moral climate where agreements are kept and the threat of being double-crossed is reduced. States are more inclined to approach a potential partner whose reputation for reliability is beyond reproach than one who suffers from a history of fraudulent promises. Mutually beneficial problem-solving ventures will be common and mutually rewarding goals will more readily be reached when the negotiating parties trust the agreements they reach voluntarily. In a culture where unswerving commitments to agreements are expected, resources do not have to be expended to assure compliance. Credibility can be taken as a given and pledges become largely self-enforcing. Trust, as Charles Fried (1981: 8) writes, is "a powerful tool." Indeed, trust is so remarkable "that in the end we pursue it for its own sake; we prefer doing things cooperatively when we might have relied on fear or interest or worked alone."

This does not, of course, eliminate the inherent tension between the need for reliable allies and the need to reserve the right to withdraw from dangerous commitments. The costs of both norms are substantial. But, on balance, the precept that promises should be kept, when adopted, clearly produces rewards that offset many of the costs. It allows trust to develop, which "makes it possible to enact fiduciary relationships in pursuit of shared goals" (Lewis and Weigert, 1985: 978).

Within a culture of trust, attention focuses not just on one's own interest but also on the obligation of actors to the common good. Indeed, as Michael Walzer (1970) suggests, a civil society may not be possible without this sense of obligation to the common welfare. Similarly, trust is a precondition for an effective international legal order: "Law perishes or becomes corrupt if used where no one trusts, but trust is weakened if those who have become unjustifiably distrustful have no recourse to the law and its controls" (Barber, 1983: 22). Trust permits habits of cooperation to develop and expand—a process of learning that builds still new levels of trust. In this context, U.S. Secretary of War Henry Stimson concluded: "The chief lesson I have learned in a long life is that the only way to make a man trustworthy is to trust him, and the surest way to make him untrustworthy is to distrust him and show him your distrust" (cited in Niebuhr, 1959: 264).

A culture of trust does not remove the need to ground agreements on converging interests. But mutual trust does facilitate collaboration. What Robert Keohane (1984: 88) observes about international regimes applies equally well to obligations to adhere to agreements generally: ad hoc efforts to cooperate in the absence of trust will yield inferior results compared to bargains within a culture built on the expectation of trust.

These benefits notwithstanding, suspicion remains pervasive within the contemporary international system. It is therefore no accident that the binding nature of treaties has routinely been questioned. Why should states mortgage their future to the promises of others? With the passage of time some treaties may prove detrimental to a state's national security, and in rapidly changing circumstances they may become detrimental to global stability. The tension between these incompatible needs for order and for freedom therefore is likely to persist.

MORALITY IN THE INTERNATIONAL JUNGLE

A "culture of mistrust" and a "culture of trust" describe two very different normative climates for the conduct of international relations, each based on an alternative conception of promissory obligation. Both conceptions appear to have benefits and costs associated with them, so that "alliance partners often differ in their understanding of the goals and priorities of a particular commitment . . . and nations may disagree in the assumptions they make about the general meaning of any act of commitment" (Weinstein, 1969: 39). The challenges thus posed for the scholar are to (1) discover which culture enhances the prospects for a just world order and (2) determine how that culture can be created and sustained. What is needed, in the words of Herbert Butterfield and Martin Wight (1968: 13), is an ability "to clarify the principles of prudence and moral obligation which have held together the international society of states."

Our inquiry has been motivated by a desire to discover what norms have best held the society of states together in the past so that we can make more informed choices about the code of conduct we ought to promote in the future. The evidence affirms that during any given historical era an ethos will emerge to shape the politics of that age, an ethos based on shared expectations about the probability that states will act in conformity with their agreements. We contend that the norms comprising this ethos are not irrelevant, as all nihilists and some realists (e.g., Levi, 1969) would have us believe. Norms based on different conceptions of morality are an inescapable component of international affairs. Their existence cannot be denied, for in many areas states have demonstrably achieved agreement about rules, and their frequent discussion of alleged violations testifies to the existence of these standards of behavior.[3] The influence of norms therefore cannot be dismissed: "trust . . . is a dimension of all social relationships" (Barber, 1983: 2).

One overriding reason to promote the creation of a moral consensus, our evidence suggests, is because the prospects for international peace have increased when adherence to agreements have been supported by the international community's moral vision and legal norms. History suggests that in "international affairs, payoffs often come to stable alliances; and statesmen do much to maintain these alliances" (Lieberman, 1968: 371). The statesman's instrument, observed Henry Kissinger (1973), is diplomacy—the art of relating

---

3. Consider the position of Hans J. Morgenthau in regard to the relevance of morality in world politics. On the moral underpinning of international order, and in response to his critics, who he believed underestimated the importance his realist vision placed on normative factors in history, Morgenthau argued that the will to power can be constrained by the creation of a normative consensus. In fact, he alleged that during two distinct periods of history (1648–1772 and 1815–1914) there did emerge "a consensus of common moral standards and a common civilization, as well as of common interests, which kept in check the limitless desire for power, potentially inherent, as we know, in all imperialism and prevented it from becoming a political actuality" (cited in Hare and Joynt, 1982: 39). Morgenthau argued, however, that the twentieth-century growth of nationalistic and ideological movements has eroded the consensual basis for this ethical framework.

states to one another by agreement rather than force. Whether states perceive themselves obligated to keep their agreements is determinative of the capacity of diplomacy to substitute for and prevent the use of force.

It is for this reason that Ronald P. Barston (1988: 3) has described one of the most important tasks of diplomacy as "the creation, drafting and ammendment of a wide body of international rules of a normative and regulatory kind that provide structure in the international system." Precise communication is instrumental to success in accomplishing this task. Consequently, statesmen have developed specialized language to convey their policy positions with as much clarity as possible. Diplomacy, as Adam Watson (1984) has put it, is a dialogue; and statesmen use specialized language as a symbolic means to get an audience to see the world in a particular way and to act according to that vision (Duncan, 1968). Their correspondence and speeches contain discursive elements that highlight expectations of proper action with regard to promissory obligations. Both statesmen and publicists use these terms, phrases, metaphors, and stories in a rhetorically effective vocabulary to communicate injunctions that prescribe certain actions toward treaty agreements but proscribe others. As we have attempted to show, sometimes the narrative pattern of this diplomatic discourse supports a restrictive definition of promissory obligation, and at other times it reinforces a more permissive definition.

In addition to using the written and spoken word, statesmen also communicate through nonverbal means. Certain body movements, facial expressions, and ritualistic gestures can demonstrate the strength of a commitment. As Raymond Cohen (1987: 51, 94–95) points out, the offer of an open palm by one leader to another symbolizes trust, the duration of their handshake reflects the tightness of a bond, and, in some cultures, an embrace expresses solidarity. A leader can further underscore the strength of a commitment by visiting a symbolically important location and striking a posture.

> At the Berlin wall, a frequent place of pilgrimmage for NATO leaders, a permanent vantage point has been set up from where allied visitors can peer through binoculars into East Berlin. Every American president and secretary of state since the time of John Kennedy has visited the spot to symbolize the continuing U.S. commitment to the defense of West Berlin. Similar observation posts exist at Panmunjom, on the armistice lines between North and South Korea, and at Shibetsu in

Northern Japan overlooking the Kuril Islands, occupied by the
U.S.S.R. since 1945. (Cohen, 1987: 52)

Thus while one's definition of promissory obligation is normally done
in verbal form, statesmen reinforce the message through nonverbal
communication. Taken together, words and rites form a symbolic system that may support either binding or flexible alliance norms.

As noted, the dilemma posed to statesmen by these contending
norms centers on the timeless and possibly irreconcilable problems of
freedom versus authority, and individualism versus community. As
Reinhold Niebuhr (1959: 266) expressed it: "Perhaps we are fated, for
some centuries at least, to live in a situation in which the global community appears to be a necessity because of the interdependence of
nations, but an impossibility because there are not quite enough organic forces of cohesion in the global community." Support for the
sanctity of agreements is one force for cohesion that continues to be
challenged by advocates of the norm *rebus sic stantibus.* Sadly, as can
be seen from the Fall of the House of Ichimonji in Kurosawa's *Ran,*
when commitments become brittle and allies waver, trust breaks down
and chaos overwhelms community.

Two traditions, two philosophies, have shaped diplomatic discourse
about promissory obligation. The atomistic, laissez-faire competition
that governed world politics throughout the nineteenth century was
lubricated by the widespread belief that fluid, flexible alliances
would make for a more peaceful and orderly world. In the second half
of the twentieth century, the quest for order has been pursued under a
regime restricting the sovereign freedom of states to unilaterally terminate their alliance commitments when changed circumstances made
them unrewarding. The patterns of crisis escalation and warfare displayed in these periods invites the conclusion that adherence to
commitments promotes harmony between states; the inclination to
disregard commitments does not. A world without honor is a world
without order. To keep peace, allies would be advised to keep
promises.

Epilogue: Alliance Norms and the Future of World Order

To maintain order and peace among nations which live together in a state of nature and acknowledge no superior on earth, the obligation of keeping faith with one another is as necessary as it is natural and unquestionable. . . . The trust that we have in [other's] promise is our security . . . it is the sovereign who fails to keep his promises on clearly trivial grounds who deserves to be treated as an enemy of the human race.

Emeriche de Vattel

Trust is the coin of the realm.

George Shultz

The heart of any alliance is a promise. On the face of it, the promise seems foolish: two otherwise autonomous states that have only a partial understanding of each other pledge that they will stand together when one or both face danger. To many, this would seem risky. Alliances require confidence in others despite the cloud of suspicion that generally hangs over international agreements. But without the risk of a promise, there is little prospect for assistance. There is only solitary self-help.

The problem with alliances is that they require confidence in others at precisely those times when faith in treaty compliance is most lacking. To guard against betrayal or the possibility that changed circumstances will remove the incentives for commitments to be carried out as called for by a treaty, many states have chosen either to avoid alliances altogether or have only been willing to commit themselves in a way that allows a quick exit. Yet when there is an easy way out, allies deprive themselves of the advantages to be gained by partnership. This is not to say that all alliances should survive. As can be seen in the origins of the First World War, sometimes damage can be done in maintaining agreements. But in the absence of binding commitments, the benefits that might be realized are lost.

The issue of compliance with treaty provisions has always been problematic. Though it does not fit the cynical mood pervading international relations, all states need fidelity. The intention to do what is promised, to shoulder responsibilities, is critical to the building of trust on which security rests. All fears cannot be dispelled, but uncertainties are reduced and policy planning can proceed on a more confident basis when policymakers expect that their counterparts will adhere to their agreements.

Regardless of their attendant risks, statesmen have turned to alliances throughout history as a way of responding to threats to their security. When confronted with a threat, alliance members face a strategic choice. On the one hand, they may seek external support by invoking their treaties of alliance. On the other hand, fearing entrapment, abandonment, or betrayal, they may choose to abrogate their treaty commitments and go it alone. "Alignment and dealignment," note Grace E. Iusi Scarborough and Bruce Bueno de Mesquita (1988: 87), "are the main short-term strategies for increasing security." The options consist of the decision to seek "changes in foreign policy commitments, adding or expanding relations with nations that can provide immediate increases in one's security, and eliminating or curtailing relations with nations that are a drain on security." Making these choices has seldom been easy, for it requires statesmen to weigh the potential risks against the probable advantages, with consideration given to a host of uncertainties ranging from the military strength, intentions and dependability of their allies to the capabilities, motivations and goals of their adversaries. The calculus of choice has always been informed by formal or informal assessment of prevailing norms governing the formation or termination of alliances. These norms guide the choice by structuring perceptions of the risks. Norms shape expectations about states' behavior toward one another, and reduce the uncertainties by making behavior more orderly and predictable. The urge to underwrite treaties of alliance in legal language stems from this preference for norms that constrain sovereign freedom and thereby reduce uncertainties.

Left largely unanswered, however, are the types of alliance norms most conductive to national and international security. The impulse to confine action to a specified course is powerful, but so, too, is the urge to preserve the freedom to maneuver by avoiding entangling commitments. Images of how these antithetical needs are to be met derive from reactions to previous decisions. Painful experiences are a catalyst to learning, calling into question prior policies and inviting reassessment of conventional wisdoms. "The things that hurt, instruct," Benjamin Franklin once observed. Many episodes in diplomatic history clearly have been hurtful, costly experiences (especially wars, but also disappointing or unsuccessful alliances), and from them statesmen have routinely derived instructions. But as the foregoing survey has indicated, the "lessons" that they have learned have not always been the same. The type of alliance norms promoted has varied from one period to the next as two largely incompatible views of commitment between allies have struggled with each other for dominance. Neither binding nor flexible conceptions of treaty obligations has enjoyed consensual support without eventual challenge. The norm prevailing in a given historical period has tended to give way to the opposed norm at a later point in time, so that the climate of opinion shared about the standard of conduct preferred for the performance of treaty obligations has oscillated repetitiously since 1815. A permanent consensus on which conception best serves international security has not been achieved. Alliance norms have been modified to facilitate states' efforts to act on behalf of their perceived national interests, and these perceptions have changed with global circumstances.

The analysis provided here reveals that nineteenth century statesmen generally perceived their interests served by flexibility; they supported a code of conduct that gave states the latitude to sever agreements when changed circumstances reduced the benefits of an alliance. But since the end of World War I, statesmen have supported a different code, one based on the perception that their interests were served best by norms that would help prevent a dereliction of duty by allies. In the post-World War II era, this norm was reinforced by the vigorous support exerted for it by the United States and, secondarily, by the Soviet Union. Alliance structures became highly institutionalized due to the bipolar division of the world into two tight, internally cohesive coalitions. The stability of these military configurations was reinforced by the preference of their leaders to prevent realignments. Solidified by fear, post-World War II alliances became rigid, and a treaty regime was therefore brought into place stressing the norm *pacta sunt servanda*. Such a departure from previous diplomatic practice represented a direct challenge to the legal doctrine *rebus sic stantibus*, which was embraced during the last century to facilitate rapid realignments and a fluid balance-of-power system.

This transformation represents a significant watershed. It demarcates two worlds, two historical epochs. It is possible, however, that the era of binding promissory obligations inherited from the legacies of the First and Second World Wars may be coming to an end. The rise in support for *pacta sunt servanda* was influenced by many interacting factors whose complex relationships may not persist. Hence we must contemplate the possibility that the future may not conform to the recent past, and that fundamental changes are underway in the international system that portend the advent of a new era, wherein promissory obligations between allies are given a different interpretation.

To pursue this, let us depart from the historical evidence and look to the possible future by considering the conception of promissory obligations that is likely to influence the course of alliance politics at the end of the twentieth century. We speculate on whether the code of conduct prescribing that agreements be honored has begun to erode, and, if so, what the demise of this norm portends. Is the pattern characteristic of the previous century likely to repeat itself? If so, what consequences might be predicted from this development?

TREATY COMPLIANCE IN THE CONTEMPORARY SETTING

Throughout history, alliance norms have undergone modification to facilitate states' efforts to act on behalf of their perceived national interests, and these perceptions have changed with changes in global circumstances. It is certainly too early to tell whether the changes occurring in world politics over the last several decades are forceful enough to foment changes in the "pactomania" exhibited in the two decades after World War II and revision of the binding conception of legal norms that governed alliance politics during that period. If one inspects the record of diplomatic practice and recent developments in international legal doctrine, there are strong indications that, beginning in the late 1960s and early 1970s, a new transformation of commitment norms commenced, and that with it has come a decay in support for strict adherence to promissory obligations. If inherently fragile alliances did begin to decay, and the code of conduct prescribing that treaties of alliance be honored did begin to erode, what does this demise portend?

A prominent example of these changes is seen in the increased attention given to the costs of so-called entangling alliances. Nations have always been acutely aware of the risks involved when casting their fate with allies. But in the 1970s those fears rose to new heights. Bonds can bind in unwelcomed ways, entrapping patron and client with one another in what may appear to be a mutual hostage relationship. Prudence dictates avoiding these entanglements through the preservation of flexibility, and statesmen began to reevaluate the wisdom of tying their country's future to the behavior of others. Behind all the pious rhetoric about friendship and the merits of collective defense, statesmen openly began to ask whether changing international conditions made the security interests of many allies incompatible. Nostalgia and sentimentality are not enough to resuscitate burdensome, anachronistic alliances. As Thucydides reminds us, an "identity of interests is the surest bond, whether between states or individuals."

The accelerating pace of global change had increased the risks of permanent alignments and concomitantly reduced the perceived utility of prior agreements. The emergence of conditions of complex interdependence in the 1970s also placed unprecedented burdens on the commitment of states to alliance obligations by expanding both the number of issues dividing nations and the linkages among them, therein reducing the ability to distinguish between friend and foe and raising fundamental questions about the advantages to be realized from steadfast commitments to unreliable allies. The rapidly tightening webs of global interdependence have provided incentives to breach treaties whose original purposes have been outmoded by the accelerating pace of change. *The Treaty Trap,* the title of a book by Laurence Beilenson (1969), a one-time student of alliances who became a policymaker in the Reagan administration, captured a popular sentiment (see also Sleeper, 1987).

It is difficult to document precisely when support for the binding character of treaties first began to erode. For this task it is useful to review the context in which the atmosphere for treaty compliance developed in the last decade of the twentieth century. The waning of support for the norm *pacta sunt servanda* is recognizable only against the developments that preceded it and prepared the way for its arrival.

Recall that in the aftermath of World War II, the United States and the Soviet Union strongly endorsed a view of alliance commitments that held states to abide faithfully by their agreements. Little room was left for the repudiation of pledges: neutrality was chastized, the nonaligned movement had not yet gathered momentum, and the needs of the colonial states awaiting independence were not taken into account. With the advent of the Cold War, the overriding need was for collective defense pacts resting on assured compliance with treaty agreements, and for this purpose a norm preaching the inviolability of commitments was required (Cook, 1989). But the consensus on which this regime rested was precarious. Its political foundations were fragile and dependent on the continuation of a highly concentrated distribution of military power. With the dispersion of military capabilities and the advent of multiple centers of autonomous political decision, the first tears in the web of Cold War alliances became visible.

As the post-World War II era unfolded, references to the costs of entangling alliances increasingly entered the diplomatic discourse, and nascent enthusiasm began to be voiced for the benefits of avoiding alliances, or for a norm releasing allies from their commitments when vital interests were threatened. Among NATO members, for instance, the issue of credibility was discussed by concerned individuals on both sides of the Atlantic. Would the United States sacrifice New York to defend German territory east of the Rhine? Would a government in Bonn, eager to improve relations with the German Democratic Republic, be willing to make concessions to Moscow that ultimately compromised the defense of Central Europe? In short, alliance accords were perceived as instruments that could diminish as well as increase the security of their members by drawing them into conflicts they would prefer to avoid. Concentrated attention on those potential dangers recommended withdrawal from alliance commitments, "dealignment" as a recommended policy (Kaldor and Falk, 1987), and corresponding attention to the benefits of unilateral action.

To be sure, creation of a laissez-faire alliance system under which commitments could be broken simply on the grounds of expediency was not advocated. Instead, the applicability of flexible alliance norms was proposed only for those cases where calculations of national interest showed the costs of compliance outweighing the benefits. Still, the drift toward a revised, more permissive code of conduct was becoming more and more evident. The opposition voiced to this normative development attested to the strength, not the weakness, of the new trend. For we can assume that when states find it necessary to expend political capital to defend *pacta sunt servanda,* it is because the norm has already come under serious challenge and support for its maintenance has begun to erode. Decision makers, like most people, defend values most vigorously when the possibility becomes real that they may be lost.

It is thus clear that in many respects the end of the 1960s represented a transition in alliance politics (see Kegley and Raymond, 1991). Conflicting interests arose from deep structural changes within the international system, and policy opinion began to swing toward emphasis on the entangling dangers of alliances. Likewise, the proclaimed right of states to unilaterally renounce the promises contained in treaties of alliance was increasingly supported.

To support this thesis, let us briefly examine three sets of indicators. Evidence that the obligation of states to adhere to their alliance agreements has eroded since the late 1960s is exhibited in (1) the changing normative temper of international law, (2) state practices generally, and (3) the policies and conduct of the United States.

International Treaty Law

Support for the legal doctrine of *rebus sic stantibus* became increasingly frequent during the 1960s. For example, in the International Law Commission's 1966 ruling that although the obligation to abide by agreements remained, support was also voiced for the doctrine *rebus sic stantibus* in order to accommodate the perceived need for greater flexibility in the law of treaties. Support for that doctrine was "so considerable that it [seemed] to indicate a recognition of a need for this safety-valve in the law of treaties" (Weinstein, 1969: 43). The new regime gave states relatively more freedom to shed undesired or obsolete commitments that no longer served the original purposes for which those alliances had been constructed in a rapidly changing global system.

The shift in alliance norms was dramatically signalled by the Vienna Conference on the Law of Treaties, which concluded its deliberations and issued its final report in 1969. The Draft Convention of the International Law Commission and the positions articulated by the delegates to the Vienna Conference revealed the extent to which the contest between the two opposed interpretations of treaty obligations had once again surfaced.[1] The debate between proponents of *pacta sunt servanda* and advocates of *rebus sic stantibus* was intense; it was the primary issue, "the main battleground" (Gormley, 1970: 367), on which the dialogue in Vienna centered. Although left unresolved, the Draft Convention weakened "the moral force exerted by *pacta sunt servanda*:" acceptance of *rebus sic stantibus* "represent[ed] a setback for *pacta sunt servanda*," and "the retreat . . . [showed] the shifting emphasis in international law" (Gormley 1970: 368, 380, 384). These negotiations unquestionably opened the door for a more relaxed definition of the duties of allies to adhere to their promises. As one careful student of this legal dialogue framed the matter, "The crucial

---

1. The International Law Commission gave explicit credence to the doctrine *rebus sic stantibus*, defining it boldly as an "objective rule of law." But it also acknowledged the continuing importance of the principle *pacta sunt servanda*, recognizing that the binding character of treaties is the basis for international law. Its statements thus captured the tension between these contending norms. As Anthony Carty (1986: 81) noted, "The International Law Commission itself said that state practice shows a wide acceptance of the view that a fundamental change may justify a demand for the termination or revision of a treaty but also shows a strong disposition to question the right of a party to denounce a treaty unilaterally on that ground."

issue in the problematic of treaty obligations [is] the manner in which one is to react to a State's claim that adherence to a treaty is no longer compatible with its national interest. . . . How far can a state pledge its word when it has no guarantee that the evolving 'dynamic' of international relations will not make it 'unreasonable' to expect it to keep its word, given that this 'dynamic' is not itself subject to any legal constraints?'' (Carty, 1986: 67–68).

By this time, the "dynamic of international relations" had clearly evolved in fundamental ways and exerted pressure for revising international legal rules. *Opinio juris* now began to reflect a new permissive mood about treaty obligations. The right of states to unilaterally modify or withdraw from a treaty on the ground of changed circumstances thus became an increasingly prominent theme in legal and diplomatic discourse. The shift in the climate of opinion set in motion at that time has not lost its momentum. The new regime gave states relatively more freedom to shed undesired or obsolete commitments that no longer served the purposes for which those alliances were originally constructed.

State Practices

Rules tend to codify state practice. Since the late 1960s, that practice has reinforced the movement away from the legal obligation of states to abide by their treaties of alliance. States began to exhibit a reluctance to tie their security to the promises of others, and sought through both words and deeds to liberate themselves from prior commitments. For this purpose, the *clausula rebus sic stantibus* was well-suited. It provided a rationale for the dissolution of those agreements that changed circumstances had rendered disadvantageous.

A catalyst in this process was the shift of the international system away from tight bipolarity. With the diffusion of political, economic, and military capabilities, the need for rigid, cohesive bloc structures receded. Both the policies of states and the norms they supported underwent modification. The consensus about the community of interests on which alliances are predicted began to crumble. As doubts about their cost-effectiveness began to surface, the edifice of alliances constructed earlier began to splinter. "Whole alliance systems (including SEATO and CENTO) have come and gone since World War II, and even the strongest relationships (such as NATO) seem continually prone to tension and crisis" (Deibel, 1987a: 100). Changed international circumstances provoked reassessments of national interests, and these reassessments reduced the perceived utility of a code of conduct prohibiting the renunciation of entangling commitments. American serverance of its promise to protect Taiwan in 1980, and the dispute between the United States and New Zealand over the issue of the harboring of U.S. nuclear ships, which led to the disintegration of the ANZUS Pact, are representative of this trend. Strained and broken relations between present or former alliance partners—the U.S. with Iran, the Philippines, Nicaragua, Vietnam; the U.S.S.R. with Afghanistan, the People's Republic of China, Ethiopia, and Egypt—attest to the fragility of alliances whose permanence was assumed when they were forged. As Deibel (1987a: 113–114) notes, "The only remembrances of Dulles' schemes are pale, proxy alliances like ASEAN, the Gulf Cooperation Council, or the Organization of Eastern Caribbean States, which enjoy only U.S. support, not direct American commitment." Instead of formal alliances, states began to show a "tendency toward casual commitment" (Claude, 1981). Trade negotiations among the United States, Japan, and Western Europe also typified the heightened level of contention surrounding the issue of whether parties to agreements were abiding by their terms.

Another example of this trend can be seen in the decline in NATO cohesion. Détente, the rise of Euroneutralism, the prospect of a nuclear-free European theater, and the transition from an offense-dominated to a defense-oriented deterrence strategy threaten to remove the basis for unity within an alliance whose members had long been divided over such troublesome issues as burden sharing.[2] Indeed, disarray became so deeply rooted that by the late 1980s NATO resembled "a phantom alliance" (Draper, 1988) whose main continuity was a "continuity of discord" (Jackson, 1985). As one observer warned: "unless Atlantic relations are fundamentally reordered, the alliance may collapse amid bitter recrimination. But [reformers'] proposals will not stave off the threats to NATO's cohesion. The reformers speak the language of change, but their proposals would leave the current Atlantic situation unaltered" (Layne, 1987: 22). NATO had become weakened by the perception that it no longer provided members with enough benefits. Even supporters on the right—long asso-

---

2. An example of the recurrent strains within NATO can be seen in the 1988 debate within Denmark over nuclear policy. Although Denmark has had a peacetime nuclear ban, it did not demand that visiting NATO ships declare whether they are carrying nuclear weapons. During the spring of 1988, however, the Danish parliament surprised the conservative-led coalition government of Paul Schlueter by passing a resolution on a vote of 75 to 58 that required the government to inform visiting ships of its peacetime nuclear weapons ban.

ciated with defense of the Western Alliance—found it relevant to address the question of whether it had become time for NATO to "call it a day" (Gray, 1987–1988).

Nor was this metamorphosis unfolding only in the Western Alliance. The Soviet Union under Gorbachev also began to weaken its grip on its satellites, which in 1988 and 1989 were not hesitant in their efforts to visibly reduce their dependence on the U.S.S.R. Paradoxically, this splintering was facilitated by the Soviet Union, whose efforts at "restructuring" at the time seemed to invite more relaxed relations with its allies. A comparison of treatises authored by Soviet publicists, from Kozhevnikov to Levin to Tunkin, reveals a gradual acceptance of the *clausula rebus sic stantibus*. According to György Haraszti (1975: 31), "The headway that the clause [made] in the Soviet literature on international law . . . had some influence on Soviet diplomatic practice." But as in the West, acceptance of a more elastic definition of commitment raised a specter: bloc members might reduce their allegiance to the bloc leader. Hence it is not surprising that speculation about the reliability of Warsaw Pact members became a common part of both scholarly (e.g., Volgyes and Herspring, 1980; Nelson, 1984) and popular (e.g., Hackett, et. al., 1978) writing on Eastern Europe.

"Global unilateralism" is the current code word for the effort of states to detach themselves from existing treaty obligations. It "implies withdrawal from any and all alliances," but "more properly and soberly understood, it means little more than a partial disengagement from many of the extravagant . . . commitments that are embodied in truly 'entangling alliances' " (Kristol, 1986: 20). Irony, and, perhaps danger, resided in the fact that alliance durability declined at precisely the same time when the scope of international obligations in the realm of "low politics" and economic relations had expanded so dramatically (Brewin, 1988).

Closely related to the resurgence of unilateralism was the attack on the liberal international philosophy which heretofore had driven the effort to build bridges among independent states. Many observers (e.g., Hughes, 1985–1986) spoke of "the twilight of internationalism," an eclipse in the "ethos that values and pursues international cooperation in all its diverse forms . . . as at least a potential locus of moral loyalty" (Sizemore, 1988: 213–214).

The decay of liberal internationalism can be linked to the decay of trust. Faith in the dependability of other states had begun to break down, and with its deterioration the issue of treaty compliance as-

sumed a prominent place on the global agenda. It was not coinciden-
tial that, in the absence of trust, "confidence-building measures" and
risk reduction centers became such a large part of the lexicon in arms
control treaty negotiations. Nor was it happenstance that Ronald Reagan chose to repeatedly quote a Russian proverb to General Secretary
Gorbachev: "Trust, but verify." Clearly, treaty compliance had become "a crisis of enormous proportions;" "virtually all the major
nuclear arms agreements of the 1970s [were] unraveling" (Schear,
1985: 141) amidst the breakdown of faith in the observance of agreements. Similarly, many nonnuclear arms agreements showed signs of
stress. For example, the Reagan administration charged that the Soviet Union had violated the 1972 Biological and Toxic Weapons Convention by using mycotoxins in Laos, Cambodia, and Afghanistan. In
addition, it claimed that the Soviets violated the Helsinki Final Act
during the 1981 Polish crisis when they conducted a military maneuver exceeding 25,000 ground troops without providing required notification and information.

The INF treaty showed the world that possibilities still existed for
meaningful arms control, but it also demonstrated how dependent
those bargains are on the ability of the negotiators to build a modicum of mutual trust and back them with expectations that commitments will be honored. Reaching future agreements appeared
contingent upon the building of the trust that is a precondition to the
control of the arms race, which was widely assumed to be in everyone's interest (for a review and critique, see Kruzel, 1991).

The erosion of trust[3] had been reinforced by the growth of support
for flexible alliance norms. Taken together, distrust and a permissive
legal order undermined the capacity of states to negotiate agreements,
weakened the cohesion of existing alliances, and reduced the faith
that members of alliances placed in their fungibility. The result was a

---

3. Robert J. Einborn (1981–1982: 29) summarized the mood by noting "Americans do
   not trust the Russians, and this deep-seated distrust has contributed to the belief that
   the Soviets cannot be trusted to live up to their obligations under arms control agreements." To illustrate, he quoted Eugene Rostow's congressional testimony in July,
   1981, when Rostow was Director of the Arms Control and Disarmament Agency:
   "No arms control agreement can contribute to the goal of a peaceful world unless we
   have confidence that the Soviet Union is abiding by its terms." It can be added that
   the Soviets, themselves highly distrustful of U.S. intentions to observe treaty agreements, might concur with the thesis that the absence of trust lies at the core of the
   problem. It would appear that in a culture of mistrust confidence-building measures
   are required to rescue arms control (see Borawski, 1986).

world of suspicious countries absorbed with worries that fickle allies would abandon them when they would be most needed.

American Foreign Policy and Norm Revision

The code of conduct that prevails at any given point in time within the international system has always been influenced by the rules supported by the system's most powerful members. "Singly or jointly, the great powers are responsible for managing the international system," observes Inis L. Claude (1986: 727). Their postures toward treaties in general and toward the members of the alliances over which they preside reinforce the norms which others follow. The Reagan administration's erratic behavior with respect to more than forty treaty commitments the United States had forged with its allies in the postwar period and the Soviet Union's strained relations with its nominal allies undermined the image of alliances and reduced faith in their capacity to afford protection. Its record across a broad spectrum of cases demonstrated a clear intent "to pressure the international legal system into changing" by violating generally accepted rules. According to Stuart S. Malawer (1988), the Reagan administration's rejection of the Law of the Sea Treaty, interventions in Nicaragua, withdrawal from UNESCO, nonpayment of budget obligations to the United Nations, and withdrawal from the compulsory jurisdiction of the International Court of Justice all fit this pattern.

Issues of treaty compliance dominated diplomatic discourse in the United States during the late 1980s precisely because adherence to agreements was perceived to be so uncertain. Ronald Reagan elevated the issue when, as a presidential candidate, he accused Jimmy Carter "of a weakness and vacillation that had prompted U.S. allies to reluctantly conclude that America is unwilling or unable to fulfill its obligations. . . . Accordingly, [Reagan] assured American allies in his first inaugural address that the United States would 'match loyalty with loyalty' " (Deibel, 1987b: 54). Yet Reagan practiced the very behavior he berated. His administration announced that the United States would no longer be bound by the provisions of Strategic Arms Limitation Talks (SALT II) treaty, despite the protests of alarmed members of NATO (see Gwertzman, 1986) who were unpersuaded by Secretary of State George Shultz's "contention that the accord had become obsolete" (Gordon, 1986). In addition, the Reagan administration defiantly chose to abrogate the Anti-Ballistic Missile (ABM) Treaty amidst considerable controversy (see Clark, 1987). In a similar fashion, the Reagan administration sanctimoniously accused (see the

Congressional Record, March 6, 1986: S2180–2199) its Soviet competitor of engaging in the same kind of treaty violation that the United States has threatened to practice toward international institutions (UNESCO, the World Bank, the International Monetary Fund, the United Nations) it once led in creating. As a consequence, the status of long-standing commitments was clouded by suspicion and doubts about their durability. American foreign policy fed the growing level of uncertainty afflicting international politics rather than reducing it.

Part of the U.S. posture undoubtedly stemmed from the American preference for and willingness to "go it alone." Washington had rediscovered the virtues of autonomous action. "American attempts to marshall multilateral action at critical times [had] produced a long and dismaying list of failures," noted Charles Krauthammer (1985: 18), and in response the United States chose to extricate itself from its dependence on reluctant allies who allegedly refused to abide by their promises for concerted action. An uninterrupted series of events in which American initiatives failed to receive allied support (e.g., intervention in Grenada, counterterrorist tactics in the Middle East, and the Yamberg Pipeline) led the United States to depreciate the value of its allies and chastize them for their insubordination. The pervasive fear that the United States intended to decouple Europe from its security umbrella punctuated the mistrustful mood.

In disengaging itself from these commitments, the United States adopted the same preference for seeking security unilaterally and reserving the right to liberally define the extent of its treaty obligations that it previously had found so objectionable when practiced by its allies. The Reagan administration sought to mask the disengagement from its treaty obligations, resorting to a "series of misstatements followed by repudiations superseded by disavowals . . . every step informed by one maxim: interpret now, justify later" (McCaffrey, 1988: 154). This equivocation belied what was becoming readily apparent to many observers: that "the United States [seemed] increasingly content to be perceived by other nations as indifferent to its most solemn treaty obligations . . . [and was willing to display] cavalier indifference to [its] own gross violations of treaties that the rest of world [took] seriously" (Franck, 1988: 67). The place of alliance obligations in American foreign policy was decidedly different in the 1980s than it was in the 1950s: "Compared with the Truman and Eisenhower treaties, the Carter-Reagan security relationships [seemed] to be pale alliances that hardly deserve the name" (Deibel, 1987: 57).

In refusing to uphold principled standards of conduct, the United States contributed to the processes through which these standards hemorrhaged. Its conduct weakened the foundation of those binding commitments it previously had fought to promote and preserve. Its conduct, moreover, threatened to become an *erga onmes* rule, applicable to all.

Related to the quest for unilateralism and attendant rejection of commitments linking American interests to the policies of allies was the quest to escape the confines of international law (Farer, 1988). When perceived interests were threatened in the 1980s, the United States behaved as if it was justified in acting beyond the law (although it judged with alacrity the propriety of others' conduct by reference to those same standards). The Reagan administration made this attack on international legal institutions a defining attribute of its foreign policy. "The erosion of American concern about a world of law," writes Arthur M. Schlesinger, Jr. (1986: 84), "intensified after 1980."[4] The endorsement of the precept *salus populi suprema lex est*, as symbolized in the disregard the United States showed the World Court in the aftermath of the court's ruling on the Nicaraguan case, further undercut the stature of international law and the principles of adherence on which it rests. Indeed, the claim that the United States should not be bound by those rules of law respected by others ran counter to the core values upon which international law is based.

In an environment where the structure of international legal institutions is challenged by the world's most powerful state, the status of the fundamental principle that treaties are to be honored, which underpins the whole system of positive international law (Suganami, 1983: 41) and on which all other treaty norms depend (Gormley, 1970), is exposed to direct challenge. Whether the precept that states must keep their word can survive as a ground norm under this attack remains to be seen.

As the distribution of global power became dispersed, the multilateral alliance systems based on the sanctity of commitments began to

---

4. The blatant attack on international law and multilateral institutions launched by the Reagan administration may be interpreted as an attack by an insecure state on its loss of global influence. That loss was particularly evident in the World Court and the United Nations. In attacking these international entities the United States may have undermined its own national interests and demonstrated its impotence, not its power. Its actions reduced the nation's moral standing in the community of nations, and that was not a negligible loss. As Walter Lippmann (cited in Schlesinger, 1986: 85) warned, "A policy is bound to fail which deliberately violates our pledges and our principles, our treaties and our laws."

collapse. Part of this disintegration can clearly be traced to the symbolic loss of influence by the United States following the Vietnam War (and also by the Soviet Union as a result of its unsuccessful intervention in Afghanistan). But whatever the cause, nearly all observers have accepted that the international system began in the 1980s to move through a period of fundamental readjustment, a historical conjuncture or watershed. The authority of the world leader began to wane (see Calleo, 1987; Mead, 1987; and Kennedy, 1987), and with the unraveling of the American "empire" had come the disintegration of alliances and deterioration of the norms previously supported by the United States to bolster bloc cohesion. The "high fidelity" characterizing alliance politics since the end of World War II broke into discordant chords. A quest for sovereign autonomy, accompanied by a propensity to terminate onerous commitments, loomed on the diplomatic horizon.

THE TWILIGHT OF TRUST

Diplomacy cannot be divorced from the normative climate in which it occurs. As policymakers attempt to fashion norms to govern the relationships of states, it seems highly probable that the emphasis placed in the international legal order on binding interpretations of alliance obligations will recede further. As the lessons dervied from the experiences of the First and Second World Wars fade from memory, international law can be expected to undergo additional readjustment in the position taken toward the long-standing question of whether states should abide by formal treaty commitments. It has been said that the "contemporary international law of any period, including both legal treatises and international agreements, contains aspirations for reform as well as descriptions of customary practice" (Tillema and Van Wingen, 1982: 241). The last decade of the twentieth century is unlikely to be an exception. International norms showed clear signs of change during the last quarter of the twentieth century in response to the visible efforts of states to release themselves from prior agreements. A permissive legal order began to form. Once again, a period of reconceptualization commenced. Compliant, faithful allies became rare, and their support could not be taken for granted. The widespread expectation that allies would abandon their commitments and defect from their promises had moved the world closer to a culture of mistrust.

To the extent that there are entrenched cyclical rhythms in world politics, it is possible that the world is passing through a phase very similar to ones that have occurred previously. The 1990s bear a striking resemblance to the conditions that prevailed a century earlier. As before, so once again "no international moral consensus exists in sufficient depth and strength to sustain a comprehensive and binding morality" (Schlesinger, 1986: 73)

"The further back you look," Winston Churchill is said to have remarked, "the further forward you can see." The likely consequences of this return to *rebus sic stantibus* are not reassuring. Now, as in the late nineteenth century, flexible conceptions of alliance commitments have gained renewed support and power has become increasingly diffused. Once solid blocs are beginning to dissolve and "new alliances are forming that seemed impossible twenty years ago" (Bergesen, 1983: 264).

These developments do not portend the maintenance of international order. The reassertion of *rebus sic stantibus* thinking may be a prelude to the next global war, just as the permissive posture toward alliance obligations was a potent catalyst a century ago to the global war that erupted in 1914 (Bergesen, 1983: 264–267). On January 1, 1888, the *Neue Freie Press* spoke ominously of "the cracking of the walls of an unsound house that usually precedes catastrophies" (cited in Fleming, 1968: 68). At the end of the 1980s the sounds of cracking alliances echoed through the streets and plazas of national capitals. Are they the sounds of catastrophe?

Comfort cannot be taken in the fact that support for the belief that changes in those conditions that existed at the signing of an alliance treaty free the parties from their obligations has often been followed by a period of systemic conflict. As we have demonstrated, nonbinding alliance norms have been associated with the outbreak of international violence. The prophesy of the outbreak of another global war early in the twenty-first century, presaged today by the reduced normative constraints on promissory obligations, is an apocalyptic scenario. It is rooted in deterministic logic and teleological reasoning (Ray, 1983). Trend is not destiny; humans have a demonstrated capacity to shape their fates. Nonetheless, past historical patterns cannot be discounted, and, if heeded, can even inform policymakers of the path to liberate themselves from the repeated mistakes that have exerted their paralyzing grip on history. This is a test of statesmanship. "A statesman," former British Ambassador to the United States Sir Oliver Wright reflected in 1988, "does what is necessary, while a politician does what is popular." If a catastrophic war is to be averted, it may be essential for statesmen to come forward to do what is necessary but unpopular—uphold commitments and the sanctity of the promissory obligations that undergrid them.

Freedom and order are inextricably linked. Contrary to the pessimistic theories of moral nihilists, support for the binding character of treaties historically has been medicinal: when norms have restricted states' freedom to renounce promissory obligations, the prospects for the maintenance of order has improved. Stated differently, freedom from external attack has expanded when states have voluntarily restricted their sovereign freedom to breach treaties. Liberating states to abandon their commitments when changed circumstances make them burdensome is not a viable formula for a more orderly world. Order is a product of restricted freedom.

Adherence to commitments may not guarantee peace; but foreign policy derives from "states of mind," and in the absence of the expectation in the minds of statesmen that agreements will be observed, aggressors will be less inhibited to choose the use of force. A diplomatic culture that condones broken promises and the breach of treaties is a culture likely to experience armed conflict. States turn to the sword when they fail to stand resolutely by their word. Although national leaders are well advised not to make commitments recklessly, once made their interests are advanced in honoring those commitments.

REFERENCES

Abolfathi, Farid, John J. Hayes, and Richard E. Hayes. 1979. "Trends in United States Response to International Crisis," in Charles W. Kegley, Jr., and Patrick J. McGowan, eds., *Challenges to America,* pp. 57–85. Beverly Hills: Sage.

Adler-Karlsson, Gunnar. 1968. *Western Economic Warfare, 1947–1967: A Case Study in Foreign Economic Policy.* Stockholm: Almqvist & Wiksell.

Ailleret, Charles. 1968. "Directed Defense," *Survival* 10 (February): 38–43.

Albrecht-Carrié, René. 1968. *The Concert of Europe.* New York: Harper & Row.

Alighieri, Dante. 1957. *On World Government,* trans. by Herbert W. Schneider. Indianapolis: Bobbs-Merrill.

Alker, Heyward R., Jr. 1965. *Mathematics and Politics.* New York: Macmillan.

Allott, Antony. 1980. *The Limits of Law.* London: Butterworths.

Alperovitz, Gar. 1985. *Atomic Diplomacy: Hiroshima and Potsdam—The Use of the Atomic Bomb and the American Confrontation with Soviet Power,* rev. ed. New York: Penguin.

Altfeld, Michael F. 1984. "The Decision to Ally: A Theory and Test," *Western Political Quarterly* 37 (December): 523–544.

Altfeld, Michael F., and Won K. Paik. 1986. "Realignment in ITOs: A Closer Look," *International Studies Quarterly* 30 (March): 107–114.

Andrews, Bruce. 1975. "Social Rules and the State as a Social Actor," *World Politics* 27 (July): 521–540.

Ardal, Pall S. 1968. "And That's A Promise," *Philosophical Quarterly* 18 (July): 225–237.

Aron, Raymond. 1966. *Peace and War: A Theory of International Relations,* trans. by R. Howard and Annette Baker Fox. New York: Praeger.

——— . 1968. "The Anarchical Order of Power," in Stanley Hoffmann, ed., *Conditions of World Order,* pp. 25–48. New York: Simon & Schuster.

Ashley, Richard K. 1980. *The Political Economy of War and Peace.* New York: Nichols.

——— . 1990. "Social Will and International Anarchy: Beyond the Domestic Analogy in the Study of Global Collaboration," in Heyward R. Alker, Jr., and Richard K. Ashley, eds., *Anarchy, Power, Community: Understanding International Collaboration.* (forthcoming).

Atiyah, Patrick. 1979. *The Rise and Fall of Freedom of Contract.* Oxford: Oxford University Press.

Austin, John L. 1962. *How to Do Things with Words.* London: Oxford University Press.

Axelrod, Robert. 1984. *The Evolution of Cooperation.* New York: Basic Books.

———. 1986. "An Evolutionary Approach to Norms," *American Political Science Review* 80 (Winter): 1095–1111.

Axelrod, Robert, and Robert O. Keohane. 1986. "Achieving Cooperation Under Anarchy," in Kenneth A. Oye, ed., *Cooperation Under Anarchy,* pp. 226–254. Princeton, NJ: Princeton University Press.

Back Impalliomeni, Elisabeth. 1974. *Il principio* rebus sic stantibus *mella Convenzione di Vienna sul diritto dei trattati.* Milan: A. Giuffrè.

Bailey, F. G. 1969. *Strategems and Spoils: A Social Anthopology of Politics.* New York: Scholken.

Baker, C. Ashford. 1988. *The Ultimate Dilemma: Obligation Conflicts in Wartime.* London: University Press of America.

Barber, Bernard. 1983. *The Logic and Limits of Trust.* New Brunswick, NJ: Rutgers University Press.

Barkun, Michael. 1968. *Law Without Sanctions: Order in Primitive Societies and the World Community.* New Haven: Yale University Press.

Barnet, Richard J. 1988. "An Absence of Trust: Roots of Discord in the Soviet-American Relationship," in Charles W. Kegley, Jr., and Eugene R. Wittkopf, eds., *The Global Agenda,* pp. 127–137. New York: Random House.

Barry, Brian. 1970. *Sociologists, Economists, and Democracy.* London: Collier Macmillan.

Barry, Donald. 1980. "The Politics of 'Exceptionalism:' Canada and the United States as a Distinctive International Relationship," *Dalhousie Review* 60 (Spring): 114–137.

Barston, Ronald Peter. 1988. *Modern Diplomacy.* London: Longman.

Barton, R. F. 1930. *The Half-Way Sun.* New York: Brewer & Warren.

Becker, Carl L. 1932. *The Heavenly City of the Eighteenth Century Philosophers.* New Haven: Yale University Press.

Beer, Francis A. 1981. *Peace Against War: The Ecology of International Violence.* San Francisco: W. H. Freeman.

———, ed. 1970. *Alliances.* New York: Holt, Rinehart and Winston.

Beilenson, Laurence W. 1969. *The Treaty Trap.* Washington, DC: Public Affairs Press.

Beitz, Charles. 1979a. "Bounded Morality," *International Organization* 33 (Summer): 405–424.

———. 1979b. *Political Theory and International Relations.* Princeton, NJ: Princeton University Press.

Beres, Louis René. 1972. "Bipolarity, Multipolarity, and the Reliability of Alliance Commitments," *Western Political Quarterly* 24 (December): 702–710.

Bergesen, Albert. 1983. "1914 Again? Another Cycle of Interstate Competition and War," in Pat McGowan and Charles W. Kegley, Jr., eds., *Foreign Policy and the Modern World-System,* pp. 255–273. Beverly Hills: Sage.

Berkowitz, Bruce D. 1983. "Realignment in International Treaty Organizations," *International Studies Quarterly* 27 (March): 77–96.

Bernholz, Peter. 1985. *The International Game of Power.* Berlin: Mouton.

Bilder, Richard. 1981. *Managing the Risks of International Agreement.* Madison: University of Wisconsin Press.

Binder, Guyora. 1988. *Treaty Conflict and Political Contradiction: The Dialectic of Duplicity.* New York: Praeger.

Bishop, William W., Jr. 1962. *International Law,* 2d ed. Boston: Little, Brown.

———. 1967. "Law of Treaties," *American Journal of International Law* 61 (October): 990–992.

Blalock, Hubert. 1968. "The Measurement Problem: The Gap Between the Language of Theory and Research," in Hubert Blalock and Ann Blalock, eds., *Methodology in Social Research,* pp. 5–27. New York: McGraw Hill.

Blechman, Barry M., and Stephen Kaplan. 1978. *Force Without War.* Washington, DC: Brookings Institution.

Bonanate, Luigi. 1976. *Teoria politica e relazioni internazionali.* Milan: Comunita.

———. 1979. "Il Sistema Internazionale," in Luigi Bonanate, ed., *Politica Internazionale,* pp. 352–397. Florence: La Nuova Italia.

Borawski, John. 1986. "Confidence-Building Measures," *Fletcher Forum* 10 (Winter): 111–131.

Boyle, Francis Anthony. 1985. *World Politics and International Law.* Durham, NC: Duke University Press.

Bozeman, Adda B. 1960. *Politics and Culture in International History.* Princeton, NJ: Princeton University Press.

Brecher, Michael, and Patrick James. 1986. *Crisis and Change in World Politics.* Boulder, CO: Westview Press.

Brecher, Michael, and Jonathan Wilkenfeld. 1982. "Crises in World Politics," *World Politics* 34 (April): 380–417.

———. 1989. *Crisis in the Twentieth Century: The Analysis of International and Foreign Policy Crisis,* vol. 3. Oxford: Pergamon Press.

Brecher, Michael, Jonathan Wilkenfeld, and Sheila Moser. 1988. *Crises in the Twentieth Century: Handbook of International Crises,* vol. 1. Oxford: Pergamon Press.

Brewin, Christopher. 1988. "Liberal States and International Obligations," *Millennium* 17 (Summer): 321–338.

Brickman, Philip. 1974. *Social Conflict.* Lexington, MA: D. C. Heath.

Brierly, James Leslie. 1955. *The Law of Nations*, 5th ed. New York: Oxford University Press.

————. 1963. *The Law of Nations*, 6th ed. New York: Oxford University Press.

Briggs, Herbert W. 1949. "*Rebus Sic Stantibus* Before the Security Council," *American Journal of International Law* 43 (October): 762–769.

Brinton, Alan. 1986. "Ethotic Argument," *History of Philosophy Quarterly* 3 (July): 245–258.

Brown, D. Mackenzie. 1954. "Indian and Western Realism," *Indian Journal of Political Science* 15 (October): 265–272.

Brown, Seyom. 1987. *The Causes and Prevention of War*. New York: St. Martin's Press.

————. 1988. *New Forces, Old Forces, and the Future of World Politics*. Glenview, IL: Scott, Foresman.

Brucan, Silviu. 1984. "The Global Crisis," *International Studies Quarterly* 28 (March): 97–109.

Buchan, Alastair. 1965. "Problems of an Alliance Policy: An Essay in Hindsight," in Michael Howard, ed., *The Theory and Practice of War*, pp. 293–310. Bloomington: Indiana University Press.

Bueno de Mesquita, Bruce. 1975. "Measuring Systemic Polarity," *Journal of Conflict Resolution* 22 (June): 187–216.

————. 1978. "Systemic Polarization and the Occurrence and Duration of War," *Journal of Conflict Resolution* 22 (June): 241–267.

————. 1981. *The War Trap*. New Haven: Yale University Press.

Bueno de Mesquita, Bruce, and J. David Singer. 1973. "Alliances, Capabilities, and War: A Review and Synthesis," in Cornelius Cotter, ed., *Political Science Annual*, vol. 4, pp. 237–280. Indianapolis: Bobbs-Merrill.

Bull, Hedley. 1968. *Systems, States, Diplomacy and Rules*. New York: Cambridge University Press.

————. 1977. *The Anarchical Society: A Study of Order in World Politics*. New York: Columbia University Press.

Bullough, Vern L. 1957. "The Roman Empire vs. Persia, 363–502: A Study of Successful Deterrence," *Journal of Conflict Resolution* 7 (March): 55–68.

Burgess, Philip M., and David W. Moore. 1972. "Inter-Nation Alliances, An Inventory and Appraisal of Propositions," in James A. Robinson, ed., *Political Science Annual*, vol. 3, pp. 339–383. Indianapolis: Bobbs-Merrill.

Burgess, Philip M., and James A. Robinson. 1969. "Alliances and the Theory of Collective Action," in James N. Rosenau, ed., *International Politics and Foreign Policy*, pp. 640–653. New York: Free Press.

Burklin, Wilhelm. 1987. "Why Study Political Cycles?" *European Journal of Political Research* 15 (No. 2): 131–143.

Burns, Arthur Lee. 1968. *Of Powers and Their Politics*. Englewood Cliffs, NJ: Prentice-Hall.

Butterfield, Herbert. 1962. *The Statecraft of Machiavelli.* New York: Collier.

————. 1968. "The Balance of Power," in Herbert Butterfield and Martin Wight, eds., *Diplomatic Investigations: Essays in the Theory of International Politics,* pp. 132–175. Cambridge, MA: Harvard University Press.

Butterfield, Herbert, and Martin Wight., eds. 1968. *Diplomatic Investigations: Essays in the Theory of International Relations.* Cambridge, MA: Harvard University Press.

Calleo, David. 1987. *Beyond American Hegemony: The Future of the Western Alliance.* New York: Basic Books.

Callières, François de. 1963. *On the Manner of Negotiating with Princes,* trans. by A. F. Whyte. South Bend, IN: University of Notre Dame Press.

Campbell, Donald T. 1963. "From Description to Experimentation: Interpreting Trends as Quasi-Experiments," in Chester Harris, ed., *Problems in Measuring Change,* pp. 212–245. Madison: University of Wisconsin Press.

Carr, E. H. 1937. *International Relations Since the Peace Treaties.* London: Macmillan.

————. 1939. *The Twenty-Years' Crisis, 1919–1939: An Introduction to the Study of International Relations.* London: Macmillan.

————. 1948. *International Relations Between the Two World Wars, (1919–1939).* London: Macmillan.

Carson, Robert C. 1969. *Interaction Concepts of Personality.* Chicago: Aldine.

Carty, Anthony. 1986. *The Decay of International Law?* Manchester: Manchester University Press.

Castren, Erik Johannes Sakari. 1954. *The Present Law of War and Neutrality.* Helsinki: Annals Academical Scientiarum Fennical.

Chagnon, Napoleon A. 1968. *Yanomamo: The Fierce People.* New York: Holt, Rinehart and Winston.

Chan, Steve. 1984. "Mirror, Mirror, on the Wall . . . Are the Freer Countries More Pacific?," *Journal of Conflict Resolution* 28 (December): 617–648.

Charney, Jonathan I. 1986. "The Power of the Executive Branch of the United States Government to Violate Customary International Law," *American Journal of International Law* 80 (October): 913–922.

Chase-Dunn, Christopher. 1981. "Interstate System and Capitalist World-Economy," *International Studies Quarterly* 25 (March): 19–42.

Chi, Hsi-Cheng. 1968. "The Chinese Warlord System As an International System," in Morton A. Kaplan, ed., *New Approaches to International Relations,* pp. 405–425. New York: St. Martin's Press.

Chihiro, Hosoya. 1976. "The Tripartite Pact," in James W. Morley, ed., *Deterrent Diplomacy,* pp. 201–240. New York: Columbia University Press.

Cicero, M. Tullius. 1913. *De Officiis,* trans. by W. Miller. Loeb Classical Library. London: Heinemann.

Clark, G. N. 1966. "European Equilibrium in the Seventeenth Century," in Laurence W. Martin, ed., *Diplomacy in Modern European History,* pp. 23–30. New York: Macmillan.

Clark, Ian. 1980. *Reform and Resistance in the International Order.* Cambridge: Cambridge University Press.

Clark, Mark T. 1987. "The ABM Treaty Interpretation Dispute," *Global Affairs* 2 (Summer): 58–79.

Clark, Ronald W. 1971. *Einstein: The Life and Times.* New York: Crowell.

Claude, Inis L., Jr. 1962. *Power and International Relations.* New York: Random House.

———. 1981. "Casual Commitment in International Relations," *Political Science Quarterly* 96 (Fall): 367–379.

———. 1986. "The Common Defense and Great-Power Responsibilities," *Political Science Quarterly* 101 (Winter): 719–732.

Clemens, Diane Shaver. 1970. *Yalta.* New York: Oxford University Press.

Cohen, Marshall. 1987. "Moral Skepticism and International Relations," in Kenneth Kipnis and Diana T. Meyers, eds., *Political Realism and International Morality,* pp. 15–34. Boulder, CO: Westview.

Cohen, Raymond. 1980. "Rules of the Game in International Politics," *International Studies Quarterly* 24 (March): 129–150.

———. 1981. *International Politics: The Rules of the Game.* London: Longman.

———. 1987. *Theatre of Power: The Art of Diplomatic Signalling.* London: Longman.

Coll, Alberto R. 1985. *The Wisdom of Statecraft.* Durham, NC: Duke University Press.

Collett, Peter. 1977. "The Rules of Conduct," in Peter Collett, ed., *Social Rules and Social Behavior,* pp. 1–27. London: Macmillan.

Cook, Don. 1989. *Forging the Alliance: The Birth of the NATO Treaty and the Dramatic Transformation of U.S. Foreign Policy Between 1945 and 1950.* New York: Arbor House/William Morrow.

Cook, Thomas, and Malcolm Moos. 1954. *Power Through Purpose: The Realism of Idealism as a Basis for Foreign Policy.* Baltimore: Johns Hopkins University Press.

Coplin, William D. 1965. "International Law and Assumptions About the State System," *World Politics* 17 (July): 615–634.

———. 1966. *The Functions of International Law.* Chicago: Rand McNally.

———. 1970. "Current Studies of the Functions of International Law," in James A. Robinson, ed., *Political Science Annual,* vol. 2, pp. 149–207. Indianapolis: Bobbs-Merrill.

Cowhey, Peter F., and Edward Long. 1983. "Testing Theories of Regime Change: Hegemonic Decline or Surplus Capacity?," *International Organization* 37 (Spring): 157–188.

Craig, Gordon A. 1965. "The World War I Alliance of the Central Powers in Retrospect: The Military Cohesion of the Alliance," *The Journal of Modern History* 37 (September): 336–344.

———. 1966. "Problems of Coalition Warfare: The Military Alliance Against Napoleon," in Gordon A. Craig, ed., *War, Politics, and Diplomacy*, pp. 22–45. New York: Praeger.

Craig, Gordon A., and Alexander L. George. 1983. *Force and Statecraft.* New York: Oxford University Press.

Creel, H. G. 1953. *Chinese Thought: From Confucius to Mao Tse-Tung.* New York: Mentor.

Croce, Benedetto. 1945. *Politics and Morals,* trans. by Salvatore J. Castinione. New York: Philosophical Library.

Crozier, Brian, Drew Middleton, and Jeremy Murray-Brown. 1985. *This War Called Peace.* New York: Universe Books.

D'Amato, Anthony. 1987. "The President and International Law: A Missing Dimension," *American Journal of International Law* 81 (April): 375–377.

David, Arie E. 1975. *The Strategy of Treaty Termination: Lawful Breaches and Retaliations.* New Haven: Yale University Press.

David, René. 1984. "The Sources of Law," in International Association of Legal Science, ed., *International Encyclopedia of Comparative Law,* vol. 2, pp. 4–404. The Hague: Martinus Nijhoff.

Degan, V. D. 1963. *L'interpretation des Accords en Droit International.* La Haye: Martinus Nijhoff.

De Gaulle, Charles. 1959. *The War Memoirs of Charles De Gaulle,* vol. 2. New York: Simon & Schuster.

———. 1960. *The Edge of the Sword.* New York: Criterion.

———. 1964. *Major Addresses, Statements and Press Conferences of General Charles de Gaulle.* French Embassy, Press and Information Division, New York.

———. 1966. *French Foreign Policy: Official Statements, Speeches and Communiques.* French Embassy, Press and Information Division, New York.

———. 1971. *Memoirs of Hope: Renewal and Endeavor,* trans. by Terence Kilmartin. New York: Simon & Schuster.

Dehio, Ludwig. 1962. *The Precarious Balance,* trans. by Charles Fullman. New York: Knopf.

Deibel, Terry L. 1978. "A Guide to International Divorce," *Foreign Policy* 30 (Spring): 17–35.

———. 1987a. "Alliances for Containment," in Terry L. Deibel and John Lewis Gaddis, eds., *Containing the Soviet Union,* pp. 100–119. Washington, DC: Pergamon-Brassy's.

————. 1987b. "Hidden Commitments," *Foreign Policy* 67 (Summer): 46–63.

DeLupis, Ingrid Detter. 1967. *Essays on the Law of Treaties.* London: Street and Maxwell.

————. 1986. "Treaties in the Modern Era," in Ervin Laszlo and Jong Youl You, eds., *World Encyclopedia of Peace,* vol. 2, pp. 429–482. Oxford: Pergamon.

————. 1987. *The Concept of International Law.* Stockholm: Norstedts.

DePorte, A. W. 1968. *De Gaulle's Foreign Policy, 1944–1946.* Cambridge, MA: Harvard University Press.

Derian, James Der. 1987. "Mediating Estrangement: A Theory for Diplomacy," *Review of International Studies* 13 (April): 91–110.

Derrida, Jacques. 1977. *Of Grammatology,* trans. by G. C. Spivak. Baltimore: Johns Hopkins University Press.

————. 1982. *Dissemination,* trans. by Barbara Johnson. London: Athlone Press.

Deutsch, Karl W., and Morton A. Kaplan. 1964. "The Limits of International Coalitions," in James N. Rosenau, ed., *International Aspects of Civil Strife,* pp. 170–184. Princeton: Princeton University Press.

Deutsch, Karl W., and J. David Singer. 1964. "Multipolar Power Systems and International Stability," *World Politics* 16 (April): 390–406.

Deutsch, Morton. 1958. "Trust and Suspicion," *Journal of Conflict Resolution* 2 (December): 265–279.

Dhrymes, P. J. 1971. *Distributed Lags: Problems of Estimation and Formulation.* San Francisco: Holden-Day.

Dingman, Roger V. 1979. "Theories of, and Approaches to, Alliance Politics," pp. 245–266 in Paul G. Lauren, ed., *Diplomacy: New Approaches in History, Theory, and Policy.* New York: Free Press.

Dinnerstein, Herbert S. 1965. "The Transformation of Alliance Systems," *American Political Science Review* 59 (September): 589–601.

Doran, Charles F. 1983a. "Power Cycle Theory and the Contemporary State System," in William R. Thompson, ed., *Contending Approaches to World System Analysis,* pp. 165–182. Beverly Hills: Sage.

————. 1983b. "War and Power Dynamics: Economic Considerations," *International Studies Quarterly* 27 (December): 419–441.

Doran, Charles F., and Wes Parsons. 1980. "War and the Cycle of Relative Power," *American Political Science Review* 74 (December): 947–965.

Doyle, Michael W. 1986. "Liberalism and World Politics," *American Political Science Review* 80 (December): 1151–1169.

Draper, Theodore. 1988. "Coalition Dynamics: NATO, the Phantom Alliance," in Charles W. Kegley, Jr., and Eugene R. Wittkopf, eds., *The Global Agenda,* pp. 150–158. New York: Random House.

Dubois, Pierre. 1956. *The Recovery of the Holy Land,* trans. by Walther I. Brandt. New York: Columbia University Press.

Duncan, George T., and Randolph M. Siverson. 1982. "Flexibility of Alliance Partner Choice in a Multipolar System: Models and Tests," *International Studies Quarterly* 26 (December): 511–538.

Duncan, Hugh D. 1968. *Symbols and Society.* New York: Oxford University Press.

Dworkin, Ronald. 1986. *Law's Empire.* Cambridge, MA: Harvard University Press.

Eckstein, Harry. 1975. "Case Study and Theory in Political Science," in Fred I. Greenstein and Nelson W. Polsby, eds., *Handbook of Political Science,* vol. 7, pp. 79–138. Reading, MA: Addison-Wesley.

Eco, Umberto. 1980. *The Name of the Rose,* trans. by William Weaver. New York: Harcourt Brace Jovanovich.

Eijk, Crees vander, and Robert Philip Weber. 1987. "Notes on the Empirical Analysis of Cyclical Processes," *European Journal of Political Research* 15 (No. 2): 271–280.

Einborn, Robert J. 1981–1982. "Treaty Compliance," *Foreign Policy* 45 (Winter): 29–47.

Eisenstadt, S. N. 1959. "Primitive Political Systems: A Preliminary Comparative Analysis," *American Anthropologist* 61 (February): 200–220.

Ekirch, Arthur A., Jr. 1966. *Ideas, Ideals, and American Diplomacy.* New York: Appleton-Century-Crofts.

Elazer, Daniel J. 1970. *Cities of the Prairie.* New York: Basic Books.

Elrod, Richard B. 1976. "The Concert of Europe: A Fresh Look at an International System," *World Politics* 28 (January): 159–174.

Eppstein, John. 1984. "Motives and Morality in International Relations," *NATO Review* 32 (October): 14–19.

Evans, Gary. 1964. "Effect of Unilateral Promise and Value of Rewards Upon Cooperation and Trust," *Journal of Abnormal and Social Psychology* 69 (November): 587–590.

Falk, Richard A. 1968a. *Legal Order in a Violent World.* Princeton: Princeton University Press.

———. 1968b. *The Six Legal Dimensions of the Vietnam War.* Princeton: Center for International Studies, Princeton University.

———. 1970. *The Status of Law in International Society.* Princeton: Princeton University Press.

———. 1971. "Bipolarity and the Future of World Society," in B. Landheer, J. H. M. M. Loenen and F. L. Polak, eds., *Worldsociety,* pp. 103–114. The Hague: Martinus Nijhoff.

————. 1980. "Anarchism and World Order," in Richard A. Falk and Samuel S. Kim, eds., *The War System*, pp. 37–57. Boulder, CO: Westview Press.

Farer, Tom J. 1988. "International Law: The Critics Are Wrong," *Foreign Policy* 71 (Summer): 22–45.

Fedder, Edwin. 1968. "The Concept of Alliance," *International Studies Quarterly* 12 (March): 65–86.

Felperin, Howard. 1985. *Beyond Deconstruction: The Uses and Abuses of Literary Theory*. Oxford: Clarendon Press.

Fenwick, Charles G. 1965. *International Law*, 4th ed. New York: Appleton-Century-Crofts.

Ferguson, Yale H., and Richard W. Mansbach. 1988. *The Elusive Quest: Theory and International Politics*. Columbia: University of South Carolina Press.

Ferrell, Robert H. 1952. *Peace in Their Time: The Origins of the Kellogg-Briand Pact*. London: Oxford University Press.

Ferris, Wayne H. 1973. *The Power Capabilities of Nation-States*. Lexington, MA: D. C. Heath.

Field, G. Lowell. 1949. "Law as an Objective Political Concept," *American Political Science Review* 43 (April): 229–249.

Fischer, Dietrich. 1984. *Preventing War in the Nuclear Age*. Totowa, NJ: Rowman & Allanheld.

Fisher, Roger D. 1961a. "Bringing Law to Bear on Governments," *Harvard Law Review* 74 (April): 1130–1140.

————. 1961b. "Constructing Rules that Affect Governments," in Donald Brennan, ed., *Arms Control, Disarmament, and National Security*, pp. 56–68. New York: Braziller.

————. 1981. *Improving Compliance with International Law*. Charlottesville: University Press of Virginia.

Fisher, Walter R. 1987. *Human Communication as Narration*. Columbia: University of South Carolina Press.

Fleming, D. F. 1968. *The Origins and Legacies of World War I*. Garden City, NY: Doubleday.

Folly, Martin H. 1988. "Breaking the Vicious Circle: Britain, the United States, and the Genesis of the North Atlantic Treaty," *Diplomatic History* 12 (Winter): 59–77.

Fortes, Meyer, and Edward Evan Evans-Pritchard, eds. 1940. *African Political Systems*. London: Oxford University Press.

Foucault, Michel. 1979. *Power, Truth, Strategy*. Sydney: Feral Publications.

Franck, Thomas. 1988. "Taking Treaties Seriously," *American Journal of International Law* 82 (January): 67–68.

Franck, Thomas M., and Edward Weisband. 1972. *Word Politics: Verbal Strategy Among the Superpowers*. New York: Oxford University Press.

Franke, Winfried. 1968. "The Italian City-State System as an International System," in Morton A. Kaplan, ed., *New Approaches to International Relations,* pp. 426–458. New York: St. Martin's Press.

Freedman, Lawrence. 1988. "Managing Alliances," *Foreign Policy* 71 (Summer): 65–85.

Frey, Frederick W. 1970. "Cross-Cultural Survey Research in Political Science," in Robert T. Holt and John E. Turner, eds., *The Methodology of Comparative Research,* pp. 173–294. New York: Free Press.

Fried, Charles. 1981. *Contract As Promise.* Cambridge, MA: Harvard University Press.

Fried, John H. E. 1965. "For a New Image of International Law," *Main Currents in Modern Thought* 21 (May-June): 106–108.

Friedheim, Robert L. 1968. "The 'Satisfied' and 'Dissatisfied' States Negotiate International Law," in Richard A. Falk and Wolfram F. Hanrieder, eds., *International Law and Organization,* pp. 68–88. Philadelphia: J. B. Lippincott.

Friedman, Julian R. 1970. "Alliance in International Politics," in Julian R. Friedman, Christopher Bladen, and Steven Rosen, eds., *Alliance in International Politics,* pp. 3–32. Boston: Allyn and Bacon.

Friedman, Wolfgang. 1964. *The Changing Structure of International Law.* New York: Columbia University Press.

Friedrich, Carl J., and Charles Blitzer. 1957. *The Age of Power.* Ithaca, NY: Cornell University Press.

Fromkin, David. 1981. *The Independence of Nations.* New York: Praeger.

Frost, Mervyn. 1986. *Towards a Normative Theory of International Relations.* Cambridge: Cambridge University Press.

Furniss, Edgar S., Jr. 1960. *France, Troubled Ally.* New York: Harper & Brothers.

Gaddis, John Lewis. 1972. *The United States and the Origins of the Cold War.* New York: Columbia University Press.

——— . 1982. *Strategies of Containment.* New York: Oxford University Press.

——— . 1986. "The Long Peace: Elements of Stability in the Postwar International System," *International Security* 10 (Spring): 99–142.

——— . 1987. *The Long Peace: Inquiries Into the History of the Cold War.* New York: Oxford University Press.

Gallois, Pierre. 1961. *The Balance of Terror: Strategy for the Nuclear Age,* trans. by Richard Howard. Boston: Houghton-Mifflin.

Garner, James W. 1927. "The Doctrine of Rebus Sic Stantibus and the Termination of Treaties," *American Journal of International Law* 21 (July): 509–516.

Garnham, David. 1976a. "Dyadic International War, 1816–1965," *Western Political Quarterly* 29 (June): 231–242.

Garnham, David. 1976b. "Power Parity and Lethal International Violence, 1964–1973," *Journal of Conflict Resolution* 20 (September): 379–394.

Geertz, Clifford. 1973. "Thick Description: Toward An Interpretive Theory of Culture," in Clifford Geertz, ed., *The Interpretation of Cultures,* pp. 3–30. New York: Basic Books.

George, Alexander L. 1979. "Case Study and Theory Development: The Method of Structured, Focused Comparison," in Paul Gordon Lauren, ed., *Diplomacy: New Approaches in History, Theory and Policy,* pp. 43–68. New York: Free Press.

——— , ed. 1983. *Managing U.S.-Soviet Rivalry: Problems of Crisis Prevention.* Boulder, CO: Westview.

——— . 1986. "US-Soviet Global Rivalry: Norms of Competition," *Journal of Peace Research* 23 (September): 247–262.

——— . 1987. "Ideology and International Relations: A Conceptual Analysis," *The Jerusalem Journal of International Relations* 9 (March): 1–21.

Gibbs, Jack P. 1965. "Norms: The Problem of Definition and Classification," *American Journal of Sociology* 70 (March): 586–594.

——— . 1966. "The Sociology of Law and Normative Phenomena," *American Sociological Review* 31 (June): 315–323.

Gilpin, Robert. 1981. *War and Change in World Politics.* Cambridge: Cambridge University Press.

——— . 1984. "The Richness of the Tradition of Political Realism," *International Organization* 38 (Spring): 287–304.

Gochman, Charles, and Russell J. Leng. 1983. "Realpolitik and the Road to War," *International Studies Quarterly* 27 (March): 97–120.

Gochman, Charles S., and Zeev Maoz. 1984. "Militarized Interstate Disputes, 1816–1976: Procedures, Patterns, and Insights," *Journal of Conflict Resolution* 28 (December): 585–615.

Goldberg, Andrew C. 1989. "Offense and Defense in the Postnuclear System," in Charles W. Kegley, Jr., and Eugene R. Wittkopf, eds., *The Nuclear Reader,* pp. 121–128. New York: St. Martin's Press.

Goldmann, Kjell. 1971. *International Norms and War Between States.* Stockholm: Laromedelsforlagen.

Goldstein, Joshua S. 1988. *Long Cycles: Prosperity and War in the Modern Age.* New Haven: Yale University Press.

Goodman, Elliot R. 1975. *The Fate of the Atlantic Community.* New York: Praeger.

Gordon, Michael R. 1986. "Reagan and Arms Treaty: A Sharp Shift in Policy," *The New York Times* (May 30): 8A.

Gordis, Robert. 1984. "Religion and International Responsibility," in Kenneth W. Thompson, ed., *Moral Dimensions of American Foreign Policy,* pp. 33–49. New Brunswick, NJ: Transaction Books.

Gormley, W. Paul. 1970. "Codification of *Pacta Sunt Servanda* by the International Law Commission: The Preservation of Classical Norms of Moral Force and Good Faith," *Saint Louis University Law Journal* 14 (Spring): 367–428.

Gottlieb, Gidon. 1968. *The Logic of Choice: An Investigation of the Concepts of Rule and Rationality.* New York: Macmillan.

Gould, Wesley L. 1957. *An Introduction to International Law.* New York: Harper.

Gould, Wesley L., and Michael Barkun. 1970. *International Law and the Social Sciences.* Princeton: Princeton University Press.

Gralnick, Alexander. 1988. "Trust, Deterrence, Realism, and Nuclear Omnicide," *Political Psychology* 9 (March): 175–188.

Granovetter, Mark. 1978. "Threshold Models of Collective Behavior," *American Journal of Sociology* 83 (May): 1420–1443.

Gray, Colin S. 1987–1988. "NATO: Time to Call it a Day?," *The National Interest* 10 (Winter): 13–26.

Grey, Edward. 1925. *Twenty-Five Years, 1892–1916.* New York: Frederick Stokes.

Gross, Leo. 1969. "The Peace of Westphalia, 1648–1948," in Leo Gross, ed., *International Law in the Twentieth Century,* pp. 25–46. New York: Appleton-Century-Crofts.

Grosser, Alfred. 1965. *French Foreign Policy Under de Gaulle.* Boston: Little, Brown.

Guerlac, Henry. 1943. "Vauban: The Impact of Science on War," in Edward Mead Earle, ed., *Makers of Modern Strategy: Military Thought From Machiavelli to Hitler,* pp. 26–48. Princeton: Princeton University Press.

Gulick, Edward Vose. 1955. *Europe's Classical Balance of Power.* Ithaca, NY: Cornell University Press.

Gurr, Ted Robert. 1972. *Politimetrics: An Introduction to Quantitative Macropolitics.* Englewood Cliffs, NJ: Prentice-Hall.

Gwertzman, Bernard. 1986. "NATO Faults U.S. on Intent to Drop 1979 Arms Treaty," *The New York Times* (May 30): 1A, 8A.

Haas, Ernst B. 1969. *Tangle of Hopes: American Commitments and World Order.* Englewood Cliffs, NJ: Prentice-Hall.

———. 1980. "Why Collaborate? Issue-Linkage and International Regimes," *World Politics* 32 (April): 357–405.

Haas, Michael. 1970. "International Subsystems: Stability and Polarity," *American Political Science Review* 64 (March): 98–123.

Hackett, John, et al. 1978. *The Third World War.* New York: Macmillan.

Hackworth, Green H. 1953. *Digest of International Law,* vol. 5. Washington, DC: U.S. Government Printing Office.

Haggard, Stephan, and Beth A. Simmons. 1987. "Theories of International Regimes," *International Organziation* 41 (Summer): 491–517.

Hampson, Fen Osler. 1988. "The Divided Decision Maker," in Charles W. Kegley, Jr., and Eugene R. Wittkopf, eds., *The Domestic Sources of American Foreign Policy,* pp. 227–247. New York: St. Martin's Press.

Hanrieder, Wolfram, and Graeme P. Auton. 1980. *The Foreign Policies of West Germany, France, and Britain.* Englewood Cliffs, NJ: Prentice-Hall.

Haraszti, György. 1975. "Treaties and the Fundamental Change of Circumstances," *Recueil Des Cours* 146 (No. 3): 1–93.

Hardin, Garrett. 1980. *Promethean Ethics: Living with Death, Competition, and Triage.* Seattle: University of Washington Press.

Hardin, Russell. 1982. *Collective Action.* Baltimore: Johns Hopkins University Press.

Hare, J. E., and Carey B. Joynt. 1982. *Ethics and International Affairs.* New York: St. Martin's Press.

Harf, James E., David G. Hoovler, and Thomas E. James, Jr. 1974. "Systemic and External Attributes in Foreign Policy Analysis," in James N. Rosenau, ed., *Comparing Foreign Policies,* pp. 235–249. New York: Wiley.

Harrer, Heinrich. 1959. *The White Spider,* trans. by Hugh Merrick. London: Rupert Hart-Davis.

Hays, Richard E. 1973. "Identifying and Measuring Changes in the Frequency of Event Data," *International Studies Quarterly* 17 (December): 471–493.

Hart, H. L. A. 1961. *The Concept of Law.* London: Oxford University Press.

Hartmann, Frederick H. 1983. *The Relations of Nations,* 6th ed. New York: Macmillan.

Healy, Brian, and Arthur Stein. 1973. "The Balance of Power in International History: Theory and Reality," *Journal of Conflict Resolution* 17 (March): 33–61.

Henkin, Louis. 1979. *How Nations Behave: Law and Foreign Policy.* New York: Columbia University Press.

Herkin, Greg. 1980. *The Winning Weapon: The Atomic Bomb and the Cold War, 1945–1950.* New York: Random House.

Hermann, Charles F., ed. 1972a. *International Crises.* New York: Free Press.

———. 1972b. "Some Issues in the Study of International Crisis," in Charles F. Hermann, ed., *International Crises,* pp. 3–17. New York: Free Press.

Herz, John H. 1951. *Political Realism and Political Idealism.* Chicago: University of Chicago Press.

Hill, Chesney. 1934. "The Doctrine of 'Rebus Sic Stantibus' in International Law," *The University of Missouri Studies* 4 (July): 1–95.

Hinde, Robert. 1987. "Trust, Co-operation, Commitment and International Relationships," *Current Research on Peace and Violence* 10 (No. 2–3): 83–90.

Hoebel, E. Adamson. 1954. *The Law of Primitive Man*. Cambridge: Harvard University Press.

———. 1960. *The Cheyenne: Indians of the Great Plains*. New York: Holt, Rinehart and Winston.

Hoffmann, Stanley. 1961. "International Systems and International Law," in Klaus Knorr and Sidney Verba, eds., *The International System: Theoretical Essays*, pp. 205–237. Princeton: Princeton University Press.

———. 1965. *The State of War*. New York: Praeger.

———. 1968. "Introduction," in Lawrence Scheinman and David Wilkinson, eds., *International Law and Political Crisis*, pp. xi–xix. Boston: Little, Brown.

———. 1969. "The Study of International Law and the Theory of International Relations," in Leo Gross, ed., *International Law in the Twentieth Century*, pp. 150–159. New York: Appleton-Century-Crofts.

———. 1971. "International Law and the Control of Force," in Karl Deutsch and Stanley Hoffmann, eds., *The Relevance of International Law*, pp. 34–66. Garden City, NY: Doubleday-Anchor.

———. 1981. *Duties Beyond Borders: On the Limits and Possibilities of Ethical International Politics*. Syracuse: Syracuse University Press.

Holsti, Kalevi J. 1970. "National Role Conceptions in the Study of Foreign Policy," *International Studies Quarterly* 14 (September): 233–309.

———. 1982. "Restructuring Foreign Policy: A Neglected Phenomenon in Foreign Policy," in Kalevi J. Holsti, ed., *Why Nations Realign: Foreign Policy Restructuring in the Postwar World*, pp. 1–20. Boston: Allen & Unwin.

———. 1988. *International Politics*, 5th ed. Englewood Cliffs, NJ: Prentice-Hall.

Holsti, Ole R. 1969. *Content Analysis for the Social Sciences and Humanities*. Reading, MA: Addison-Wesley.

———. 1972. *Crisis Escalation War*. Montreal: McGill-Queen's University Press.

———. 1976. "Alliance and Coalition Diplomacy," in James N. Rosenau, Kenneth W. Thompson, and Gavin Boyd, eds., *World Politics*, pp. 337–372. New York: Free Press.

Holsti, Ole R., P. Terrence Hopmann, and John D. Sullivan. 1973. *Unity and Disintegration in International Alliances: Comparative Studies*. New York: John Wiley.

Holsti, Ole R., and John D. Sullivan. 1969. "National-International Linkages: France and China as Nonconforming Alliance Members," in James N. Rosenau, ed., *Linkage Politics*, pp. 147–195. New York: Free Press.

Hoover, Robert A. 1980. *Arms Control: The Interwar Naval Limitation Agreements*, University of Denver Monograph Series in World Affairs, Vol. 17, Denver.

Hopple, Gerald W., Paul J. Rossa, and Jonathan Wilkenfeld. 1980. "Threats and Foreign Policy: The Overt Behavior of States in Conflict," in Pat McGowan and Charles W. Kegley, Jr., eds., *Threats, Weapons, and Foreign Policy*, pp. 19–53. Beverly Hills: Sage.

Houweling, Henk, and Jan G. Siccama. 1988. "Power Transitions as a Cause of War," *Journal of Conflict Resolution* 32 (March): 87–102.

Howard, Michael. 1984. "Men Against Fire: Expectations of War in 1914." *International Security* 9 (Summer): 41–57.

Huang, Ting-Young. 1935. *The Doctrine of Rebus Sic Stantibus in International Law*. Shanghai: Comacrib Press.

Hughes, Charles C. 1966. "From Contest to Council: Social Control Among the St. Lawrence Island Eskimos," in Marc J. Swartz, Victor W. Turner, and Arthur Tuden, eds., *Political Anthropology*, pp. 255–264. Chicago: Aldine.

Hughes, Thomas L. 1985–1986. "The Twilight of Internationalism," *Foreign Policy* 61 (Winter): 25–48.

Hurst, Michael. 1972. *Key Treaties for the Great Powers, 1814–1914*, vol. 1. London: David and Charles.

Ikenberry, G. John. 1987. "The Spread of Norms in the International System." Paper presented at the annual meeting of the American Political Science Association.

Isard, Walter, and Christine Smith. 1980. "Matching Conflict Situations and Conflict Management Procedures," *Conflict Management and Peace Science* 5 (Fall): 1–25.

———. 1982. *Conflict Analysis and Practical Conflict Management Procedures*. Cambridge, MA: Ballinger.

Jacobini, H. B. 1962. *International Law*. Homewood, IL: Dorsey.

Jackson, Robert J. 1985. *Continuity of Discord: Crises and Responses in the Atlantic Community*. New York: Praeger.

Jackson, William D. 1977. "Polarity in International Systems: A Conceptual Note," *International Interactions* 4 (No. 1): 87–96.

James, Alan. 1986. *Sovereign Statehood: The Basis of International Society*. London: Allen & Unwin.

James, Patrick, and Michael Brecher. 1988. "Stability and Polarity," *Journal of Peace Research* 25 (March): 31–42.

Jameson, Fredric. 1972. *The Prison-House of Language*. Princeton: Princeton University Press.

Jellinek, Georg. 1880. *Die Rechtliche Natur der Staatenvertrage*. Vienna: A. Holder.

Jenks, C. Wilfred. 1958. *Pacta Sunt Servanda, The Common Law of Mankind*. New York: Praeger.

Jervis, Robert. 1978. "Cooperation Under the Security Dilemma," *World Politics* 30 (January): 186–213.

———. 1982. "Security Regimes," *International Organization* 36 (Spring): 357–378.

Job, Brian L. 1976. "Membership in Inter-Nation Alliances, 1815–1965: An Exploration Using Mathematical Probability Models," in Dina A. Zinnes and John V. Gillespie, eds., *Mathematical Models in International Relations*, pp. 74–109. New York: Praeger.

———. 1981. "Grins Without Cats: In Pursuit of Knowledge of International Alliances," in P. Terrence Hopmann, Dina A. Zinnes, and J. David Singer, eds., *Cumulation in International Relations Research*, pp. 39–64. University of Denver Monograph Series in World Affairs, vol. 18. Denver.

Joll, James. 1984. *The Origins of the First World War*. London: Longman.

Jönsson, Christer. 1981. "Bargaining Power: Notes on an Elusive Concept," *Cooperation and Conflict* 16 (No. 4): 249–257.

———. 1984. *Superpower: Comparing American and Soviet Foreign Policy*. London: Frances Pinter.

Jordan, Amos A., and William J. Taylor, Jr. 1984. *American National Security*. Baltimore: Johns Hopkins University Press.

Joyner, Christopher. 1988. "The Continuing Relevance of International Law," in Charles W. Kegley, Jr., and Eugene R. Wittkopf, eds., *The Global Agenda*, pp. 186–197. New York: Random House.

Kahler, Miles. 1979–1980. "Rumors of War: The 1914 Analogy," *Foreign Affairs* 58 (Winter): 374–396.

Kahn, Herman. 1960. "The Arms Race and Some of Its Hazards," *Daedalus* 89 (Autumn): 744–780.

Kaldor, Mary, and Richard Falk, eds. 1987. *Dealignment: A New Foreign Policy Perspective*. New York: Basil Blackwell.

Kann, Robert A. 1976. "Alliances Versus Ententes," *World Politics* 28 (July): 611–621.

Kant, Immanuel. 1887. *The Philosophy of Law*. Edinburgh: T. and T. Clark.

Kantorowicz, Herman. 1958. *The Definition of Law*. Cambridge: Cambridge University Press.

Kaplan, Morton A. 1957a. "Balance of Power, Bipolarity and Other Models of International Systems," *American Political Science Review* 51 (September): 684–695.

———. 1957b. *System and Process in International Politics*. New York: John Wiley.

Kaplan, Morton A., and Nicholas deB. Katzenbach. 1961. *The Political Foundations of International Law*. New York: John Wiley.

Kaplan, Stephen S. 1981. *Diplomacy of Power*. Washington, DC: Brookings Institution.

Kaufman, Edy. 1976. *The Superpowers and their Spheres of Influence.* London: Croom Helm.

Kaufmann, Erich. 1911. *Das Wessen des Volkerrechts und die Clausula Rebus Sic Stantibus.* Tubingen: J. C. B. Mohr.

Keal, Paul. 1984. *Unspoken Rules and Superpower Dominance.* New York: St. Martin's Press.

Keeton, George W. 1929. "The Revision Clause in Certain Chinese Treaties," *British Year Book of International Law* 10: 111–136.

Kegley, Charles W. 1970. "Observations on Legal Vis-à-Vis Moral Thought and Life," *The Personalist* 51 (Winter): 58–84.

Kegley, Charles W., Jr. 1975. "Measuring the Growth and Decay of Transnational Norms Relevant to the Control of Violence: A Prospectus for Research." *Denver Journal of International Law and Policy* 5 (Fall): 425–439.

———. 1982. "Measuring Transformation in the Global Legal System," in Nicholas Greenwood Onuf, ed., *Law-Making in the Global Community,* pp. 173–209. Durham, NC: Carolina Academic Press.

———. 1988. "Neo-Idealism: A Practical Matter," *Ethics and International Affairs,* vol. 2: 173–197.

———, ed. 1991. *The Long Postwar Peace.* Chicago: Scott, Foresman/Little, Brown.

Kegley, Charles W., Jr., and Gregory A. Raymond. 1981. "International Legal Norms and the Preservation of Peace, 1820–1964: Some Evidence and Bivariate Relationships," *International Interactions* 8 (March): 171–187.

———. 1982. "Alliance Norms and War: A New Piece in An Old Puzzle," *International Studies Quarterly* 26 (December): 572–595.

———. 1983. "Civil War and Great Power Intervention: A Statistical Reexamination," *Korea and World Affairs* 7 (Fall): 455–460.

———. 1984. "Alliance Norms and the Management of Interstate Disputes," in J. David Singer and Richard J. Stoll, eds., *Quantitative Indicators in World Politics,* pp. 199–226. New York: Praeger.

———. 1986. "Normative Constraints on the Use of Force Short of War," *Journal of Peace Research* 23 (September): 213–227.

———. 1991. "Alliances and the Preservation of the Postwar Peace: Weighing the Contribution," in Charles W. Kegley, Jr., ed., *The Long Postwar Peace.* Chicago: Scott, Foresman/Little, Brown.

Kegley, Charles W., Jr., and Eugene R. Wittkopf. 1987. *American Foreign Policy: Pattern and Process,* 3rd ed. New York: St. Martin's Press.

———. 1989. *World Politics: Trend and Transformation,* 3d ed. New York: St. Martin's Press.

Kelsen, Hans. 1952. *Principles of International Law.* New York: Rinehart and Company.

———. 1967. *The Pure Theory of Law,* trans. by M. Knight. Berkeley: University of California Press.

———. 1971. "The Essence of International Law," in Karl W. Deutsch and Stanley Hoffmann, eds., *The Relevance of International Law,* pp. 115–123. Garden City, NY: Doubleday-Anchor.

Kennan, George F. 1951. *American Diplomacy 1900–1950.* Chicago: University of Chicago Press.

———. 1979. *The Decline of Bismarck's World Order: Franco-Russian Relations, 1875–1890.* Princeton: Princeton University Press.

———. 1984. *The Fateful Alliance: France, Russia and the Coming of the First World War.* New York: Pantheon Books.

Kennedy, Paul M. 1984. "The First World War and the International Power System," *International Security* 9 (Summer): 7–40.

———. 1987. *The Rise and Fall of the Great Powers.* New York: Random House.

Kennedy, Robert F. 1971. *Thirteen Days.* New York: Norton.

Keohane, Robert O. 1980. "The Theory of Hegemonic Stability and Changes in International Economic Regimes, 1967–1977," in Ole R. Holsti, Randolph M. Siverson, and Alexander L. George, eds., *Change in the International System,* pp. 131–162. Boulder, CO: Westview.

———. 1984. *After Hegemony: Cooperation and Discord in the World Political Economy.* Princeton: Princeton University Press.

———. 1986a. "Reciprocity in International Relations," *International Organization* 40 (Winter): 1–27.

———. 1986b. "The Study of International Regimes and the Classical Tradition in International Relations." Paper presented at the annual meeting of the American Political Science Association.

Keohane, Robert O., and Joseph S. Nye, Jr. 1988. "Complex Interdependence, Transnational Relations, and Realism: Alternative Perspectives on World Politics," in Charles W. Kegley, Jr., and Eugene R. Wittkopf, eds., *The Global Agenda,* pp. 257–271. New York: Random House.

Khadduri, Majid. 1964. "The Islamic Philosophy of War," in Joel Larus, ed., *Comparative World Politics,* pp. 166–174. Belmont, CA: Wadsworth.

———. *The Islamic Law of Nations, Shaybānī's Siyar.* Baltimore: Johns Hopkins University Press.

Kiesler, Charles A. 1971. *The Psychology of Commitment: Experiments Linking Behavior to Belief.* New York: Academic Press.

Kindleberger, Charles P. 1973. *The World in Depression, 1929–1939.* Berkeley: University of California Press.

———. "Dominance and Leadership in the International Economy," *International Studies Quarterly* 25 (June): 242–254.

Kissinger, Henry A. 1973. *A World Restored: Metternich, Castlereagh and the Problem of Peace, 1812–1822.* Boston: Houghton Mifflin.

Kohl, Wilfrid. 1971. *French Nuclear Diplomacy.* Princeton: Princeton University Press.

Kohn, Alfie. 1986. *No Contest.* Boston: Houghton Mifflin.

Krasner, Stephen D. 1976. "State Power and the Structure of International Trade," *World Politics* 28 (April): 317–347.

———. 1982. "Structural Causes and Regime Consequences," *International Organization* 36 (Spring): 185–206.

Krass, Allan S. 1985. "Verification and Trust in Arms Control," *Journal of Peace Research* 22 (No. 4): 285–288.

Kratochwil, Friedrich. 1984. "The Force of Prescriptions," *International Organization* 38 (Autumn): 685–708.

———. 1987. "Norms and Values: Rethinking the Domestic Analogy," *Ethics and International Affairs,* vol. 1: 135–159.

Krauthammer, Charles. 1985. "The Multilateral Fallacy," *The New Republic* (December 9): 17–20.

Kristol, Irving. 1986. " 'Global Unilateralism' and 'Entangling Alliances,' " *The Wall Street Journal* (February 3): 20.

Krummenacher, Heinz. 1985. *Internationale Normen und Krisen: Die Normative Dimension Internationales Politik.* Grusch: Ruegger.

Kruzel, Joseph. 1991. "Arms Control, Disarmament, and the Stability of the Postwar Era," in Charles W. Kegley, Jr., ed., *The Long Postwar Peace.* Chicago: Scott, Foresman/Little, Brown.

Kuechler, M. 1986. "The Utility of Surveys from Cross-National Research." Paper presented at the 11th World Congress of the International Sociological Association, New Delhi.

Kuhn, Thomas S. 1970. *The Structure of Scientific Revolutions.* Chicago: University of Chicago Press.

Kulski, W. W. 1966. *De Gaulle and the World.* Syracuse: Syracuse University Press.

Kunz, Josef L. 1945. "The Meaning and the Range of the Norm *Pacta Sunt Servanda*," *American Journal of International Law* 39 (April): 180–197.

LaFeber, Walter. 1985. *America, Russia and the Cold War, 1945–1984,* 5th ed. New York: Alfred A. Knopf.

Lake, David A. 1984. "Beneath the Commerce of Nations: A Theory of International Economic Structures," *International Studies Quarterly* 28 (June): 143–170.

Lammasch, Heinrich. 1918. *Das Volkerrecht nach dem Kriege.* Nysaard: H. Ascheoug.

Langer, William L. 1956. *European Alliances and Alignments, 1871–1890.* New York: Alfred A. Knopf.

Langsam, Walter Consuello. 1954. *The World Since 1919.* New York: Macmillan.

Lasswell, Harold D., and Richard Arens. 1967. "The Role of Sanction in Conflict Resolution," *Journal of Conflict Resolution* 11 (March): 27–39.

Lauren, Paul Gordon. 1983. "Crisis Prevention in Nineteenth-Century Diplomacy," in Alexander L. George, ed., *Managing U.S.-Soviet Rivalry,* pp. 31–64. Boulder, CO: Westview.

Lauterpacht, Hersch. 1933. *The Function of Law in the International Community.* Oxford: Clarendon.

———. 1970. *International Law,* vol. 1. Cambridge: Cambridge University Press.

———. 1975. *International Law,* vol. 2. Cambridge: Cambridge University Press.

Lawrence, Thomas J. 1915. *The Principles of International Law,* 6th ed. Boston: D.C. Heath.

Lawson, Frederick H. 1976. "Alliance Behavior in Nineteenth Century Europe," *American Political Science Review* 70 (September): 932–934.

———. 1983. "Hegemony and the Structure of International Trade Reassessed," *International Organization* 37 (Spring): 317–338.

Layne, Christopher. 1987. "Atlanticism Without NATO," *Foreign Policy* 67 (Summer): 22–45.

Lebow, Richard Ned. 1981. *Between Peace and War: The Nature of International Crisis.* Baltimore: The Johns Hopkins University Press.

Leffler, Melvyn P. 1986. "Adherence to Agreements," *International Security* 11 (Summer): 88–123.

Leive, David M. 1976. *International Regulatory Regimes.* Lexington, MA: Lexington Books.

Leng, Russell J. 1983. "When Will They Ever Learn? Coercive Bargaining in Recurrent Crises," *Journal of Conflict Resolution* 27 (September): 379–419.

———. 1984. "Reagan and the Russians: Crisis Bargaining Beliefs and the Historical Record," *American Political Science Review* 78 (June): 338–355.

Leng, Russell J., and Hugh B. Wheeler. 1979. "Influence Strategies, Success and War," *Journal of Conflict Resolution* 23 (December): 655–684.

Levi, Werner. 1969. "The Relative Irrelevance of Moral Norms in International Politics," in James N. Rosenau, ed., *International Politics and Foreign Policy,* pp. 191–198. New York: Free Press.

———. 1974. "International Law in a Multicultural World," *International Studies Quarterly* 18 (December): 417–449.

———. 1981. *The Coming End of War.* Beverly Hills: Sage.

Levy, Jack S. 1981. "Alliance Formation and War Behavior: An Analysis of the Great Powers, 1495–1975," *Journal of Conflict Resolution* 25 (December): 581–613.

———. 1983. *War in the Modern Great Power System, 1495–1975.* Lexington: University of Kentucky Press.

————. 1985a. "The Polarity of the System and International Stability: An Empirical Analysis," in Alan Ned Sabrosky, ed., *Polarity and War: The Changing Structure of International Conflict*, pp. 41–66. Boulder, CO: Westview.

————. 1985b. "Theories of General War," *World Politics* 37 (April): 344–374.

Levy, Jack S., and T. Cliff Morgan. 1984. "The Frequency and Seriousness of War," *Journal of Conflict Resolution* 28 (December): 731–749.

Lewis, J. David, and Andrew Weigert. 1985. "Trust As A Social Reality," *Social Forces* 63 (June): 967–985.

Li, Richard, and William R. Thompson. 1978. "The Stochastic Process of Alliance Formation Behavior," *American Political Science Review* 72 (December): 1288–1303.

Lieber, Robert J. 1982. "Cohesion and Disruption in the Western Alliance," in Daniel Yergin and Martin Hillenbrand, eds., *Global Insecurity*, pp. 320–348. New York: Penguin.

Lieberman, Bernhardt. 1968. "*i*-Trust: A Notion of Trust in Three-Person Games and International Affairs," in Louis Kriesberg, ed., *Social Processes in International Relations*, pp. 359–371. New York: John Wiley & Sons.

————. 1975. "Coalitions and Conflict Resolution," *American Behavioral Scientist* 18 (March/April): 557–581.

Lijphart, Arend. 1974. "The Structure of the Theoretical Revolution in International Relations," *International Studies Quarterly* 17 (March): 41–74.

Lindskold, Svenn. 1978. "Trust Development, the GRIT Proposal, and the Effects of Conciliatory Acts on Conflict and Cooperation," *Psychological Bulletin* 85 (July): 772–793.

Link, Arthur S. 1965. *Wilson the Diplomatist*. Chicago: Quadrangle.

Lippmann, Walter. 1952. *Isolation and Alliances*. Boston: Little, Brown.

Liska, George. 1962. *Nations in Alliance: The Limits of Interdependence*. Baltimore: Johns Hopkins University Press.

————. 1968. *Alliances and the Third World*. Baltimore: John Hopkins University Press.

Lissitzyn, Oliver J. 1967. "Treaties and Changed Circumstances (Rebus Sic Stantibus)," *American Journal of International Law* 61 (October): 895–922.

Little, Richard. 1975. *Intervention*. London: Martin Robertson.

Locke, Don. 1972. "The Object of Morality and the Obligation to Keep a Promise," *Canadian Journal of Philosophy* 2 (September): 135–143.

Lockhart, Charles. 1978. "Flexibility and Commitment in International Conflicts," *International Studies Quarterly* 22 (December): 545–568.

Luard, Evan. 1976. *Types of International Society*. New York: Free Press.

Luhmann, Niklas. 1979. *Trust and Power*. New York: Chichester.

Luttwak, Edward. 1980. *Strategy and Politics*. New Brunswick, NJ: Transaction Books.

MacCormick, Neil. 1972. "Voluntary Obligations and Normative Powers," *Proceedings of the Aristotelian Society* 46 (Supp. Volume) (July): 59–78.

MacIntyre, Alasdair. 1981. *After Virtue: A Study in Moral Theory*. Notre Dame, IN: University of Notre Dame Press.

de Madariaga, Salvador. 1929. *Disarmament*. New York: Coward McCann.

Magnetti, Donald L. 1978. "The Function of the Oath in the Ancient Near Eastern International Treaty," *American Journal of International Law* 72 (October): 815–829.

Mahoney, Robert B., Jr., and Richard P. Clayberg. 1980. "Images and Threats: Soviet Perceptions of International Crises," in Pat McGowan and Charles W. Kegley, Jr., eds., *Threats, Weapons, and Foreign Policy*, pp. 55–81. Beverly Hills: Sage.

Maine, Henry Sumner. 1861. *Ancient Law: Its Connection with the Early History of Society and its Relation to Modern Ideas*. Boston: Beacon Press.

Mair, Lucy. 1964. *Primitive Government*. Baltimore: Penguin.

Malawer, Stuart S. 1988. "Reagan's Law and Foreign Policy, 1981–1987: The Reagan Corollary of International Law," *Harvard International Law Journal* 29 (Winter): 85–109.

Manning, C. A. W. 1962. *The Nature of International Society*. New York: Wiley.

Mansbach, Richard W., and John A. Vasquez. 1981. *In Search of Theory: A New Paradigm for Global Politics*. New York: Columbia University Press.

Manuel, Frank E. 1951. *The Age of Reason*. Ithaca, NY: Cornell University Press.

Maoz, Zeev. 1982. *Paths to Conflict: International Dispute Initiation, 1816–1976*. Boulder, CO: Westview Press.

Maoz, Zeev, and Dan S. Felsenthal. 1987. "Self-Binding Commitments, The Inducement of Trust, Social Choice and the Theory of International Cooperation," *International Studies Quarterly* 31 (June): 177–200.

Marshall, Lorna. 1967. "!Kung Bushman Bands," in Ronald Cohen and John Middleton, eds., *Comparative Political Systems*, pp. 15–43. Garden City, NJ: Natural History Press.

Masters, Roger D. 1961. "A Multi-Bloc Model of the Internation System," *American Political Science Review* 55 (December): 780–798.

———. 1969. "World Politics as a Primitive Political System," in James N. Rosenau, ed., *International Politics and Foreign Policy*, pp. 104–118. New York: Free Press.

Mattingly, Garrett. 1971. *Renaissance Diplomacy*. (Sentry Edition.) Boston: Houghton Mifflin.

May, Ernest R. 1973. *"Lessons" of the Past*. London: Oxford University Press.

McCaffrey, Stephen C. 1988. "The ABM Treaty Interpretation Resolution," *American Journal of International Law* 82 (January): 151–165.

McClelland, Charles A. 1968. "Access to Berlin: The Quantity and Variety of Events, 1948–1963," in J. David Singer, ed., *Quantitative International Politics*, pp. 159–186. New York: Free Press.

————. 1972. "The Beginning, Duration, and Abatement of International Crisis," in Charles F. Hermann, ed., *International Crises*, pp. 83–105. New York: Free Press.

McCormick, James M. 1978. "International Crises: A Note on Definition," *Western Political Quarterly* 31 (September): 352–358.

McDonald, H. Brooke, and Richard Rosecrance. 1985. "Alliance and Structural Balance in the International System," *Journal of Conflict Resolution* 29 (March): 57–82.

McDougal, Myres S., and Harold D. Lasswell. 1959. "The Identification and Appraisal of Diverse Systems of Public Order," *American Journal of International Law* 53 (January): 1–29.

McDougal, Myres S., and Florentino P. Feliciano. 1961. *Law and Minimum World Order.* New Haven: Yale University Press.

McDougal, Myres S., Harold D. Lasswell, and James C. Miller. 1967. *The Interpretation of Agreements and World Public Order.* New Haven: Yale University Press.

McGowan, Pat, and Charles W. Kegley, Jr., eds., 1980. *Threats, Weapons, and Foreign Policy.* Beverly Hills: Sage.

McGowan, Patrick J., and Robert M. Rood. 1975. "Alliance Behavior in Balance of Power Systems: Applying a Poisson Model to Nineteenth Century Europe," *American Political Science Review* 69 (March): 859–870.

McKeown, Timothy J. 1983. "Hegemonic Stability Theory and Nineteenth Century Tariff Levels in Europe," *International Organization* 37 (Winter): 73–92.

McKinlay, Robert D., and Richard Little. 1986. *Global Problems and World Order.* Madison: University of Wisconsin Press.

McNair, Arnold Duncan. 1948. *Legal Effects of War.* Cambridge: Cambridge University Press.

————. 1961. *The Law of Treaties.* Oxford: Clarendon Press.

McNeilly, F. S. 1972. "Promises Demoralized," *Philosophical Review* 81 (January): 63–81.

McWhinney, Edward. 1964. *Peaceful Coexistence and Soviet-Western International Law.* Leyden: A. W. Sythoff.

Mead, Walter Russell. 1987. *Mortal Spendor: The American Empire in Transition.* Boston: Houghton Mifflin.

Messer, Robert L. 1982. *The End of an Alliance: James F. Byrnes, Roosevelt, Truman, and the Origins of the Cold War.* Chapel Hill: University of North Carolina Press.

Middleton, John, and David Tait. 1958. *Tribes Without Rulers*. London: Routledge & Kegan Paul.

Midlarsky, Manus I. 1975. *On War*. New York: Free Press.

Midlarsky, Manus I. 1984. "Preventing Systemic War," *Journal Conflict Resolution* 28 (December): 563–584.

———. 1988. *The Onset of World War*. Boston: Unwin Hyman.

Miller, Lynn H. 1985. *Global Order: Values and Power in International Politics*. Boulder, CO: Westview Press.

Miner, Steven Merritt. 1988. *Between Churchill and Stalin: The Soviet Union, Great Britain, and the Origins of the Grand Alliance*. Chapel Hill: University of North Carolina Press.

Modelski, George. 1963. "The Study of Alliances: A Review," *Journal of Conflict Resolution* 7 (December): 769–776.

———. 1974. *World Power Concentrations: Typology, Data, Explanatory Framework*. Morristown, NJ: General Learning Press.

———. 1978. "The Long Cycle of Global Politics and the Nation-State," *Comparative Studies in Society and History* 20 (April): 213–235.

———. 1982. "Long Cycles and the Strategy of U.S. International Economic Policy," in William P. Avery and David P. Rapkin, eds., *America in a Changing World Political Economy*, pp. 97–116. New York: Longman.

———. 1983. "Long Cycles of World Leadership," in William R. Thompson, ed., *Contending Approaches to World System Analysis*, pp. 115–139. Beverly Hills: Sage.

———. 1984. "A Sequence of Long Cycles with Succession of Lead Powers in the Modern World System," *Man, Environment, Space and Time* 4 (Fall): 55–77.

———. 1986. "Long Cycles, Macrodecisions, and Global Wars." Paper presented at the conference on "The Origins and Prevention of Major Wars," Durham, New Hampshire.

———. 1987a. *Long Cycles in World Politics*. Seattle: University of Washington Press.

———. 1987b. "A System Model of the Long Cycle," in George Modelski, ed., *Exploring Long Cycles*, pp. 112–128. Boulder, CO: Lynne Rienner.

Modelski, George, and Patrick Morgan. 1985. "Understanding Global War," *Journal of Conflict Resolution* 29 (September): 391–417.

Modelski, George, and William R. Thompson. 1987. "Testing Cobweb Models of the Long Cycle," in George Modelski, ed., *Exploring Long Cycles*, pp. 85–111. Boulder, CO: Lynne Reinner.

Morgenthau, Hans J. 1951. *In Defense of the National Interest*. New York: Alfred A. Knopf.

———. 1959. "Alliances in Theory and Practice," in Arnold Wolfers, ed., *Alliance Policy in the Cold War*, pp. 184–212. Baltimore: Johns Hopkins University Press.

————. 1960. *The Purpose of American Politics*. New York: Alfred A. Knopf.

Morgenthau, Hans J. 1985. *Politics Among Nations: The Struggle for Power and Peace*, 6th ed., rev. by Kenneth W. Thompson. New York: Alfred A. Knopf.

Morris, Richard T. 1956. "A Typology of Norms," *American Sociological Review* 21 (October): 610–613.

Morse, Edward L. 1973. "Crisis Diplomacy, Interdependence, and the Politics of International Economic Relations," in Raymond Tanter and Richard L. Ullman, eds., *Theory and Policy in International Relations*, pp. 123–150. Princeton: Princeton University Press.

Most, Benjamin A., and Randolph M. Siverson. 1987. "Substituting Arms and Alliances, 1870–1914," in Charles F. Hermann, Charles W. Kegley, Jr., and James N. Rosenau, eds., *New Directions in the Study of Foreign Policy*, pp. 131–160. Boston: Allen & Unwin.

Most, Benjamin A., and Harvey Starr. 1989. *Inquiry, Logic and International Politics*. Columbia: University of South Carolina Press.

————. 1987. "Polarity, Preponderance and Power Parity in the Generation of International Conflict," *International Interactions* 13 (No. 3): 225–262.

Moul, William Brian. 1988. "Balances of Power and the Escalation to War of Serious Disputes Among the European Great Powers, 1815–1939: Some Evidence," *American Journal of Political Science* 32 (May): 241–275.

Murphy, Cornelius F., Jr. 1982. "The Grotian Vision of World Order," *American Journal of International Law* 76 (July): 477–498.

————. 1985. *The Search for World Order*. Dordrecht: Martinus Nijhoff.

Nader, Laura, 1965. "The Anthropological Study of Law," *American Anthropologist* 67 (Special Issue) (December): 3–32.

Namenwirth, J. Zvi, and Robert Philip Weber. 1987. *Dynamics of Culture*. Winchester, MA: Allen & Unwin.

Nardin, Terry. 1983. *Law, Morality, and the Relations of States*. Princeton: Princeton University Press.

Nelson, Daniel N. 1984. *Soviet Allies: The Warsaw Pact and the Issue of Reliability*. Boulder, CO: Westview.

Nelson, Randall H. 1958. "The Termination of Treaties and Executive Agreements by the United States," *Minnesota Law Review* 42 (April): 879–906.

Neustadt, Richard E. 1970. *Alliance Politics*. New York: Columbia University Press.

Neustadt, Richard E., and Ernest R. May. 1986. *Thinking in Time: The Uses of History for Decision Makers*. New York: Free Press.

Newman, Charles. 1987. "What's Left Out of Literature," *New York Times Book Review* (July 7): 1, 24–25.

Niebuhr, Reinhold. 1932. *Moral Man and Immoral Society: A Study in Ethics and Politics*. New York: Charles Scribner's Sons.

————. 1959. *The Structure of Nations and Empires.* New York: Charles Scriber's Sons.

Nish, Ian H. 1972. *Alliance in Decline.* London: Athlone Press.

Nogee, Joseph L. 1975. "Polarity: An Ambiguous Concept," *Orbis* 18 (Winter): 1193–1224.

North, Robert C., Ole R. Holsti, M. George Zanimovich, and Dina A. Zinnes. 1963. *Content Analysis.* Evanston, IL: Northwestern University Press.

Northrop, F. S. C. 1954. *The Taming of The Nations: A Study of the Cultural Bases of International Policy.* New York: Macmillan.

Numelin, Ragnar. 1950. *The Beginning of Diplomacy: A Sociological Study of Intertribal and International Relations.* London: Oxford University Press.

Obinyakov, V. 1987. "Treaties Must Be Observed," in John T. Rourke, ed., *Taking Sides,* pp. 213–216. Guilford, CT: Dushkin.

Ogden, Charles K., and I. A. Richards. 1938. *The Meaning of Meaning.* New York: Harcourt, Brace and Company.

Olson, Mancur, Jr. 1965. *The Logic of Collective Action.* Cambridge: Harvard University Press.

Olson, Mancur, Jr., and Richard A. Beer. 1970. *Alliances: Latent War Communities in the Contemporary World.* New York: Holt, Rinehart & Winston.

Olson, Mancur, Jr., and Richard Zeckhauser. 1966. "An Economic Theory of Alliances," *Review of Economics and Statistics* 48 (August): 266–279.

Onuf, Nicholas Greenwood. 1982a. "Global Law-Making and Legal Thought," in Nicholas Greenwood Onuf, ed., *Law-Making in the Global Community,* pp. 1–81. Durham, NC: Carolina Academic Press.

————, ed. 1982b. *Law-Making in the Global Community.* Durham, NC: Carolina Academic Press.

————. 1989. *World of Our Making: Rules and Rule in Social Theory and International Relations.* Columbia: University of South Carolina Press.

Opp, Karl-Dieter. 1982. "Evolutionary Emergence of Norms," *British Journal of Social Psychology* 21 (June): 139–149.

Oppenheim, Lassa Francis Lawrence. 1955. *International Law: A Treatise,* 8th ed., ed. by Hersch Lauterpacht. London: Longmans, Green.

Orbell, John M., Peregrine Schwartz-Shea, and Randall T. Simmons. 1984. "Do Cooperators Exit More Readily than Defectors?" *American Political Science Review* 78 (March): 147–162.

Oren, Nissan, ed. 1984. *When Patterns Change: Turning Points in International Politics.* New York: St. Martin's Press.

Organski, A. F. K., and Jacek Kugler. 1980. *The War Ledger.* Chicago: University of Chicago Press.

Osgood, Robert Endicott. 1968. *Alliances and American Foreign Policy.* Baltimore: Johns Hopkins University Press.

Ostrom, Charles, Jr., and John H. Aldrich. 1978. "The Relationship Between Size and Stability in the Major Power International System," *American Journal of Political Science* 22 (November): 743–771.

Ostrom, Charles, Jr., and Francis W. Hoole. 1978. "Alliances and Wars Revisited," *International Studies Quarterly* 22 (June): 215–236.

Padelford, Norman Judson, and George A. Lincoln. 1967. *The Dynamics of International Politics.* New York: MacMillan.

Parry, Clive. 1965. *The Sources and Evidence of International Law.* Manchester: Manchester University Press.

———. 1968. "The Function of Law in the International Community," in Max Sørensen, ed., *Manual of Public International Law,* pp. 1–54. New York: St. Martin's Press.

Parsons, Talcott. 1960. *Structure and Process in Modern Societies.* Glenco, IL: Free Press.

———. 1961. "Order and Community in the International System," in James N. Rosenau, ed., *International Politics and Foreign Policy,* pp. 120–129. New York: Free Press.

Paskins, Barrie. 1978. "Obligation and the Understanding of International Relations," in Michael Donelan, ed., *The Reason of States: A Study of International Political Theory,* pp. 153–170. London: Allen & Unwin.

Pearson, Frederic S. 1981. *The Weak State in International Crisis.* Washington, DC: University Press of America.

Perelman, Chaim. 1980. *Justice, Law and Argument: Essays in Moral and Legal Reasoning.* Dordrecht, Holland: D. Reidel.

Perkins, John A. 1981. *The Prudent Peace: Law as Foreign Policy.* Chicago: University of Chicago Press.

Perroux, François. 1948. "Esquisse d'un Theorie de l'Economie Dominante," *Economie Applique* 1 (April-September): 2–3.

Pfister, J. W. 1974. *The Compulsion to War.* Beverly Hills: Sage.

Phillimore, Walter Frank George. 1917. *Three Centuries of Treaties of Peace.* London: John Murray.

Pierre, Andrew J. 1982. *The Global Politics of Arms Sales.* Princeton: Princeton University Press.

Pindyck, Robert S., and Daniel L. Rubinfeld. 1975. *Econometric Models and Economic Forecasts.* New York: McGraw-Hill.

Platt, John. 1969. "What We Must Do," *Science* 166 (November): 1115–1120.

Plessis, Armand-Jean du. 1961. *Political Testament,* trans. by Henry Bertram Hill. Madison: University of Wisconsin Press.

Powell, Charles A., Helen E. Purkitt, and James W. Dyson. 1987. "Opening the Black Box: Cognitive Processing and Optimal Choice in Foreign Policy Decision Making," in Charles F. Hermann, Charles W. Kegley, Jr., and

James N. Rosenau, eds., *New Directions in the Study of Foreign Policy,* pp. 203–220. Boston: Allen & Unwin.

Prichard, Harold A. 1957. *Moral Obligation: Essays and Lectures.* Oxford: Clarendon.

Puchala, Donald J., and Raymond F. Hopkins. 1983. "International Regimes: Lessons from Inductive Analysis," in Stephen D. Krasner, ed., *International Regimes,* pp. 61–91. Ithaca, NY: Cornell University Press.

Pye, Lucian W. 1971. "Political Culture and National Character," in Gilbert Abcarian and John W. Soule, eds., *Social Psychology and Political Behavior,* pp. 80–97. Columbus, OH: Charles E. Merrill.

Pye, Lucian W., and Sidney Verba. 1965. *Political Culture and Political Development.* Princeton: Princeton University Press.

Quinn, T. J. 1981. *Athens and Samos, Lesbos and Chios: 478–404 B.C.* Manchester: Manchester University Press.

Radcliffe-Brown, A. R., and Daryll Forde. 1952. *Structure and Function in Primitive Society.* New York: Free Press.

Ramberg, Jan. 1970. *Cancellation of Contracts of Affreightment on Account of War and Similar Circumstances.* Goteberg: Elanders Boktryckkeri Aktiebolag.

Randle, Robert F. 1973. *The Origins of Peace.* New York: Free Press.

Rapkin, David, and William R. Thompson. 1980. "A Comparative Note on Two Alternative Indexes of Bipolarization," *International Interactions* 6 (No. 4): 377–386.

Rapkin, David, and William R. Thompson with Jon A. Christopherson. 1979. "Bipolarity and Bipolarization in the Cold War Era," *Journal of Conflict Resolution* 23 (June): 261–295.

Rasler, Karen A., and William R. Thompson. 1989. *War and Statemaking: The Shaping of the Great Powers.* Boston: Unwin Hyman.

Rawls, John. 1955. "Two Concepts of Rules," *Philosophical Review* 64 (January): 3–32.

Ray, James Lee. 1983. "The 'World System' and the Global Political System: A Crucial Relationship," in Pat McGowan and Charles W. Kegley, Jr., eds., *Foreign Policy and the Modern World-System,* pp. 13–34. Beverly Hills: Sage.

Raymond, Gregory A. 1977. "The Transnational Rules Indicators Project: An Interim Report," *International Studies Notes* 4 (Spring): 12–16.

——— . 1980. *Conflict Resolution and the Structure of the State System: An Analysis of Arbitrative Settlements.* Monclair, NJ: Allanheld and Osmun.

——— . 1987a. "Canada Between the Superpowers: Reciprocity and Conformity in Foreign Policy," *American Review of Canadian Studies* 17 (Summer): 221–236.

———. 1987b. "Evaluation: A Neglected Task for the Comparative Study of Foreign Policy," in Charles F. Hermann, Charles W. Kegley, Jr., and James N. Rosenau, eds., *New Directions in the Study of Foreign Policy,* pp. 96–110. Boston: Allen & Unwin.

Raymond, Gregory A., and Charles W. Kegley, Jr. 1985. "Third Party Mediation and International Norms: A Test of Two Models," *Conflict Management and Peace Science* 9 (No. 1): 33–52.

———. 1987. "Long Cycles and Internationalized Civil War," *Journal of Politics* 49 (May): 481–499.

Raz, Joseph. 1972. "Voluntary Obligations," *Proceedings of the Aristotelian Society* 46 (supp. vol.) (July): 79–102.

Remark, Joachim. 1967. *The Origins of World War I, 1871–1914.* Hinsdale, IL: Dryden Press.

Richardson, James L. 1988. "Crisis Management: A Critical Appraisal," in Gilbert R. Winham, ed., *New Issues in International Crisis Management,* pp. 13–36. Boulder, CO: Westview Press.

Richardson, Lewis F. 1960. *Arms and Insecurity.* Pittsburgh: Boxwood Press.

Richelson, Jeffrey T., and Desmond Ball. 1985. *The Ties That Bind.* London: Allen & Unwin.

Riker, William H. 1962. *The Theory of Political Coalitions.* New Haven: Yale University Press.

Robinson, James A. 1972. "Crisis: An Appraisal of Definitions and Theories," in Charles F. Hermann, ed., *International Crises,* pp. 20–38. New York: Free Press.

Robinson, Thomas W. 1969. "National Interests," in James N. Rosenau, ed., *International Politics and Foreign Policy,* pp. 182–190. New York: Free Press.

Rohn, Peter H. 1976. *Treaty Profiles.* Santa Barbara, CA: Clio Books.

Rommetveit, Ragmar. 1955. *Social Norms and Roles.* Minneapolis: University of Minnesota Press.

Rood, Robert M., and Patrick J. McGowan. 1974. "Flexibility in Balance of Power Systems and International War." Paper presented at the annual meeting of the Peace Science Society (International)/South.

Rose, Lisle. 1973. *Dubious Victory: The United States and the End of World War II.* Kent, OH: Kent State University Press.

Rosecrance, Richard. 1963. *Action and Reaction in World Politics.* Boston: Little, Brown.

———. 1966. "Bipolarity, Multipolarity, and the Future," *Journal of Conflict Resolution* 10 (September): 314–327.

———. 1987. "Long Cycle Theory and International Relations," *International Organization* 41 (Spring): 283–301.

Rosenau, James N. 1986. "Before Cooperation: Hegemons, Regimes, and Habit-Driven Actors in World Politics," *International Organization* 40 (Autumn): 879–884.

Rosenne, Shabtai. 1970. *The Law of Treaties: A Guide to the Legislative History of the Vienna Convention.* Leyden: A. W. Sijthoff.

————. 1984. *Practice and Methods of International Law.* London: Oceana.

————. 1985. *Breach of Treaty.* London: Grotius Publications.

Rothgeb, John M., Jr. 1981. "Loose vs. Tight: The Effect of Bloc Structure Upon Foreign Interactions," *Journal of Politics* 43 (May): 493–511.

Rothstein, Robert L. 1966. "Alignment, Nonalignment, and Small Powers, 1945–1965," *International Organization* 20 (Summer): 397–418.

————. 1968. *Alliances and Small Powers.* New York: Columbia University Press.

Rotter, Julian B. 1971. "Generalized Expectancies for Interpersonal Trust," *American Psychologist* 26 (May): 443–452.

Royce, Josiah. 1908. *The Philosophy of Loyalty.* New York: Macmillan.

Rubenstein, Robert A. 1988. "Cultural Analysis and International Security," *Alternatives* 13 (October): 529–542.

Ruddy, Francis Stephen. 1975. *International Law in the Enlightenment.* Dobbs Ferry, NY: Oceana.

Rummel, R. J. 1985. "Libertarian Propositions on Violence Within and Between Nations: A Test Against Published Research Results," *Journal of Conflict Resolution* 29 (September): 419–455.

Russell, Frank M. 1936. *Theories of International Relations.* New York: Appleton-Century-Crofts.

Russett, Bruce M. 1974. *Power and Community in World Politics.* San Francisco: W. H. Freeman.

Russett, Bruce, and Harvey Starr. 1989. *World Politics: The Menu for Choice,* 3d ed. San Francisco: W. H. Freeman.

Sabrosky, Alan Ned. 1980a. "Allies, Clients, and Encumbrances," *International Security Review* 5 (Summer): 117–149.

————. 1980b. "Interstate Alliances: Their Reliability and the Expansion of War," in J. David Singer, ed., *The Correlates of War II: Testing Some Realpolitik Models,* pp. 161–198. New York: Free Press.

————. 1985a. "Alliance Aggregation, Capability Distribution, and the Expansion of Interstate War," in Alan Ned Sabrosky, ed., *Polarity and War: The Changing Structure of International Conflict,* pp. 145–189. Boulder, CO: Westview Press

————. 1985b. "The Role of Alliances in U.S. Foreign Policy," in Jeffrey Salmon, James P. O'Leary, and Richard Schultz, eds., *Power, Principles & Interests,* pp. 373–384. Lexington, MA: Ginn Press.

Sagan, Scott. 1986. "1914 Revisited: Allies, Offense and Instability," *International Security* 11 (Fall): 151–175.

Sampson, Martin W., III. 1987. "Cultural Influences on Foreign Policy," in Charles F. Hermann, Charles W. Kegley, Jr. and James N. Rosenau, eds., *New Directions in the Study of Foreign Policy*, pp. 384–408. Boston: Allen & Unwin.

Sanders, David. 1986. *Lawmaking and Cooperation in International Politics.* New York: St. Martin's Press.

Scarborough, Grace E. Iusi, and Bruce Bueno de Mesquita. 1988. "Threat and Alignment," *International Interactions* 14 (No. 1): 85–93.

Schear, James A. 1985. "Arms Control Treaty Compliance: Buildup to a Breakdown?," *International Security* 10 (Fall): 141–182.

Scheingold, Stuart A. 1974. *The Politics of Rights: Lawyers, Public Policy and Political Change.* New Haven: Yale University Press.

Scheinman, Lawrence. 1965. *Atomic Energy Policy in France Under the Fourth Republic.* Princeton: Princeton University Press.

Scheinman, Lawrence, and David Wilkinson, eds. 1968. *International Law and Political Crisis.* Boston: Little, Brown.

Schelling, Thomas C. 1960. *The Strategy of Conflict.* Cambridge, MA: Harvard University Press.

———. 1966. *Arms and Influence.* New Haven: Yale University Press.

———. 1978. *Micromotives and Macrobehavior.* New York: Norton.

———. 1984. *Choice and Consequence.* Cambridge, MA: Harvard University Press.

Schlesinger, Arthur M., Jr. 1967. "Origins of the Cold War," *Foreign Affairs* 46 (October): 22–52.

———. 1986. *The Cycles of American History.* Boston: Houghton Mifflin.

Schmidt, Bruno. 1907. *Uber die volkerrecht clausula rebus sic stantibus.* Leipzig: Van Duncker und Humblot.

Schroeder, Paul W. 1976. "Alliances, 1815–1945: Weapons of Power and Tools of Management," in Klaus Knorr, ed., *Historical Dimensions of National Security Problems*, pp. 227–262. Lawrence: University Press of Kansas.

Schuman, Frederick L. 1969. *International Politics: Anarchy and Order in the World Society*, 7th ed. New York: McGraw-Hill.

Schwarzenberger, George. 1951. *Power Politics.* New York: Praeger.

Scott, John F. 1971. *The Internalization of Norms.* Englewood Cliffs, NJ: Prentice-Hall.

Sederberg, Peter C. 1984. *The Politics of Meaning: Power and Explanation in the Construction of Social Reality.* Tucson: The University of Arizona Press.

Selltiz, Claire, et al. 1976. *Research Methods in the Social Sciences.* 3d ed. New York: Holt, Rinehart and Winston.

Seneca, L. Annaeus. 1935. *De Providentia*, trans. by J. W. Basore. London: Heinemann.

Senghass, Dieter. 1983. "The Cycles of War and Peace," *Bulletin of Peace Proposals* 14 (No. 2): 119–124.

Serfaty, Simon. 1968. *France, De Gaulle, and Europe*. Baltimore: Johns Hopkins University Press.

Service, Elman R. 1975. *Origins of the State and Civilization: The Process of Cultural Evolution*. New York: Norton.

Sheikh, Ahmed. 1974. *International Law and National Behavior*. New York: John Wiley and Sons.

Sherry, Michael. 1977. *Preparing for the Next War*. New Haven: Yale University Press.

Sherwin, Martin J. 1973. *A World Destroyed: The Atomic Bomb and the Grand Alliance*. New York: University Books.

Singer, David. 1961. "The Level-of-Analysis Problem in International Relations," in Klaus Knorr and Sidney Verba, eds., *The International System*, pp. 77–92. Princeton: Princeton University Press.

———. 1968. "Man and World Politics: The Psycho-Cultural Interface," *Journal of Social Issues* 24 (July): 127–156.

———. 1971. *A General Systems Taxonomy for Political Science*. New York: General Learning Press.

———. 1980. "Accounting for International War: The State of the Discipline," *Journal of Peace Research* 18 (No. 1): 1–18.

———. 1982. "Variables, Indicators, and Data: The Measurement Problem in Macropolitical Research," *Social Science History* 6 (Spring): 181–217.

Singer, J. David, Stuart Bremer, and John Stuckey. 1972. "Capability Distribution, Uncertainty, and Major Power War, 1820–1965," in Bruce M. Russett, ed., *Peace, War, and Numbers*, pp. 19–48. Beverly Hills: Sage.

Singer, J. David, and Melvin Small. 1966a. "Formal Alliances, 1815–1939: A Quantitative Description," *Journal of Peace Research* 3 (January): 1–32.

———. 1966b. "National Alliance Commitments and War Involvement, 1818–1945," *Papers of the Peace Research Society (International)* 5: 109–140.

———. 1968. "Alliance Aggregation and the Onset of War: 1815–1945," in J. David Singer, ed., *Quantitative International Politics: Insights and Evidence*, pp. 247–286. New York: The Free Press.

———. 1969a. "Formal Alliances, 1816–1965: Extension of the Basic Data," *Journal of Peace Research* 6 (No. 3): 257–282.

———. 1969b. "National Alliance Commitments and War Involvement, 1815–1945," in James N. Rosenau, ed., *International Politics and Foreign Policy*, pp. 513–542. New York: Free Press.

———. 1972. *The Wages of War*. New York: Wiley.

Singer, J. David, and Michael Wallace. 1970. "Intergovernmental Organization and the Preservation of Peace, 1816–1965: Some Bivariate Relationships," *International Organization* 24 (Summer): 520–547.

Singham, A. W., and Shirley Hune. 1986. *Non-Alignment in An Age of Alignments.* Westport, CT: Lawrence Hill.

Sinha, Bhek Pati. 1966. *Unilateral Denunciation of Treaty Because of Prior Violations of Obligations by Other Party.* The Hague: Martinus Nijhoff.

Siverson, Randolph M. 1980. "War and Change in the International System," in Ole R. Holsti, Randolph M. Siverson, and Alexander L. George, eds., *Change in the International System,* pp. 211–232. Boulder, CO: Westview Press.

Siverson, Randolph M., and George T. Duncan. 1976. "Stochastic Models of International Alliance Initiation, 1885–1965," in Dina A. Zinnes and John V. Gillespie, eds., *Mathematical Models in International Relations,* pp. 110–131. New York: Praeger.

Siverson, Randolph M., and Joel King. 1979. "Alliances and the Expansion of War," in J. David Singer and Michael Wallace, eds., *To Auger Well,* pp. 37–49. Beverly Hills: Sage.

———. 1980. "Attributes of National Alliance Membership and War Participation, 1815–1965," *American Journal of Political Science* 24 (February): 1–15.

Siverson, Randolph M., and Michael P. Sullivan. 1983. "The Distribution of Power and the Onset of War," *Journal of Conflict Resolution* 27 (September): 473–494.

Siverson, Randolph M., and Michael Tennefoss. 1982. "Interstate Conflicts: 1815–1965," *International Interactions* 9 (No. 2): 147–178.

Sizemore, Russell F. 1988. "The Prudent Cold Warrior," *Ethics and International Affairs,* vol. 2: 199–217.

Skinner, Richard A., and Charles W. Kegley, Jr. 1978. "Correlates of International Alignment," *Journal of Political Science* 5 (Spring): 97–108.

Sleeper, Raymond S., ed. 1987. *Mesmerized by the Bear: The Soviet Strategy of Deception.* New York: Dodd, Mead.

Small, Melvin, and J. David Singer. 1976. "The War-Proneness of Democratic Regimes," *Jerusalem Journal of International Relations* 1 (Summer): 50–69.

———. 1982. *Resort to Arms: International and Civil Wars, 1816–1980.* Beverly Hills: Sage.

Smith, Michael. 1984. *Western Europe and the United States: The Uncertain Alliance.* London: Allen & Unwin.

Smith, Theresa C. 1982. *Trojan Peace: Some Deterrence Propositions Tested.* University of Denver Monograph Series in World Affairs, vol. 19. Denver.

Snidal, Duncan. 1985. "The Limits of Hegemonic Stability Theory," *International Organization* 39 (Autumn): 579–614.

Snell, John L., ed. 1956. *The Meaning of Yalta: Big Three Diplomacy and the New Balance of Power.* Baton Rouge, LA: Louisiana State University Press.

Snyder, Glenn H. 1984. "The Security Dilemma in Alliance Politics," *World Politics* 36 (July): 461–495.

Snyder, Glenn H., and Paul Diesing. 1977. *Conflict Among Nations*. Princeton: Princeton University Press.

———. 1988. "The Anatomy of International Crises," in Charles W. Kegley, Jr., and Eugene R. Wittkopf, eds., *The Global Agenda*, pp. 87–95. New York: Random House.

Snyder, Richard C., H. W. Bruck, and Burton Sapin, eds. 1962. *Foreign Policy Decision Making*. New York: Free Press.

Sorokin, Pitirim A. 1944. *The Crisis of Our Age: The Social and Cultural Outlook*. New York: Dutton.

Soroos, Marvin A. 1986. *Beyond Sovereignty: The Challenge of Global Policy*. Columbia: University of South Carolina Press.

Spanier, John. 1975. *Games Nations Play*. New York: Praeger.

Sprout, Harold, and Margaret Sprout. 1965. *The Ecological Perspective on Human Affairs*. Princeton: Princeton University Press.

Stein, Arthur A. 1982. "Coordination and Collaboration: Regimes in an Anarchic World," *International Organization* 36 (Spring): 299–324.

———. 1984. "The Hegemon's Dilemma: Great Britain, the United States and the International Economic Order," *International Organization* 38 (Spring): 355–386.

Stein, Arthur A., and Bruce M. Russett. 1980. "Evaluating War: Outcomes and Consequences," in Ted Robert Gurr, ed., *Handbook of Political Conflict*, pp. 399–422. New York: Free Press.

Stein, Janice Gross. 1988. "The Managed and the Managers: Crisis Prevention in the Middle East," in Gilbert R. Winham, ed., *New Issues in International Crisis Management*, pp. 171–198. Boulder, CO: Westview Press.

Stoessinger, John G. 1986. *The Might of Nations*, 8th ed. New York: Random House.

Strayer, Joseph R. 1955. *Western Europe in the Middle Ages*. New York: Appleton-Century-Crofts.

Suganami, Hidemi. 1979. "Why Ought Treaties To Be Kept?" in George W. Keeton and George Schwarzenberger, eds., *The Yearbook of World Affairs*, pp. 243–256. London: Stevens and Son.

———. 1983. "A Normative Enquiry in International Relations: The Case of 'Pacta Sunt Servanda,' " *Review of International Studies* 9 (January): 35–54.

Sullivan, John D. 1974. "International Alliance," in Michael Haas, ed., *International Systems: A Behavioral Approach*, pp. 100–122. New York: Chandler.

Sullivan, Michael P., and Randolph M. Siverson. 1981. "Theories of War," in P. Terrence Hopmann, Dina A. Zinnes, and J. David Singer, eds., *Cumulation in International Relations Research*, pp. 9–37. University of Denver Monograph Series in World Affairs, vol. 18. Denver.

Taylor, A. J. P. 1954. *The Struggle for Mastery of Europe, 1848–1918*. Oxford: Oxford University Press.

Teune, Henry. 1987. "Comparing Nations: What Have We Learned?" Paper presented at the annual meeting of the International Studies Association.

Teune, Henry, and Sig Synnestvedt. 1965. "Measuring International Alignment," *Orbis* (Spring): 171–189.

Theoharis, Athan G. 1970. *The Yalta Myths: An Issue in U.S. Politics, 1945–1955*. Columbia: University of Missouri Press.

Thompson, Kenneth W. 1960. *Political Realism and the Crisis of World Politics*. Princeton: Princeton University Press.

———. 1980. "Tensions Between Human Rights and National Sovereign Rights," in The Center for Study of the American Experience, ed., *Rights and Responsibilities: International, Social and Individual Responsibilities*, pp. 113–158. Los Angeles: University of Southern California Press.

Thompson, William R. 1983. "Cycles, Capabilities, and War," in William R. Thompson, ed., *Contending Approaches to World System Analysis*, pp. 141–163. Beverly Hills: Sage.

———. 1985. "Cycles of General, Hegemonic, and Global War," in Urs Luterbacher and Michael D. Ward, eds., *Dynamic Models of International Conflict*, pp. 462–488. Boulder, CO: Lynne Rienner.

———. 1986. "Polarity, the Long Cycle, and Global Power Warfare," *Journal of Conflict Resolution* 30 (December): 587–615.

———. 1988. *On Global War: Historical-Structural Approaches to World Politics*. Columbia: University of South Carolina Press.

Thompson, William R., Karen A. Rasler and Richard P. Y. Li. 1980. "Systemic Interaction Opportunities and War Behavior," *International Interactions* 7 (No. 1): 57–85.

Thompson, William R., and Gary Zuk. 1986. "World Power and the Strategic Trap of Territorial Commitments," *International Studies Quarterly* 30 (September): 249–267.

Thrupp, Sylvia L. 1970. "Diachronic Methods in Comparative Politics," in Robert T. Holt and John E. Turner, eds., *The Methodology of Comparative Research*, pp. 343–358. New York: Free Press.

Tillema, Herbert K. 1989. "Foreign Overt Military Intervention in the Nuclear Age," *Journal of Peace Research* 26 (May): 179–196.

Tillema, Herbert K., and John R. van Wingen. 1982. "Law and Power in Military Intervention: Major States After World War II," *International Studies Quarterly* 26 (June): 220–250.

Tobin, Harold J. 1933. *The Termination of Multipartite Treaties*. New York: Columbia University Press.

Toulmin, Stephen. 1950. *An Examination of the Place of Reason in Ethics*. Cambridge: Cambridge University Press.

Toynbee, Arnold J. 1954. *A Study of History*. London: Oxford University Press.

————. 1967. "Anarchy in Treaties, 1648–1967," in Fred L. Israel, ed., *Major Peace Treaties of Modern History, 1648–1967*, pp. xii–xxix. New York: Chelsea.

Triandis, Harry C. 1972. *The Analysis of Subjective Culture.* New York: Wiley-Interscience.

Tuchman, Barbara W. 1984. *The March of Folly.* New York: Ballentine.

Tung, William L. 1968. *International Law in an Organizing World.* New York: Crowell.

Ullmann-Margalit, Edna. 1977. *The Emergence of Norms.* Oxford: Oxford University Press.

U.S. Department of State. 1987. "Soviet Noncompliance with Arms Control Agreements," *Special Report* No. 175. Washington, DC: Bureau of Public Affairs.

Valesio, Paolo. 1980. *Novanthiqua: Rhetorics as a Contemporary Theory.* Bloomington: Indiana University Press.

Vamvoukos, Anthanassios. 1985. *Termination of Treaties in International Law.* Oxford: Clarendon.

Van Dyke, Vernon. 1966. *International Politics,* 2d ed. New York: Appleton-Century-Crofts.

Van Evera, Stephen. 1984. "The Cult of the Offensive and the Origins of the First World War," *International Security* 9 (Summer): 58–107.

————. 1985. "Why Cooperation Failed in 1914," *World Politics* 38 (October): 80–117.

Vasquez, John A. 1986. "Capability, Types of War, and Peace," *Western Political Quarterly* 39 (June): 313–327.

————. 1987a. "Foreign Policy, Learning, and War," in Charles F. Hermann, Charles W. Kegley, Jr., and James N. Rosenau, eds., *New Directions in the Study of Foreign Policy,* pp. 366–383. Boston: Allen & Unwin.

————. 1987b. "The Steps to War: Toward A Scientific Explanation of Correlates of War Findings," *World Politics* 40 (October): 108–145.

Vattel, Emeriche de. 1916. *The Law of Nations,* Book 2, trans. by Charles Fenwick. Washington, DC: Carnegie Institution.

Väyrynen, Raimo. 1988. "The Devolution of Military Alliances: Theoretical and Empirical Perspectives." Paper presented at the annual meeting of the International Studies Association.

Virally, Michel. 1968. "The Sources of International Law," in Max Sørensen, ed., *Manual of Public International Law,* pp. 116–174. New York: St. Martin's Press.

Visscher, Charles de. 1968. *Theory and Reality in Public International Law,* trans. by Percy Corbett. Princeton: Princeton University Press.

Volgyes, Ivan. 1988. "Troubled Friendship or Mutual Dependence? Eastern Europe and the USSR in the Gorbachev Era," in Charles W. Kegley, Jr., and Eugene R. Wittkopf, eds., *The Global Agenda*, pp. 159–162. New York: Randon House.

Volgyes, Ivan, and Dale R. Herspring. 1980. "Political Reliability in the Eastern European Warsaw Pact Armies," *Armed Forces and Society* 6 (Winter): 270–296.

von Glahn, Gerhard. 1981. *An Introduction to International Law*, 4th ed. New York: Macmillan.

von Wright, Georg Henrick. 1963. *Norm and Action: A Logical Inquiry*. London: Routledge & Kegan Paul.

Vyasa. 1964. *The Mahābhārata*, trans. by Protap Chandra Roy, in Joel Larus, ed., *Comparative World Politics*, pp. 262–265. Belmont, CA: Wadsworth.

Waismann, Friedrich. 1951. "Verifiability," in Anthony Flew, ed., *Essays on Logic and Language*, pp. 117–144. New York: Philosophical Library.

Walker, David M. 1980. *The Oxford Companion to Law*. Oxford: Clarendon Press.

Walker, Richard L. 1953. *The Multi-State System of Ancient China*. New Haven, CT: Shoe String Press.

Wallace, Michael D. 1972. "Status, Formal Organization, and Arms Levels as Factors Leading to the Onset of War, 1820–1964," in Bruce M. Russett, ed., *Peace, War, and Numbers*, pp. 49–69. Beverly Hills: Sage.

————. 1973. "Alliance Polarization, Cross-Cutting, and International War, 1815–1964: A Measurement Procedure and Some Preliminary Evidence," *Journal of Conflict Resolution* 17 (December): 575–604.

————. 1979. "Arms Races and Escalation: Some New Evidence," *Journal of Conflict Resolution* 23 (March): 3–16.

————. 1980. "Some Persisting Findings: A Reply to Professor Weede," *Journal of Conflict Resolution* 24 (June): 289–292.

————. 1982. "Armaments and Escalation: Two Competing Hypotheses," *International Studies Quarterly* 26 (March): 37–51.

Wallensteen, Peter. 1984. "Universalism vs. Particularism: On the Limits of Major Power Order," *Journal of Peace Research* 21 (No. 3): 243–257.

Wallerstein, Immanuel. 1984. *The Politics of the World-Economy*. Cambridge: Cambridge University Press.

Walt, Stephen M. 1985. "Alliance Formation and the Balance of World Power," *International Security* 9 (Spring): 3–43.

————. 1987. *The Origins of Alliances*. Ithaca, NY: Cornell University Press.

Waltz, Kenneth. 1954. *Man, the State and War*. New York: Columbia University Press.

————. 1964. "The Stability of a Bipolar World," *Daedalus* 93 (Summer): 881–909.

——— . 1967. "International Structure, National Force, and the Balance of World Power," *Journal of International Affairs* 21 (No. 2): 215–231.

——— . 1979. *Theory of International Politics.* Reading, MA: Addison-Wesley.

Walzer, Michael. 1970. *Obligations.* Cambridge, MA: Harvard University Press.

——— . 1977. *Just and Unjust Wars.* New York: Basic Books.

Ward, Michael D. 1982. *Research Gaps in Alliance Dynamics.* University of Denver Monograph Series in World Affairs, vol. 19. Denver.

Watson, Adam. 1984. *Diplomacy: The Dialogue Between States.* London: Methuen.

——— . 1987. "Hedley Bull, State Systems and International Societies," *Review of International Studies* 13 (April): 147–153.

Wayman, Frank. 1984. "Bipolarity and War: The Role of Capability Concentration and Alliance Patterns Among Major Powers, 1816–1965," *Journal of Peace Research* 21 (No. 1): 61–77.

——— . 1985. "Bipolarity, Multipolarity, and the Threat of War," in Alan Ned Sabrosky, ed., *Polarity and War: The Changing Structure of International Conflict,* pp. 115–144. Boulder, CO: Westview Press.

Weber, Max. 1958. "Introduction," in Hans H. Gerth and C. Wright Mills, eds., *From Max Weber,* pp. 3–74. New York: Free Press.

Weede, Erich. 1976. "Overwhelming Preponderance as a Pacifying Condition among Contiguous Asian Dyads, 1950–1969," *Journal of Conflict Resolution* 20 (September): 395–411.

——— . 1984. "Democracy and War Involvement," *Journal of Conflict Resolution* 28 (December): 649–664.

Wehberg, Hans. 1959. "Pacta Sunt Servanda," *American Journal of International Law* 53 (October): 775–786.

Weigert, Andrew J. 1981. *Sociology in Everyday Life.* New York: Longman.

Weinstein, Franklin B. 1969. "The Concept of Commitment in International Relations," *Journal of Conflict Resolution* 13 (March): 39–56.

Weisband, Edward. 1986. "Ethics in World Politics," *News for Teachers of Political Science* 51 (Fall): 13–14.

Weyer, E. M. 1967. "The Structure of Social Organization Among the Eskimos," in Ronald Cohen and John Middleton, eds., *Comparative Political Systems,* pp. 1–13. Garden City, NJ: Natural History Press.

Wight, Martin. 1946. *Power Politics.* London: Royal Institute of International Affairs.

——— . 1968. "Western Values in International Relations," in Herbert Butterfield and Martin Wight, eds., *Diplomatic Investigations: Essays in the Theory of International Politics,* pp. 89–131. Cambridge, MA: Harvard University Press.

Wildavsky, Aaron. 1987. "Choosing Preferences by Constructing Institutions: A Cultural Theory of Preference Formation," *American Political Science Review* 81 (March): 3–21.

Will, Clifford M. 1986. *Was Einstein Right? Putting Relativity to the Test.* New York: Basic Books.

Williams, Fischer. 1928. "The Permanence of Treaties," *American Journal of International Law* 22 (January): 89–104.

Williams, Glanville L. 1945. "International Law and the Controversy Concerning the World Law," *British Year Book of International Law.* London: Oxford University Press.

Williams, Phil. 1976. *Crisis Management: Confrontation and Diplomacy in the Nuclear Age.* New York: John Wiley.

Williams, Raymond. 1976. *Keywords: A Vocabulary of Culture and Society.* London: Croom Helm.

Williamson, Oliver E. 1983. "Credible Commitments: Using Hostages to Support Exchange," *American Economic Review* 83 (September): 519–540.

Williamson, Samuel R., Jr. 1969. *The Politics of Grand Strategy.* Cambridge, MA: Harvard University Press.

Wolfers, Arnold, 1962. *Discord and Collaboration.* Baltimore: Johns Hopkins University Press.

——— . 1968. "Alliances," in David L. Sills, ed., *International Encyclopedia of the Social Sciences,* pp. 268–271. New York: Macmillan.

——— . 1959. "Stresses and Strains in 'Going It with Others'," in Arnold Wolfers, ed., *Alliance Policy in the Cold War,* pp. 1–14. Baltimore: Johns Hopkins University Press.

Woolsey, Lester H. 1926. "The Unilateral Termination of Treaties," *American Journal of International Law* 20 (April): 346–353.

Wright, Quincy. 1953. "The Outlawry of War and the Law of War," *American Journal of International Law* 47 (July): 365–376.

——— . 1961. *The Role of International Law in the Elimination of War.* New York: Oceana Publications.

——— . 1965. *A Study of War.* Chicago: University of Chicago Press.

Yergin, Daniel. 1977. *Shattered Peace: The Origins of the Cold War and the National Security State.* Boston: Houghton Mifflin.

Young, Oran R. 1968a. "Political Discontinuities in the International System," *World Politics* 20 (April): 369–392.

——— . 1968b. *The Politics of Force: Bargaining During International Crisis.* Princeton: Princeton University Press.

——— . 1977. *Compliance and Public Authority.* Baltimore: Johns Hopkins University Press.

——— . 1978. "Anarchy and Social Choice: Reflections on the International Polity," *World Politics* 30 (January): 241–263.

————. 1980. "International Regimes: Problems of Concept Formation," *World Politics* 32 (April): 331–356.

Zelikow, Philip. 1987. "The United States and the Use of Force: A Historical Summary," in George K. Osborn, Asa A. Clark IV, Daniel J. Kaufman, and Douglas E. Lute, eds., *Democracy, Strategy, and Vietnam,* pp. 31–81. Lexington, MA: Lexington Books.

Zinnes, Dina A. 1980a. "Three Puzzles in Search of a Researcher," *International Studies Quarterly* 24 (September): 315–342.

————. 1980b. "Why War? Evidence on the Outbreak of International Conflict," in Ted Robert Gurr, ed., *Handbook of Political Conflict: Theory and Research,* pp. 331–360. New York: Free Press.

Zinnes, Dina A., Joseph L. Zinnes, and Robert D. McClure. 1972. "Hostility in Diplomatic Communications," in Charles F. Hermann, ed., *International Crises,* pp. 139–161. New York: Free Press.

Zoppo, Ciro E. 1966. "Nuclear Technology, Multipolarity and International Stability," *World Politics* 18 (July): 579–606.

Name Index

Subject Index

Aetolians, the, 91
Afghanistan, 272, 274, 278
Agadir crisis, 67n
Age of Reason, 15, 32n
Algerian civil war, 162
Alliances, military: as a universal component of interstate relations, 45; defined, 52; types of, 52–53; determinants of, 54–55, 57–58; life cycle of, 59; levels of aggregation, 171–172; cohesion of, 171, 173–174; methods of maintaining cohesion, 56; reliability of, 63–64; association with war, 218–222
Allied Control Council, 161
Almon lag model, 199
Anarchy, 9, 39, 40; properties of anarchic systems, 9–11, 54; bounded anarchy and partially structured conflict relationships, 2, 13–14
Anomie, 10, 13–14
Antarctica, 17
Anti-Ballistic Missile Treaty, 275
Antimony, legal, 88
ANZUS, 142, 272
Appeasement, 42
Arab League, 64
Arms races, 10, 234–239
ASEAN, 272
Athens, 8, 67, 222
Atlantic Charter, 207
Australia, 142, 182
Austria-Hungary, 1, 17, 66, 67n, 91, 132, 136, 223; as member of major power subsystem, 225n
Austro-Italian/Sardinian War, 132
Austro-Prussian War, 132
Auxiliary theory, 108

Balance of power, 9, 36, 51, 69, 127, 132, 133, 136–138, 161, 195, 208, 214, 220, 266. *See also* Realism

Bandwagoning, 65–66
Bargaining power, 55
Batoum, 91
Bavaria, 18
Belgium, 17, 55, 91, 236
Berlin, 262; Congress of, 17; Treaty of, 91, 137
Billiard ball model, 239
Biological and Toxic Weapons Convention, 274
Blocs. *See* Alliances, military; Polarization
Bosnia, 91
Breslau, 91
Brezhnev Doctrine, 31, 56
Brinkmanship, 215
Bulgaria, 137, 209
Burgundian Confederation, 223

Cambodia, 274
Canada, 22–23, 214
Canon law, 153
Carthage, 67
Central Treaty Organization (CENTO), 271
Chaldeans, the, 88
Cheyenne (of North America), 14
China, Imperial, 88, 91; Chou dynasty, 9, 67
China, People's Republic of, 142–143, 272
China, Republic of, 142, 272
Civil wars, internationalized, 205n
Cobweb processes, 122
Coercive diplomacy, 234
Cold War, 142, 207–216, 268
Collective security, 9, 138. *See also* Idealism; League of Nations
Commitment, situational versus nonsituational, 244n
Complex interdependence, 268
Concert of Europe, 128, 131, 133

332